An Unholy Alliance

SPORTS AND RELIGION

A Series Edited by Joseph L. Price

This series explores the academic study of the connection of religion and sports. The series will include books that examine sports through various disciplines and cultural forms (literature, history, music, poetry, among others) and that consider how sports challenge, inspire, or function as religion.

Titles

Joseph L. Price, ed., *From Season to Season: Sports as American Religion*

Allen Hye, *The Great God Baseball: Religion in Modern Baseball Fiction*

Robert J. Higgs and Michael C. Braswell, *An Unholy Alliance: The Sacred and Modern Sports*

An Unholy Alliance

The
Sacred
and
Modern
Sports

Robert J. Higgs
and
Michael C. Braswell

Mercer University Press
Macon, Georgia 2004
25th Anniversary

ISBN 0-86554-923-0 (cloth)
0-86554-956-7 (paperback)
MUP/H648/P304

© 2004 Mercer University Press
1400 Coleman Avenue
Macon, Georgia 31207

First Edition.

∞The paper used in this publication meets the minimum requirements of American National Standard for Information Sciences—Permanence of Paper for Printed Library Materials, ANSI Z39.48-1992.

Library of Congress Cataloging-in-Publication Data

CIP data are available from the Library of Congress

To our families:

Reny, Julia, Laura, Igor, Sheldon, and Molly

Susan, Scott, and Matt

One of Thoreau's favorite aims was what he called *multum in Parvo*, much in little. It was as relevant to the form in which he expressed his thoughts as it was to the immediate tangible goods he sought. And so when he once wrote in his journal, "Many a man goes fishing all his life without realizing that it is not the fish he was after," he offered a small example of a great truth: Many a civilization has sought wealth, power, even knowledge, and a high standard of living without realizing that they were after none of these but after a "good life"—which they mistakenly identified with one or all of these things.

Joseph Wood Krutch, "Who Was Henry David Thoreau?' *Saturday Review of Literature* (19 August 1967) 46.

Contents

Preface

In the last few years, a spate of books has appeared that might be classified by a genre called "Sports Apologetics," that is, arguments defending or celebrating the familiar and ongoing alliance in America between sports and religion. Among treatments sympathetic to this relationship are *Religion and Religions* by Catherine Albanese, *Muscular Christianity: Evangelical Protestants and the Development of American Sports* by Tony Ladd and James A. Mathisen, *In the Zone: Transcendent Experience in Sports* by Michael Murphy and Rhea A. White, *The Joy of Sports: End Zones, Bases, Baskets, Balls and the Consecration of the American Spirit* by Michael Novak, *Religion and Sport: The Meeting of the Sacred and Profane* by Charles S. Prebish, and more recently *From Season to Season: Sports as an American Religion* edited and coauthored by Joseph L. Price.

Using the help of a number of distinguished scholars, including theologians and professors of religious studies, and drawing upon previous studies such as those listed, Price attempts to cement the argument by proclaiming that sports are not merely like a religion but are an authentic religion themselves. He and others make this assertion not by showing connections with the teachings of Buddha, Jesus, Mohammed, or Moses but by paralleling the rites of modern games with those of preliterate man that were "religious" because they were designed to propitiate powers and ward off evil for the tribes who employed them. Price's main source on mythology is Mircea Eliade, who is praised for looking at the "sacred in its entirety." Sports, it is claimed, meet the requirements of the sacred in that games are "set apart" in terms of place and time and because they provide "flow" experiences. Such experiences evoke in participants and fans feelings of "ultimacy" that are close to, or even identical with, those traditionally associated with the holy.

Religion, it is argued, does not necessarily involve the worship of a transcendent god nor always reflect "compassionate" and "humanistic" ethics. Price and his colleagues identify several apparent advantages in sports to any society, such as a means of structuring culture and celebrating the joy of being and achieving. The main value identified in athletics is found in the idea of the flow, an autotelic feeling of ultimacy sought and cherished by athletes and inspirational to fans and admirers. Sports apologists find this "religion" at least compatible with traditional religions so that the two can coexist on peaceful and even rhythmic terms.

Our book, *An Unholy Alliance*, offers a dissenting view. We suggest that while sports are good, they are not inherently divine. We do not focus on widespread abuse in sports as evidence for our counterargument. We do take apologists to task for the values and ethics advanced, and we question the use of mythological parallels from prehistory as evidence of the argument for viewing sports as a religion. There are several reasons for our skepticism, including the fact that prehistorical rites, much like many of our own, were sometimes notoriously violent, a feature often overlooked in apologetic texts. No mention is made in those texts of *Violence and the Sacred*, a highly acclaimed but neglected work by Rene Girard. If sports are a religion as claimed, they are a religion of power. This helps explain their exploitation by militant religions such as Shintoism and the Church of the Third Reich, which played significant roles in the impetus toward World War II.

Instead of judging sports in light of conventional religion, sports apologists tend to look at sports qua sports and seek to find meaning in the activities themselves. From our perspective this approach, while valuable, is not sufficient to prove the case that sports are indeed a new religion. For a fuller understanding of the implications of a religion of sports, more comparisons and contrasts with established religions are necessary. We endeavor to do this not exhaustively but enough, we hope, to suggest the need for more evaluation along these lines, especially in terms of mysticism, ethics, art, and humor. Some apologists seem to take a dim view of comparative analysis of sports, but we know no other way to proceed. If sports are a religion as is increasingly claimed, then it is sensible to see how sports might qualify in that regard. All scholarship and understanding involve two elements. Otherwise, discourse would be merely descriptive instead of critical, like a study of Nazism qua Nazism. The situation is well summarized by a joke in science fiction. The captain of a spaceship lost amid the galaxies goes before a super computer and asks, "Where are we?" "In reference to what?" the computer responds.

Thus, much depends on the meanings of terms used, for example, "holy," "sacred," "religion," "sports," "spirit," and "soul," which is why in our argument we give considerable attention to definitions, distinctions, and metaphors. In our rebuttal, we focus not only on the idea of the sacred, an idea we find troubling, but also upon an idea examined by Rudolf Otto, that of the holy. Otto's *The Idea of the Holy* is another book rarely mentioned by sports apologists. In the Price book, Otto is dismissed since it is claimed he sees the holy as "irrational," a puzzling statement since Otto viewed the mystery in religion not as irrational but as "non-rational," a term that appears in his first chapter. The holy or "wholly other" is a legitimate if not necessary consideration in any study of religion since that quality, as Otto says, is "peculiar to the sphere of religion.[1]" As belligerent as religions often have been and remain, they all share one thing in common—a quest of the holy, which is not a pursuit, at least not a primary one, in the world of sports.

Though the sacred and holy are often used interchangeably, they are by no means identical as we demonstrate repeatedly in our text. The holy spirit and the sporting spirit may have a single *arche* or source, but they are by no means synonymous and may in territorial sports even approach the soul from different directions. We will dare to suggest that this may not be the case with the comic spirit in relation to the holy. Again, this is not to deny sports their due or many of their highly publicized virtues. Rather, we question the role of sports in reflecting "ultimacy," to use the language of the apologists in describing transcendent experiences of athletes, and we contrast the idea of "ultimacy," a triumphal notion, with that of "intimacy," a more appropriate term for the surrender that seems necessary for traditional mystical experiences. The term "sacred," a key word in apologetic texts, does not even appear in the Bible, unlike the word "holy" and its variants, which appear hundreds of times, including in the title, the *Holy Bible*.

Sacred means "set apart," an elitist idea that makes it a concept applicable to politics and sports as well as to religion. The holy, a democratic idea often exploited by high priests of all times, is a word much abused these days as in "holy wars" and in the "holy shit" journalism recommended by the late Ben Bradlee of the *Washington Post*. Of the Holy Roman Empire of his day, Voltaire (1694–1788) said it was neither "Holy, nor Roman, nor an Empire." Otto treats the holy as a noun as something

---

[1] R. Otto, *The Idea of the Holy* Trans. John W. Harvey (New York: Oxford University Press, 1958) 5.

very different from holy as an adjective. *The holy* is a divine quality unattainable, "inconceivable" or "unknowable" by mortals that leaves in those who encounter it a feeling of utter "humility" and sometimes of abounding joy. It is the "wholly other"—that which is set apart from everything, not simply one thing set apart from another as in the case of the "sacred." The holy, as an attribute of God, is even set apart from the angels.

In our age, what has happened to "holy" semantically reflects an occupational hazard of terms once considered admirable. In *The Broken Covenant: American Civil Religion in a Time of Trial* (1975), Robert N. Bellah remarks that the word "bad" is often used to mean "good." Even in the nineteenth century Henry David Thoreau, to whom we refer often in this book, said that if there was anything he repented of, it was his "good behavior." Since Thoreau was a classic nonconformist, we know what he meant just as we do when he said he had never met "a worse person" than himself. He was not trying to show how "bad" he was by such a claim. After discussing the possibility that we have met people "worse" than we are, we are pretty sure that has been the case, but not enough by any means to elevate us to a position of saintliness or prophecy. What we intend as far as genre is not a sermon on literally a holy topic, but, in the spirit of Robert Pirsig in *Zen and the Art of Motorcycle Maintenance*, a Chautauqua as defined by him:

> What is in mind is a sort of Chautauqua…like the traveling tent show Chautauquas that used to move across America, *this* America, the one we are now in, in an old time series of popular talks intended to edify and entertain, improve the mind, and bring culture and enlightenment to the ears and thoughts of the hearers. The Chautauquas were pushed aside by faster-paced radio, movies, and TV, and it seem to me that the change was not entirely an improvement. Perhaps because of these changes the stream of national consciousness moves faster now but it seems to run less deep. The old channels cannot contain it and in its search for new ones there seems to be growing havoc and destruction along its banks.

Instead of asking the question "What's new?" Pirsig says he is concerned with the question "What is best?" That is the same question we would like to ask as we consider the relation between mind, body, and soul in current American culture in relation to the emergent Religion of Sports. Another matter we wish to address is the possibility of something even beyond the "best" in this world, what we think of as the holy, which Whitman seems to have in mind in Section 5 of "Song of Myself" as he speaks to his soul: "Not words, not music or rhyme I want, not custom or lecture, not even the best, Only the lull I like, the hum of your valved voice."[2]

What is there, if anything, that appears to be better than the "best" that mystics like Whitman and now athletes seem to have encountered as an "other" and wish to repeat for the sake of experience? If one had to identify a single object, a "vehicle" so to speak, that symbolized the transmission of culture of mind, body, and soul across the vast hinterland of America, the hands-down choice would be the tent, the tent of the Chautauquas, the big tent of the circus, and the ones that covered the sawdust trails of the evangelical band. So we invite you to come into our little tent as we try to make sense of where we have been in mind, body, and soul in America, where we might be at present, and what might be the prospects for change.

Sports may be sacred, but so are many other things around the world, such as the bloody flags of nations engaged in perpetual violence. Hence the explanation for our title: *An Unholy Alliance: The Sacred and Modern Sports*. We point to these distinctions throughout the text not in a spirit of self-righteousness, but in the interest of a better understanding of the terms that seem to lie at the root of violence and war as opposed to peace and justice. Now we see the words "holy" and "sacred" batted around in the world of sports, further confusing their meaning and in the case of the holy diluting the idea of it and even perhaps the experience of it.

We do not say with Howard Cossell that sports belong only to the "toy department," nor do we think Paul meant we should put away *all* childish things, especially a sense of play, as we mature. We do not subscribe, at least not entirely, to Thorstein Veblen's trenchant view of sports as presented in *Theory of the Leisure Class*:

> Sports of all kinds are of the same general character, including prize-fights, athletics, shooting, angling, yachting, and games of skill, even where the element of destructive physical efficiency is not an obtrusive feature. Sports shade off from the basis of hostile

---

[2] (Bantam: New York, 1984) 7.

combat, through skill, to cunning and chicanery, without it being possible to draw a line at any point. The ground of an addiction to sports is an archaic spiritual institution—the possession of the predatory emulative propensity in a relative high potency. A strong proclivity to adventuresome exploit and to the infliction of damage is especially pronounced in those employments which are in colloquial usage specifically called sportsmanship. [3]

Instead of regarding sports as one of the invidious habits of a class consciousness, apologists turn such thinking on its head by saying that sports *is* a religion thanks to the patterns of ancient rituals and other features apparent in our games. In Veblen's view sports "were an archaic spiritual institution" and remain so in modern times. Throughout our book, we trust that our argument will be clear: we believe that sports are (or certainly can be) a *good idea* but not a *divine idea.* In responding to apologetic texts, we will attempt to draw a bigger circle around the debate to bring into play a variety of additional themes. The most prominent of these is war, since sports cannot only provide a substitute for war but can also be a rehearsal of war.

We frequently cite Scripture throughout the text, remembering that this is a practice both of the saint and Satan, and while we cannot claim imitation of the former, we are aware of mortal affiliation with the latter. We are also aware of the dangers and implications of biblical citations as identified and illustrated in *The Bible Tells Me So: Uses and Abuses of Holy Scripture* by Jim Hill and Rand Cheadle. We will have frequent occasion to mention the word "God," but here too we are mindful of Carl Jung's observation that there is a difference between God and the "God idea" or, as Wallace Stevens says in a poem called "The Pure Good of Theory," "It is never the thing but"[4] God is much in the news these days and the subject of endless books, but all are "ideas" or "versions" of the unknowable, many of them sacred versions in constant war with other sacred versions. We cannot know with finality. All we can do is seek with as much humility as we can muster and, we might be bold enough to add, as much humor as seriousness might tolerate. Humor and humility have much in common, including, as we shall see, a history that remains unappreciated.

[3] Thorsten Veblen, *Theory of the Leisure Class* (NewYork: MacMillian Co., 1953) 170.
[4] *The Collected Poems of Wallace Stevens* (New York: Alfred H. Knopf, 1961) 332.

Recently a mutual friend of ours and a member of one of the discussion groups to which we belong called one of us late at night. He said he had finally identified the thorn in Saint Paul's side. In a voice of excitement he announced, "It's the desire to be right!" Whether or not our friend was accurate about Saint Paul, he identified a human problem, the same that is addressed in a tale attributed to Nasreddin Hodja, a legendary figure in Turkey in the late middle ages. According to some accounts, Nasreddin was the son of an Imam (religious leader) and became one himself as well as a dervish for two Islam mystics of the thirteenth century, a university professor, and a judge. As a judge, Nasreddin one day heard a case in court, and after the prosecutor made his argument, he said, "I believe you are right." Nasreddin repeated his comment after the defense made its case. "Your honor," someone said in the back of the courtroom, "they both cannot be right." "I believe you are right!" said Nasreddin. From our perspective, we find ourselves in a similar situation in the debate on sports as a religion.

On this theme of sports as a religion, as on all others, we see through a glass darkly. At best, as Whitman said, in "When I Read the Book," we proceed "by faint clews [sic] and indirections." This is especially true in any discussion of the holy—the "inconceivable." In regard to the holy there are no answers, only questions and responses. What we have, in addition to respect for those of other persuasions on the topic, is an abundance of questions that may or may not give themselves to clear answers. We hope our arguments, whether on the side of right or wrong, will be clear, and just as we cannot claim moral authority for the positions we take, neither can we claim special knowledge by background or training. We are neither theologians nor historians of religion. As far as the religion of sports is concerned, we are members of the laity with several questions for defenders of that faith not because we are interested in becoming members of the Church of Sports, but simply because inquiring minds want to know more about a religion that is at once so strange, so new, and so very, very old.

In this study Much use will be made of definitions of terms which, unless specified otherwise, came from *Webster's Ninth Intercollegiate Dictionary*. Biblical references, unless otherwise indicated are taken from the *King James Version*.

While we take full responsibilities for flaws and shortcomings in this book, any value it may have is due in large measure to contributions of a number of people over the years who have opened our minds to the many ramifications of the topic, referred us to bibliography or areas of further research and investigation, or facilitated communication with other scholars working in the field. Among them are Alex Aronis, Bill Baker, Susan Bandy, Dan Brown, the late Morton Brown, George Buck, Tom Burton, Drake Bush, Dick Crepeau, Charles Daughaday, Mick Davenport, Anne Darden, the late Richard B. Davis, Joyce Duncan, Toney Frazier, Ron Giles, Hershel Grubb (with thanks too for loan of his books on the sacred) Styron Harris, Tom Hearn, Bomar Herrin, Jean Hendricks, Neil and Ellen Isaacs, Don Johnson, Bill Kapetan, Tom Lane, Jeff Lokey, Anne LeCroy, Skip Matherly, Tim Morris, the late Lyle Olsen, Bonny Stanley, Reverend Bedford Transou, Ralph Turner, Ambrose Manning, Andy Kozar, and John Whitehead. We are grateful to all as we are to the entire staff of the Charles Sherrod Library at East Tennessee State University for various forms of assistance over the past few decades.

Foreword

Interest in the convergence of sports and religion has begun to swell among distinct American audiences at the beginning of the twenty-first century. In newspapers and periodicals, stories abound about the public testimonies of athletes and their on-field gestures of devotion, about the history of sports curses and the efficacy of superstitious behavior by players and fans to overcome the imprecations, and about the seemingly simple question, "Does God care who wins a game, round, match, or contest?" Similar stories glut internet websites, from pieces professionally written by journalists to chatty reflections by bloggers.

In the academy of higher education, sessions and panels at professorial conferences—meetings of the American Academy of Religion, the Society for the Scientific Study of Religion, the Sports Sociology Society, and the American Culture Association, for examples—have explored how sports might function as a religion or quasi-religion in contemporary American culture. Since the turn of the century, Harvard Divinity School has sponsored a program on "Baseball and Religion," and the University of Chicago Divinity School has featured lectures and published essays related to the intermingling of sports and religion. And now Mercer University Press has initiated a series of works on sports and religion in order to focus and expand conversations and analyses in this emerging interdisciplinary field of inquiry.

The purpose of the Mercer Series on Sports and Religion is to present academic studies that use various disciplinary methodologies and cultural forms to explore connections between religion and sport, considering, for example, how sports might challenge, inspire, or function as religion. The newest issue in the series, *An Unholy Alliance,* suggests the range of perspectives and voices that will be included in the series. In this work Jack Higgs and Michael Braswell contravene the thesis of the initial volume in the series. Drawing upon Rudolf Otto's astute insights in *The Idea of the Holy*, Higgs and Braswell consistently point out the incapacity of sports to lead athletes and fans to the holy itself. In their own words, "the function of sports as a category of human endeavor is not to connect us to that which is holy or even to remind us of the idea of the holy." Grounded in Christian faith and biblical familiarity, the authors distinguish the holy, which, as "wholly other," is the transcendent power that is the source and goal of true faith and religion, from the sacred, which are concrete objects that are set apart and that might represent the holy. Central to their critique of the alignment of sports with religion, Higgs and Braswell emphasize the ways in which the holy instills humility in persons; by contrast, they note, sports appeal to and promote one's ego.

Often witty and conversational in tone, *An Unholy Alliance* expands the discussion on sports and religion by articulating a theistic criticism of the works and perspectives of scholars whom the authors identify as apologists for the consideration of sports as religion. Although they deny that sports constitute a religion, Higgs and Braswell identify various ways that sports, as "an authentic archetype of human action," share common elements with religion, even as do works of art and acts of war. But rather than establishing an alliance between religion and either war or sports, the authors argue, religion should provide their check.

In an earlier work, *God in the Stadium: Sports and Religion in America*, Higgs analyzes the network of connections between sports, war, and religion in America. In *An Unholy Alliance*, he and Braswell explore the interplay of sports, art, and religion, for at their best, the authors assert, sports are "living art often breathtaking in their beauty." Inspired by this aesthetic richness in sports, the authors make allusions time and again to literary and artistic works to support their argument. In so doing they provide a text about sports and religion that is itself a work of art.

Joseph L. Price
Editor, Sports and Religion

Chapter 1

Sports and Religion: Peanut Butter and Jelly or Oil and Water?

Deion Sanders expressed something of the popular belief in the easy and natural alliance of sports and religion when he proclaimed that the two go together "like peanut butter and jelly." This could have been what Jesus left off when he said we shall "not live by bread alone," that is, that "we must also have peanut butter and jelly." If there were the opportunity for a CNN poll on the subject, our wager is that the majority queried would agree with Sanders. Further, a growing number of scholars and theologians, as mentioned in the preface, are arriving at essentially the same conclusion.

In one of the most recent works, *From Season to Season: Sports as American Religion,* Joseph Price, professor of theology at Whittier College, is a playing manager since he is editor and author of seven of the fifteen essays in the text, each affirming the modern "commingling" of sports and religion.[1] In the spirit of the book's title, Price examines "The Rhythmic and Religious Significance of American Sports Seasons," "The Pitcher's Mound as Cosmic Mountain: The Religious Significance of Baseball," "The Super Bowl as Religious Festival," and the "The Final Four as Final Judgment: The Religious and Cultural Significance of the NCAA Basketball Championship." As suggested by the title, the volume is largely arranged according to seasons and representative sports of the seasons: baseball/ spring and summer; football/fall; basketball/winter.

---

[1] Price, *From Season to Season: Sports as American Religion* (Macon GA: Mercer University Press, 2001) 8.

Subsidiary themes in *From Season to Season* focus on the kinship of sports and religion examined in earlier texts. The most provocative is that sports can be called a religion because of similarities between attributes of modern games, mainly territorial sports, and the "sacred rites and myths of previous, religiously oriented cultures." This bold argument almost begs for challenge, which in the interest of dialectic if not dogma we are willing to provide. Our hope is not so much victory, the sine qua non in modern American sports, as clarity in debate on this profound topic fraught with incalculable significance.

The thematic structure of *An Unholy Alliance: The Sacred and Modern Sports* is centered on the idea of ritual drama based upon our reading of the celebrated work by Lord Raglan, *The Hero: A Study in Tradition, Myth, and Drama*. Simply put, we see ritual drama as the universal manifestation of collective power in which rites pertaining to sports, war, religion, and the body politic are distinguishable but intertwined. In *The Theory of the Leisure Class*, Thorstein Veblen sees all these categories of human organization as "occupations" of predatory cultures and forms of honorific distinction both in archaic times and modern, all exhibiting in his view conspicuous consumption, leisure, and waste regardless of time or place. In our book, a comparison and contrast of sports and religion informs every chapter, but we also look at both in relation to war, media, mysticism, ethics, aesthetics, and humor in terms of the sacred and the holy.

Drawing upon several sources, theological and literary, we suggest that the holy, while "Wholly Other," is ironically everywhere in "smallest things— / Things overlooked before," in the words of Emily Dickinson in "The Last Night that she lived." Conversely, the "sacred," especially in territorial sports, religion, and nationalism, tends toward the "monumental" in scope and influence as in the case of the Super Bowl, an event in our culture that spectacularly weaves around football all other aspects of our culture—advertising, entertainment, patriotism, pagan rituals, religiosity, and especially money. If a hymn should ever be created to honor this day as in the case of the "Olympic Hymn," its title could be "Amazing Green: How Sweet the Touch!"

By definition sports are conspicuous activities since the athlete is one who competes for a prize or honor in a public place. For prehistoric man, all ritual was enactment or display, what today in our movies, stage productions, and daily news we regard as theater or show business. Hence sports have become "theater" on the playing field and "soap opera" off the field in the lives of athletes as celebrities, as has televangelism with Thespian pastors. For both religion and sports, there are separate channels, but on the remote they are only a click or two away from each other, almost symbolically to underscore their common origin in prehistoric ritual.

Similarly, war and politics are forms of theater brought to us daily as sensationally as possible with all the flashing colors and blaring sound that the technology of shock and awe of Ben Bradlee's kind of journalism can muster. For some time "theater of war" has been an entry in the latest edition of *Webster's*, and it is currently the title of a book by Louis Lapham. Even the word "theater" indirectly smacks of religious significance since its etymology includes the Greek *theasthai*, "to view," which is akin to *thauma* for "miracle" as in "thaumaturgy," the performance of miracles, especially magic. To be sure, television may be miraculous in the "virtual" world but scarcely holy. Its programming is limited, as far as we can tell, to sacred sermons and rites of various competing denominations, especially of an evangelical character that sometimes approaches sporting events in the theatrical display of emotion.

Whether sports with all their expenditure of energy, injuries, and rising costs are wasteful has been a matter of debate from ancient days to the present, but their attraction for large numbers of humankind endures from age to age. Sports are a paradox. Whenever and wherever they have flourished, owing to their special appeal and qualities conducive to heroism, they have been set apart in stadia and courts and invested with sacred significance. The more they are set apart, however, the more they become mutually involved with conventional religions, powers of state, and preparations for war. Sports, especially at the professional level, become sacred because of the strength and beauty in their form and function, godly features since ancient days, and because of the service to the state as magnificent symbols of success in all aspects of culture. The sacredness of nations is always before our eyes in the forms of flags and banners, honored sites for exaltation of triumphs of earlier times, and even in the symbols on national currency. The holy, in contrast, is hidden, unknowable, and mysterious. Yet somehow in certain hands the holy offers a touchstone for judgment on the arrogance of the world as reflected in the comment by Flannery O'Conner in *Mystery and Manners* that humility is not a visible trait in any national character.

Sports, our most popular form of theater, and television, the primary medium of theater, were always a marriage waiting to happen, but it is a marriage made on earth and not in heaven. It is a sacred marriage but far from holy, owing primarily to the mindlessness inherent in the union that accounts for its immense popularity. This is not to say that sports are not complex or that they do not require intelligence. The more important point is that they do not through their function serve the purposes of intellect, what Richard Hofstadter in *Anti-Intellectualism in American Life* called the critical, contemplative, and meditative side of mind. We are talking about the difference between athletics and the athletes who may, we readily admit, be individuals of noted intellect and intelligence as well as genuine seekers in matters of the spirit.

Still, we hold to the view that however remarkably well certain athletes may unify mind, body, and soul, and there are many we know who do, there is still no argument for elevating to divine status the games in which they participate. An absurd analogy, but one that holds, would be the proclamation of the study of literature as a new religion and identifying certain lecture halls on campus as sacred owing to the repeated demonstration by one or more students of critical insight into texts and extraordinary skill in expression. The links between literature and religion are many and profound as illustrated in a text of that name by Hans Kung and Walter Jens and in many other books. While this connection is recent compared to that between sports and religion, it is certainly distinguished in the literate history of all lands as reflected in the Bible and the Odes of Pindar, regardless of the different gods who inspired the literature.

At present the human body may well be having its finest hour. Since the advent of the electronic age and the proliferation of sports, advertising seems to run uninterrupted for the body's supposedly endless needs, as if prophets and ancient philosophers themselves could not have done without aspirin and underarm deodorant. Primarily because it is viewable on television and in other media, the body has assumed a tyranny over the soul undreamed of by our ancient or even recent ancestors. What seems to be literally happening is that we are losing our minds, as in intellect, over our bodies and perhaps our souls as well, forgetting that if body, mind, and soul are to be one, they must first be equal in importance. The role of sports in the transformation of emphasis, or perhaps degeneration, has not been insignificant. Not only have we idolized athletes to the point of celebrity-hood, but now we see before our eyes a proposal, endorsed on several fronts in the halls of academe, to regard sports as a religion in and of itself.

The Super Bowl may be a good thing in some ways, but we are reluctant to describe it as our "high holy day." If it is a "religious festival" as Joseph Price has called it—if it is religious at all—it is the religious as "sacred" rather than holy, sacred in its expressions of pride, power, and nationalism. It is a conspicuous extravaganza analogous to those of Rome at its pinnacle that by holy standards meant its nadir. What we watch on television on Super Sunday is not the sacred in its best form with humble connections to the holy but the sacred in its gaudiest dress, the sacred as "surreal" as in theater of the absurd, the sacred gone wild as has regularly occurred at imperial celebrations throughout history.

Our doubt about any holiness present at the Super Bowl does not stem from a distaste of sports. Indeed we have watched the Super Bowl with some regularity over the last several decades and participated in or watched and enjoyed all kinds of sports throughout our lives. We simply do not see why sports have to be anything other than activities to which we turn for enrichment and from which we turn to find the same blessings in other bounties of creation. Little seems to be gained by the apparent obsession to surround them with metaphors of religion or to categorize them as religions.

There is tremendous irony in our attachments to our monumental and increasingly sacramental sporting events. On the one hand it would seem that the Super Bowl, the World Series, the Final Four, and the PGA Tournament would, especially considered together, tell us just about all we would want to know about ourselves. Ironically they tell us relatively little about our day-to-day lives. The holy might suggest that sports at best should be only a part of our lives, and maybe a small part at that, not an end in itself. Similar to the question posited by the sexual revolution of the seventies,[2] we might ask, "What do we do after the game?" "What do we do for the rest of the week?"

Among those to whom the task is given of responding to those kinds of questions are, as always, poets, the famous and the not-so-famous writing about the hidden, the overlooked, the commonplace, and "smallest things." They may be athletes as well, novelists, scholars, or insurance executives like Wallace Stevens, but whoever they are or whatever else they do, winning for them is "not the only thing"—perhaps as George Leonard used to say, "it is nothing."

---

[2] "What do we do after the orgasm?"

In the hands of poets, a covenant is kept with consciousness and with one of the injunctions on the Temple at Delphi, "Know Thyself." If we read this famous axiom correctly, it means knowing, or attempting to know, the inner self as well as the outer, the little things as well as large, and the world outside the boundaries of courts and fields of play. "Know Thyself" has a commonsense relation to the unity suggested by the caveat over the other portal on the Temple, "Nothing in Excess," which "monumentalism" as in big games always challenges.

Sports and Religion:
The Heritage of Athens, Jerusalem, and Rome

These credos displayed at Delphi are not identical in meaning to that of the first commandment, but it can be argued that all have something in common. In this study it will be necessary to keep in mind not only the athletic legacy of Greece but also the philosophic legacy as contained in the three-volume work *Paideia: The Ideals of Greek Culture* by Werner Jaeger. On the book cover Edmund Wilson spoke of this collection as "God's gift to educators," and Edith Hamilton wrote that it is "the most illuminating work on Greece I have ever read.... I wish it could be required reading for all the multitudes today who are drawing up schemes for a new world." Among many other things, Jaeger shows how central the athlete was to the Greek concept of *arête* (excellence) and to Greek art (especially sculpture) and how under the weight of professionalism the athletic ideal degenerated into "mere sport."[3]

Jaeger is also the author of a slim but important book titled *Paideia and Christianity*, which shows how initially the philosophic heritage of Greece related to the ideals of the upstart religion coming out of Israel. The way "mere," meaning "pure" and "unmixed," relates to *arête* of the heroic age of Greece and to early Christianity is intriguing. Ironically, the more "pure" athletics were among the Greeks, the more they "mixed" with art and philosophy just as the more "pure" early Christianity was, as reflected in *Lost Christianity* by Jacob Needleman and *Mere Christianity* by C. S. Lewis, the more that embryonic faith mixed with and appealed to the suffering humanity in the Roman empire. The question might be asked how "mere" relates to the religion of sports. Again there is an irony. There is an

---

[3] Jaeger, *Archaic Greece: The Mind of Athens*, Vol. 1 of *Paideia: The Ideals of Greek Culture*, 2d ed., trans. Gilbert Highet (New York: Oxford University Press, 1945) 205–208.

admixture going on to be sure, but the ingredients are mere sport and mere religion, the kind Dietrich Bonhoeffer believed we could do without when he spoke of the need for a "religionless Christianity."

The religion of sports is even a step down from "Sportianity," Frank Deford's term for Muscular Christianity, and even a purification of that denomination since "Muscular Christianity" retained remnants of the old faith, the felt need on the part of winning athletes to "witness and testify for the Lord." Such a need demonstrated a sincere but misplaced trust since it opened the door to a religion based on the same militancy as primitive man practiced in his tribal ceremonies. In time there may not even be a nod to established faiths but rather an imitation of what Edith Hamilton called "the bloody games of Rome" in her praise of the conquered Greeks for rejecting them. "'Before you admit the gladiators,' cried one Athenian, 'come with me and destroy the altar of pity' and the people with one voice declared that their theatre should never be so defiled."[4]

Roman barbarism was one cause for the decline of the sporting spirit, and another was Christian piety of those in control. The Olympics began in Greece in 776 B.C. in honor of one god, Zeus, and were banned in A.D. 351 in the name of a Christian God by the emperor Theodosius I, who considered them "pagan idolatries."[5] They were revived in 1896 by Baron de Coubertin in honor of some god one cannot identify—unless it is the Baron himself, an argument he might not have disputed.

If there is one thing history teaches, it is that neither one's inherited culture nor religion comes *solely* and unchanged from one land or region. For instance, fundamentalists often say or at least suggest that everything we cherish in the way of beliefs and practices comes out of the "Holy Land" of the Middle East, yet the same folk are often among the biggest fans in sports and see no contradiction between their enthusiasm for sports and the spirit of the Gospels. This is not to decry any participation or love of sports by anyone of any faith but only to say that if we believed an interaction between cultures was inevitably degrading to both, then fundamentalist Christians would decry athletics altogether as both emperors Theodosius did in the fourth and fifth centuries. The influence of Jerusalem and Athens, often competitive, upon western civilization is immeasurable, and if either

---

[4] *The Roman Way* (New York: W.W. Norton, 1970) 130.
[5] Rudolph Brasch, *How Did Sports Begin? A Look at the Origins of Man at Play* (New York: David McKay Co., 1970) 414.

influence were removed, what remained of our culture would be severely diminished and unrecognizable.

Further, to what extent we deify sports will depend in large measure on how we integrate and separate the dual heritage of our civilization and indeed that of Rome, which conquered Greece and Israel. On a grand scale, Rome specialized in sports and religion for entertainment at home, the theater of bread and circuses, and conquest abroad in the theater of war. Again, as in the case of Greece and Israel, if we took away from our culture the contributions of Rome, say in architecture, law, language, and literature and including military sport, ideals of duty, honor, and country (common to other ancient states, especially Sparta), the remains would be skeletal. Indeed other countries have helped shape us and make us what we are. Still, in terms of the ongoing relation between sports, state, and religion, we turn to Athens, Jerusalem, and Rome to understand the history of the conflict and the wisdom for dealing with it.

Considering all the nations of the world, it would appear that we have plenty of armies and plenty of religions as well. From our perspective, the challenge is to do a better job with the religions we have rather than dragging still another, a Religion of Sports, onto a crowded field and attributing to it holy virtues it may not inherently possess. At the same time, this is not to deny sports qualities of high value that potentially could play a significant role in creating a good and just society. Socrates seems to address that possibility when in the *Republic* he remarks, "The best is he/she who mingles music [literally music and academic disciplines] and gymnastic [athletics] and attunes them to the soul."[6]

Sports and the Soul: The American Heritage

A primary question we address in this study concerns the issue of the balance of mind, body, and soul in individuals rather than in the body politic. Historian Henry Adams thought the question of proportion was basic to values in a democracy. In a section called "American Ideals" in his *History of the United States During the Administration of Thomas Jefferson*, he imagines Jefferson saying these words:

---

[6] *Plato, Republic: Book III, Five Great Dialogues*, trans. Benjamin Jowett (New York: Walter J. Black, 1942) 300.

If we can bring it about that men are on the average an inch taller in the next generation than this; if they are an inch larger around the chest; if their brain is an ounce or two heavier, and their life a year or two longer—that is progress. If fifty years hence the average man shall invariably argue from two ascertained premises where he now jumps to a conclusion from a single supposed revelation—that is progress! I expect it to be made here, under our democratic stimulants, on a great scale, until every man is potentially an athlete in body and an Aristotle in mind.

The imagined response of the New Englander, John Adams, was this, stunning in its brevity and insight: "What will you do for moral progress?" Henry Adams remarks that "Jefferson held the faith that men would improve morally with their physical and intellectual growth."[7]

There are two great dangers implied in this imaginary dialogue. One is that the ancient ideal of *mens sana in corpore sano* (sound mind in a sound body) is all a nation needs for moral growth. The other is that religion with its professed attention to the soul can provide the necessary influence to shape and attune mind and body into a harmonious whole. Perhaps religion can do that, unless it cultivates a theocracy that inevitably leads to oppression. Our opinion is that making a religion of sports only complicates matters. In their traditional secular form, sports provide fun, create widespread interest and excitement, and regularly dazzle by their physical grace and beauty.

Sanctification moves them even further away from the world of intellect and further from traditional religion. As much as Jefferson and Adams differed on any number of issues, we cannot imagine either endorsing a religion of sports, Jefferson even going so far as to say that the "game of ball" did little toward forming character. Adams's question about "moral progress" does not go away. In contrast to behaviorists like B. F. Skinner, Adams takes for granted the existence of the soul, which allows him to ask implicitly about the church's role in developing it, and mind and body as well. Conversely, another question has recently emerged or reemerged: What is the role of sports in the context of education and

---

[7] H. Adams, "American Ideals," *History of the United States During the Administration of Thomas Jefferson* (New York: A. and C. Boni, 1939) 1:179.

learning as conceived by Jefferson and in the care of the soul as envisioned by Adams?

Like the weather, to which they may be compared in their ubiquity, sports are deeply rooted in nature, which we suspect accounts for their lasting appeal. We are not abstractions but humans rooted in places, which, as Michael Novak has observed in *The Joy of Sports* (1976), is why we "root." Whatever successes the Enlightenment might have had, it failed to yank us completely out of nature, which is what Walt Whitman wanted us to cherish along with the soul. He, like Jefferson and Adams, was aware of the dangers threatening the idea of wholeness in America. For this reason, he never tired of calling himself and reminding others that he, Walt Whitman, was "the poet of the body and the poet of the soul" and would have neither exercising dominion over the other.

For Whitman, as for Homer, *arête* (excellence) must exist, if it exists at all, in the light of common day, amid those who plow, cook, sail, box, wrestle, run races, and throw the discus—amid, Whitman would add, all the "Occupations." For Whitman as for Homer, the soul is inseparable from the body, even indistinguishable from it, as D. H. Lawrence remarks:

> Whitman was the first to smash the old moral conception, that the soul of man is something "superior" and "above" the flesh. Even Emerson maintained this tiresome superiority of the soul. Even Melville could not get over it. Whitman was the first heroic seer to seize the soul by the scruff of the neck and plant her among the potsherds.
>
> "There!" he said to the soul. "Stay there!"
>
> Stay there. Stay in the flesh. Stay in the limbs and lips and in the belly. Stay in the breast and in the womb. Stay there, O Soul, where you belong.[8]

Not everyone has been pleased with what Whitman did with the soul or more perhaps with the elevation of the body. Randall Stewart in *American Literature and Christian Doctrine* places Whitman along with Emerson outside of Christian orthodoxy and Hawthorne and Melville within it; Stewart felt that the latter two recognized and wrote about the mystery of

---

[8] Lawrence, *Studies in Classic American Literature* (Garden City: Doubleday and Company, 1951) 184.

iniquity while Emerson and Whitman deified man. It may be that Stewart's own view is too simplistic or too general, but one thing is certain—all these great writers and poets, orthodox or heretical, knew the Bible, which Stewart calls "the single greatest influence on our literature."[9] Whitman was soaked in the knowledge of it though the lessons learned from Scripture, other readings, and experiences which led him away from the camps of doctrine of his day. This is easily inferred in his poem, "To Him Who Was Crucified": "My spirit to yours dear brother, / Do not mind because many sounding your name do not understand you, / I do not sound your name, but I understand you."[10]

Whitman claimed not to have read the "Orientals," but in *Whitman in the Light of Vedantic Mysticism,* V. K. Chari states that in *Leaves of Grass* Whitman describes the essential soul of Vedanta without ostensibly attempting to do so. Dr. Richard Bucke saw him as a splendid example of cosmic consciousness, the title of Bucke's famous book, in the tradition of Moses, Jesus, Saint Paul, Shakespeare, Balzac, Buddha, and others. Harold Bloom in the *Western Canon* places him at the center of the American canon. Did Whitman have a "position" on the connection between sports and religion? Yes, but a broad one indeed. If Homer in the *Odyssey* was the first poet to use the word "athlete," Walt Whitman in *Leaves of Grass* was the first and perhaps only poet to make the claim that he was "the teacher of athletes." "Yes," we can hear Randall Stewart saying, "that is precisely something he would say." One of the issues we wish to examine is the relation between the new Religion of Sports and the "the deification of man" that, in Stewart's view, took deep root in America in the transcendental thinking and writing of both Emerson and Whitman, *who in that process, Stewart argues, dismissed the idea of evil and removed all barriers to the limits of egos of mortals.*

Here we mention Whitman's achievements and the longstanding controversy about him for one purpose—to ask in an imaginative way what Walt Whitman, the freest of free spirits, singing upon the open road in our own time, would do and say if on a Friday afternoon before a football game, he came upon a pep rally around a flagpole in front of a small-town high school in the American South, and then heard prayers led by football players

---

[9] Stewart, *American Literature and Christian Doctrine* (Baton Rouge: Louisiana State University Press, 1958) 3.

[10] *Walt Whitman: Complete Poetry and Selected Prose*, ed. James E. Miller (Boston: Riverside Press) 271–72.

followed by the singing of "Onward Christian Soldiers," considering that Walt believed he made "holy" whatever he touched? Perhaps he would smile and not answer at all, much like Christ when asked by the Grand Inquisitor in *The Brothers Karamazov* why he did not turn the stone into bread.

We suspect he might surprise us as he might in regard to another question regarding which simile concerning the relation of sports and religion is most apt. Would he agree with Deion's perception that they are like peanut butter and jelly, or with ours, that they do not mix as the case of oil and water? We will hold our imagined version of his response until the end of the book after competing evidence from all sides has been examined and fairly presented.

Though Whitman clearly loved sports and sang their praises, including the praise of "athletic mothers," he would be puzzled by the effort to make a religion of sports as would Socrates, as we might guess from his comments on the need for balance between all sides of the human being. Saint Paul used metaphors of sports but made no effort to raise sports to a divine status. Though sports abounded in the ancient world, Jesus as far as we know never mentioned them. The same is true of Moses and Buddha. There is, though, one set of gods and heroes who are clapping wildly, immensely pleased at all they see—Zeus and his children, Apollo, Hercules, Nike, and Mercury. One can hear their cheers and the Olympian laugh of the father.

In response to these issues, our hope is not for definitive answers, certainly not dogmatic ones, but for a well-informed discussion.

Shining Bright and Staying Quiet:
Two Stars Named Sanders

We began this chapter with a simile by "Neon" Deion Sanders that sports and religion go together like peanut butter and jelly. "Neon" is a name that resonates widely in popular culture with the name "Jesus" as in 'Neon Jesus' signs, "Neon Jesus" musical contests, and a wide assortment of commercial products such as Plush Bears holding embroidered hearts which says "Jesus Loves You" and each in a neon color. Apparently for Deion, the glory of Christ and his own are symbiotic. Neon Deion would point to the sky, thanking God for his success. A question might be raised by Deion's metaphor when his endorsement of Tim Green's acclaimed book, *The Dark Side of the NFL*—"Shows the realness of life in the NFL without exaggeration"—is taken into account.

Interestingly, another super star by the name of Sanders took a different approach. We refer to Barry Sanders, who ranks third of all time in rushing yardage behind Emmet Smith and Walter Peyton and who was inducted into the Pro Football Hall of Fame in 2004. Nicknamed "Sweetness," Sanders writes in his book, "I've never been fond of public attention or of dealing with the media. I don't mean to sound aloof; being in the spotlight just isn't my nature.... I never valued the record so much that I thought it was worth my dignity...to pursue it." Deeply and quietly religious, Sanders, when he signed a 2.1 million-dollar bonus, gave a tenth to Paradise Baptist Church in Wichita, Kansas, and "continued to give ten percent of his salary to charity throughout his career."[11]

From a distance, Barry Sanders appears to be what Jim Whitehead in *Joiner*, a novel about professional football, calls a "secret Christian," while Deon is certainly a public one. This is no attempt to judge Deion in light of Barry or vice versa since we do not know either man, but the overwhelming conspicuousness of Deion's behavior seems to fall within the public domain. Such public displays of religion may well cast doubts about the growing kinship between sports and religion such as those registered by sports columnist Richard Crepeau in "Holy Touchdown":

> In a recent interview, Deion Sanders, the Billy Sunday of Jesus jocks, said he doesn't see how he could have sports in his life without religion: "They go together like peanut butter and jelly."
>
> If you find Deion's imagery a bit thin in theological clout, then the merchandise available at Catholic Supply of St. Louis might be a bit more to your liking. Here you will find an array of items mixing sport and religion in the most banal, yet somehow aggressively tasteless, fashion. It seems that when it comes to merchandising religious kitsch, there is no bottom.
>
> Let us explore the abyss.

Among the items offered by Catholic Supply and noted by Crepeau are the following among the 6-inch Jesus Sports Statues:

---

[11] John Wiebusch, "Running into Greatness," AOL Exclusive: http://poptop.hypermart. net/testbs2.html 25 November 2003.

In baseball, Jesus helps a young boy with his swing while another as catcher stands behind them without a mask, which "safety freaks" will notice. The gospel song "Jesus at the Home Plate" comes to mind.

The Soccer Jesus is in a running pose with a ball on his toe, moving it forward to two other boys. Robes and sandals seem to be no problem for this Pele divinity.

For the track, Jesus is assisting in passing the baton from one boy to another. I don't think this is what the Rev. Malcolm Boyd had in mind when he wrote, "Are you running with me, Jesus?"

For the hockey statuette, Jesus is the third man in the faceoff. This not only pushes the rulebook but is an aesthetic violation: Three sticks in a faceoff is very messy.

In football, Jesus is seen handing off to a young boy. Take this ball and run with it, Johnny. What is surprising and troubling is that another boy is tackling Jesus.

I don't want to offend anyone here, but it seems to me that all this mixing of sport and religious merchandise from Catholic Supply is evidence of the corruption of American Catholicism by the purveyors of Positive Thinking of Protestantism. The poorly veiled mix of Bruce Barton and Norman Vincent Peale platitudes has penetrated the Catholic mainstream. It is a derivative of what Jonathan Edwards called "Smiling Christianity," a form of comfortable theology made available in New England for the new burgeoning middle class merchants of the early 18th century. It now has arrived for the new century in all of its American merchandising glory and splendor.

Pass the peanut butter and jelly.[12]

The Cross and the Coliseum: How Stands the Union?

In our thinking, the simile or metaphor that best expresses the relation between sports and religion is oil and water, which seems analogous to Jesus' metaphor of the things of Caesar and the things of God. The terms

---

[12] Richard C. Crepeau, "Holy Touchdown! Forget coaches. With God on their side, how could young athletes go wrong?" <http://www.poppolitics.com/articles/2001-07-31-holy. shtml> (20 February 2004).

peanut butter and jelly, of course, do not appear in Scripture, while references to oil and water abound both in terms of practical and symbolic use. In reference to biblical passages about Jesus, we will attempt to follow the advice of Albert Schweitzer to look at Jesus in the historical context of his own time. That being the case, we find no evidence that he was a sports fan any more than Saint Paul was.

While such figures as Buddha, Moses, Mohammed, and Jesus are central to "churchly" religions and even affiliates such as Fellowship of Christian Athletes, Athletes in Action, and all that was once implied by "Sportianity," the relation between them and the Church of Sports is ambiguous, especially in the case of Jesus. On the one hand there seems to be little influence of Jesus or other founders of traditional faiths upon the tenets of the Religion of Sport, which pleads its case on parallels between modern games and sacred rites of preliterate cultures. Yet above the stadium on the jacket of the latest book on sports apologetics, *From Season to Season* (by Joseph Price), there stands the cross. Why? Essentially, the remainder of *An Unholy Alliance* is our response to this question.

The relation between the cross and the coliseum is old and troubled, not as chummy as they have appeared in recent years. To us, they are more like oil and water than peanut butter and jelly. We want to be fair, though, and represent Deion's case as well as our own and those of apologists. In our final chapter we will, as we said, ask for a nonbinding ruling by the greatest of all American poets and "teacher of athletes," Walt Whitman. In an undertaking like this, no one can be defeated, for even those who are "wrong" contribute as much to understanding as those who may be "right." Or in the words of Old Walt, in section 18 of "Song of Myself" "Vivas to those who have fail'd![13]"

---

[13] New York: Knopf, 1968. The idea of the "Secret Christian" pervades this novel as it does the works of Dietrich Bonhoeffer see, for example *Letters and Papers from Prison* (New York: Macmillan, 1953) 188. The notion of "the secret Christian" relates to Bonhoeffer's "Religionless Christianity" which will be examined in more detail in a later chapter.

Chapter 2

What's in a Name? Working Definitions of Sports and Religion

Essential in a project of this nature is a common understanding in the meaning of terms used in discussion. On H-Arete, the online service of the Sports Literature Association (SLA), there has been of late a spirited exchange regarding the definition of sports. Huizinga informed us that we cannot know with certainty what sport is (*Homo Ludens* 212), and the same appears true in the case of religion, especially if we consider the testimony of Scripture, which reminds us that we can never fathom the mind of the central figure in many if not most religions, the being called "God" as made clear in the Judeo-Christian tradition in Job 11:7, 21:14, 36:26; Psalm 77:19; and Romans 11:33. Such a notion runs contrary to the assertions of a host of television evangelists who would have us believe that such an undertaking is *no problem* since they are in constant touch with the almighty, omniscient, and the infinite, even in matters of weather predictions and presidential elections.

Students of the literature of sports appear more cautious about what we are doing and dealing with. Considerable emphasis is placed upon the quest for clearer definitions in the spirit of philosophy, at least of the Aristotelian kind. According to Enrico Berti in a lecture at the University of Creta, "In conclusion, we may affirm that all the branches of Aristotelian philosophy, logic and physics, biology and psychology, metaphysics, ethics, politics and rhetoric continue to be at the center of attention of contemporary philosophers and to provide a true arsenal of conceptual tools, i.e. definitions, distinctions, connections, classifications, for the philosophy of today. This is true even if nobody today would like to define himself an

Aristotelian."[1] In sports-as-religion texts, there is a general weakness in the quality and precision of "conceptual tools," especially in "definitions" and "distinctions," but it is an understandable flaw considering the magnitude of the problem.

While we cannot define with exactness either sports or religion, any more than Tennyson could a "flower in the crannied wall" or Whitman the "grass," we might come to understand better the nature of both through a comparison of characteristics apparently common to both. Indeed, this is an underlying assumption on our part, an epistemological method with distinguished endorsement running all the way back to Aristotle and onward through Goethe ("connect, only connect"), E. M. Forster (the name of the Forster web site is "Only Connect"), and Leslie Fiedler who in *No! In Thunder* speaks of the inability to connect as "the endemic disease" of this age.

We need to remember that the function of the scholar, as Emerson said, is to show similarities amid differences and differences amid similarities. In the case of several scholars writing about sports and religion, the emphasis is upon similarities, i.e. "connections" between sports and religion rather than "differences" between them. Today the "commingling" of sports and religion and the confusion of both make the challenge of definitions much greater than just a few decades ago, when categories of cultural phenomena such as sports and religion were more compartmentalized and at least easier to identify if not to define.

Indeed logic itself sometimes becomes bereft in efforts to equate them. In the world of big-time college and professional sports, logic does not appear to be as valuable as marketability. In such an environment, almost any commingling of religion and football, regardless of rational connection, leads to further popularity and increase in economic advantage. In analyzing why the Southeastern Conference leads all other conferences in NCAA violations in football, Bobby Bowden said it was because in the South football is a religion. Perhaps acts of hellfire and damnation on the gridiron by opposing teams lead to an increase in football's "holiest of holies" in Sports World, the foundation's treasury.

Is Bowden's assertion a connection or a "disconnect" (a verb-become-noun now popular on television)? Could it be that the breaking of rules is

---

[1] Enrico Berti, "The Present Relevance of Aristotle's Thought," <http://www.rcs.re.it/banfi/olimpo/rilevance.htm> (2 March 2004).

analogous to sin and the South has more sinners per capita than the rest of the nation? Could it be that the acknowledgment of such sin is the surest sign of the presence nearby of traditional religion? Is Bowden's comment another way of expressing Flannery O'Connor's observation in *Mystery and Manners* that while the South is not "Christ-centered" it is certainly "Christ-haunted"? In such a context, it could be that the religion of football is a leading cause for record-breaking performances in violation of NCAA rules, which are contained in a text of "Thou Shall Nots" as complicated in its own way as Deuteronomy and other parts of holy Scripture.

Conceptual Tools, Definitions, and Distinctions

With the need for "conceptual tools" in mind for such a bold and complicated mission as undertaken in his book, Joseph Price makes a discernible effort in describing boundaries and providing ground rules. While he is aware of the need for defining terms, we do not discover what he means by "religion" until his final chapter, though we have had clues all along. "Although religions do not necessarily involve the worship of 'God' or 'gods,' they do orient their followers towards an ultimate force or pantheon of powers, whether personalized as 'gods' or whether identified in abstracted ways, for example, Buddhism's path of enlightenment or Shinto's abiding sense of family and tradition."[2]

While Price focuses upon the presence of religious myth evident in American sports, his general understanding of "religion" in the text differs significantly from that suggested by the first definition in *Webster's Unabridged* (2d edition): "The service and adoration of God or a god as expressed in forms of worship, in obedience to divine commands, especially, as found in sacred *writings* [ital. added] or as declared by recognized teachers and in the pursuit of a way of life regarded as incumbent upon true believers, as ministers of *religion*." Note that while Price does not box himself in by limiting religion to the worship of a "God or gods" but expands possibilities to include the idea of an ultimate force or pantheon of powers, he goes far beyond "sacred writings" to sacred myths of prehistory that he and others still find in modern sports and that invite comparative analysis. There are other more secondary definitions including "systems of belief" that seem more closely aligned to the thinking of all

---

[2] Price, *From Season to Season: Sports as American Religion* (Macon GA: Mercer University Press, 2001) 228.

apologists. Not only is Price broad-minded and tolerant in his definition, but he winds up on common ground with *Webster's* and standard sources in theology.[3]

Defining "religion" and agreeing on what it is seems almost simple compared to the same challenge presented by "sports." In the middle of the eighteenth century, Dr. Samuel Johnson in the first English dictionary essentially equated "sport" with "play," which to him was "diversion, game, frolic and tumultuous merriment." The last phrase has a lasting charm if not the scope to encompass everything now generally passing under "sport" or the plural thereof as in the wide-ranging definition in *Webster's Sports Dictionary*: "A recreational or competitive activity which involves a degree of physical exertion or which requires skill in the playing of an object (as a ball, disk, or shuttlecock) for scoring." The *Sports Dictionary* acknowledges "a wide divergence of opinion as to what constitutes a sport, but for the purpose of the dictionary the term encompasses races, athletic contests in which the outcome is in doubt, and outdoor physical recreations such as hunting and fishing, hiking and sailing, but excludes board and card games and children's games."

Volumes such as *From Season to Season* are not about sport in the sense of hunting and fishing but *sports*, plural, also known as "athletics," which according to *Webster's* are "exercises, sports, and games engaged in by athletes." Who are "athletes"? "Those trained or skilled in exercises, sports, or games requiring physical strength or stamina." Even *Webster's* seems to err on the side of caution since common experience tells us, as the Greek roots *athlein* (to contend for a prize) and *athlon* (prize or contest) clearly indicate, that athletes are those who meet the criteria of the basic definition but who also compete for *prizes* in *public* places. In modern American sports, the prizes are often substantial financially and the public places famous indeed, including the annual sites of the World Series, the Super Bowl, and the Final Four.[4]

---

[3] See, for example, *The Westminster Dictionary of Christian Theology*

[4] For more on the complexity of definitions of "sport" and the distinctions between "sport," "play," and "game," see part 1 and part 2 of *Philosophic Inquiry into Sport,* ed. William J. Morgan and Klaus V. Meier (Champaigne IL: Human Kinetics Publishers, 1988). See also Allen Guttman, *Ritual to Record: The Nature of Modern Sports* (New York: Columbia University Press, 1978) 1–14.

The Religion of Sports and the Theology of Play

The assertions made in *From Season to Season* on the several connections between sports and religion reverberate throughout the text to the point that after a while, the Bed of Procrustes begins to hove into view in spite of a wide diversity of subjects by the contributors. This hammering of the overall thesis, though, is an editorial matter instead of one of theme and content. On the plus side, we know where Price stands on the subject, and his fellow theologians traveling other paths generally endorse the main argument. At least there are no apostates as far as we can tell.

All the contributors offer engaging views, but one message is always the same. If we are to understand modern sports, we had better look at them as varieties of religious experience, even as a religion itself, a "Popular Religion" in Price's terms or "Folk Religion" in James Mathisen's essay. Previous apologists such as Novak have spoken of sports as a "Natural Religion," and Catherine Albanese includes sports and play under "Cultural Religion," but the common term uniting them all would be a "Religion of Sports," not to be confused with a "Theology of Play" that has been much discussed in recent years.[5] While there is overlap between the two, there are important distinctions. The "Religion of Sports" is built on a high degree of competition or "gratuitous difficulty"—what Caillois in *Man, Play, and Games* calls "Ludus"—while a "Theology of Play" emphasizes "Paideia" or the unfettered and unregulated play of childhood. The former is agonic while the latter is edenic.[6]

All these modifiers—" Cultural," "Folk," "Natural," and "Popular"— illustrate a phenomenon at work in *From Season to Season*, the inexplicable tendency of the word "religion" to capture adjectives of one kind or another and to align itself over millennia with festivals, tournaments, and athletics and often, unfortunately, self-righteousness and arrogance. The alliance is baffling since hardly any other category of human experience qualifies for

---

[5] For a summary of discussion and arguments on this theme, see Robert J. Higgs, ch. 14, "Philosophy and Religion," especially 210–25, in *Sport: A Reference Guide* (Greenwood, 1982); Ronnie D. Kliever, "Theologies of Play," 124–52, 224–27, in *The Shattered Spectrum* (Richmond: John Knox Press, 1981); and Kliever's essay, "Gods and Games in Modern Culture," in Price, *From Season to Season*.

[6] See Robert J. Higgs, "The Agonic and the Edenic: Sport Literature and the Theory of Play," in *The Achievement of American Sport Literature: A Critical Appraisal*, ed. Wiley Lee Umphlett (Madison, NJ: Fairleigh Dickinson, 1991).

the almost universal praise and even sanctification rendered unto sports, even religion itself.

A person who reads too much is a "bookworm," one eating too much or having too much sex is an "addict," one obsessed by drink an "alcoholic," and obsessed by work a "workaholic." Even a person holding too conspicuously to a single point of view in a particular faith is a "fanatic," but one overindulging in "sports" either as a player or a fan, is practicing a "religion." In the *Joy of Sports*, Michael Novak would have us believe that, increasing fan violence throughout Sports World notwithstanding, the word "fan" itself, if not of divine origin, has an etymology that borders on the sacred: "To be a fan is totally in keeping with being a man. To have particular loyalties is not to be deficient in universality." We never heard anyone deny this. Novak goes on to note that a root word of fan is "fantastic" as well "fanatic," and he notes the connection of "fan" to *fanun*, "the temple of the god of the place."

In religion the term "fanatic" is derogatory enough that anyone so described would be offended. On the other hand, sports fans, or at least the many we know, jokingly acknowledge their fanaticism about a team or sport. Today sports fanaticism, school or town "spirit," appears innocent and harmless while religious fanaticism conjures up memories of witch trials of the seventeenth century and images of suicide bombers on the evening news.

One reason for such a symbiotic relationship between sports and religion is that both are so old that some of the best scholars such as Johan Huizinga and Rene Girard differ on which came first, much like the question of the chicken and the egg. They are so ancient that at one time in "great antiquity," as the encyclopedias state, perhaps 3,000 years ago, they were inseparable from magic and combat, even murder, as in the story of the "King of the Wood" at Nemi in the Alban Hills of Italy as marvelously described in the opening pages of Frazer's classic, *The Golden Bough*.

Based on Genesis and logic, one might say that the freedom of play, as opposed to the competition of sports, came first since unfettered play certainly appears to have been a prominent feature of Eden, whereas religion only came on the scene *after* the sin of the fall, which brought about the necessity not only to labor but to *hunt,* a form of competition between man and nature. Now that "sin" has again disappeared, as discussed by Karl Menninger in *Whatever Happened to Sin?* (1983), the state of religion itself is in question with no less an authority than Bill Maher saying he has no respect for any religion. Not so with the sports apologists who not only pay respect to and acknowledge the good of traditional religions, though in a limited space, but also assume they are doing a favor to the world of sports by elevating them to the status of religion in and of themselves. Are they, though, devaluing both sports and traditional religion by seeking a common currency between the two? Instead of being like peanut butter and jelly, are sports and religion more like oil and water as earlier suggested?

Theology Versus Mythology

While several theologians have written on the religion of sports, it is not strictly speaking a subject of "theology," "the study of religious faith, practice, or experience; *esp*: the study of God and his relationship to the world" (*Webster's*), nor can it be classified as a study of "ideology" ("visionary theorizing") except perhaps indirectly according to the secondary definition of that term, "a systematic body of concepts esp. about human life and culture." What is called a religion of sports involves first and foremost a study in "mythos" or "mythology," "a *pattern* [italics added] of beliefs expressing often symbolically the characteristics or prevalent attitudes in a group or culture." Several sports apologists know this and practice it with considerable skill even while straining to squeeze their often impressive commentary into the procrustean bed of religion.

"Mythos," according to Lord Raglan in *The Hero*, means "out of the mouth," suggesting an oral heritage from preliterate societies quite different from the literate and literary traditions on which most conventional religions *appear* to be based as well as "theology" or a study of them. It is true that literature is often a vehicle of myth originating in time out of mind. Indeed, common sense, never mind the theories of science, tells us that the bedrock of all religions and all other categories of human society extends "backward" into the mists of primordial time. In the caves of our souls, each of us, like Job, is a "brother to dragons and a companion of owls" (Job 30:29), seeking light from knowledge that holy (healing or saving) words might offer. The first step, like that of Job, is admitting our condition and dependency on knowledge greater than our own. Like the literature of nations, that of religions arose "out of the mouth," the word spoken by the sword of the tongue before committed to paper by the sword of the pen and too often expressed at the point of a literal sword.

The distinctions between "mythology" and "theology" used here are essentially the same as those Joseph Campbell makes concerning his own studies as seen most notably in *The Power of Myth* with Bill Moyers. Price's book is about the "Power of Myth" in American sports throughout a year, that is, every year. Please note that it is not necessarily a good thing to turn myth into a creed, a system of belief, to turn the nonrational into the rational, an effort that often backfires, as we hope will be the case with a religion of sports.

In the discussion with Campbell on these topics, Moyers makes the following statements that are in effect questions for Campbell to address:

"Religion begins with a sense of wonder and awe and the attempt to tell stories that will connect us to God. Then it becomes a set of theological works in which everything is reduced to a code, to a creed."

Campbell responds: That's the reduction of mythology to theology. Most of the myths are self-contradictory. You may find four or five myths in a given culture, all giving different versions of the same mystery. Then theology comes along and says it has got to be just this way. Mythology is poetry, and poetic language is very flexible.

"Religion turns poetry into prose. God is literally up there, and this is literally what he thinks, and this is the way you've got to behave to get into proper relationship with that god up there."[7]

Today finger pointing is more popular than ever, especially with the right index finger, which is accusatory and symbolic of the spear according to Elias Canetti in *Crowds and Power*. When it is pointing upward, as often seen in games of baseball and football, it is a signal of thanks to God for providing power and skill in making a touchdown or hitting a home run. When whole stadiums of people shake their fingers upward, it is usually a sign of drunkenness of spirit celebrating their victory over opponents. Sore losers in contests, taunted by victors, have been known to respond by use of another finger. On the whole, it can be said with some confidence that behavior of fans at ball games is less civilized than congregants at religious services, though possibly not less civilized than some of the same members at monthly business meetings of the church. Humor aside, some "fans" of religions or religious fanatics are capable of atrocities the ordinary sports enthusiasts could not imagine unless, like the rest of us, seeing such proof all too often on the evening news.

The relationship of myth to religion and of both to art and sport (as in hunting) is older than we can imagine. In a paraphrase of some of

---

[7] Moyers, *Power of Myth,* ed. Betty Sue Flowers (New York: Doubleday, 1988) 141–42.

Campbell's commentary in the introduction to *The Power of Myth*, Bill
Moyers writes,

> Out there somewhere beyond the physical plane of existence,
> was the 'animal master,' who held over human beings the power of
> life and death. Early societies learned that 'the essence of life is that
> it lives by killing and eating; that's the great mystery that myths
> have to deal with.' The hunt became a ritual of sacrifice, and the
> hunters in turn performed acts of atonement to the departed spirits
> of the animals, hoping to coax them into returning to be captured
> again. The beasts were seen as envoys from that other world, and
> Campbell surmised a 'magical, wonderful accord' growing between
> the hunter and the hunted, as if they were locked in a mystical,
> timeless cycle of death, burial, and resurrection. Their art—the
> paintings on cave walls—and oral literature gave form to the
> impulse we call religion.[8]

Representatives of the cave painting Moyer refers to are those in the Grotto
of Lascaux in Southern France.[9]

Traces of the ancient rites of atonement can be found in grace or thanks
before meals in homes and in communion in churches, while all other kinds
also associated with the hunt and war are evident in sports all around us,
especially in the territorial sports such as baseball, basketball, football, and
hockey. Rituals of competition or the myths they inspire are expressed in
team names, chants, cheers, camaraderie, intensity of commitment, and
celebration of victory, from the taunting chop of the "Tomahawk" at Atlanta
Braves baseball games to elaborate dances in end zones by receivers and
runners following a touchdown in the NFL. The question remains: Are these
and similar rites "religious"?

Perhaps they are and perhaps not, depending upon definitions and their
malleability. Where possible we will attempt to be heretical in regard to this
emerging new orthodoxy of the religion of sports, keeping in mind that
heresies, as Hans Kung has stated in *The Church,* only make established
faiths stronger through self-examination or, as sometimes happens, create
fissures that may bring lasting schisms or even collapse. The landscape of

---

[8] Ibid., xvi–xvii.
[9] Ibid., 68.

history is dotted with the rise and fall of both heresies and religions. It is impossible to imagine one without the other and hard to imagine either as being absolutely right about everything. Whether the religion of sports will become another casualty of time and circumstance remains to be seen. It has no chance of success, though, without undergoing the toughest scrutiny possible.

The Latest Apology: The Significance of "As"

Instead of concentrating upon expressions of traditional forms of worship at games—that is, pre-game and half-time prayers and witnessing of players through verbal testimony and acts of thanks, pointing upward when they score, and the like—Price and company in *From Season to Season* do something quite different and even more provocative than debating issues over relations between church and state or sports and state. They look upon patterns of competition in major American sports as expressions of ancient religious myth, as inevitable as the seasons, and even provide a calendar for them. They are not blind to the several abuses in our big games, but the advantages in their view outweigh the burdens by providing practical structural myths that give order, coherence, and meaning to our culture or at least to a sizeable portion of it.

Though *From Season to Season* is a study of sports and religion, the structure of the book, as opposed to theme and argument, is similar to that of *Anatomy of Criticism* by Northrop Frye. Perspectives are offered on Genres (the various sports or "denominations" as well as categories of major sporting events, "spectacle," "festival," "ritual," and "game"), Myths ("Eternal Return" and the significance of the seasons), Symbols, ("McGwire's Balls," the pitcher's mound as Omphalos, Halls of Fame), and Modes (varieties of heroes and the heroic, Matty, Gehrig, and Clemente). This is a "polysemus" approach that Frye endorsed and that is evident in Price's statement of intention in the opening essay called "Fervent Faith: Sports as Religion in America."

Says Price,

> In this collection the essays analyze and celebrate sports *as* religious in two ways, always considering sports as religious rather than looking at the impact of sports on ecclesiastical traditions or trying to decipher the ways in which a peculiar form of religious ethics is challenged by or buttressed by sporting competition....A

second way of construing the relation between sport and religion is one that emerges out of the sorts of analysis frequently undertaken by sociologists and historians in their discussion of civil religion. In this regard several of the essays direct attention to Catherine Albanese's discussion of sports (in *America: Religion and Religions* as one manifestation of "Cultural Religion" in her imaginative survey of American religious history and experience).[10]

The importance of Albanese's book for *From Season to Season*, and of Eliade's work in turn, can be easily inferred from Price's comments in his essay "From Sabbath Proscriptions to Super Sunday Celebrations":

> Combining emphases from Johan Huizinga, a theoretician of play, and Mircea Eliade, historian of American religion, Albanese points out that "both play and ritual are satisfying for their own sake.... Sports and deliberate religious rituals, through their performances, create an 'other' world of meaning complete with its own rules and boundaries, dangers and successes." In other words, both sports and religious rituals establish a sense of order by creating a "world." "By setting up boundaries and defining the space of the game, sports have helped Americans fit a grid to their own experience in order to define it and give it structure," Albanese continues.[11]

Though it is not used in the passage cited above, a key word in this text is "as," which Price makes clear at the outset. With Price's use (and overuse in our view) of the word "as"—it appears ten times in the sense of simile between pages seven and nine—we would argue that there is an accompanying "if," as in "as if." We suspect we all know that sports, at least since the development of religious texts in literate times, do not truly constitute what we normally call a religion, but we might gain a better knowledge of their significance by considering them "as if" they are, a legitimate stratagem and perhaps something of a game, but at least a phrase with something of a religious connection. The Calvinist, when asked how he

---

[10] Ibid., 7–8.
[11] Ibid., 36.

could know he was among the elect since only God knew beforehand who was destined for heaven or hell, replied that he lived *as if* he were.

Throughout the essays, the use of "as" as simile serves its intended function, but by the end, by the last sentence in the book, "as" has become an "is" or the equivalent of "is" in the closing argument, which, stated again for emphasis to counteract disbelief, is as follows: "In America, quite simply, sports constitute a form of popular religion."[12] Is this a credo to make us joyful about our competitive nature, one that hints at a faint dread without a name, or maybe both at once?

The danger of attempting to make sport a religion, even one qualified by the word "popular," is the distinct possibility of an opposite effect, legitimizing religion as sports, trivializing the grand purposes of religions in spite of failures that all human institutions experience. Having the world's largest congregation or Sunday school, becoming top dog in the manner of national champions, and providing services for membership can easily become more important than providing services for "the least of these" in a community. Like sports organizations, who notoriously support causes and then advertise their charity on television as the NFL does in regard to the United Way, churches too become boastful of their charities when in fact, according to the teaching of Jesus, generosity is supposed to be anonymous, partly to keep any of us from thinking ourselves more generous than we actually are, a holy injunction. In its extreme manifestation, religion has become a blood sport as we see every night on the news in the box scores and body counts from around the globe in contests for economic prizes and sacred territory.

To have any chance of understanding the rapid transformation taking place in our culture, we need to understand as best we can the differences, as opposed to the similarities, between the holy, the "inconceivable," that which according to Otto is "peculiar to the sphere of religion," and the sacred, that which is held in special esteem in *any* field of human endeavor, and of the distinctions between both the "secular" and the "profane."

---

[12] Ibid., 229.

Chapter 3

The Sacred and the Holy
Distinguishing the Indefinable

Most of us normally think of two elements when religion comes to mind: ethics or commandments and the rites of worshiping a transcendent being. In books on sports apologetics, there is not a great deal of attention paid to either element. Instead, there is much talk about the transcendence of the athlete that causes "religious" responses in athletes and fans, which happens in the "sacred" setting of games in "sacred" time, as opposed to routine time in profane places where we daily labor. If there is a linchpin term in the emerging orthodoxy of sports as religion, it is the word "sacred," as in the title of Mircea Eliade's book *Sacred and Profane.*

The pattern among theologians of sports is to contrast the exciting and transformative world of sports with the weary, humdrum, everyday world of the "profane," from *pro* and *fanum* or "before a temple," and with the "secular," from *seacularis,* "coming once in an age," and *saeculum,* "generation." In our book we will move in an opposite direction toward more difficult territory and with a different purpose, contrasting the "sacred" with another idea, that of the "holy." Webster's offers "secular" as a synonym for "profane," but they are not identical any more than the "sacred" is to the "holy." Certainly, they occasionally overlap, but not as much as we tend to assume.

Speaking in Metaphor:
The "Vehicle" and the "Tenor" and the Mandalora

Possibly in no other realm of human endeavor is meaning of words so disputed as in religions where symbols represent ideas and ideals. A step forward in dealing with this complicated issue was the work of Charles Kay

Ogden and Ivor Armstrong Richards, which culminated in a book called *The Meaning of Meaning* (1923). Since the sacred and the holy are abstractions that require myths and symbols for comprehension and understanding, we will frequently find it helpful to draw upon the discussion of metaphors, especially by Richards. A metaphor, he says, consists of two parts, "the tenor" and the "vehicle." The tenor is the idea expressed in the metaphor, and the vehicle is the image by which the idea is conveyed. In the sentence "The Lord is my shepherd," the tenor is "Lord" and the vehicle is "shepherd," the image by which the main idea is conveyed.

One symbolic purpose of the sacred is to remind us of the holy, not with pride allied with nationalism, ethnicity, or gender but with humility before the everlasting and the inconceivable. The figure of speech that seems most helpful in understanding the proper role of the sacred comes from literary criticism. *Synecdoche* means a part that stands for a whole but literally is not the whole, as "hand" stands for a worker or "sail" for a ship. The relation of the sacred to the holy may also be likened unto a Venn Diagram with two intersecting circles. The area of partial overlap is where the sacred and the holy might coincide, but a complete identity between them seems impossible, just as does the complete identity between sports and religion.

As Robert A. Johnson points out in *Owning Your Own Shadow*, the intersected area is known as a "mandalora" (the Italian word for "almond"). Like the mandala, itself a holy symbol that reminds us in Johnson's words "of our unity with God and all living things," the mandalora is a healing symbol. It "binds together that which was torn apart and made unwhole—unholy. It is the most profound religious experience we can have in life." The mandalora, says Johnson, "is the place of poetry."

It is the duty of the true poet to take the fragmented world that we find ourselves in and to make unity of it. In *Four Quartets*, T.S. Eliot writes, "The Fire and the Rose are one." By overlapping the two elements of fire and a flower, he makes a mandalora. We are pleased to the depth of our soul to be told that the fire of transformation and the flower of rebirth are one and the same. All poetry is based upon the assertion that *this* is *that*. When the images overlap we have a mystical statement of unity. We feel there is safety and sureness in our fractured world, and the poet has given us the gift of synthesis.[1]

From our perspective, we would modify the idea that *this is that* to say that *this is partially that*, which we believe is what Robert Frost means when in "Education by Poetry" he says that "all metaphor breaks down somewhere. That is the beauty of it…. Greatest of all attempts to say one thing in terms of another is the philosophical attempt to say matter in terms of spirit, or spirit in terms of matter. That is the greatest attempt that ever failed…. But it is the height of poetry, the height of all thinking, the height of all poetic thinking, that attempt to say matter in terms of spirit and spirit in terms of matter."[2] In connections between the sacred and the holy, even overlap cannot occur unless the sacred is sufficiently humble and not top-heavy with some kind of national or ethnic pride such as Sam Keen identifies when God and country or God and political cause are viewed as mirror images each of the other.

So much has the word "God" been overused in connection with political and ideological goals that Keen recommends silence on the subject and even the use of alternative forms:

For instance, instead of God: The Quantum Leaper. Being-Becoming-Itself. The Whence and Whither. The Subject that Encompasses All Predicates. The Great Whomever or Whatever that is Within-Without-Beside-Before-After-and-During. The Verb that Activates All Other Verbs. The Cosmic DNA. …Notice what happens when your imagination is forced to coin new language? It becomes poetic, makes a raid on the inarticulate and returns with new metaphors. It must consult raw experience and ask "what exactly do I mean when I speak about G--? What kinds of experience make me want to use this word?"[3]

---

[1] *Owning Your Own Shadow: Understanding the Dark Side of the Psyche* (San Francisco: Harper, 1991) 102–103.

[2] *Selected Prose of Robert Frost*, ed. Hyde Cox and Edward Connery Lathem (New York: Collier Books, 1957) 41.

[3] Sam Keen, "A Time for Silence: On Not Speaking About G--," *Spirituality and Health: The Body/Soul Connection*, <http://www.spiritualityhealth.com/newsh/items/article/item_ 3478.html> (2 March 2004).

Like "God" or the "God Idea," the word "Holy" has been severely wounded, as we have shown, by what Keen calls "theospeak" and, considering Ben Bradlee's comments, by "Newsspeak."

Keen goes on to say that "the task of authentic religion is to keep this world a sacred place, to remind us to wander, to tread reverently on the humus and be compassionate to all sentient beings. I believe we do this best by remembering: In the beginning was Silence." We agree with his purpose of "authentic religion" but add that in keeping the world "sacred" as Keen envisions the sacred, another purpose, and perhaps an even higher one for an "authentic religion," is to help others seek the holy, keeping in mind that the sacred and the holy are not identical. While the world can be confusing, one thing seems clear to us—leading participants to the holy is not a function of sports. At best, sports might help keep the world sacred, though we are doubtful of that. There is nothing wrong with being secular, at least in activities by which we earn our daily bread. Sacred folks should always remember that without the secular, there would be no money for collection plates or booster clubs or even advertisements that surround our fields of play. Here is an irony: if we sincerely seek the holy, we are more inclined to remember with gratitude what and who provides for our physical needs.

The Rational and Nonrational

In this regard, Otto's reasoning makes perfect sense and seems a fair and balanced perspective. Religion consists of two elements: (1) a rational element including ethics, rules, and commandments that adherents can clearly understand and choose whether or not to follow and (2) a nonrational element that is transcendent, mysterious, subliminal, and completely beyond the comprehension of mortals, yet the source of unspeakable joy and terror. The rejection or acceptance of either element affects the course of history, or in Jung's words, "called or not, God is there."

Generally, the rational side of religion tends to become sacred, that is, authoritative and sometimes heavy-handed in application, as in Bible sword drills for youngsters and the stone monument inscribed with the Ten Commandments and erected outside a court of law in Montgomery, Alabama. Such a sacred action is precisely what one might expect in an age of television that despises reading, not only of Scripture but of just about anything. Sacred people tend to suggest that if we can get a few rules down and follow them, then we have a good grasp of the totality of God. Hundreds of prophets, saints, mystics, and other seekers from every religion on earth provide compelling testimony that this is not exactly the case, that the fires of truth in the being called God are unquenchable. In Emerson's words, in "The Divinity School Address" "God is, not was; …God speakth, not spake."

Ironically the sense of the holy, the nonrational element of religion that unsettles things, as Emerson himself liked to do, seems to come as much from naturalists as from ministers. Chet Raymo reminds us that the holy in our lives may be all around us all the time, a matter of the senses as much as anything else: "The earth moves. And stones fall from heaven. Perseids clatter to the earth like hailstones. They embed themselves in arctic icecaps. They sprinkle the forest of the Amazon with fine cometary dust. Meteors clatter at my feet and I dance in the road. 'Up noble soul!' cried Meister Eckhardt. 'Put on your jumping shoes which are intellect and love.' I put on my jumping shoes and go jumping between the hedgerows."[4] Much in the same vein considering the joy and even dangers of the awakened state, Annie Dillard writes, "It is madness to wear ladies' hats to church. We all should be wearing crash helmets. Ushers should issue life preservers and signal flares. They should lash us to our pews. For the sleeping God may awake some day and take offense; or the waking God may draw us out to where we can never return."[5]

Whereas religion has commandments, sports have rules both for on the field and off the field, far more probably than most religions, but just as commandments are not all there is to religion, so sports are far more than a compilation of rules, rites of preparation, and dramatic spectacle. Among other phenomena are transcendent experiences similar to those related by religious mystics but, as we will suggest, different in nature. Clearly sports are like religion in basic ways, but this does not make them identical in nature to religion as Charles Prebish in Religion and Sport: The meeting of religion as Charles Prebish.[6]

Even though sports are not a religion, they are not necessarily less valuable to the human experience. Their functions and purposes are different, but each is subject to the higher laws of the great ideas—truth,

---

[4] Chet Raymo, *The Road Within*, ed. Sean O'Reilly, James O'Reilly, and Tim O'Reilly (San Francisco: Travelers' Tales, 2002) 16.

[5] *Quotations for the Soul*, ed. Rosalie Maggio (Paramus NJ: Prentice Hall, 1997) 56.

[6] *The Sacred and Profane* (1993) (Maintained over a decade ago, note: the view has since become a popular one among other sports apologists)

goodness, and beauty, liberty, equality, and justice, and God.[7] This is not to claim that God is merely chief of a set of ideas, but that God and the archetypal ideas are closely related, as Emily Dickinson observes.

Truth—is old as God—
His Twin identity
And will endure as long as He
A Co-Eternity—

And perish on the Day
Himself is borne away
From Mansion of the Universe
A Lifeless Deity.[8]

The pursuit of the holy is simply not among the justifications for sports. We question whether or not sports are even sacred, but we will grant that they are to sports apologists. Even so, we contend that sports do not meet the standards of the holy, as some apologists claim, because holiness is another matter altogether as we will try to illustrate in the following definitions and distinctions.

According to *Webster's*, "sacred" comes from the past participle of the French *sacren* (to consecrate) meaning "dedicated or *set apart* for the service or worship of deity (a *tree* sacred to the gods)" (italics added). Whereas primitive men identified caves and hunting grounds as "sacred," we do the same, the argument goes, not only for churches and national monuments but for stadia as well where we enter into "sacred time" when the action starts.

The first part of the definition of "sacred" as that "set apart" applies to sports, but there is little about the sacred in regard to worship of a deity as in the Westminster Catechism—"The chief end of man is to worship God and enjoy him forever." This kind of catechism belongs in the domain of traditional religion but would not necessarily, according to some sports apologists, conflict with the new or rather the new-old religion of sports. The thesis advanced by apologists is that "with historians of religion like

---

[7] See the discussion of these great ideas and others in Mortimer J. Adler, *Six Great Ideas* (New York: Collier Books, 1984).

[8] *Final Harvest: Emily Dickinson's Poems, ed. Thomas H. Johnson* (Boston: Little, Brown and Company, 1961) 209.

Mircea Eliade…it is possible for persons to be simultaneously religious in apparently competing ways, then a new respect for pluralism might arise, we could appreciate the rhythmic or antagonistic forces for allegiance among devoted fans who are also faithful followers of an established religious tradition."[9]

The idea of holding in the mind contrary or competing opinions, the basic tenet of open-mindedness and critical thinking, is not new, as the words of Whitman in *Leaves of Grass* (1855) remind us. "Do I contradict myself? Very well, I contradict myself. I contain multitudes." Whitman referred to paradoxes inherent in the cosmos, but what we see taking place in sports apologetics is not so much a paradox as the usurpation of traditional religion. In the old forms of faith now passing into oblivion, emphasis was upon personal remorse, redemption, and salvation; in the religion of sports, redemption becomes a matter of trying harder and running faster rather than turning around or walking off playing fields of a certain kind, and salvation becomes a matter of success rather than grace, a prize to be won rather than a gift to be received.

Cultures of Shame and Cultures of Guilt

Basically there are two types of cultures, those of shame and those of guilt. The Greek culture was centered on shame, so losing was a terrible thing. Fear of losing was perhaps the major kind of shame, but another kind lay at the heart of the Greek athletic ideal, the quality of *aidos,* which according to E. Norman Gardiner wins the athlete the favor of the gods and averts their jealousy:

> That jealousy is excited by all excess, by pride, by insolence. *Aidos* is the exact opposite of insolence…. It is a feeling of respect for what is due to the gods, to one's fellow men, to oneself; the feeling of reverence, modesty, honor. It distinguishes the athlete from the bully. Strength may tempt a man to abuse it; success may begat "braggart insolence." But *aidos* puts into the heart "valor and the joy of battle." No sport demands so high a standard of honor as boxing and wrestling and none are so liable to corruption. But *aidos* makes a man "a straight fighter," the epithet by which Pindar

---

[9] Price, *From Season to Season: Sports as American Religion* (Macon GA: Mercer University Press, 2001) 229.

describes Diagoras of Rhodes "who walks in a straight path that abhors insolence." It is a feeling incompatible with the commercial spirit, for "*aidos* is stolen away by secret gain." It is akin to that typical Greek virtue of self-control, Sophrosyne, but is something more subtle and indefinite.[10]

To Edith Hamilton, it is not a pejorative shame but the shame that holds men back from wrongdoing." It is "reverence" but also the "feeling a prosperous man should have in the presence of the unfortunate—not compassion, but a sense that the difference between him and those poor wretches is not deserved."[11] According to Werner Jaeger, it is dedication to an ideal: "In Homer the real mark of the nobleman is his sense of duty. He is judged and proud to be judged by a severe standard. And the nobleman educates others by presenting to them an eternal ideal to which they have a duty to conform. His sense of duty is 'aidos.'"[12] As such it has connection with a sense of guilt, what one might feel if he or she failed to do what was expected of a noble nature in order to win a worldly prize.

Perhaps all cultures reflect the same dilemma: on the one hand, the temptation to win honor anyway one can in order to avert shame, and on the other to avert guilt by abandoning social, cultural, and religious restraints, often in Jewish and Christian culture those stemming from the law and the prophets.

These two forces, shame and guilt, are alike though different as Ernest Kurtz explains: "Guilt, as transgression, always involves aggression: One feels guilty about the aggression. Shame, although it may involve an aspect of aggression, arises over the attempt's failure rather than over the attempt itself."[13] Interestingly, Kurtz uses a football field to illustrate further the differences and similarities between guilt and shame:

> To be human is to be surrounded by boundaries: It is somewhat like standing in the middle of a football field. As on a football field, there are two kinds of boundaries: sidelines and endlines. The

---

[10] *Athletics of the Ancient World* (London: Clarendon Press, 1930) 70.

[11] *Mythology* (Boston: Little, Brown and Company, 1942) 37–38.

[12] *Paideia: The Ideals of Greek Culture,* trans. Gilbert Highet (New York: Oxford Univ. Press, 1945) Vol. I, 7.

[13] Ernest Kurtz, *Shame and Guilt: Characteristics of the Dependency Cycle* (Center City MN: Hazelden, 1981) 22.

sidelines are containing boundaries: to cross them is "to go out of bounds," to do something wrong. The endlines are goal lines: the purpose of the game is to attain them and cross them. One feels "bad" (guilty) when one crosses the sideline, the restraining boundary. Feeling "bad" about the goal line arises not from crossing it but for not crossing it, from failing to attain it.[14]

If there is a Church of Sports, it is one based upon shame rather than guilt. Any sense of sin players may have will come directly or indirectly from a traditional religion. In the Church of Sports there is no sin, only regret for losing as a team. It is too complex to state with certainty how our culture changed from a guilt culture to one based on shame, but who can deny that sports played a significant part in that transformation? Certainly sports are the most obvious symbol of the pursuit of fame, and the shame that occurs when we fail to achieve is evident in stark contrasts of the moods in the dressing rooms of winners and losers, whether on the professional level or in little league. There are many clichés like it, such as MacArthur's "there is no substitute for victory," but in the modern world "winning is the only thing" arose in the arena of sports and remains the number-one credo of commercial cultures. To invest it with the aura of religion seems a huge step backward in the direction of Rome.

A logical parallel in regard to sacrifice and effort and spectators presents itself in the performance of a minister in the pulpit. "Fans" in the pews, like fans in the bleachers, listen and watch but don't participate except by criticism or cheering with a chorus of "amens." Anyone familiar with the rigors of public speaking knows what pastors endure on a regular basis with preparation and performance only to be "repaid" by parishioners who sleep, a practice developed into a high art form by some students who attend class in body while their minds are AWOL. We know that it may well have happened, but we have never heard of anyone going to sleep at an actual game, though it happens endlessly in easy chairs in front of television sets with boring or one-sided contests.

One characteristic sports and religion traditionally have in common is the *agon* or struggle, real in the case of religion with endless stories of martyrdom, sacrifice, and violence and imitative in sports, though any number of athletes can be identified as martyrs off the field. However, these

---

[14] Ibid., 6.

off-the-field actions by themselves, while perhaps admirable and heroic, do not change the essence of sports or bring them any closer to that of religion. For sincere participants in religion and sports, there is an element of pain gladly embraced in the interest of meaning, as different as the meaning of one might be from that of the other. For some significant numbers of fans in each, meaning comes in the form of pleasure and comfort from the "standing" of the team or church in the community and less and less in the form of effort or *agon*. In such cases, fans are more concerned with having the world's largest Sunday school or winningest team than with sacrificing what they have in order to help the least of those in their communities.

Increasingly, the word "club" applies as much to church as to ball teams. All clubs appear to meet the criterion of the sacred in that they are set apart, but all too often they are set apart by indifference to the conditions of others, society, and the earth itself, offering ease and exclusivity at the expense of involvement at the street level. Just as wearing a jersey of a favorite athlete to a sporting event does not require any sweat, neither does wearing a gold cross around the neck or carrying around a Holy Bible with one's name on it require sacrifice in the cause of one's faith. In spite of these and other similarities between sports and religion, there remain fundamental differences between the two.

In religion, one goal for the good of our souls is to help others, *anybody* if we read Scripture correctly, while the goal of sports—let's face it—is to beat others for the good of our egos. We will even schedule contests with those we are sure we can beat in order to make seasons look good, a regular practice of Bob Neyland at Tennessee, who learned the technique from Knute Rockne. In Neyland's book *Coaching*, the Rock advises other coaches to play "the hardest game last, with approximately three other hard games interspersed with games which should be so easy that a team can win with most of the second and third teams...."[15] The trickery in scheduling has become a virtue in a culture where winning (ball games) has become "the most important thing," the surest way, experience has shown, of holding at bay that monster known as shame.

Of course, religion may be no more altruistic than sports if the befriending of others is limited to members of one's own congregation or denomination, members perhaps of "one's club." Helping first one's own

---

[15] Andrew J. Kozar, *Football As A War Game: The Annotated Journals of R. R. Neyland* (Nashville: Falcon Press, 2002) 12.

kind or maybe even only one's own kind may happen as a matter of course in some churches, but we know of none where that is considered a policy. In sports, the situation is entirely different. In football, we may offer a hand to the person we just tackled, but both know that every effort will be made on the part of the tackler to repeat the same action the next play.

It can be argued that there is nothing wrong with "a little good, clean violence" as in the title of Ivan M. Kaye's book on the history of college football, but it is violence nevertheless, usually far more than "a little" in practices and games. We must be honest with ourselves: football does not seem like something Jesus, Moses, Buddha, or Mohammed would do. Not many people would enjoy it if it were played in the woods without spectators. The great appeal of football to young and old alike is its theatricality, not its quest for the good, the true, the beautiful, and the holy, but an ardent quest for victory in the presence of others.

In the religion of sports, joy does not come from consolation found in private prayer while sitting still in a room, the inability to do so the cause of all man's problems in Pascal's view. Instead "the joy of sports" comes from intense involvement in the *experience* of competitive play itself or the witnessing of that play. Athletes, it might be said, worship with body, mind, and spirit, and fans enjoy their services, the display of extraordinary physical skills. Athletes strive mightily to transcend themselves, and fans watch them with undeniable enthusiasm. *Enthusiasm*, apologists might remind us, is a word that comes from *en theos* and means to be "in god." To this we say there are many other things full of "enthusiasm": business, sex, and war. In the past it was the purpose of religion to restrain or at least to moderate such enthusiasms that they would not, like sports, become religions in themselves. "Joy," like "sacred" and "redeem"—e.g., "Vols redeem themselves against Cats"—has been co-opted by Sports World to provide the impression that whatever religion once offered, sports can do the same but better, not by bringing joy to the world but joy to the victors. Let the losers build character this week, as the joke goes in the Religion of Sports.

Thus, religion has lost principle ownership of the word "joy," so that it is now ever present in the realm of the natural and secular as in the titles of books, *The Joy of Sex*, *The Joy of Cooking*, and *The Joy of Sports* by Novak. If the setting for sports can be "sacred," why can't the same hold true for the bedroom and kitchen? Why can't we declare a Religion of Sex that might also qualify as a Cultural Religion, a Folk Religion, a Natural Religion, and no doubt a Popular Religion much like the cult of Baal that "provided chambers for sacred prostitution by male prostitutes (*kedishim*) and sacred harlots (*kedeshoth*) (1 Kings 14:23, 24; 2 Kings 23:7)." According to *Unger's Biblical Dictionary*, "The gaiety and licentious character of Baal worship always had a subtle attraction for the austere Hebrews bound to serve a holy God under a rigorous moral code."[16] That conflict, mysteriously, is eternal. The Baal cult is an example of the endless variety of what humans have considered "sacred," what we have at one time or another "set apart," sometimes for sex, sometimes for sports, sometimes for religion, and sometimes for two or more of them at once, which does not make such activities holy no matter how sacred they may appear. Why, though, would there be a popular outcry, in contrast to the proclamation of a religion of sports, if distinguished scholars started beating the drums for recognition of a religion of sex or a religion of food?

We suspect the answer is not obvious. Sex and food remind us of Eden, a prelapsarian place where longing is unknown (excepting the longing for knowledge) but delight in the senses unending. Sports, like war and religion, belong to a fallen world, a world of becoming, a place for struggle in body and spirit or both at once, a realm where meaning must be gained and regained, an arena not for delight in the senses but for heroics of the self.

What affords parallels between stadium and church is that both are public places in contrast to bedroom and kitchen, which, as a rule, are places of privacy. Further, both sports and religion are communal and ritualistic in nature, which, however, does not necessarily make the stadium sacred nor does it make it profane in contrast to the ground of the church. The idea of the sacred needs the idea of the profane, but the idea of the holy does not need either. Herein lies a major difference between sacred and holy: the possibilities of the holy exist everywhere in the world of the secular and profane—bedroom, kitchen, garden, bar, parking lot, sidewalk, shopping mall as well as in church or ball field, wherever the "holy spirit" decides to roam.

The sacred depends upon the idea of the holy, but the holy does not depend on the sacred as a human creation and certainly not upon the idea of victory in sports and war. The sacred requires authoritarian approval by powers on earth for the erection of the Washington Monument, the Statue of

---

[16] Merrill F. Unger, *Unger's Bible Dictionary* (Chicago: The Moody Institute of Chicago, 1970) 413 (see "Gods, False").

Lenin or Saddam Hussein, St. Peter's Basilica, the Bear Bryant Museum. The holy, at least as discussed by Otto, is subject to no authority in spite of heralded claims to the contrary by all religions on earth, now including that of football.

We fully acknowledge the difficulty of distinguishing between the sacred and the holy. As stated previously, they are often used interchangeably and, more troubling, in ways almost opposite to our way of seeing, which makes tentativeness essential on all sides. For example, in his fine article "Recovering a Sense of the Sacred in Sport," Shirl Hoffman, long a voice of reason on the subject, uses the term "sacred" in a way that we would find closer to the idea of the holy.

After describing the questionable aspects of the kinship of sports and religion, which we would call features of the sacred that tend to sanctify sports (for example, pre-game prayer), Hoffman shows how a different kind of religious expression has been appearing on the horizon of sports:

> The most obvious is the growing number of athletes who talk about the existential implications of their performance, bona fide jocks who seem more concerned with sport as a medium for opening mind and soul to new spiritual vistas than with appropriating religion as a bandage "to protect a soul made bloody by circumstance." The horde of Sunday morning joggers immediately comes to mind, ascetic adherents of *cultus aerobicus* who claim to have found on the roads passing by the church what they could never find within the walls.[17]

To us, sports as a medium makes more sense than sports as a religion with its own rites recapitulated from prehistory. Also we see in the term "new spiritual vistas" an indication of the holy that is always new *and* ageless, beyond time. The sacred is bound by time as a sacred holiday or a time of battle commemorated by setting aside land where it was fought. The suffering experienced in any battle on both sides is holy, but the sacred is concerned primarily with who won or who lost, with victory or defeat. However we define the terms "sacred" and "holy," the challenge to conventional religion comes as much from athletes who see sports as a

---

[17] Shirl J. Hoffman, "Recovering a Sense of the Sacred in Sports," *Sport and Religion*, ed. Shirl J. Hoffman (Champaign: Human Kinetics Books, 1992) 157.

medium as from those who see religion as an ally of sports or who see sports itself as a new religion, as Hoffman makes clear.

As we endeavor to distinguish between the sacred and the holy, we are reminded of Tallyrand's problem with zeal and Whitman's advice, previously mentioned, to proceed by "faint clews [*sic*] and indirections." In an age, though, in which the idea of the holy, in contrast to the growing sacredness of nations and religions, has all but disappeared and often been shorn of its traditional meaning, some thundering, we hope, might be pardonable in our effort to bring it back at least on the edge of the radar of modern thought and reflection.

Qualities and Effects of the Holy as Distinct from the Sacred

One purpose of the sacred is to empower us through inspiration to emulate the religious, political, or sporting examples set before us. The holy, though, overwhelms everything with which it is compared as Eliade himself remarks in his praise of Otto for *The Idea of the Holy*. Citing Otto's text, Eliade too sees the holy as the "'wholly other' (*ganz andere*); radically and totally different. It resembles nothing either human or cosmic. In relation to it, man has the feeling of his utter 'nothingness,' the feeling of being 'no more than a creature'; that is, to use the words in which Abraham addresses the Lord, of being no more 'than dust and ashes' (Genesis 18:27)."[18]

In the realm of sacred idealization, trophies and plaques are displayed in places of prominence; in the realm of the holy, they, like their winners, also return to dust and ashes. We cling to the comfortable illusion that sacred symbols, like halls of fame, are permanent, but the holy reminds us that only spirit, what was here from the beginning, is all that lasts; wood rots, metal rusts, and stones crumble.

Perhaps the chief feature of the holy, according to Otto, is what he called the *numinous*, a word coined from the Latin *Numen*, "command" or "assent," and from *Omen* from which we get "ominous." The *numinous* appears to be that aspect of the "Wholly Other" on which mortals depend with or without acknowledgment. It appears similar to what Paul Tillich called "the ground of being," the basis upon which all objects and people participate in being and without which or whom there would be no being, neither time nor space. With reference to Abraham in the passage in Genesis

---

[18] *Myths, Dreams, and Mysteries: The Encounter Between Contemporary Faiths and Archaic Realities* (New York: Harper and Row, 1960) 124.

cited by Eliade, Otto writes, "There you have a self-confessed 'feeling of dependence,' which is yet at the same time far more than, and something other than, *merely* a feeling of dependence. Desiring to give it a name of its own, I propose to call it 'creature-consciousness' or 'creature-feeling.' It is the emotion of a creature, submerged and overwhelmed by its own nothingness in contrast to that which is supreme above all creatures."[19]

The other quality of the holy contributing to the effect of humility is what Otto calls *mysterium tremendum,* "the most fundamental element in all strong and sincerely felt religious emotion," that beyond "faith unto salvation, trust, love…. The feeling of it may at times come sweeping like a gentle tide, pervading the mind with a tranquil mood of deepest worship…. It may become the hushed, trembling, and speechless humility of the creature in the presence of—whom or what? In the presence of that which is a *mystery* inexpressible and above all creatures." The one American writer who comes immediately to mind in reading about the holy in Otto is Jonathan Edwards, perhaps our greatest philosopher, in his descriptions of a "Divine and Supernatural Light" in contradistinction to things worldly. Parallel concepts may also be found in *I and Thou* by Martin Buber.

Why do we take time to invoke the idea of the holy in books about the religion of sports? For two simple reasons: either its general absence or its misuse. The presence of Otto's idea of the holy would seem required by a sentence at the beginning of his chapter 2, "'Holiness,'—the holy—is a category of interpretation and valuation *peculiar to the sphere of religion."* The sacred, in contrast, can be and often is appropriated for use and exploitation in politics, business, government, entertainment, and sports. The holy is far removed from all of these but instructive to all if its existence, or even the possibility of its existence, is noted.

If sports are a religion, then more ought to be said about their holy aspects. Though sports apologists do not hesitate to identify holy possibilities in sports in connection with "ultimacy," their main emphasis is upon sports as sacred, which from our perspective they confuse with the holy. Of course, this is easy to do; many of us often confuse the sacred and the holy. In *From Season to Season* there is further confusion in the use, or misuse of the terms "irrational" and "nonrational." This is common, but

---

[19] Otto, *The Idea of the Holy: An Inquiry into the Non-Rational Factor in the Idea of the Divine and Its Relation to the Rational,* ed. John W. Harvey (New York: Oxford University Press, 1958) 12-13.

knowing the difference between the terms is crucial to understanding Otto's idea of the holy. Note the beginning of Professor Miller-McLemore's discussion of "Sacred and Profane" in her article "Through the Eyes of Mircea Eliade: United States Football as a Religious Rite de Passage": "Distinct from Rudolph Otto's classic study of the nature of religious encounters as irrational, Eliade holds immense respect for the human experience of the 'sacred in its entirety."[20]

The term Otto uses in this regard is "nonrational," not "irrational." Obviously aware of the possibility of this kind of confusion, Otto goes to great pains to make the distinction between the nonrational, the realm of the holy, and the rational, the perspective by which most of us view the human world. Indeed the distinction is explained in section 1 of the foreword titled "The Rational and the Non-Rational."

The "irrational" is yet a third category of mentation, and while *Webster's* speaks of it as "not rational," it is by no means synonymous with the "nonrational," which means completely and totally and *absolutely* beyond human reason or understanding, that is, the Holy, which may be experienced but not understood. The "irrational" in contrast is an aberration ("unsoundness or disorder of the mind") of the rational, as *Webster's* goes on to say, "Not endowed with reason or understanding.... Lacking usual or normal mental clarity and coherence. Not governed by or according to reason." Since putting words in the mouth of God is a favorite pastime these days, we are going to try that ourselves, imagining the distinction God might make relative to the difference between the "irrational" and the "nonrational," which might go something like this: "I never said I was crazy; that is irrational. I just said you could not understand my ways, that I am nonrational or perhaps 'suprarational' if you prefer. Humans are the ones who are crazy because they cannot learn or practice humility in all things which my nature—often referred to as Holiness—absolutely requires."

To repeat, Eliade is highly respectful of the work of Otto and is careful to make the distinctions between Otto's work and his own. "Otto's analyses," he says, "have not lost their value; readers of this book [*Idea of the Holy*] will profit by reading and reflecting on them. But in the following pages we adopt a different perspective. We propose to present the phenomenon of the sacred in all its complexity, and not only insofar as it is

---

[20] Price, 117.

irrational. What will concern us is not the relation between the rational and the non-rational but the sacred in its entirety."[21]

This is a perfectly legitimate and valuable undertaking for a distinguished scholar such as Eliade, and Miller-McLemore is within bounds to extrapolate his findings and apply them where possible to modern professional football. It may be a matter of phrasing of complex issues, but her indication that Otto saw "religious encounters" as "irrational" is not the case. Note that it is Eliade who makes the connection between the sacred and the irrational, though not in all aspects. Eliade made clear what he was doing and so does Miller-McLemore in the body of her essay. The distinction between the Holy of Otto and the Sacred of Eliade, however, needs to be grasped more fully.

"The first possible definition of the sacred is that it is *the opposite of the profane*," says Eliade. Thus, each with respect to the other is a *ganz andere* (wholly other), but the holy in relation to both, and all else, is the *ganz andere*. It is true that the elements of the holy and sacred have been commingled throughout history and certainly confused, but all the elements of the sacred that ever existed, compared to the holy or its "Inconceivableness," are like the flickering flame in the tail of a lightning bug compared to the whirling balls of fire of the super galaxies.

In appendix X of *The Idea of the Holy*, "The Expression of the Numinous in English," translator John W. Harvey leaves no doubt about the distinction that Otto saw between the holy and the sacred or of his own distinction between the two: "The deciding factor in the choice of the *holy* rather than the *sacred* as the regular rendering of *Helig* was the fact that it is the Biblical word, found especially in those great passages (e.g. Isa.vi) of which this book makes repeated use, and which seems central to its argument. *Holy* will be felt, I believe, to be a distinctly more numinous word than *sacred*: It retains about it more markedly the numinous atmosphere."[22]

Unlike the holy, the sacred depends on concrete correlatives to express its mysterious power—a stone, a tree, a door, a cross, a statue of Lenin or of George Washington or for that matter a championship football trophy. With the holy, these symbols cut no ice. The holy is not about America, Russia, China, or Great Britain, capitalism or communism, or even about

---

[21] Eliade *Sacred and Profane: The Nature of Religion,* trans. Willard R. Trask (New York: Harcourt Brace Jovanovich, 1959) 10.

[22] Otto, *The Idea of the Holy*, 216.

Christianity, Islam, Judaism, or Buddhism. Now that we have supposedly outgrown religion centered around trees, stones, mushrooms, and caves, we are able to see consciously what the holy has always been, "Inconceivableness" that, properly regarded, can create in mortals the quality Ben Franklin saw in both Socrates and Jesus and advised us to practice. It is a virtue that would affect our attitudes toward contests we invest with such great significance.

Miller-McLemore, Mircea Eliade, and certainly others seem to lament that our age is nonreligious since we have lost the sense of the sacred that abounded in the primitive world. They feel that we are left with only the secular and the profane. However, we are not in our present condition on this little planet because we at last discovered that sacred objects like rocks and trees, with all due respect, did not have the efficacious power of sympathetic magic we once attributed to them; we are in our condition because we lost faith in the idea of the holy and the ability to distinguish between it and the sacred. Because the holy is an idea like truth, goodness, beauty, liberty, equality, and justice, and not a sacred stone or monument, we in a thoroughly materialistic age lost faith in it as an invisible entity and relegated it to the junkyard of history. In the meantime, the sacred is more prominent than ever and keeps killing us day after day as it always has in the tribal wars it sparks and refuels. Now it is being exploited in the endeavor to make sports a religion, as is the idea of the holy itself. It is good in a way to see the idea of the holy alive somewhere, but there are so many other places where its power could better serve us all.

Since sports apologists invoke the idea of the holy, the holy invites itself into our discussion as a common theme of the debate, for contrast with the sacred and especially since it is an essential quality "peculiar to the sphere of religion." The holy would seem to figure in definitions of religion devised by many theologians of either sports or play since, while not synonymous with "God" or gods, it is certainly a quality of them. "The Lord our God is holy (*Psalm* 99:9)."

The holy in Otto's treatment is a "thing" "ineffable" and unique that we mortals in bad grammar, bad theology, and unimaginative humor insist on using as a modifier in terms like "holy smoke," "holy cow, "holy terror," and the like. Unlike several authors in *From Season to Season* who draw upon him almost reverentially for his ideas of the sacred, Eliade, to his credit, pays homage to the idea of the holy instead of dismissing it in the interest of identifying as a religion an old human category of action, namely sports, because of supposedly sacred qualities found within them even in the space age.

In texts of sports apologetics, the idea of the sacred is central since sports, especially territorial sports and face-to-face sports, require a wide array of symbols on both sides in the way of mascots, team names, team colors, uniforms, and specialization of roles and assignments. This is much in the manner of war, one of the most "sacred" and self-righteous activities of our times and of all times, as witnessed in the sacrifice of martyrs and heroes commemorated by sacred rites in sacred places, sometimes at the 50-yard lines of football games. Almost invariably the sacred, and especially sacred games, are aligned with or dependent upon the dominant political power in the place where games are played, commercial interests or patronage, and often religious affiliation exemplified in any number of proselytizing Christian ministries.

The holy stands aside from such mergers and enterprises of mutual interests, choosing to speak, if it speaks at all, to individuals who appear to reflect a great inner need of one kind or another, including the humble desire for knowledge. Thoreau, who seemed on good permanent terms with the holy, said that if someone would bring him a list of all the organizations in the world, he would resign from all of them at once. There does not appear to be any rational reason why the holy would not converse with anyone heavily involved in clubs or organizations, but neither is membership in any required, even membership in churches. What is troubling about all organizations, especially universities, is the self-congratulatory posture each and every one seems to assume.

The same type of posturing is present in many churches and with businesses of every stripe, each attempting to show eminence and worthiness at a sacred level, that is, a level set apart by distinction and adopting an endless array of symbols of service, plaques, trophies, certificates of merit, bejeweled crosses, and commemorative wristwatches. In our culture the refrain is not so much bitch, bitch, bitch as brag, brag, brag. Finding humility nowhere and hearing her names cast in the sewer, the holy hides, perhaps sleeps, and of course waits.

Anything sacred must of necessity out-boast other things sacred in order to be set apart in a more distinctive manner, to gain prestige for members, to raise the stock in the field of honor, perhaps to raise stock in money, the most sacred of all symbols in all governments, capitalistic as well as socialistic. Where there is unabashed competition for recognition as with colleges, the world religions, nations, and sports teams, there is violence, especially in territorial sports such as football. In his highly acclaimed book *Violence and the Sacred*, Rene Girard effectively shows beyond doubt that the connections between them in all spheres of human endeavor are inevitable, as we shall see.[23] This is not a stumbling block to nonviolent sports such as Shirl Hoffman finds in running or in the exploratory and playful walking of Thoreau. Sports apologists, though, still have a way to go in explaining the benefits and virtues of making face-to-face sports sacred, to say nothing of calling them holy. If the idea of the holy were used as a touchstone (that which is peculiar to religion), the inherent violence in some sports, boxing for example, would not make any more sense as a religion than any religion now makes in the advocacy of terror or wars.

That kinship between violence and the sacred, in contrast to any between violence and the holy, unless the sacred is misnamed and called the holy, lies at the heart of a religion of combative sports, as seen even in the consecration of ground in stadia in memory of those who died for their tribe in the endless wars on our planet. It can be demonstrated that those of militant faith have a tendency to make sacred special sites and structures such as political statues and stadia as reminders of those who through sacrifice served their faith or the country or both. The more crosses we place over stadia, as on the jacket for the cover of *From Season to Season*, the more flyovers we will have at half-time and the more frequent the occasion to remember and honor the war dead. Such consciousness is that of the Christian Crusader knight and the young Muslim strapping bombs to his chest in contrast to the Shepherd in all cultures, who sees the sacred nowhere but the holy everywhere, even or especially in the barren desert where prophets liked to go for a deeper knowledge of self and God.

The sacred, thus, is *set apart* by humans and its significance highlighted by manmade symbols and rites, while the holy is set apart by itself or God and yet embraces all of creation. The holy is a reality wholly beyond our power. The sacred is always indicated by place, time, object, or

---

[23] Trans. Patrick Gregory (The Johns Hopkins University Press: Baltimore & London, 1989.)

word, while the holy is beyond place and time and language, that before which "words and understanding recoil."[24]

Reportedly the holy, like God, cannot be seen. It is revealed not as a thing but as an "insight" or awareness, consciousness, or knowledge, according to Otto. With the sacred there is always something primitive, totemic, magical, and superstitious, but the amulet is in no way required for a quest of the holy. Symbols sacred to nations and to religions go to war and often breed pride; the holy requires that we yield to it and sacrifice, if need be, even ourselves for the cause of peace and reconciliation, as impossible as that seems.

A few other major distinctions between the sacred and the holy need to be made. The sacred sells; the holy cannot be marketed, only an idea of the holy such as a "holy sword" used in a "holy war," as most wars at one time or another are thought to be. There seems little difference between any "sacred object" that is also called a "holy object," but the gulf between the holy and the sacred as a complete identity may well be unbridgeable. According to impressive testimony over the millennia, the holy is totally beyond our comprehension, while the sacred is forever on display and even in the daily service of business and commerce and spiritual tourism as, for example, an ABC ("Another Bloody Cathedral") tour in Europe and nearby a gift shop with endless displays of sacred objects for sale.

So may "holy objects" be for sale, from bottled holy water to prayer beads to crosses of gold or silver, maybe even studded with diamonds. Regardless of the role objects play or don't play in reaching a state judged to be holy, the objects themselves, even if vehicles for the transformation of consciousness to a new realm, remain separate from the experience or awareness attained, a condition independent of all our traditional concepts of time, place, speech, or materiality.

The Day of Pentecost and frontier camp meetings, where credible accounts tell of 500 people undergoing "holy falling" at once as if swept by the artillery of heaven, are evidence that the holy spirit in one form or another can descend upon a crowd, that, like a wind, it "bloweth where it listeth" (John 3:8), outdoors or indoors. It can ride the words of prophetic orators like Martin Luther King Jr. or the notes of mighty maestros, leaving

---

[24] Rudolph Otto, *Mysticism East and West: A Comparative Analysis of the Nature of Mysticism*, trans. Bertha L. Bracy and Richenda C. Payne (New York: Collier Books, 1962) 48–49.

audiences rapt and transformed if only for while. It can come upon us like a category 5 tornado, a holy terror indeed, or it can come, perhaps most notably, in a whisper to whomever it chooses—fools, clowns, idiots, or the most brilliant among us. It has what appears to be a subtle side, almost shy and maybe even flirtatious, like a reluctant lover insisting upon privacy and solitude before making himself known to those worthy of his blessings and boons. Einstein, himself a mystic as well as a rationalist, caught the elusive nature of the divine when he said, "God is not mean; He is just subtle."

Finally, the sacred attempts to make the holy conform to concrete realities of human experience, but the holy of course will have none of it, judging us all by its silence in a world gone mad by self-glorification from every corner. To reiterate our total incapacity regarding the behavior of the holy or plans thereof, we wish to say that as far as we ourselves know, the holy may descend "from above" or "rise up from within" at any time or any place, public or private, at a ball game, in a bathtub, regardless of pedigree, education, means of employment, if any, or even criminal record. Who would have thought that a persecutor like Paul would have had a holy encounter or that Job, an extraordinarily good man, would have been subjected to such suffering in his own holy encounter? We have read about a wide variety of apparent holy experiences, but even if we had all of them tabulated throughout time, that would be no assurance that the holy would ever react in the same ways again, or even react at all.

Secular Humanists, Sacred Conservatives, and Holy Poets

Keep in mind that we do not consider the terms "secular" or "secular humanism" as horrific. By definition, "secular humanism" would appear no more divine than sports, which is not to deny the contribution to civilization on the part of both. In fact, both sports and humanism, long associated with schools for centuries, occupy a sort of no-man's land between the sacred and the secular, generating debate about where they belong. Frederick Edwards wrote, "Secular humanists often refer to Unitarian Universalists as 'Humanists not yet out of church habit.' But Unitarian Universalists sometimes counter that a secular Humanist is simply an 'unchurched Unitarian.'"[25] One is reminded of the middle state that a student inflicted on Dante when he wrote that the great poet was a transitional figure who stood

---

[25] Frederick Edwords, "What Is Humanism?" *Common Dreams News Center*, <http://www.jcn.com/humanism.html> (5 October 2003), 3.

with one foot in the Middle Ages while with the other he saluted the rising star of the Renaissance.

In the last several decades, some religious fundamentalists have attempted to castigate the idea of the secular as in "secular humanism." Such demonization seems to apply to any liberal idea that is in apparent conflict with biblical literalism, inerrancy, and football. It is not our intent to demonize the sacred since it has an important symbolic purpose to remind us of the holy. In this regard we would all be better served if the sacred were less a symbol of national and other kinds of pride and more a symbol of humility before the everlasting and the inconceivable. Making a religion of sports seems to move the idea of the sacred in an opposite direction toward an attitude of questionable pride that borders on arrogance. Certainty in politics, sports, and religion has, judging from history, a tendency to coalesce into a sacred nationalism of monolithic proportions that may hold at bay enemies of the state but also the humility that the holy demands for the good of our individual and collective souls, whatever our country.

Secularism Humanism in its devotion to "Saint Socrates," to use Erasmus's term, and Socrates' ironic method of inquiry can be as doctrinaire as the most conservative religious denomination, even diminishing the spiritual side of Socrates by emphasizing his skepticism as if rational seeking would yield information about the nonrational. Socrates spoke at length about the soul, and while he could never penetrate the mystery of the holy in relation to the gods, he did not deny the possibility of its existence as seen in the *Euthyphro*. On the other hand, fundamentalists of all religions could profit from the rational scrutiny and good will for humanity that humanists of all denominations proclaim instead of conveying the impression that "secular humanism" is an evil disease infiltrating universities throughout the world. It may be true that Socrates was "at ease in Zion" as Thomas Carlyle remarked, according to Randall Stewart, but Carlyle was also at ease in regard to slavery, which Emerson definitely was not.

Together both of us authors know or have taught or known thousands of students and faculty in our years as teachers, and we have yet to meet a single person who calls himself or herself a "secular humanist." We know "secularists" aplenty, but "secular humanists" is a term almost never heard except from the pulpits of dogmatists who, it often appears, are scanning the horizon for some group, real or imagined, to identify as scapegoats, from the word "*pharmakos*," those who "poison" a culture. Scapegoating is not as easy as it used to be since it is no longer fashionable to tag ethnic minorities in such a way, but intellectuals, artists, and scientists of whatever background remain fair game since in every age they have been known to question the sacred doctrine of politics, religion, and science, as seen in the examples of Galieo, Kepler, and Robert J. Oppenheimer, whose words about science apply perfectly to sports: "Science is not everything but science is very beautiful." If there is a lesson to be learned from the best relation between the sacred and the holy, it is that no one thing is the only thing, including winning.

In contrast to artists, intellectuals, and scientists, who are always a little suspect to true believers in regard to any sacred doctrine, athletes, especially "good ole boys," have been easy picking by proselytizing religions since they are viewed as popular symbols of power and loyalty uncorrupted by ambiguities inherent in intellectual pursuits. For the last several decades, Sports World USA has been rocked by one scandal after another of every description from illegal gambling to murder, but one listens in vain for a peep of any condemnation from the religious right, even from the Billy Graham Crusade, its eponym having made it virtually taboo to criticize sports. That task has been left to disgruntled academics, carping journalists, and whistle-blowing athletes themselves, all of whom might easily be tagged as "secular humanists." The term, no matter how inaccurate, would certainly not apply to street evangelists and mountain pastors outside the mainstream of religion and critical of the alliance it has made with high-profile sports.

In the myriad problems of athletics in the country, the established churches have been as silent as sheep. What the older churches embraced, the sporting establishment, and in effect regarded as sinless is now becoming a church in itself, winning attendance competition Sunday after Sunday. Here is a perfect example of what Jung called *enantiodromia*, the tendency of what one regards as a virtue to become a vice. We could say that the chickens are coming home to roost, but another metaphor is more applicable, that of the Trojan horse within the domain of the church, with its knights disembarking to secure the target of the invasion.

The importance of the secular in any society cannot be overemphasized since by that term we are talking about clean air and water and good roads and school buildings, efficient fire departments, police protection, and a thousand other things essential for a functioning society. It too by definition is neither sacred nor holy, which is not to imply by any means that the secular is without worth. The sacred too has worth unless it blinds us to the possibility of the holy instead of suggesting ways the holy might be experienced. When the sacred becomes a substitute for the holy, as is the case with flags, state creeds, sports, science, and even religions, the condition is known as "warping," one definition of heresy that we believe is what happens when sports are considered a religion. We are not, however, advocating any punishments or persecutions of "heretics." That has always been the lamentable jobs of sacred churches, governments, and academic institutions.

If "secular humanists" is a tag name for academic and political liberals, then "sacred conservatives" is a fair name for fundamentalists often aligned against them on the national scene as we see daily on debates between "talking heads" from the left and the right on belligerent news programs such as "Cross Fire" and "Hard Ball." Though within each of these categories there is a wide variety of opinion, theological and otherwise, positions generally taken may be summarized as follows: Sacred conservatives want to keep government out of business; secular humanists want to keep religion out of the schools. Sacred conservatives want government help in private education; humanists want government aid for public education. Neither group seems averse to government grants.

While common ground may exist between them, we can be sure that sacred conservatives always have at least one nostalgic eye on the past—revered traditions, national heroes, and the sacred constitution. Their theme song could be the old favorite in World War II, "The Bible on the Table and the Flag upon the Wall." Without discrediting values and symbols of the past, secular humanists have at least one Utopian eye on the future, stressing the need for change and collective action, their theme song, "Oh Brother, Where Art Thou?"

Sacred conservatives seem to think that our cultural decline could be arrested if we restored prayer in the school and at football games, kept the Ten Commandments ever before us on plaques and monuments in public places, and ceased abortions. Secular humanists stress the importance of jobs and environment and curtailing lobbying for special interests. Sacred conservatives emphasize patriotism and a strong national defense; secular humanists stress love of the earth and a national defense based on a strong system of public education. When debate gets heated with both sides talking at the same time, we think of "Meathead" of the left and Archie Bunker on the right, one consolation being the realization that all of it is probably another network device to entertain rather than to inform.

The debate in America between the left and the right is both old and distinguished, reaching back to the correspondence, real and imagined, between Jefferson and Adams and between Thomas Paine, a classic liberal, and again John Adams and other fathers who objected to Paine's views on religion in *Age of Reason*. Religion is almost always involved in controversies as in the long divide between Emerson and Harvard following Emerson's "Divinity School Address" in 1838. Perhaps the classic example of cultural conflict is found in the polar views of Mark Twain and Theodore Roosevelt on just about everything and certainly including issues of sports and play, Roosevelt the great advocate of the former and Mark Twain our champion of play in all its varieties, one wanting to display our flag around the world and the other the head of the Anti-Imperial League. Teddy's motto was to "speak softly and carry a big stick;" Twain would agree if it were nothing more than a cue stick.

There is a third group in America whose writings are not limited to sacred and secular concerns. We call them "holy poets." The term is representative rather than exclusive. Neither is it suggested that holy poets are oblivious to what we call the secular and the sacred, but their vision is not limited to the here and now. It seems safe to say, though, that promotion of good citizenship in any country is not their main mission. If there is a principal theme, it would be that of awakening consciousness that transcends not only daily events in any nation but time itself. Since sports have been called holy, we will call on the services of holy poets to help us in understanding that idea and to make informed judgments about such claims.

The poet who perhaps best articulates the significance of the holy in our lives is a scientist, Loren Eiseley, who in turn gives credit to another for reminding us of an idea that had been lost owing to the barbarism of modern warfare and the reductive thinking of modern science. In an essay titled "Science and the Sense of the Holy," Eiseley writes,

> Over six decades before the present, a German Theologian, Rudolf Otto, had chosen for his examination what he termed *The Idea of the Holy (Das Heilige)*. Appearing in 1917 in a time of bitterness and disillusionment, the book was and still is widely read. It cut across denominational divisions and spoke to all those concerned with that *mysterium tremendum,* that very awe before the

universe which Freud had sighed over and dismissed as irrational. I think it safe to affirm that Freud left adult man shrunken and misjudged—misjudged because some of the world's scientists and artists have been deeply affected by the great mystery, less so the child at one's knee who frequently has to be disciplined to what in India has been called the "opening of the heavenly eye."[26]

To Eiseley, "the opening of the heavenly eye" is the task of the poet, and in his estimation we have had many in America worthy of that challenge, among them geniuses of the American Renaissance, Emerson, Thoreau, Melville, and Whitman, on whom he draws frequently to illustrate the idea of the holy. With Otto, Eiseley assumes, in contrast to Freud and some students of sports and religion, that the search for the holy is "nonrational" instead of "irrational." If we may say so, it is the bickering between the left and the right in modern media that is irrational, while poetry, using symbolic reasoning, is clearly nonrational. While creeds, doctrines, and platitudes of sacred institutions in politics, sports, and religion are literally rationalized, poetry functions symbolically, suggesting transcendent truths rather than declaring them blatantly. This is the difference between hymns and professions of faith.

Holy poetry "makes nothing happen" as proclaimed by W. H. Auden in his "In Memory of W. B. Yeats"(1939), one holy poet honoring another. "It survives in the valley of its making where executives / Would never want to tamper...." Ironically, sacred verse, religious doggerel, sloganeering, and singsong jingoism tragically turn the world, as illustrated in *Patriotic Gore: The Literature of the American Civil War* by Edmund Wilson. The effect of such self-righteousness upon religion and politics is evident in a study by C. C. Goins, *Broken Churches, Broken Nation*, about our national tragedy. Inevitably in war, civil or otherwise, truth is the first casualty, and the second is art or popular art anyway, which tends toward bellicosity on all sides, hardly a holy endeavor. As always, the great poets such as Herman Melville and Walt Whitman are called upon to give meaning to great tragedy like the Civil War and to suggest ways of healing, as in Whitman's sublime elegy, "When Lilacs Last in the Dooryard Bloom'd." Today, unfortunately, poetry does not have much of an impact upon American

---

[26] *The Star Thrower*, intro. by W. H. Auden (New York: Harcourt Brace Jovanovich, 1978) 189.

culture, especially sports, but during the nation's darkest hour poetry, especially Whitman's, may have played more of a role in providing the much-needed faith in national unity than previously imagined.[27]

The eternal problem inherent in the sacred is that of pride, formerly known as the unpardonable sin and as hubris, but in our sporting, corporate, militarized world, it has become the chief virtue of success or more accurately excess, seen regularly in the form of running up the score on hapless opponents for the purpose of national ranking. We intend to attempt to put the sacred back in its rightful place, but without any malice toward the "sacred" in its proper role in the natural or even divine order. What we have said about the sacred holds true for sports, which, like the sacred, have become a false idol and often a dumb one. Sports too need to be put back into their proper place for their own good. Both the sacred and sports are suffering from a drunkenness of spirit, and for both a sober reckoning is long overdue.

With all the moral problems that beset us in the new global village, we are not, at least in our view, anywhere close in America to the sorry state of sports and religion in the days of the Empire of Rome and those of the Third Reich. It is, though, time for a fundamental assessment not merely of highly publicized and sensational cases in the sports world but of a radical review of the values and assumptions claimed as common to religion. It is highly ironic, as modes of conduct in sports become more and more questionable, that sports, especially some of the more violent among them, are increasingly labeled "religious." Even more ironic is the argument that ethics are not a determining factor in comparing sports and religions since some religions don't seem to emphasize ethics as in "humanistic" and "pacifistic." One is reminded of the Jay Leno joke about the proposed code of conduct for television evangelists. He said, "I thought they had one called the Ten Commandments."

---

[27] See Daniel Mark Epstein, *Lincoln and Whitman: Parallel Lives in Civil War Washington* (New York: Ballantine Books, 2004).

Chapter 4

Wisdom and Strength:
Two Faces of the Holy

The fear of the LORD is the beginning of wisdom, and the knowledge of the holy is understanding. (Proverbs 9:10)

Thus far, in addition to announcing our thesis, we have attempted to present working definitions and to distinguish between the idea of sacred and the idea of the holy. Before proceeding further, we wish to shed what light we can on the mystery of the holy by drawing comparisons between the "holy" and "wisdom," also beyond the reach of mortals. On the one hand the ways of God and the holy are beyond our knowing, and on the other we are not only driven but commissioned, as it were, to seek understanding of them. The central mystery of the universe includes the question whether God is "there" or not. However, the Hubble Telescope may have less application in this regard than we might at first assume. Searching primarily for patterns of matter and energy and even signs of intelligent life, so visibly lacking on our own planet, the Hubble is not looking for transcendent spirit and may not be equipped to communicate such a discovery to us. In seeking for the nature of spirit, we might be better off looking in the wilderness still left on earth or the wilderness within the galaxies of the self than in the burning chill of the surrounding skies.

Whether looking within or without, we are alternately driven by faith and doubt so that the stronger one is proclaimed, the other is there beside it. Like Siamese twins, they live and die together or, in the words of Tennyson in *In Memoriam,* "There lives more faith in honest doubt, believe me, than in half the creeds." Indeed, for how can there be faith in any religion, political system, sports team, or whatever without doubt, which in the words of Frederick Buechner "is the ants in the pants of faith?" Our dilemma is acknowledged in

Scripture in the words of the father of the child with the "dumb spirit." "Lord, I believe; help thou mine unbelief" (Mark 9:14).

First and foremost, there does not appear to be any answer to the mystery of God. Instead, there are only responses, one of which is denial, and that, strangely, is a form of acknowledgment of God. Even for those of us who accept the existence of God, there is no rational answer to the mystery but rather a matter of living the question. All we know is that in whatever time in whatever culture, the idea (or ideal) of God has been clothed in the qualities of strength and wisdom, *Sapientia et Fortitudo,* also the virtues attributed to epic heroes.

A Literary and Cultural History
of the Divine and Heroic Ideal

The ideal of wisdom and strength did not evolve overnight. Both qualities were worshiped some 8,000 years ago in Egypt in the respective forms of Apis the bull and Isis the bird. Even earlier in Crete, the bull was a revered symbol of power as evident in bullfights that were religious as well at sporting events. The preoccupation with the same themes is evident in the Old Testament. Only now strength and wisdom are attributes of an invisible god rather than those of creatures of the natural world. God bestows all power (Isa 40:29). He "made the earth by his power" (Jer 10:12; 51:15), "ruleth by his power forever" (Ps 66:7), has the "power to help" (2 Chr 25:8) and power over the grave (Ps 49:15). He is a "refuge and strength" for those who believe in him (Ps 46:1), and blessed is the man whose strength is in him (Ps 84:5). This human strength, however, is not an effective force of action but an effective force of attitude; it is strength that gives peace of mind rather than the satisfactions of domination or performance symbolized by a piece of gold. This strength is not diminished by loss or failure.

Equally numerous are references to wisdom, which is the soulmate and playmate of power but more importantly the checkmate. Without wisdom, power is arrogance. Wisdom, it is said, was with God in the beginning and ever shall be. Wisdom recognizes and awards competence, excellence, and skill; but it is receptive and kind to incompetence as well. It is playful but recognizes its own limits and those of power. "The fear of the LORD is the beginning of wisdom" (Prov 9:10). Still, wisdom is tolerant and not dogmatic and certain, for "Wisdom of this world is foolishness unto God" (1 Cor 3:19). It knows tears and is well acquainted with grief; it "is better than gold" (Prov 16:16). To a real degree, the Bible, just as we learned in Sunday school, is a story of divine power and holy wisdom and our reaction to them. God is the being in whom apparent opposites are harmonized in ways eternally beyond our knowing. With God is "wisdom and strength" (Job 12:13).

The ideal of God, wisdom and strength, *Sapientia et Fortitudo*, was also the formula for the Old Testament prophets and leaders—Moses, Joshua, and Samson—and also for epic heroes of other cultures—Gilgamesh, Odysseus, Aeneas, and Beowulf. The formula abounds in the Koran where repeatedly we learn that God is "mighty and wise" (e.g., 43, 232, 233). However, by the seventh century A.D., the ideal had become a *topos*, a cliché, in western culture.[1] The problem with the fallen angels in *Paradise Lost* is that they want God's power but not his wisdom. Of Moloch, "the strongest and fiercest spirit / that fought in heaven," Milton writes, "His trust was with the Eternal / to be deemed equal in strength, / and rather than be less / cared not to be at all...."[2] The title hero in *Samson Agonistes* laments after his bitter experience with Dalila, "O impotence of mind in body strong / But what is strength without a double share of wisdom?" The Philistines, worshipers of Dagon, are "only set on sport and play." In their "idolatrous rites" are "sword-players, and every sort of gymnic artists, wrestlers, riders, runners, / Jugglers and dancers, antics, mummers, mimics..."[3]

Because the Philistines disdain what Milton, anticipating Kierkegaard, called "the living Dread" and had no sense (wisdom) of the limits of power, they unwittingly cause their own destruction when Samson, inwardly illuminated and renewed in strength, brings down their temple. Notice in both classics that power corrupts in two ways, from the want of more power by Satan in *Paradise Lost* and from idolatrous play by the Philistines in *Samson Agonistes*. What is missing in both instances is restraint, the essence of shepherd-wisdom, what Rilke called "patience." Nowhere is playfulness categorically indicted but only the form of play that has become an end in itself

---

[1] Robert E. Kaske, "*Sapientia et Fortitudo* as the Controlling Theme in *Beowulf*," *Studies in Philology* 55 (July 1955): 423–57. Says Kaske, "Ernst Curtius has sketched the development of the *Sapientia et Fortitudo* ideal in Graeco-Latin-Christian tradition, its supposed origin in Homer and adaptation in Virgil, and its decline to a rhetorical commonplace." Other scholars point to its presence in *The Epic of Gilgamesh.*

[2] John Milton, book 2, *The Complete Poetical Works of John Milton*, ed. Harris Francis Fletcher (Cambridge: Riverside Press, 1941) 174. (lines 46–48)

[3] Ibid, lines 1323-25.

or a form of worship. In both instances, arrogance and excess are punished by the avenging will of God characterized by divine strength and wisdom.

This Puritan story is repeated at Merry Mount in Massachusetts with Myles Standish, the little captain playing the role of Samson—he, that is, who brings the games at Mount Dagon to a halt. This Maypole of Merry Mount theme abounds in American literature, a sobering reminder of some kind of inevitable counteraction whenever play is perceived as license or when individuals take the law into their own hands as does Ishmael Bush in Cooper's *The Prairie*. In effect contrasting himself with the Bush family, Natty Bumppo says, "The law is needed, when such as have not the gifts of strength and wisdom are to be taken care of." Natty Bumppo has been called "the Christian knight" transferred to the American prairie, and knight Myles Standish would wholeheartedly agree with his pronouncement about strength and wisdom, as would most people.

There is a trick here, though—as there usually is with the knight—in our siding too readily with Myles Standish and Natty Bumppo. This does not mean that one approves therefore of the freewheeling, self-serving Thomas Morton or brutal and equally self-serving Ishmael Bush. The point is this—that what we have wound up celebrating has not been law, the shepherd's balance of strength and wisdom, but the perceived protector of law, the Christian knight who, like Natty Bumppo and Myles Standish, has been more intent upon maintaining class or privilege or, like Sylvester Stallone's Rambo, gaining revenge rather than spreading justice. The Christian knight neither fathered the law nor embodied it.

The law at its best is not concerned with purity and the display of strength but with justice and the moderation of strength. It is both spirit and letter and, like the Lord, it gives and takes away. The strength that yields achievement makes use of excellence of the forces of the body—the excellence of performance. The strength that yields patience, endurance, and acceptance makes use of excellence and skill if it can, but it also makes use of the force of conviction and trust, belief and belonging. Wisdom that yields knowledge makes use of order and fit, sequence and consequence, hierarchy and degree. Wisdom that yields virtue makes use of hope and care.

Why has knighthood with its endless sacred rituals become *the* public model of excellence in business, the military, sports, science, and even religion, which has as many levels of ranking as any army on earth? It is grounded neither in the patterns of the natural world, as is the shepherd's life, nor in the religious idealism of early Christianity. Even if the idea of a just war is morally acceptable, there is no justification in Scripture for constant celebration of athletic prowess or military might as annually demonstrated at the Super Bowl. There are few statues of wise men and women among us (thankfully in one sense), but endless monuments to knights and supporters of lost causes, athletic trophy cases, and athletic halls of fame on every corner. The poor muses remain in the shadows. Who wants to be learned when all the betting is on the swift and strong? We have made even Socrates and Jesus into warriors when in fact, as Benjamin Franklin observed, they are models of humility, the essence of shepherd-wisdom. Franklin had this characteristic, doing everything he could to prevent war with England before becoming a one-man army in support of the Revolution with his diplomacy.

The Paradox of Wisdom and Strength

What is literally killing us in the world is the illusion of "certainty," an obsessive disease that inflicts us all at one time or another and that is widespread and growing around the planet, not a new disease like SARS but perhaps the oldest of all. In matters of scholarship, in contrast to sports and war, winning victories in this world is not the only thing. There is not necessarily any correlation between victory or being right and virtue. In fact being wrong or losing is often as important as being right. According to Albert Camus in his essay "The Myth of Sisyphus," "the admission of ignorance and the rejection of fanaticism" are in themselves virtues. Clearly this is an opinion shared by Jacob Bronowski in reflecting on tragic consequences of certainty. At the crematorium of Auschwitz where members of his family died, he posed a question of science and of any group claiming "absolute knowledge and power," "I beseech you, in the bowels of Christ, think it possible you may be mistaken?"[4] One wonders if Oliver Cromwell, who asked the question centuries earlier, as Bronowski notes, had doubt about his own religious convictions.

With reference to this chapter's epigraph, how does one go about seeking "knowledge of the holy," the "inconceivable," the incomprehensible, that which is infinite in inner and outer space and beyond time and eternity? What are the human attributes of God, who, according to prophets (themselves adjudged holy), cannot be fathomed, a "wholly other" from the human world yet the creator of that world and by no means indifferent to it as taught by all faiths. Here is a paradox as defined by G. K. Chesterton, "truth standing on her

---

[4] *The Ascent of Man* (Boston: Little, Brown and Company, 1973) 374.

head to attract attention." What is *truth* that often seems to stand on its head in science, art, and religion? *Webster's*, as usual avoiding paradox as much as possible, says simply, "sincerity in action, character, and utterance, the body of real things, events, and facts, a transcendental fundamental or spiritual reality."

Wisdom and strength, roughly parallel to the "knowledge of the holy" and the "fear of the Lord" as perhaps in "fear and trembling," are primary values esteemed in politics, sports, and religion. They are so readily asserted as a joined pair of ideals that they often seem almost a single concept as *sapientia et fortitude,* the virtual "formula" for ancient heroism. Wisdom and strength are qualities attributed to God by other terms as in "omniscience" and "omnipotence" and in effect to Jesus who grew in "stature and wisdom" (Luke 2:52). At the divine level, they seem appropriately harmonious yet at the same time two different sides of the holy. On the one hand they comprise that which is unspeakably fearful, the overwhelming power of the almighty that left Abraham repentant in dust and ashes, and on the other hand the sweeping sense of consolation, peace, joy, and understanding experienced by legions in all faiths, including geniuses in the creative worlds of art and science.[5]

Together strength and wisdom are often supposed to be sufficient to define and produce the "good life" we all long for. Yet, in spite of any presumed symmetry between them, strength and wisdom in human hands may work against one another. Thus, the cliché that dominates the world of sports, "winning is the only thing"—that is, the idolization of power, prestige, ranking, and standing—may symbolize the spiritual crisis of our times especially since as a credo it has replaced the judgment of Proverbs: "Wisdom is the principle thing: *therefore* get wisdom: and with all thy getting get understanding" (4:7). In other words, the wisdom of the day stresses *standing*; that of the ages stresses *under*standing (italics added).

While we posit a harmony between wisdom and strength, our religious and cultural heritage clearly shows in its history an ambiguity that the formula "strength and wisdom" does not display. This ambiguity is at the center of the dilemma of modern sports. The contrast is both clear and significant. If the good life is defined as a life lived with human quality derived at least in part from strength and wisdom, there remains a possible confusion between two different interpretations or styles of fulfillment of this rough definition. For one

---

[5] See Arthur Koestler, appendix 2, "Some Features of Genius," in *Act of Creation: A Study of the Conscious and Unconscious Processes of Humor, Scientific Discovery, and Art* (New York: MacMillan Company, 1964) 674–708.

view, the ideal of strength and wisdom engages expertise, domination and control, authority and order, and certain knowledge—as in Ronald Reagan's absolute certainty, often repeated, that strength is the road to peace. Perhaps it is the road to peace if one is referring to an inner fortitude of spirit as opposed to an externalized strength of body. Reagan's supporters would say that both kinds of strength are necessary and that such strength is wise.

From another perspective, strength and wisdom as a singular ideal engages common sense, compassion, cooperation, humility, and a knowledge that accepts limits. One view emphasizes universal values with success defined as achievement or effectiveness; for the other, more concrete and immediate, success is more like harmony or affiliation. One is closed and absolute, the other open to change and surprise. One definition of success is a CEO of a corporation with a government contract of astronomical proportions or a football coach with several hundred victories to his credit and endorsements for the sale of potato chips. Thoreau offers an alternative definition: "if the day and the night are such that you greet them with joy, and life emits a fragrance like flowers and sweet-scented herbs, is more elastic, more starry, more immortal—that is your success. All nature is your congratulation, and you have cause momentarily to bless yourself."[6] In the world of athletics, business, and war, the former is the dominant mode. It is first and foremost a Greek idea gloriously praised by poets in honor of Olympic victors. In this system, wisdom is left to philosophers, not to the valiant athletes who strive for prizes in public places.

In either case, the importance of these ideas is almost universally recognized. Repeatedly in Hebrew Scripture, wisdom and strength together are celebrated as an eternal ideal and the divine qualities of God. Whatever wisdom is, we know that God loves it and that humans ought to pursue it as some quality that both restrains strength and uses it in the edification of the best human life possible. God thus is a philosopher—a lover of wisdom—whether humans are or not.

What mortal, though, can say what wisdom is? "For the wisdom of the world is foolishness unto God" (1 Cor 3:19). If wisdom cannot be defined, why even talk about it? Perhaps the wise are those, like Socrates, who know that for humans there is no wisdom. Yet wisdom remains an honorific prize esteemed in every culture where the "wise ones" advise and evaluate and explain and

---

[6] Henry David Thoreau, *Walden*, ed. Joseph Wood Krutch (New York: Bantam Books, 1965) 265.

justify the lives of those of us who are less wise. As elusive as wisdom may be, it seems related to learning, long experience, consideration of the past, compassion, humility, fear, and often sorrow. "In much wisdom is much grief" (Eccl 1:18). In an age of super powers (athletic, military, and economic), the idea of wisdom has come upon hard times. Philosophy—the love of *Sophia* or wisdom—has been pushed into the shadows in favor of power constantly demonstrated in arena, marketplace, and battlefield.

The Feminine as Holy and as Wisdom

While wisdom and the holy do not appear synonymous, they may share some equivalency in meaning as in various Renaissance paintings of Madonna and Child, also symbolic of divine love. Sculptures, like masks, are meant both to reveal and to hide, which they always do. The same is true with poetry and prose and other kinds of art.

In the holy there is a unity quite unlike the discord wrought by sacred beliefs around the world. The great ideas or ideals, for instance, are much like what Tolstoy said of happy families—they are all alike or in some measure anyway. In John 14:15–17, 26, when Jesus is speaking to his disciples there does not seem to be much difference between "another comforter," "the holy spirit," and the "spirit of truth." In the poem by Emily Dickinson cited in chapter 3 above, "Truth" is a "co-eternity" with God. Many of the great ideas are also alike in the sense that they are classically symbolized by the feminine: Beauty by Helen, Freedom by Lady Liberty, Humor by the shepherd muse Thalia, Justice by the lady with a blindfold, Love by Aphrodite, Sophia and Wisdom by Athena and Mary.

Men on the other hand are symbolized by figures of conquest as in the statues of the "nine worthies" of the ancient world, warriors or knights, who hold up the huge stone mantle in the Academic Board Room at West Point, three Jews (Joshua, David, and Judas Maccabeus), three pagans (Hector, Caesar, and Alexander), three Christians (Arthur, Charlemagne, and Godfrey of Bouillon).[7] This is not to suggest the need for a unified ideal of wisdom and strength along the lines of gender with all the wisdom coming from women and all the strength from men. At this point in the evolution of the species, it should be clear that men and women everywhere need *both* strength and wisdom.

---

[7] See Higgs, *God in the Stadium: Sports and Religion in America* (Lexington: University Press of Kentucky, 1995) 96–97.

It is almost humanly impossible to reflect upon the nonrational, transcendent world of ideas and ideals without the use of metaphors, which, as mentioned, have two devices, "vehicle" and "tenor." The "tenor" is the idea being expressed—"Wisdom," for example—and the "vehicle" the means of conveying the idea—Athena or Mary. For the idea of the holy as love and beauty, the "vehicle" is Madonna with Child or without child as in *Birth of Venus.* For the idea of the holy as awesome and overwhelming, the "vehicle" is the image of Abraham repenting in dust and ashes.

In *Playboy*, the Playmate of the Month has never been pictured, as far as we know, with a baby in her arms; there is also the idea of love, self-love or narcissism, always a feature of the sacred. Hugh Hefner, a self-proclaimed lover with thousands of pictures to prove it, has built a sacred empire replete with shrines and palaces for adherents and worshipers, not a secular empire as he would like us to think in his endless and pitifully outdated rebellion against Puritanism. Sex, a part of life, has come to stand for the whole of life, or at least the most important part, a different attraction from that of Madonna and Child. Sex itself is sacred, set apart and highly revered, but love is holy as suggested in the idea of "holy matrimony" and, like the "holy" itself, some would say it is impossible to achieve.

None of this is to suggest that the holy cannot be depicted symbolically in the female nude without the presence of a child. Note what Sir Kenneth Clark has to say in this regard about the *Birth of Venus* by Botticelli (1445–1510):

> Every movement is related to every other by a line of unbroken grace, and Botticelli, like a great dancer, cannot make a gesture without revealing the harmonious perfection of his whole being.... Flow on line is the most visual element in the visual arts, continually urging us on in time, and this gives a unity to the form and content of Botticelli's Venus. For her head is even further than those of the *Three Graces* from the expressionless, time-free pumpkins of antique sculpture. The word "wistful" that comes to the lips of every tourist who tries to describe her is correct and cannot be translated into Greek or Latin. It is the same head that Botticelli uses for his Madonnas, and this fact, at first rather shocking, is seen, on reflection, to reveal *a summit of the human mind, shining in the pure air of the imagination.* That the head of our Christian goddess, with all her *tender apprehension and scrupulous inner life,* can be set on a

naked body without a shadow of discord is the supreme triumph of Celestial Venus.[8]

Here in Clark's words, italicized above, are recurring qualities of the holy. The terms "tender apprehension" and "scrupulous inner life" seem precisely apt for the purity and innocence of a kingdom within. As for the word "imagination," it is the sine qua non of poets and prophets in attempts to express the inexpressible and the unthinkable, the miracle of divine creation as in the spine-tingling language of Loren Eiseley, a scientist-poet: "Before time was or act existed, imagination grew in the dark." Or, as he asked, "Why did the dust arise and walk?" With this, he asked in effect the Ontological Question: Why is there something rather than nothing? In the language of the holy, the word "imagination" keeps occurring as does another word, "shining," and the implication of these two terms is enormous, pointing to the nonrational side of the holy rather than to the rational on which religions base their creeds for repetition by the faithful. If we understood this difference, we might not be so quick to indict others as "atheists," especially if we knew more about what was going on in inside their minds nonrationally as opposed to public pronouncements about belief.

The difference between rational "belief" and "imagination" is well illustrated in the case of one of the leading philosophers of the twentieth century. Bertrand Russell is the author of *Why I Am Not a Christian* in which, among other matters, he pays homage, as we think most Christians would, to "ordinary virtues of tolerance, kindness, truthfulness, and justice."[9] That is well and good but not the point here. Note what he wrote at age eighty-nine: "I must, before I die, find some means of saying the essential thing which is in me, which I have not yet said, a thing which is neither love nor hate nor pity nor scorn but the very breath of life, *shining and coming from afar*, which will link into human life the immensity, the frightening, wondrous, and implacable forces on the non-human."[10] We are not saying that Russell, since his ethics seem admirable and since he had a keen sense of the "Other," is a Christian but didn't know it or acknowledge it, but simply that we should not be so quick to judge others on arguments about "beliefs" when they do not seem to coincide with our own.

---

[8] *The Nude: A Study in Ideal Form* (Garden City: Doubleday, 1956) 155 (italics added).

[9] Bertand Russell, *Why I Am Not a Christian* (New York: Simon & Schuster, 1967) 178.

[10] Quoted in Koestler, "Some Features of Genius," in *Act of Creation*, 262 (italics added).

Just as no claim is made that the female figure cannot symbolize the holy without child in arms, neither is it here argued that the female figure in any art must reflect qualities limited to Christianity. It may well be that Christianity popularized the idea of the holy as much or even more than any other religion, but the idea of the holy has been around a long time before the Christian era. It was well established as far back as the Paleolithic era as abundantly revealed in more than 200 plates and drawings in Erich Neumann's landmark study *The Great Mother: An Analysis of the Archetype*. The illustrations of mother and child dating from 1700 B.C. to "Madonna and Child of Henry Moore," 1943, come from all parts of the world and also reflect feminine archetypes other than the "mother," herself many-sided, at one extreme the "Terrible Mother" and at the other "the highest feminine figure, the Sophia." How Neumann sees the transformation of ancient figurines of woman from "vehicle" to "tenor" is worthy of note in our effort to distinguish between sacred and holy, a relationship not of stasis but of endless evolution toward higher consciousness that, ideally, comes with understanding of the difference between the versions of the thing in disparate cultures and the supreme thing itself generating endless responses to it.

> Just as in the elementary phase of the nourishing stream of the earth flows into the animal and phallic power of the breast flows into the receiving child, so on the level of spiritual transformation the adult human being receives the "virgin's milk" of Sophia.... And at this highest level there appears a new symbol in which the elementary character and the transformative character of nourishment achieve their highest spiritual stage: the heart spring of Sophia, the nourishment of the middle. This central stream flows from Sophia in our Philosophia, in the Ecclessia, and also in the representation of the Indian World Mother. A new "organ" becomes visible, the heart that sends forth the spirit-nourishing "central" wisdom of feeling, not the upper wisdom of the head.[11]

The reason mother and child is the holiest of images seems clear: the parts are united into a whole that symbolizes the binding force of love in all

---

[11] Bolingen Series fourty-seven, trans. Ralph Manheim (Princeton: Princeton University Press, 1974) 329–30.

of life. This "central" wisdom" of the heart, an intuited wisdom as opposed to that of the head or the ego, makes us aware of a higher power such as that which reduces Abraham to utter dependence and which the Mighty Achilles recognizes if only briefly when in the *Iliad*, Athena, goddess of wisdom, yanks him by the hair of the head in order to restrain him from action she considers rash and foolish. There are more similarities in theme between the literature of Greece and that of Israel than we are often inclined to admit. In both there is one major theme, the use and abuse of power, which may well be the dominant theme in all literature. Without the idea of wisdom, we would have no clue when abuse occurs.

Up to some point wisdom is the enabling ally of power needed by all of us in order to function in the world; beyond that certain point when wisdom is abandoned, which can only be revealed in story, power becomes despotic reflective of a condition the Greeks called hubris. Until recent times, hubris was known in the Judeo-Christian heritage as "sin." In the world of sports, sin has not so much disappeared as it has been transformed into something called "losing." Lady Wisdom allows a wide field of play as seen in muses devoted to dance, song, lyric poetry, and comedy, but she is wary of box seats where, if prizes are big and serious enough, another feminine archetype garners all the attention, the one William James called "the Bitch Goddess of Success" who never consoles or satisfies but asks for more and more of the same effort, the striving for victory day after day, season after season.

The consideration of the two "devices" in symbolic thinking, the "vehicle" and the "tenor," allows us a way to approach and deal in this text with one of the most famous and complex symbols in Christendom, the holy grail, an obvious feminine symbol, a holy vessel of wisdom. In our perspective, the story of the grail, the subject of medieval legend, focuses upon the sacred object of the grail itself rather than the idea of the holy. Here the holy becomes the adjectival vehicle that conveys glory upon the tenor, supposedly the cup from which Jesus drank at the Last Supper. The grail, a symbol, becomes more significant than what it symbolizes. Emphasis, thus, is placed upon what the lips of Jesus touched, a sacred idea, rather than upon what they spoke, a holy idea. The Holy Spirit itself gets confused with the martial spirit of manliness of the knights of the Round Table, which is the way knights of all clime view the world, a place requiring two hearts—one as soft as wax and the other hard as stone as required in tournament or war.

A question raised by the "Jesus Seminar" concerns, among other matters, which of the red letter words Jesus actually spoke, but a deeper question for professing believers is this: How much *truth* in the same words would remain if it could be proven conclusively that Jesus never spoke any of them? Schweitzer concludes in *Search for the Historical Jesus* that Jesus comes to us as "One unknown." What would happen to Christian faith if it were discovered that Jesus' words of wisdom came from sources "unknown"? Such questions reveal immediately the importance of a physical person or personality in matters both sacred and holy. In sacred practices and beliefs, heavy emphasis is placed upon the senses, especially that of touching and tasting as in communion, a nonrational but not irrational rite. It seems perfectly possible for the sacred and the holy to blend harmoniously, but the sacred rite is always the device. The holy is the goal or purpose of the rite, a transcendent idea that, it seems reasonable to assume, can be sought in meditation and prayer by sitting still in a room or walking alone in the woods (the essential idea of the hymn "In the Garden") without the aid of sacred ritual.

It is our view that the idea of the holy did indeed originate in sacred rituals of our preliterate ancestors, a contribution by the sacred that almost by itself justifies its presence in the world, but its time has come not to vanish but to recede from view. It has brought us a glimpse of the whole and the holy on a shrinking planet in the presence of an unspeakably complex universe, not just the physical world from atoms to super galaxies but of the infinite soul in each of us and in "the spiritual universe," the title of Physicist Fred Allen Wolf's fascinating book. The purpose of the sacred is to suggest the idea of the holy rather than to preach it or go to war over the rightness of its depiction of the holy. It is time for the sacred to abandon its lavish and ornate vehicle and turn to simpler and more economical models or, ideally, to walk again so that the idea of the holy all around it can be enjoyed by seekers and sojourners.

The visibility of the sacred vis-à-vis the holy is analogous to that between the artist and the artist's work as suggested in *A Portrait of the Artist as a Young Man* by James Joyce. As viewers stand in front of a painting, the artist, Joyce thinks, should be behind it cleaning his nails, a metaphor reflective of Joyce's own relation to his art and of Picasso's to his. In "Picasso and His Art," Carl Jung sees Joyce as the "literary brother" of Picasso and both as questers of genius into the world of the unconscious as much as into the visible world, both worlds seemingly infinite and inexplicable. Great art, like Scriptures of many tongues, is always focused upon the many-sidedness of the whole of being, its horrors as well as possibilities.

Herein lies a fundamental difference between art and the ministry, between showing and telling, between painter and preacher, which is not to say that sermons cannot be forms of art as many are. The more preaching and proselytism are bounded by sacred doctrine of denominations and warring faiths, the more the world will sound like the Tower of Babel and the harder insight into the holy will be. In this insight lies the hope that we can still all live together without trying to convert each other to our own thinking or going to war as an acceptable and sacred alternative. The last thing we need is to make sacred and holy the world of sports, the very symbol of conspicuous victory over others that is always followed by thanks to God for such glory.

"I dwell in possibility" is the first line of one of Emily Dickinson's well-known poems that concludes as follows: "The spreading wide my Narrow hands/To gather Paradise." Repeatedly we see this same message in her verse and in that of her contemporaries, Emerson, Thoreau, Whitman, Hawthorne, and Melville. "Infinity," Emily says, is both ahead of her and behind her, and she is "term between." Here is still another marvelous metaphor illustrating the difference between the holy and the sacred, the "term between." Each of us is a "term between" of inestimable value since without the "term" we would not even be conscious of the infinite swirling around us and inside us. The "possibility" inside us is as amazing as anything we witness through the lens of the Hubble. As Goethe put it in *Life Lines* concerning a lens far older than that in Hubble, "If the eye were not sun-lit, it could not see the sun." Goethe employs the metaphor of the awakened state or awakening as did two major American writers, Jonathan Edwards and Henry David Thoreau. Whether one looks at the idea of the holy in the orthodox tradition as seen in Edwards or in the unorthodox as in Thoreau, the qualities of an elevated consciousness in each are clearly evident. Both Edwards and Thoreau acknowledged the power of the visible world—the sun, for example—but each was aware of another light within, called "divine and supernatural" by Edwards and by Thoreau a "higher light" as in his journal entry for 1856: "It is by obeying the suggestions of a higher light within you that you escape from yourself and...travel totally new paths...."[12] The mysticism of Edwards, a perfectly orthodox Christian, and Thoreau, a representative Transcendentalist, have much more in common than either or both with the mysticism being reported these days from the playing fields, a subject of later discussion.

Whenever the word "holy" is used as an adjective for anything earthly or material, whether for dung, blood, smoke, journalism, sword, cloak, or cup, it is sometimes robbed of its power as a transcendent idea. As a sacred modifier for the "grail," it becomes so burdened with the imaginary freight of fetishism, magic, superstition, allegory, chivalry, and competition for power as to lose all traditional meaning. The same is true with the mythological journey of holy splinters of the cross, holy bones of saints, the holy shroud of Christ, the sword of the Roman soldier that pierced his side. Fetishism is always a form of sacred, like the baseball knocked out of a ballpark by Mark McGuire, Sammy Sosa, or Barry Bonds and scrambled over by fanatics. Even the hand of Francis Xavier that baptized thousands and is still preserved by the church in Rome under glass is sacred, though the effect it wrought on others may well have been holy.

The "cup" as used in the Scripture is a helpful vehicle for understanding the distinctions between secular practices and sacred and holy rituals. This is evident in such marvelous phrasing as, on the one hand, "cup of trembling," or "reeling, intoxication," "cup of astonishment and desolation," "cup of fury," "cup of indignation," "cup of demons," and on the other hand "cup of consolation," "cup of salvation," "cup of blessing," and "cup of the Lord." Readings about the uses and abuses of the "cup in Scripture are every bit as entertaining. Readings about the uses and abuses of the "cup" in Scripture are every bit as entertaining and instructive as tales of combat and derring-do of commissioned knights in heavy armor in search of the grail. One thing we learn is that the people of the holy land, whether they were using alcohol for secular or holy purposes, were not Prohibitionists.

We are always giving God the credit for the beauty of design of sacred buildings, churches, cathedrals, temples, statues, stadia, and the like, for victory in battle, for winning beauty pageants, hitting home runs, and scoring touchdowns, without ever considering the possibility that God, for all we know, may prefer outdoor worship, maybe even in the rain, despise

---

[12] Walter Harding, "Thoreau's Ideas," *A Thoreau Handbook* (New York: New York University Press, 1959) 135. For many correlations between "awakenings" and the "holy" or "holy spirit," see the index in George M. Marsden, *Jonathan Edwards: A Life* (New Haven: Yale University Press, 2003).

architecture, beauty contests, and every form of sports imaginable. Hints appear in Scripture that this might at least be a possibility; for example, "For my thoughts are not your thoughts, neither are your ways my ways, (Isa. 55:8)

Two Kinds of Wisdom, Two Kinds of Power

Faced with the paradox inherent in wisdom and strength, the best we might be able to do is take note of the different kinds of wisdom and power. In the human world there are two kinds of each, the first set being dictatorial and closed and the second democratic and open. The first type stresses the cult of power supported by authority, the second the openness of wisdom supported by the strength of caring and community. In the first, power is the principle thing ("Winning is the only thing") with "wisdom" taking the form of dogma and cliché. In the second, wisdom is the principle thing, the playmate of power that here means endurance and commitment.

Model 1 **Dictatorial and Demonic**	
"Strength"	"Wisdom"
Authority, Domination	Certainty Dogma
Obedience, Manliness	Pride
(Sports as instrument—serving state, wealth, and religion)	
Model 2 **Democratic and Divine**	
Strength	Wisdom
Patience, Endurance	Receptivity, Compassion,
Faith, Playfulness,	Communion, Restraint,
Virtuous character	Humility, Hope
(Sports as aim —serving individuals' health and happiness)	

In Model 1, wisdom and strength are an illusion. The closure and scope acquired by certainty in Model 1 is not available to human understanding. Thus to speak of God's "wisdom and strength" is little more than a flag-waving gesture. The source for what we think may even be a heresy in the religion of modern sports, and perhaps traditional religions as well, is the presumption of possessing wisdom that only a god could empower. We simply do not know ultimate truth. But having presumed to have that total understanding and having presumed to speak from the authority it *would* command, the only recourse is to presume also to the power that omniscience would allow. Then that "omniscient" strength—which is constantly tested and threatened and thus constantly vigilant—becomes a proof of the presumption. Might makes right, or one might say might makes might.

The threat to Model 2 comes always with the certainty and closure of Model 1 and the power, usually political, that short views and demagoguery inevitably generate. Just because one holds in hand a leatherbound, gold-lettered copy of the Bible does not necessarily mean that one understands or speaks God's word. Throughout both the Old and New Testaments there is constant warning *against* certainty, dogma, and pride. Again, "Wisdom of this world is foolishness with God."(1 Cor 3:19) "The foolishness of God is wiser than man" (1 Cor 1:25). "Be not wise in your own conceits" (Rom 12:16). "Woe unto them that are wise in their own eyes" (Isa 5:21). "Be not wise in thine own eyes" (Prov 3:7).

David Miller in *Gods and Games* points out the association of play and wisdom in both Greek and Hebrew texts, and Greek drama, like the Bible, warns of the dangers of pride, "wisdom" in the form of certainty, dogma, and overweening. In *Antigone* by Sophocles, the title character, Tierasis, and Choragos all try to get Creon to show reason, common sense, compassion, or patience, but he does not change until it is too late, causing Choragos to chant a message that, with little adjustment, would be at home in Proverbs or the writings of Saint Paul: "There is no happiness where there is no wisdom / No wisdom but in submission to the gods. / Big words are always punished, / Proud men in old age learn to be wise."[13]

All prophecy in the Old Testament and Greek literature centered on the abuse of power, the indictment of hubris, and one does not have to look far in twentieth-century writing to find the same theme, as, for example, in "Cassandra" by E. A. Robinson written in 1914: "The power is yours, but not the sight; / You see not upon what you tread; / You have the ages for your guide, / but not the wisdom to be led."[14]

---

[13] Sophocles, *Antigone*, trans. Dudley Fitts and Robert Fitzgerald, in *Introduction to Literature*, 7th ed., ed. Sylvia Barnet, Morton Berman, William Burto (Boston: Little, Brown & Company, 1981).

[14] E. A. Robinson, in *Twentieth Century American Writing,* ed. William T. Stafford (New York: Odyssey Press, 1965) 22.

In Robinson's view, the crowd can be as guilty of pride and idolatry as single dictators, which, from experience, we know to be true.

Lest it be assumed that the knightly ideal of wisdom and strength is invoked only by Puritans or Neo-Puritans, let us point out that it is evident even in the comics. All the fumbling and ineffectual but well-meaning and wise Clark Kent has to do to become strong is to find a phone booth wherein to change clothes, and all Billy Bateson has to do to become a marvel with the rank of captain is to invoke the magical (and divine) formula, SHAZAM—S for the wisdom of Solomon, H for the strength of Hercules, etc. Both Billy Bateson and Clark Kent reverse the situation in the Christian story. Instead of God becoming incarnate in man, they are men who become as gods, acquiring in the process the wondrous qualities of wisdom and strength. Today the ideal is more of a cliché than ever, but something of its essence can still be glimpsed even in popular culture. When as a child one of us was telling a friend about the power of Jesus in order to get him to come to church, the besieged friend announced that Jesus didn't seem like much compared to Superman! Today's church seems to have solved that problem by transforming Jesus *into* Superman, one who can leap tall buildings in an instant or score a touchdown in a flash.

As a glance at any sports page reveals, sports are a story of power. We speak of "powerhouses" and "perennial powers" in leagues; also, in recent years "strength coaches" have been added to staffs in order to add muscle to the teams. In big-time college sports and in professional sports, it is an "arms" race to see which team can develop the most brawn and skill, even the quarterback with the strongest arm. The closest thing to a "wisdom" coach presumably is the athletic tutor, usually a graduate assistant who visits the athletic dorm once or twice a week during "study hall"—not with the intention of helping the athletes gain wisdom, but merely to help them remain eligible. In professional ranks, a consultant is sometimes hired, usually a psychiatrist or psychologist, to help keep the team's head straight. College coaches may respond that it is also the task of the faculty to make students wise, but the teachers then explain that this is difficult to do for athletes when all we hear and see in society is that winning games is "the only thing" instead of the scriptural injunction that "wisdom is the principle thing."

The power required in sports must be exercised in concert with virtues. Only then can sports remain free from abuse, as Robert Frost has observed in "Perfect Day—a Day of Prowess," an account of a baseball game in "Clark Griffith's old gem of a field":

Prowess comes first, the ability to perform with success in games, in the arts, and come right down to it, in battle. The nearest of kin to the artists in college where we all become bachelors of arts are their fellow performers in baseball, football and tennis. That's why I am so particular college athletics should be kept from corruption. They are close to the soul of culture. At any rate the Greeks thought so. Justice is a close second to prowess. When displayed toward each other as antagonists in war and peace, it is known as the nobility of noble natures. And I mustn't forget courage for there is neither prowess nor justice without it. My fourth, if it is important enough to be brought in, is knowledge, the mere information we can't get too much of and can't ever get enough of, we complain, before going into action.[15]

In sports and in art "the old verities" may be evident, but neither sports nor art should be arenas for dogmatism, any more than religion should be. Sports, as Frost implies, are forms of art. If there were as much overt proselytism going on in prose, poetry, and painting as occurs today in athletics, the whole academic community would justifiably be up in arms. As it is, not many artists are speaking out on the matter, possibly because they see sports as harmless entertainment outside the mainstream of culture. Frost saw exactly how sports relate to culture. Notice that though Frost puts prowess first, he makes it and justice dependent upon courage, another way of expressing the eternal ideal of the shepherd's wisdom and strength. Wisdom, thus, lies in courage rather than in physical strength. It is courage, for instance, that Santiago sees in the Great Dimaggio in Hemingway's *The Old Man and the Sea.* "Profiles in Courage" could as well be the title of a book about athletes as well as politicians who track another type of power.

In the emerging Church of Sports, football, we think, is the leading denomination with the Super Bowl equivalent in significance to St. Peter's Basilica at Easter or Christmas. As a symbol of the Church of Sports, the Super Bowl, we will admit with apologists, is Sacred City with theatrical rites too numerous to mention. From pre-game buzz to the victors' post-game thanks to God and the televised pseudo sorrow in the locker room of the vanquished, it may well be the mother of all conspicuous displays

---

[15] *Selected prose of Robert Frost*, eds. Hyde Cox and Edward Connery Lathem (New York: Holt Rhinehart and Winsten, 1966) 91.

excepting the Olympics. We use the term "pseudo sorrow" to express the emotional state of the losers, since real sorrow lives in hospitals and in funeral homes and indeed in ordinary homes without number.

Super This and Super That

In the world at present, our language confirms that the ideal of power dominates the ideal of wisdom, that is, restraint, more than ever. In addition to "holy," "sacred," and "redemption," numerous other religious terms have been seized and put to hard labor in broadcasts as "miraculous" so that now they are more at home in the sports pages than in the pulpit. The same is true of "great," which is used more than 500 times in Scripture but mainly known in a culture of mass media not as in "How great thou art?" but as in "great catch," "great kick," and especially "great hands," all favorites of sportscasters for football games, as if viewers are not qualified to make our own judgments. As Emerson says, "a false currency is employed when there is no bullion in the vaults." This applies to secular terms as well as to ones confiscated from Scripture. The more the word "great" is used in the religion of sports, like "awesome" among teenagers, the more the stretch marks show, which is what has happened to the word "super," as John Updike makes clear in a little poem called "Superman," an apt satire in a society where "Super Power" is the greatest compliment a nation can make to itself and where "Super Sunday" is our "Religious Festival."

> I drive my car to supermarket,
> The Way I take is superhigh,
> A superlot is where I park it,
> And Super Suds are what I buy.
>
> Supersalesmen sell me tonic—
> Super-Tone-O, for Relief.
> The planes I ride are supersonic
> In trains I like the Super Chief.
>
> Supercilious men and women
> Call me superficial—me
> Who so superbly learned to swim in
> Supercolossality.

Superphosphate-fed foods feed me;
Superservice keeps me new.
Who would dare to supercede me,
Super-super-superwho?[16]

So elusive is wisdom and so evident the apparent benefits of power that
we in our age no longer trust any achievement that doesn't come with an award
or a trophy (and a big bank account) as proof of personal worthiness. Those we
most admire and esteem are not foremost wise but successful, often wealthy,
and in any case accomplished in terms of current thinking. This seems to imply
that wisdom has been replaced by something else as our highest life-goal. Or
perhaps it is supposed that with enough strength, wisdom does not matter or
that the strong can simply declare their own wisdom without the hindrance of
legitimacy. We see this every day in oppressive governments and even in the
chatter of talk-show hosts. Philosophy has long been overshadowed in the
world by what might be called the "philagonic," love of competition, which is
now becoming a religion before our eyes. If sport as a religion does not need a
god or even ethics in a conventional sense, why should participants and fans be
bothered with philosophy or love of wisdom, the very consort of God? We
should remember too that it is not as if play is empty of possibilities. The sky is
the limit and the reasons abound for why we should play more and compete
less if at all. Before making an indignant response to that idea, one should read
No Contest: The Case Against Competition by Alfie Kohn.

The current approach to strength and wisdom is, we believe, in opposition
to our philosophical and religious heritage of all denominations and constitutes
a loss of the value of that heritage. Our hearts are turned to threat and danger,
leaving little room for care and compassion or for life at peace rather than life
at war. The idea that life contains a perpetual element of combat and
competition is undeniable as Veblen observed in *Theory of the Leisure Class*;
the question is when and by what moral authority did war and the preparation
of war become a habitual way of life.

Without wisdom, strength in human form acts with certainty and
superiority and awards itself all honor. The only question is the reach of its
power, influence, and success; one suspects that even a secondary wisdom is
threatened by impotence and failure with attendant weaknesses of compassion,

---

[16] John Updike, *The Carpentered Hen and Other Tame Creatures* (New York: Alfred Knopf, 1982) 47.

toxic shame, and chance. The knight's wisdom, if it matters at all, is spoken in the language of achievement, in the death it brings to dissent and doubt. On the other hand, the strength of the shepherd neither needs nor welcomes displays and proof and remains in alliance with its wisdom. Both Hebrew and Greek history (with some important differences) exalted a strength and wisdom that contrasts with the authority and power ideal symbolized by victors in national and international games.

In the latter myth, winning is the only thing, has been unchanged for the last few thousand years. In the former, wisdom is the principal thing, with the consolation of sorrow, perhaps of the same kind Christ endured alone at Gethsemane, another whole ball game. The former depends upon surrender, seeking intimacy with the everlasting; the latter requires strength and trickery in the conquest of another in the desire for ultimacy and that only briefly until another conqueror comes to rule the sacred ground under the golden bough in the dark of night.

We may call sports a religion if we like, but to find prototypes of that religion we need to go back several millennia, far beyond the beginning of the written word. What's wrong with that? Apologists seem to ask this question with apparent good reason, since the recorded word in traditional religions seems only to have accented tribalism. After epochs of shedding blood upon our planet, what we still have is, in the words of the prison camp warden talking to Cool Hand Luke in the classic film of the same name, "a failure to communicate," ironically echoed by Luke a few lines later. When we talk about communication, we mean the thing called "media," of which sports and religion are principal examples and driving forces.

Chapter 5

The Religion of Sports and the Media: Marshall McLuhan among the Apologists

Sports apologists and Marshall McLuhan have different agendas, but their theses intertwine in the same general direction. One might easily conclude that religion of sports could only exist in preliterate times and in modern times that are "post-literate" and, some would add, "post-Christian." While McLuhan's argument is complex, his thesis is simple as stated on the cover of *Understanding Media*: "McLuhan declares that down through the ages the means by which man communicates have determined his thoughts, his actions, his life,...that the mass media of today are decentralizing modern living, turning the globe into a village, and catapulting twentieth-century man back to the life of the tribe."[1] Some, including McLuhan up to a point, would argue that the global village is a good thing—for example, "it takes a village"—but *only if* the "tribes" of the global village make up a community.

While McLuhan focuses on media and art in culture and sports apologists on religion, some passages in *Understanding Media* could well serve as a summary for the increasing tribe of scholars who praise the merits of sports as a religion, especially the following:

> Games are dramatic models of our psychological lives pro-
> viding release of particular tensions. They are collective and popular

---

[1] McLuhan, *Understanding Media: The Extensions of Man* (New York: New American Library, 1964).

art forms with strict conventions. Ancient and non-literate societies naturally regarded games as live dramatic models of the universe or of the outer cosmic drama. The Olympic games were direct enactments of the *agon*, or struggle of the Sun god. The runners moved around a track adorned with zodiacal signs in imitation of the daily circuit of the sun chariot. With games and plays that were dramatic enactments of a cosmic struggle, the spectator role was plainly religious. The participation in these rituals kept the cosmos on the right track, as well as providing a booster shot for the tribe. The tribe or the city was a dim replica of that cosmos, as were the games, the dances, and the icons. How art became a sort of civilized substitute for magical games and rituals is the story of the detribalization which came with literacy. Art, like games, became a mimetic echo of, and relief from, the old magic of total involvement. As the audience for the magic games and plays became more individualistic, the role of art and ritual shifted from the cosmic to the humanly psychological, as in Greek drama. Even the ritual became more verbal and less mimetic and dancelike. Finally the verbal narrative from Homer to Ovid became a romantic literary substitute for the corporate liturgy and group participation. Much of the scholarly effort of the past century in many fields has been devoted to a minute reconstruction of the condition of primitive art and ritual, for it has been felt that this course offers the key to understanding the mind of primitive man. The key to this understanding, however, is also available in our new electric technology that is so swiftly and profoundly recreating the conditions and attitudes of primitive tribal man in ourselves.[2]

McLuhan says many other things about sports that would appear to sound like music to the ears of apologists, none of whom have consulted this "oracle" of our age. Note the following: "...a man or society without games is one sunk in the zombie trance of the automation. Art and games enable us to stand aside from the material pressures of routine and convention, observing and questioning. Games as popular art forms offer to all an immediate means of participation in the full life of a society, such as no

---

[2] Ibid., 210.

single role or job can offer any man."[3] "Scholars have often pointed out that
Plato conceived of play dedicated to the Deity as the loftiest reach of man's
religious impulse."[4]

"Voila!" the apologist might exclaim, "even McLuhan sees sport as
religious." This, though, is not quite the case. Much going on here will
escape both the "eye" and the "ear," to use two of McLuhan's favorite
metaphors.

It could be argued that McLuhan sees sports as at least sacred owing to
the good things, as mentioned, they are capable of providing. They are,
though, in his analysis, limited institutionally to the here and now, to
"interplay" within a culture on which, as he says, "play" depends. Sports are
"good" or can be, but this is not the same as suggesting they are innately
divine or at least any more divine than another activity. The function of
sports is social and cultural, which is a high compliment. They operate
within a certain limit of possibility or potentiality, which is not to say that
individuals cannot exceed those limits in quest of the holy on or off a field
or racetrack.

Says McLuhan, "Games, then, are contrived and controlled situations,
extensions of group awareness that permit a respite from customary matters.
They are a sort of talking to itself on the part of society as a whole. And
talking to oneself is a recognized form of play that is indispensable to any
growth of self confidence."[5]

There is no indication in his thinking that McLuhan sees games as
situations or means for talking to something "wholly other," an act central to
religion, as opposed to a society "talking to itself," which could be and we
suspect largely is "secular" talk rather than "sacred." We see nothing in
games that seems to connect to the holy, the task of the sacred, or what
should be the vehicle to the holy, which is not to suggest that this cannot
happen to individuals in games and in other "nonreligious" settings. One
meditating in the Lincoln Memorial, a sacred shrine, might well evoke the
power and mystery of the holy as conceivably might happen to one by
merely reading about Lincoln's life and death. The holy works in mysterious
ways, and no possibility in either the private or public spheres is beyond its
reach, including, we acknowledge, athletics.

---

[3] Ibid.
[4] Ibid., 215.
[5] Ibid., italics added.

What we are saying is that the function of sports as a category of human endeavor is not to connect us to that which is holy or even to remind us of the idea of the holy. Never in the history of football, we would wager, has a coach said, even following opening prayers in the locker room, "Now boys, just remember that the purpose of this game, win or lose, is to encounter the holy." Sports might make us better warriors or citizens or provide any number of other benefits often claimed for them, including a milieu for psychic experiences, but these are byproducts and not central to the goal of sports—which, strictly speaking, is to defeat other teams within the rules in a public place to gain a prize, even if the prize is only the honor of victory.

When football teams kneel in prayer at midfield following games, they may feel holiness surpassing that of St. Teresa of Avila for all we know, but that display comes after the purposes of the game have been served by determination of a winner and loser. It may be admirable in the eyes of fans but not necessary for football, especially after a game. Sports apologists, though, do not base their arguments on rituals such as public prayer before or after games but in the action itself, which recapitulates in color and drama the propitiatory rites and myths of primitive man. The book that comes to mind as we watch any sporting event in person or on television, especially territorial games, is not the Bible but, for better or worse, *Understanding Media*.

McLuhan's discussion takes place at a social or cultural level with frequent forays into the mass psychological effect of media upon minds wrought by endless trains of images spread before us. It is no accident that *Survivor* has become one of the most popular of television productions. A primal instinct, tested throughout history against unforgiving elements and the whimsy of nature, has been reduced to the subject of a soap opera where participants are more in danger of sunburn than serious injury. Since *Survivor* enacts ancient myths by design and even staging, one would have to ask if this competition, sporting in the sense of hunting and fishing and skill in trickery and deception, is also religious in nature or if the tremendous response by such large numbers of viewers is also "religious." If we had to pick one show on television that illustrated McLuhan's thesis about our return to tribalism in the global village, it would be *Survivor*, which also seems to meet criteria of some apologists for religion. It is free of ethics of common sense, and, as in televised professional wrestling, there are no gods other than the god of vanity to interfere with the abounding egos of the competitors.

Ted Turner, a mogul of modern media, predicted that by 2003, there would be no major newspaper still in circulation. Perhaps he is disappointed that many are still around, considering his impact upon modern media. He does not appear to be a seer or prophet, but his understanding is correct even if predictions are off in regard to time.

Billy Graham and the Wide World of Network Sports

The impact of television upon our culture will probably not be fully evident until print finally disappears, but the demise of print seems inevitable considering what has already happened, owing to television's effects on religion, sports, and verbal art of metaphor or poetry. With the advent of television in the middle fifties, evangelism and sports, college and professional, burst on the entertainment scene at the same time. The new medium erased old antipathies between sports and religion and made it possible for them to wrap arms around one another as seen in the Fellowship of Christian Athletes (1954), an organization blessed by Billy Graham who, at least at the time, believed that sports are good for the soul.

In a letter to a Dallas crusade convert, a former television actor and night club owner who was planning a film on the life of Christ, Billy Graham wrote, "Please get a man with great strength in his face. I have seen so many pictures of Jesus as a weakling that I am sick of it. He was no sissy and he was no weakling. No sin or mar had come near his body. He must have been straight, strong, fit, handsome, tender, gracious, courteous…." John Pollock writes that "Graham was sure Christ must have been the most perfectly developed man physically in the history of the world, 'one whose eyes could pierce the hypocrisy of a Pharisee yet had such tenderness that he could break a sinful woman's heart.'"[6] Such an image may be made to order for television but appears at odds with that of the coming messiah in the prophecy of Isaiah: "He hath no form nor comeliness; and when we shall see him, *there is* no beauty that we should desire him." Instead, "he is a man of sorrows and acquainted with grief" (53:2–3). As for the modern moral crisis about the manliness of Christ, Jerry Falwell also wants us to understand that Christ was no "sissy."

---

[6] John Pollock, *Billy Graham* (New York: McGraw Hill, 1966) 168.

One may disagree with Graham's generous opinions on sports as a soulmate of religion, but his ministry was unmarked by any hint of scandal; this is in contrast to a number of other television evangelists who succumbed to the temptation of big money that the new medium made available to them. A number of major universities also yielded to such temptation. Further, Graham has moderated over the years, becoming more compassionate and open-minded. Asked by Hugh Downs on *20/20* if he could love a child of his who was a homosexual, he said he would love that child all the more. Asked by Larry King what he would say to a Jew or Muslim about his faith, Graham replied that he would tell him to be the best Jew or Muslim he could. Billy learned many years ago, like prophets of old, that if one is to be revered as a minister, there is a limit to the time one can spend in the palaces of power. In 2002 Billy appeared on *Oprah* and, upon Oprah's request, prayed after Oprah sang "Just as I Am." No mention was made of Matthew 6:6 as an estimated twenty million viewers looked on. In the spirit of Corrie Ten Boom's book *Nestle, Don't Wrestle*, which Oprah had once read, *the show closed with Billy and Oprah nestling together.*

No one utilized television more than Graham in the interest of evangelism or did more to build an alliance between religion and sport. He *never*, though, saw sports *as* a religion. All his life, he has been awash in the sacred, not necessarily of his own making. A "stone of witness" marks the spot where in California Billy "accepted, once and for all, the absolute authority of the scriptures,"[7] and his name will have a revered place in a theme park in Charlotte devoted to evangelism. After half a century, when he is seen preaching in stadia, he seems more distinguished than handsome, more graceful than eloquent, and more peaceful than desperate in presenting his message, which hasn't changed; it is still as simple and sincere as ever. As one looks at him, there is the conviction that he has put his worldly honors in perspective and that in him the sacred and holy, if at times at odds over a long career, have nevertheless overlapped more than might sometimes be apparent.

For both religion and sports, television made possible a *hieros gamos*, a wedding made in heaven, but as far as religion goes in its relation to sports, television may well be a Trojan horse within the gates, a trick played by Zeus, god of games, on his old antagonist, Jehovah, who said he should have

---

[7] William Martin, *A Prophet with Honor: The Billy Graham Story* (New York: Morrow, 1992) 112.

no other gods before him. Jehovah, though, hadn't reckoned on leather "Easy Boy" box seats before the altar of television. In retrospect, it seems that anyone could have predicted what would happen. Once an alliance overcame the Puritan skepticism of sports as entertainment, sports broke the agreement of understanding and is now well on its way to becoming a separate religion unto itself, which, according to apologists, is just fine. Just as the purveyors and prophets of sports once needed or thought they needed academics and then ditched those concerns for all intents and purposes, so now conventional religion is unnecessary. Those pre- and post-game prayers finally wore thin, and when one thinks about it as our apologists have done, we have rites all over the place anyway. Our contests are nothing but rituals, so we must be religious without even knowing it.

Popular Art and High Art: Talking Versus Reflecting

For McLuhan, games are forms of "collective and popular art." For apologists, they comprise "a popular religion." It might be asked whether or not art and religion can coexist at the same time and in the same place as in Greek statuary displaying *kalo kagathos* (good beauty) or in any museum of religious art or beautiful churches or in sacred music, which is also art. No one has said they can't, but the response needs qualification. Otto himself sees connections between the holy and art, as we shall see, and the distinguished poet-critic John Crowe Ransom spoke of the desirability of an element called MA for the blending of the Moral and the Aesthetic in poetry. Edgar Allan Poe believed the best poetry is that which at once combines the sublime and the beautiful, two other terms for faces of God.

It would seem that McLuhan's praise of sports as popular art would link them in his mind with religion much in the manner of the apologists, but that assumption does not appear valid, as he makes clear in this distinction: "Art is not just play but an extension of human awareness in contrived and conventional patterns. Sport as popular art is a deep reaction to the typical action of the society. But high art on the other hand, is *not a reaction but a profound reappraisal of a complex cultural state.*"[8] He then goes on to cite Jean Genet's *The Balcony* as an example, essentially making the same point as Leslie Fiedler makes in *No! In Thunder: "what people,*

---

[8] *Understanding Media*, 213, italics added.

what party, what church" that is, that no society needs an enemy as long as it has a great writer in its midst.[9]

As examples, Fiedler names Tolstoy who turned on the reformers, Joyce who turned on the Irish, Nathaniel West who turned on the Jews, and Faulkner who turned on the South. The great writer inherits the role of the ancient prophet whose purpose is to awaken his or her people to a nay-saying consciousness beyond the shallow, sentimental, and unconscious yea-saying of a society talking to itself about best-sellers, ball games, television celebrities, war, violent movies, or the price of gas. Thankfully, there have been celebrated outcries against social injustices in sports and out, for example *The Revolt of the Black Athlete* by Harry Edwards (1969), but as an institution sports, like religion, tends to serve the status quo of the state, symbolizing patriotism and cultural norms and images of power. Also, like all other forms of authority, sports discourages whistleblowing, what the Greeks called *parrhesia*, "straight talk" or "honesty" as opposed to "honor."

The distinction McLuhan makes between Popular Art and High Art is an old one and perhaps an eternal one often referred to as High Brow and Low Brow or as art and artifact (defined by *Webster's* as "a handmade object [as a tool or ornament] representing a particular culture or stage of technological development, a mass produced item…usually inferior artistic work").

In the popular realm, we are, as everyone knows, subjected to an endless stream of sporting artifacts celebrating various sports, teams, and champions. Such items are on display in halls of fame now stretching across the land like an Archipelago of the celebrityhood of sweat. Always for sale or order over the Internet are imitations of sacred jerseys worn by the gods and demigods of sports, even reportedly jock straps of the mighty, and bats, balls, and other objects touched by sacred hands. The sales pitch for these is even altering the traditional imagery of religious icons. In previous times we thought of a haloed Jesus on face mirrors or calendars tenderly holding a rescued lamb or kneeling in prayer at Gethsemane on funeral home fans. Never fear—he is risen and now can be seen in figurines dunking a basketball, making a handoff in football, or on T-shirts in beard and sandals making a leaping "save" in soccer. Even the holy spirit has become "fuel for

---

[9] *No! In Thunder: Essays on Myth and Literature* (New York: Stein and Day, 1972), 9-10.

the soul" as in the ad for television sports for one of the recent model Pontiacs. Stay tuned—special offers may be coming your way soon for splinters off the recently discovered cross and autographed sandals of Jesus Christ. As in the Middle Ages and indeed all other ages, fetishism is alive and well and indistinguishable from the sacred. With the aid of television and the Internet, fetishism is having its finest hour and certainly its most profitable.[10]

McLuhan is right about what has happened and is still happening. Poetry, including the vast harvest of metaphors and hymns of the world's religions but excluding patriotic gore of every nation, is passing from view as well as an understanding of its nature and its singular importance. What makes good poetry whole is that it creates images in words as Koestler explains:

> Thinking in pictures dominates the thinking of the unconscious—the dream, the hypnotic half-dream, the psychotic's hallucination, the artist's "vision." (The "visionary prophet" seems to have been a visionary, and not a verbalizer; the highest compliment we pay to those who trade in verbal currency is to call them "visionary thinkers.")
>
> But, on the other hand, pictorial thinking is a more primitive form of mentation than conceptual thinking, which it precedes in the mental evolution of the individual and of the species. The language of the primitive (and of the child) is, to borrow Kretschmer's simile, "like the unfolding of a picture strip: each word expresses a picture, a pictorial image, regardless of whether it signifies an object or an action." In Golding's novel *The Inheritors* the Neanderthal men always say, "I had a picture" when they mean "I thought of something"; and anthropologists agree that for once the novelist got the picture right.
>
> Thus the poet who reverts to the pictorial mode is regressing to an older and lower level of the mental hierarchy—as we do every night when we dream, as mental patients do when they regress to infantile fantasies. But the poet, unlike the dreamer in his sleep,

---

[10] For a superb treatment of this phenomenon in sports see Paul C. Johnson, "The Fetish and McGuire's Balls," *From Season to Season: Sports as American Religion* (Macon GA: Mercer University Press, 2001).

alternates between two different levels of the mental hierarchy; the dreamer's awareness functions on one only. The poet thinks both in images and verbal concepts, at the same time or in quick alterations; each *trouvaille*, each original find, bisociates two matrices. The dreamer floats among the phantom shapes of hoary deep; the poet is a skin diver with a breathing tube.[11]

It is highly questionable whether film or television can function on any plane other than that of the dreamer in his sleep as suggested in the following anecdote related to the authors by Rachel Maddux, author of *A Walk in the Spring Rain*. She said that at Gatlinburg in the late 1970s during the filming of the movie based on her novel, Ingrid Bergman told the director Guy Green that she "had an idea," whereupon he replied that he could not film an idea. He was, we suspect, expressing a profound insight into the nature of media. Cameras can photograph the techniques of actors, varieties of settings, and action. Scenes and plots can be argued over as far as interpretation and meaning, but once on film they are forever "finished" in ways that poems, plays, and film scripts are never finished as long as they are read, each reader bringing an analysis to the written language as the imagination prompts one to do. Because they always require encoding and decoding, reading and listening stimulate the imagination, while film and television undermine it and consequently the play of ideas. Each reading projects an original image and vision in the mind of the reader created against the context of his or her own experience. Even radio requires the listener to conjure up images of what is happening, unlike television where the viewer receives the image and reacts. With instant replay, we are told over and over what the image is and repeatedly what the conclusion ought to be on questionable calls. Both our intelligence and judgment are called into question much as moral sensibilities tend to get blunted when we repeatedly see the same tragedy such as that of the Twin Towers.

Game analysis of television sports by experts is a kind of double-barreled overkill by the media of both the "eye" and the "ear." Since sports are by nature public events, we once thought they were performed for the benefit of *spectators*, but networks tell us we are also *auditors* who need to be told what to think about what we see. This play-by-play detail is

---

[11] Arthur Koestler, *Act of Creation: A Study of the Conscious and Unconscious Processes of Humor, Scientific Discovery, and Art* (New York: MacMillan Company, 1964) 168–69.

something new in religion, if that is what sports are in the eyes of apologists. In the Religion of Sports we see something else that is not exactly new in conventional religion but practiced on a scale and in areas the advertisers for the Gospels dare not tread—but maybe only for the moment.

We still have trouble imagining a Sunday morning worship service on television brought to us by Budweiser or Viagra, but the idea is not as far-fetched as one might imagine considering that both are already on the track in the Religion of NASCAR. The following news release for 14 February 2004 tells the story and, McLuhan would add, the story of our age in which the media is the message: "If you get the Christian community behind your film and supporting it, they're very strong at word-of-mouth and grass-roots (marketing), and bringing friends to the theater," said Melisa Richter, who runs Richter Strategic Communications and was formerly Cloud 10's public relations manager. "*Passion* has even *scored* [italics added] prime advertising on the hood of a NASCAR race car, just in time for Sunday's Daytona 500, which draws a television audience of about 11 million. Interstate Batteries Chairman Norm Miller said a friend asked him to paint the ad on his company-sponsored race car."[12]

This indeed came to pass. The ad on Bobby Labonte's car read as follows: "The PASSION of the Christ in Theaters 02.25.04."[13] The *Passion* is the Crucifixion as shock and awe in contrast with the theme of "*com*passion" in classic art, which Protestants have long objected to teaching in schools because most of it is Catholic and secular humanists have objected to because of the fear that any theme of religion might translate into doctrinal prejudice. Now we are beginning to see what strange forms our collective myopia can take. Here we had the Labonte car in the race with, among others, the Viagra car, one promising victory over sexual impotence of sexual dysfunction and the other over the impotence of mortality. The winner was Dale Earnhardt Jr., driving a car sponsored by Budweiser, makers of still another kind of passion. We doubt that one would ever see a race car with the word "compassion" emblazoned across the hood since based on the teachings of Jesus, such a concept might suggest that the car in question would have to keep the slowest race car company. We have

---

[12] "Christians and Marketing of Gibson's 'Passion,'" <http://www.abs-cbnnews.com> (14 February 2004).

[13] Paul Newberry, "Racin' and Religion...Witnessing has Moved from Revival Tent to Fast Lane," AP, *Greeneville* (TN) *Sun,* 10 February 2004, B1.

literally made of Jesus a vehicle; the identity of the tenor, whether money or the holy, appears to be a matter of opinion.

Years ago Billy Graham said, "We should be selling Jesus like soap."[14] That we have done and continue to do, forgetting that only the sacred sells. The holy is not on the market, and the price of admission to its presence, like grace, is always free. The reason sports are so conspicuous in developed societies is simple. Since they invariably involve human bodies in motion and since they are by nature a form of "showing off," they become an absolutely indispensable, irresistible, and essential subject for photographers, especially considering the beauty, drama, and power associated with them. Every other "occupation" wants the athlete on his or her team—traditional religion, the military establishment, the government in power.

The Media Is the Message:
Theme Parks and Sacred Entertainment

Televised religion and televised sports have merged into what might be called "sacred entertainment." With corporate mergers and White Knight takeovers occurring, one would not be surprised to hear that one of the networks had permanently taken over all sports, including professional wrestling, and televangelism and formed a new network altogether called SBC—not the Southern Baptist Convention but the "Sacred Broadcast Corporation" with twenty-four-hour programming. As ever, things that are private and holy remain out of sight, even hidden, from the cameras of "reality" shows and the questers of their networks who rove the land in search of meaning generally absent on television programming. Dr. Johnson was prescient in his 1755 *Dictionary* in describing a "network" as "anything reticulated or decussated, at equal distances, with interstices between the intersections."

Major territorial sports such as football have long been steeped in entertainment, especially in the advertisements, which McLuhan describes as a means of keeping "*upset* with the Joneses" (italics added). The word "upset" is common in sports language and has theatrical connotations as in "upstage" (of or relating to the rear of the stage). As an adjective, it means haughty and as a transitive verb to steal the show from and to treat snobbishly. Indeed, like sports, entertainment is, by definition, something diverting or engaging, a

---

[14] Frank Deford, "Endorsing Jesus," *Sports Illustrated*, 26 April 1976, 69.

public performance. One meaning of "entertain" is to play against an opposing team (on one's home field or court). A growing trend in sports by apologists, players, and management is to blur all distinction between other categories of human culture, on the one hand to compete with the traditional role of religion in society and on the other to outdo Broadway in song and dance. When sports become either religion or entertainment, or both at once as is usually the case, their soul is AWOL and perhaps the national soul as well. Only the form or shell remains. If proof is needed for the pattern and the consequences, look to Rome or even the movie *Gladiator*, which treats the gladiator hero sympathetically as he tries to survive with his humanity intact in a culture of decadence.

Mass media, especially television, has affected *agon*, the world of competition, but no more than it has the world of *mimesis*, or imitation, turning the world of print and individual imagination into public displays of visible objects. We refer to the widely ballyhooed pop art of our leisure class culture, ranging from that of Disney World, to Playboy's Bunny Land to Orlando's Bible Land, all revered sites and destinations of pilgrimages, all different in theme but not in form. All reflect the sentimentality and semiconsciousness that are always evident in the usual portrayal of the sacred. Hugh Hefner thinks he is in moral revolt when in fact in his bathrobe and with pipe, he is armed with a superficial sense of self-righteousness and is as much an ideologue as Cotton Mather and just as conforming in the age of television as Walt Disney ever dared to be.

Walt Disneyfied childhood, Hefner Disneyfied sex, and the builders of Bible Land have Disneyfied Scripture and the "holy lands" of the Middle East. All proceeded on the assumption that Americans at heart are babes in Toyland with money to shell out for what we have in common, the growing pains of childhood, confusion and frustration over sexuality, and a Judeo-Christian legacy of unimaginable suffering that could be sufficiently anesthetized and prettified to the point of inanity. As always the sacred sells not so much by distorting truth but by not facing all of it. For example, the language of desert prophets such as the following fires the senses and imagination instead of stifling them as imitation scenes in theme parks are prone to do: "Therefore thus sayeth the LORD God of Israel, Behold, I am bringing such evil upon Jerusalem and Judah, that whosoever shall hear of it, both his ears shall tingle...and I will wipe Jerusalem as a man wipeth a dish, wiping it, and turning it upside down." (see also Jeremiah 19:3) God "plays" but he doesn't "play around."

It can be said that all theme parks, like the one created by pop star Michael Jackson, are "Never Lands." Each is a substitute for reading, thinking, and reflecting regardless of the aesthetic, moral, and sacred vision each claims to portray. The theme in each, no matter what is being sold or promoted, is money, and the connections each enjoys with sports are evident in "sacred" time as was the last half-time celebration of the "sacred" Super Bowl on Super Sunday, our High Holy Day. On this special day the Super Bowl itself becomes a theme park of exhibitionism, highlighting the sacredness of football amid the unabashed celebration of riches and patriotic fervor by which we beseech the almighty and the conviction of America's place in the divine destiny of the world.

Brothers to Dragons and Companions to Owls

If there is anything that distinguishes the religion of sports from traditional religion, it is the language of both. The language of the old religions is metaphorical based upon that in the King James Version of the Bible and the plays of Shakespeare. If we listen to pre- and post-game testimony of athletes, commentary of coaches and fans, and analyses from the broadcast booth, we cock our ears for memorable metaphors, usually in vain excepting that of Deion Sanders likening sports and religion to peanut butter and jelly. In traditional religions, metaphors abound as the examples quoted above expressing the apocalyptic imagery of one side of the holy in contrast to that of the 23rd Psalm promising the peace that passes understanding. Sports apologists would, we suspect, tend to cry foul about any comparisons of religions of language since the religion of sports is supposedly based on field rituals during the sacred time of the game. Unfortunately, words have a way of diluting the religion of physical grace and power as in the deluge of clichés before every big game; all the while, the muses of poetry continue to fade into the darkness gathering atop Mount Parnassus.

McLuhan hits upon a key phrase when he says that "games are dramatic models of our psychological lives," meaning they are dramatic rituals such as those in religion, politics, and war. Parallels between sports, religion, stage drama, and war are plentiful as seen in the use of special dress, uniforms or costumes, the dramatis personae, lineups, orders of battle, the rehearsals, practice and training, the presence of audience, even if at a distance, the division of the performances into periods or innings analogous to "acts," "stages," "theaters of operations," and imitation of the heroic.

All of this makes sports, religion, and war eminently stageable, filmable, salable, and accountable for most of the programming on television, including newscasts that have also become entertainment competing for recognition and prizes. Some sports sell better than other sports, but overall they are the dream come true for advertisers. They flash on our television screens with drums beating, banners flying, and for the big games, a stadium full of prosperity, promising excitement and good wholesome fun. The major danger to networks is one of surfeit, which is already occurring. They serve advertisers best with spot promotions from athletes and with heroic themes from the world of sports. If Tiger Woods drives a Buick, why don't you? Have a "breakfast of champions," and for dinner cook out with friends on a George Foreman Grill. Examples are endless.

McLuhan sees games themselves as media, each with a message. The message of the media of baseball is quite different from the message of football, and these differ from the messages of golf and boxing. Football and hockey are brutal games played within limits of time, while baseball and golf are not. The latter two would be more at home before the fall, while the former two would be products of a fallen world like war to which they are related. Both football and hockey are knightly sports, baseball and golf more akin to shepherd games. Baseball, we acknowledge, is in part a face-to-face sport as between pitcher and batter, and though prone on occasion to brawls over calls or other incidents, it is still a game of great sanity, fun to play and watch without the violence of football. The very terms "infield" and "outfield" reflect their rural origins or at least associations, possibly deriving from use of those terms by the Scotch Irish in farming in America.

The other media McLuhan mentions—clothing ("extension of our skin"), number, printed word, money, ads, movies, radio, and television—are extrinsic media of display. These follow the same gradation of gratuitous difficulty in *agon* (competition) as indicated in the movement from *Paideia* (simplicity) to *Ludus* (complexity) in Caillois's classification of games.[15] An example of the varying range of competition is, on the simple end, students playing touch football on campus in T-shirts and Bermuda shorts without a clock and or spectators to, on the complex end, the Super Bowl with timeouts every few minutes for million-dollar ads that, in McLuhan's view,

---

[15] Roger Caillois, *Man, Play, and Games*, trans. Meyer Barash (New York: Free Press, 1961) 36.

are means of keeping us *"upset* with the Joneses" (italics added). When a touch football game is over, its influence ends, but the effects of Super Sunday, go on forever.

"Weapons" seems like an odd form of extrinsic media that McLuhan discusses, but more and more they are the means by which we "communicate" with one another—from sticks and stones at the simple level to weapons of mass destruction at the most complex. The inevitable flyover of military planes at the Super Bowl is a sacred reminder that, as Plato said, "only the dead have seen the end of war."

The military connection with sports is everywhere in the world of advertising, from toys such as paintball guns to war games to computer football to those directing our attention to the new SUV, which like the Hummer, resembles an army tank more than a vehicle. Dangerous times call for transportation that is both intimidating and secure. The message seems clear: I can go where I want to when I want to, and if you get in my way, I can obliterate you if I choose to do so. I am a road warrior rather than a road traveler.

The extrinsic media serve one purpose, to make the play of any game as conspicuous as possible and therefore profitable. Marketeers of televangelism learned early on the value of media extravaganza, and long before respected scholars of religion started calling sports a religion, televangelists had already made of religion a profitable sport. There is, as we have said, a theater side to religion as in all other forms of human drama, but what has distinguished it from other forms of entertainment is a private side evident in every religion on earth, the solitude needed for respite from a society talking to itself, for meditation, and—who knows?—for listening in private to something wholly other.

We see no evidence in modern sports of the avowed purpose of religions, to awaken the sense of the holy either in players or in fans. The holy does not depend on conflict either in games or war. The sacred does. Our games do not appear to exist as vehicles or pathways to the holy but as means for secular entertainment, dramatic ritual for the imitation of the heroic, instruction and illustration of the value of teamwork, pride of town or region, a way to keep society "talking to itself" in essentially mindless chatter, and, increasingly, generation of wealth and maintenance of the status quo. There is a case for this action or "reaction," as McLuhan says, as there is for playing with dogs by throwing sticks for them to chase and retrieve. However, to ascribe "ultimate" significance to them or sensationalize events as apologists do is a reach. It also fails to acknowledge that such rare experiences in sports might be only one type of encounter with the "wholly other" that engulfs us and tries to awaken us to infinite varieties of being and possibility.

George Orwell, one of the most distinguished writers of the twentieth century, wrote an article titled "The Sporting Spirit," in which he had little good to say about it. Based upon his observations in India and Burma, he wrote, "Serious sport has nothing to do with fair play. It is bound up with hatred, jealousy, boastfulness, disregard of all rules and sadistic pleasure in witnessing violence; in other words it is war minus the shooting."[16] Replying specifically to Orwell's contention, Philip Goodhart and Christopher Chataway in *War Without Weapons* (1968) say that one of the values of sports is that they are war *without the fighting*.

We will examine this matter of the question of the sublimation of violence later, but here we wish to mention one area in sports where there is no pretense at hiding possible connections with the violent world of nature. Consider our team nicknames: from animals (Bulls, Wildcats, Wolverines, Lions, Tigers, Gophers), from amphibians, reptiles, and fish (Horned Toads, Diamondbacks, Rattlers, Gators, Terrapins, Dolphins), from insects and birds (Hornets, Yellow Jackets, Wasps, Eagles, Falcons), and finally from acts of God (Cyclone, Hurricane, Tornado, and, apparently, virtual tsunamis as in Crimson Tide and the Green Wave). When we are playing or watching sports, we become, at least symbolically as Job suggests, "brothers to dragons and companions to owls," (30:29) no matter how much we might deny such kinship in debate with evolutionists.

Sports teams both in name and in athletic action represent a temporary retreat down the ladder of evolution, and their mission is never in question—to knock out the other guy, to pin an opponent, to overwhelm the other team, to do whatever is necessary within rules to win. When one reflects on the situation for a while, it becomes a mystery why anyone ever thought that groups so named could serve the causes of evangelism. Names such as "Doves" and "Lambs," which would seem perfect for proselytism, would be utter disasters, say, for football teams. "Hawks" and "Rams" would be more fitting for a game of good, clean violence.

---

[16] George Orwell, "The Sporting Spirit," <http://user.sezampro.yu/~misicb/lektira/english/spirit.htm> 2 March 2004).

If the holy is invisible, the media are secular and sacred representations of the here and now with little difference between them when it comes to making money. If the one virtue demanded by the holy is humility, the media moves in an opposite direction, hyping interest in prizes and pride as in a wide variety of contests that are competitive and compatible with working definitions of sports—fashion shows (clothes), beauty contests (ads), the stock market (money), the Oscars (movies), armaments races (weapons), and televangelism (all of the above, including the "weapon" of fear centered on the end of time).

Normally, says McLuhan, "each of the media is also a powerful weapon with which to clobber other media and other groups."[17] Sports as media, especially professional and major college sports, excel, much like televangelism, in perfect orchestration or manipulation of all other forms—numbers (identification and ranking), clothes (uniforms), radio and television (network broadcasts), and weapons (trick plays, secret planning, psychological toning)—with their special contributions in honor of the most sacred media of all, money, as the symbols on any of the coins or bills will illustrate and as confirmed by the special separation and extreme protection afforded it in the form of gold in Fort Knox. Money is not merely sacred but nothing less than the god of this world. Sports, though, is the darling of all competitions because nowhere else is victory symbolized so clearly and the boons thereof—power, popularity, rank, and money—that set champions apart, which in a religion of sports might make them sacred *but not holy*.

In the case of the sports, the thing (the contest) and the version of the thing, that is "spin," are the same between competing teams. Each team at a certain level has a public relations staff, a chaplain, a doctor or medicine man, and accountants to exalt the team in victory or defeat and reveal the community spirit of the team—pictures of the team in prayer, the players' love of small children, and community service in picking up trash. This may all be well and good, but the hard facts won't go away. The goal in sports is to win a contest in a public place, to bring glory to one's team and town, to make money for investors, and the like. Teams may consist of people who throughout the week are in constant communion with the holy, but once the game begins, we are back down to earth where winning becomes the only thing—but not the holy thing.

---

[17] McLuhan, *Understanding Media*, 34–35.

In regard to "spin," let us take for further analysis some of the most famous and controversial work of all time, especially as it relates to sports and religion, as in a state religion. We refer to the work of Leni Riefenstahl, creator of Nazi propaganda films *Olympiad, Triumph of the Will,* and *Days of Freedom.* What we will see is that often humans take on the most ferocious and destructive traits of animals when attempting to parade as models of purity and perfection.

Before Riefenstahl's *Olympische Spiele (Olympiad)* in 1936, little attention was given to aesthetic matters in sports films, as Ken Wlaschin has observed: "In truth all the Olympic films until 1936 were essentially newsreels, or at best documentary records filmed in a flat and relatively dull manner."[18] Instead of merely recording, Riefenstahl interpreted, creating widespread controversy since many believed she was still deliberately promoting the Aryan ethos as she had blatantly in *Triumph of the Will,* though few disputed her artistic skills. In the case of *Olympiad,* it is fair to point out as Wlaschin does that "the star of the film is the black American athlete Jesse Owens, winner of four gold medals, not Hitler (an ironic comment on the Nazi theories of Aryan Superiority)."

Can we not say, then, that film directors can photograph ideas? As always much depends upon definitions. As we have said, symbols can be photographed, but symbols are not exactly the same as ideas. Symbols are like husks covering the seed that blossoms into fruit once the shell is removed, leaving, in democracies, interpretations to the auditor, spectator, or reader. In *Olympische Spiele* there may not be a lot of room for argument over aesthetic treatment of material, or some might say of artful manipulation, but there is plenty of room for reactions to the moral element in the content. Film is the medium of *Olympische Spiele* but not the genre suggested in the title by *Spiele.* In German the word has a wide variety of meanings starting with "play, game, sport, playing, acting, performance," but the English word "Spiel" means "a voluble line and often extravagant talk" and "pitch."

A modern term in describing Riefenstahl's work is "spin," which is a quieter and more subtle form of propaganda but still recognizable as "patriotic gore." One television talk show brags that the spin stops with that program, but the spin never stops on anything. It is absolutely essential for

---

[18] Wlaschin, *Olympics on Film, Olympic Games: 80 Years of People, Events, and Records,* ed. Lord Killanian and John Roda (New York: Macmillan Company, 1976) 165.

sacred views in politics, religion, and sports. It has a little more class than the term "propaganda" but still the same kind of dry air. The holy has entirely different forms of media ranging from whispers to music of the spheres, to a wide range of acts of God leaving witnesses and survivors certain that in terms of physical might there is indeed a higher power, whether there is a higher wisdom or not. The question of spin is an interesting one in regard to the sacred and the holy. If there is a spin in everything, including sacred doctrine in sports, war, politics, and religion, is there anything in the center around which words in whatever arrangement always revolve? We think Robert Frost thought there was in his poem called "The Secret Sits": "We dance round in a ring and suppose, / but the secret sits in the middle and knows."[19]

Time and Money: Secular or Sacred?

Instead of connections between sacred rites of prehistory and similar patterns in modern society, Marshall McLuhan sees disconnects. What secularizes the modern age or maybe profanes it, including the world of sports, is to some extent that oft-cited villain "money" as suggested in a *Sports Illustrated* article several years ago, "Money: The Monster Ruining Sports." Yet, Paul Weiss in *Sport: A Philosophic Inquiry* was also right when he said the athlete does not sell his soul by playing for money, and this may not depend on the amount as much as we sometimes think. To be sure, money and the eternal problems associated with it are never out of the picture as a corruptive force in all categories of human interaction, including sports and religion, but as areas of philosophic speculation in values the subject has been worn threadbare without visible results in understanding. The ideal was articulated in Greece more than two and one half millennia ago that *aidos*, the central quality in the Greek athletic ideal, is stolen away by "secret gain." Money undermines the possibility of holiness in sports and even the sacredness of it not so much on the actual field of play as in the front office, which the daily news from Sports World confirms.

What secularizes sports on the athletic fields of play and tends to remove them from the realm of the sacred is not so much the question of money as the twin currency of money—time. While both are spent, how or why they are spent depends upon our ideas of the sacred and the holy. In

---

[19] *The Complete Poems of Robert Frost* (New York: Holt Rinehart and Winston, 1964) 495.

regard to the controlling effect of time, McLuhan would say something like this: "Place a cross over a stadium if you wish but don't forget the huge electric clock on one end of the gridiron regulating the time of play by the relentless march of numbers called seconds, minutes, and hours, while in the press box on the opposite side sporting scribes are dividing the action of the game into segments of the alphabet called 'words' and 'stories.'" Hear McLuhan's own words on the media of time:

> The clock dragged man out of the world of seasonal rhythms and recurrence, as effectively as the alphabet had released him from the magical resonance of the spoken word and the tribal trap. This dual translation of the individual out of the grip of nature and out of the cycle of the tribe are, under electric conditions, fatally simple. We need beware of those who announce programs for restoring man to his original state and language of the race. The crusaders have never examined the role of media and technology in tossing man about from dimension to dimension.[20]

In the sixties McLuhan was obviously pointing to groups advocating one language or a return to nature as in communal projects of one kind or another.

Sports-as-religion proponents are by no means "reformers" or "crusaders" announcing programs for "restoring man to his original state and language." Their thesis is different, one showing parallels between ancient myths and the same enactments in modern sports, and they do so with unremitting emphasis but without evangelical zeal. In *From Season to Season* Professor Miller-McLemore draws repeatedly upon the learned commentary of Mircea Eliade. Notice what McLuhan says about the same scholar, indeed the same book, that provides so much support for apologists in connection between modern sports and archaic rites: "Mircea Eliade, professor of comparative religion, is unaware, in *The Sacred and the Profane*, that a 'sacred' universe in his sense is one dominated by the spoken word and by auditory media. A 'profane' universe, on the other hand, is one dominated by the visual sense. The clock and the alphabet, by hacking the universe into visual segments, ended the music of interrelation. The visual desacralizes the universe and produces 'the nonreligious man of

---

[20] McLuhan, *Understanding Media*, 144.

modern society.'"[21] In regard to sports, we now see an idea emerging called "Muscular Secularism." It has in truth been with us for many years under sacred terms of one kind or another. Muscularism of any type always secularizes the religion to which it is connected.

In the thinking of McLuhan, what goes on in our stadia and gymnasia is as "nonreligious" as tailgate parties in parking lots before game time or in bars down the street or in millions of homes where fans are glued to television on Super Sunday. There is no escape from the laws here at work. Call Super Sunday our "high holy day" if we wish, but the game that day is as subject to the tyranny of the clock as are other face-to-face sports such as hockey and boxing and our jobs in the workaday world. Play in the Super Bowl is different from mechanic work down at the nearest garage, but even this mightiest of rituals in our sporting age cannot escape the demon of repetition, that plodding reality the Bard spoke of as "tomorrow and tomorrow and tomorrow." "If it's the Super Bowl, Hollywood Henderson asked, "Why do they have it every year?" Another to whom the same general remark is attributed is Duane Thomas of the Cowboys in 1972, as mentioned in "Super Bowls and Sisyphus: Why Do We Care Who Wins Any Contest?" by Lawrence Meredith, who bravely asks a question that is like placing a bomb in the foundation of the sacred temple of sports.[22]

How crucial is any contest? After four years telecasting with ABC's Monday Night Football, Don Meredith looked down on the San Francisco 49er game with Green Bay in Candlestick Park and said, "There must be something more important than this."

Don's comment reached far beyond mere athletic mediocrity on the field. City after city, banquet after banquet, year after year—the traveling freak show moved on. Was it weariness as an invocation to authenticity? The pornography of celebrity status could no longer energize Don's piece of the rock. Two months later *Sports Illustrated* published a feature story on "The Defection of Dandy Don." There *must* be something more important—perhaps at NBC, perhaps in film, perhaps in deepening relationship with one's family, perhaps back with ABC again, perhaps simply a dandy glass of tea in the clear air of Santa Fe. The gods say be

---

[21] Ibid.

[22] Lawrence Meredith, "Super Bowls and Sisyphus: Why Do We Care Who Wins Any Contest Anyway?" *Arete: The Journal of Sport Literature* 1/2 (Spring 1984).

careful—rebel or not—you will push some rock. Camus warns us that genius, after all, is the intelligence that knows its frontier.[23]

For our physical comforts, rapid communication, convenience in travel, and other technological marvels, we have paid a heavy price, the loss of the sense of Great Time, the time of myths and legends that stirred the soul. The sense of eternity in this world stands in contrast to the overwhelming sense of Passing Time, which creates angst by its nature, the feeling that one is attached to a hawser inevitably pulling him toward the darkness and silence of the grave, as J. B. Priestly noted several years ago in *Man and Time.* No matter how many times we watch the replay on television, it is still in the past. Time has moved on and dragged us along with it. As Bo Lozoff, cofounder of the Human Kindness Foundation, is fond of saying, "What time brings, time takes away."

It may be that instead of entering into sacred time and sacred place at stadia for big games or even into a secular place, we enter instead into a *surreal* world where time either gallops like a runaway clock if one's team is behind or drags like dog days if that team is ahead in a tight game. The definition of surrealism applies perfectly to such scenes: "The principles, ideals, or practice of producing fantastic or incongruous imagery or effects in art, literature, film or theater by means of unnatural juxtapositions and combinations." Michael Novak himself, the supreme apologist for the religion of sports, lends credence to this view by his opinion that sports fan does not just mean "fanatic" but also "fantastic." Yes, that is true, and there we have it—all we have to do is to add "sports" ("tumultuous fun") to the list of genres of the surreal mentioned in *Webster's.* Ahh—could it be that apologists of sports were on to something after all but misnaming it? Could it be that sports, instead of being religious in nature, are still aesthetic but today with a zaniness that the Greeks in their highly stylized concepts of sports and art did not develop to any pronounced degree?

The word "surreal" makes us aware of still other striking features of our games, especially championship series, "having the intense irrational reality of a dream." (Webster's Dictionary) When we look at the word "irrational," we see immediately how appropriate it is for a description of sports, especially for those with some sense of humor. It is defined, "not endowed with reason or understanding, lacking usual or normal mental clarity or coherence; not governed by or according to reason." Our guess is

---

[23] Ibid., 15.

that Joseph Price would find some sympathy for this line of reasoning judging from some of his concluding remarks in "The Final Four as Final Judgment":

> Why has the Final Four become such a religious event? Bayless suggests: "Because it's divine madness. Perfect imperfection. We've fallen head over Air Jordans for the NCAA's (tournament) because every team *does not* start five first-round draft choices and every game is *not* artfully played and every favorite does not have a fair chance to prove its superiority...." The amateur character of the tournament increases our vicarious identification with the players and their performances. By not being in the "other" category of the professional, they more nearly represent us as amateurs, and consequently, they elicit fanaticism from us.[24]

Herein lies a clue, to be pursued later, as to why the church has lost control over sports and play.

Of course, such fanaticism isn't just limited to shouting at the television or from the stands while wearing the team colors. It is also expressed more darkly through fistfights between fans or tearing down goalposts, not to mention the substantial vandalism and destruction that occur after victory in business and residential districts where the "fantastic" fire of enthusiasm expresses itself visually and literally.

Carrying *Webster's* definitions still further, that of "madness" strikes us as highly amusing in relation to the Final Four: "Any of several ailments of animals marked by frenzied behavior" as in, one might add, painting one's face, wildly flapping one's limbs, cheering and jumping insanely when a large inflated leather ball is pitched through a net or, apparently more desirable, slammed down from above the net.

A legitimate question from apologists might be: whoever said the "surreal" and the sacred—or even the surreal and the holy—are incompatible? Is not Abraham being reduced to a feeling of dust and ashes a surreal scene? What about the ordeal of Job or the scene at Golgotha? These are difficult questions, and perhaps all we can say in response, at least for the moment, is that whereas the surreal is irrational, the holy is nonrational.

---

[24]Price, 180.

Instead of seeing sports as either conspicuous waste or a new religion, Marshall McLuhan sees them as forms of media, and the media, as always, is the message. If modern sports are a religion, as apologists claim and as they certainly were in ancient Greece, they are today increasingly pagan thanks to television, which has returned us to the mentality of children, the psychological worldview of primitive man who, as Arthur Koestler, William Golding, and others confirm, looked upon the world in terms of images and pictures without aid or hindrance of language. It is acknowledged that modern American sports may be categorized as "sacred," as apologists are fond of saying, when considered as spectacle or display of the presumed virtues of a society, but the "sacred" is not the same as the holy, which apologists also claim for sports though not as frequently.

Considering the implications involved, we may ask the same question of sports as religion proponents as Tom Wolf Did about McLuhan? What if he is right – that the media is the message? If the media is the message and games are media requiring a "religious response" as in preliterate times, are conventional religions also media? If so, what do they "connect" or link or attempt to link? Man and God, many people would say. In the case of the religion of sports, the question becomes who or what is the God or gods, and if there is no deity as in some other religions, what ideals are served? If the religion of sports depends on the idea of the "sacred," what is the relation of that idea to ethics of play and, especially, to the idea of the holy? Here, to repeat, is where the dividing line occurs. We do not deny that holy experiences cannot occur in dramatic rituals such as sports, war, and politics, but it is not the purpose of these rituals to connect us with the holy, which, if it exists at all, is *peculiar to the sphere of religion* as an organized endeavor.

World War II removed all doubt from our minds about the reality of evil. What we call the good and the connection of both good and evil to the idea of God in the church of sports have not often been examined in any detail. Hence in the following chapter we will attempt to take note of the long relationship between the religion of sports and war, which modern apologists rarely note.

Chapter 6

The Cross in the Coliseum:
Sacred Ground and Battle Ground

If heaven were to do again,
And on the pasture bars
I leaned to line the figures in
Between the dotted stars,

I should be tempted to forget,
I fear, the Crown of Rule,
The Scales of Trade, the Cross of Faith,
As hardly worth renewal

For these have governed in our lives,
And see how men have warred.
The Cross, the Crown, the Scales may all
As well have been the Sword[1]

For our response to issues in this chapter, we need before us again in the interest of easy reference the view of "gods" and "powers" set forth in *From Season to Season*: "Although religions do not necessarily involve the worship of 'God' or 'gods,' they do orient their followers towards an ultimate force or pantheon of powers, whether personalized as 'gods' or

---

[1] "The Peaceful Shepherd," from the *Complete Poems of Robert Frost* (New York: Holt, Rinehart and Winston, 1964) 319.

whether identified in abstracted ways, for example, Buddhism's path of enlightenment or Shinto's abiding sense of family and tradition."[2]

The use of "or" tending to equate Buddhism and Shintoism needs modification as suggested by encyclopedia histories such as the following:

> Beginning in the 18th century, Shinto was revived as an important national religion through the writings and teachings of a number of a succession of notable scholars.... Motivated by nationalistic sentiments which took the form of reverence for Japanese antiquity and hatred of ideas and practices of foreign origins, these men prepared the way for the disestablishment of Buddhism and the adoption of Shinto as a state religion.... According to revived Shinto doctrine, the sovereignty of the emperor is exercised by divine right through his reputed descent from the sun goddess Amaterasu Omikami, who is considered to be the founder of the Japanese nation. Concomitant beliefs include the doctrines that the Japanese are superior to other peoples because of their descent from the gods, and that the emperor is destined to rule over the entire world. Until the defeat of Japan in World War II, these beliefs were of the utmost importance in assuring popular support for the military expansion of the Japanese Empire.[3]

Like a number of other religions, Shinto comes in several packages, but it is worthwhile to remember what happened to the militant branch of that religion after World War II:

> In 1946, during the American occupation of Japan...the cult was completely separated from the state by the general order of Douglas MacArthur, supreme commander for the Allied powers. Government financial support of State Shinto was eliminated, the former practice of teaching cult doctrines was abolished, and the use of Shinto symbols for nationalistic purposes was forbidden. At the same time the emperor issued a statement renouncing all claims to

---

[2] Joseph Price, *From Season to Season: Sports as American Religion* (Macon GA: Mercer University Press, 2001) 228.

[3] "Shinto," *Funk and Wagnall's*, vol. 30 (New York: Unicorn Publishers, 1952) 11,070.

divinity. Sectarian Shinto, a religion of the same status as Buddhism and Christianity, was unaffected by these changes.[4]

The preceding commentary comes from the West, but note what contemporary Japanese scholars are now saying about connections between military sports and the rise of fascism in Japan:

> A fascistic regime was almost completed before the outbreak of the Pacific War in December 1941. School gymnastics became synonymous with military training. All amateur sports organizations were reorganized into the Greater Japan Physical Education Association, which was an organ of the Ministries of Education and Health and Welfare. All youth organizations became subservient to the fascist regime.
>
> Contests and games were ritualized to indoctrinate militarism, patriotism, and above all, the ideology of the Emperor System. All kinds of physical activities were colored by *bushido* ("the Way of the Warrior") and *Yamato damashii* ("Japanese spirit"). Meanwhile play elements and the liberalism of sports were decolorized.[5]

Obviously Price was talking about this latter branch of Shinto and not the military kind, symbolized by a sword, that derived its justification from myths of the sun goddess. As in other religions with militant traditions, including Christianity, the symbolism of the sacred sword in Shintoism stands in contrast with holy sites set in nature, fields, mountains, and water. The same divide occurred in Germany in the years preceding and during WWII between traditional Christianity and Judaism on the one hand and on the other the "National Reich Church,"[6] which, like military Shinto, embraced knightly values of power and conquest as opposed to shepherd values of mercy and compassion. In both "religions," military sport was held in high esteem as a method of training and as a popular symbol of national faith and tribal superiority.

---

[4] Ibid.

[5] Ikuo Abe, Yasuharu Kiyohara, and Ken Nakajima, "Sport and Physical Education Under Fascistization in Japan," <http://ejmas.com/jalt/jaltart_abe_0600.htm> (2 March 2004). Also see bibliography for this article.

[6] William L. Shirer, *The Rise and Fall of the Third Reich* (New York: Simon and Schuster, 1960) 324–33.

Perhaps the best example of this fracturing in American culture is our Civil War, when the comity that held the nation together yielded to self-righteous pressures on both sides. It was a sacred war by sacred knights for sacred territory for sacred causes, but how holy it was in bringing about democracy is still open to question, as is the role of the churches in that catastrophe.[7] While we are somewhat removed from Germany and Japan of the thirties and forties in our current condition, it is well to keep in mind the words of Shirer: "In reality the struggle between the Nazi government and the churches was the age old one of what to render unto Caesar and what to God. So far as the Protestants were concerned, Hitler was insistent that if the 'German Christians' could not bring the evangelical churches into line under Reich Bishop Mueller then the government itself would have to take over the direction of the churches."[8]

In pre-World War II Germany we see a scene confirming the aptness of Sam Keen's observation on military metaphors in relation to economics and the world of business, metaphors similar to those of sports, especially territorial sports. "When we organize our economic life around military metaphors and words such as war, battle, strategy, tactics, struggle, contest, competition, winning, enemies, opponents, defenses...we have gone a long way toward falling into a paranoid world view."[9]

This observation is also true regarding a culture's criminal justice process and system. When we declare "war on" issues such as poverty and drugs, cynicism and retribution can too easily become the order of the day. Perhaps we might try declaring "peace on" our social ills and work with a different mind-set toward a different conclusion.

Similarly in sports, teams are always preparing for "battle" and getting ready to go to "war" against "enemies" or "opponents." The religion of sports, thus, is close to a religion of power and ranking, which is why it does not surprise us that before Christ was made a CEO in our culture he had already been a linebacker. Before that he was a soldier looking down a rifle at an enemy in World War I and in the Middle Ages a knight on horseback

---

[7] In this connection, see C. C. Goen, *Broken Churches, Broken Nation: Denominational Schisms and the Coming of the War* (Macon: Mercer University Press, 1985).

[8] Shirer, *Rise and Fall*, 329.

[9] Sam Keen Quoted in Joe Dolce, "Metamorphosis of the Warrior," *The Warrior, the Wound and Woman-hate: The Politics of Softfear, 1992*, <http://www.starnet.com.au/d women/MWintro.html> (2 March 2004).

contesting with knights of other faiths over sacred ground also called holy, indeed as far back as the sixth century.

It crosses one's mind that the world might be safer if we had an international league of religions using athletic competition instead of war to show which team was the most powerful and closest to God. This would, though, require faith in the subliminal power of sports, substituting a less violent form of one action for another even more destructive, a theory that is still open to question. We will focus more on this important issue later, but increasingly it seems that sports, instead of ventilating aggression, refuel it so that a loss or setback in sports as in war is a call for stronger retaliation. In the Church of Sports, there is no answer to this that we can see, only rivalry, revenge, and redemption from season to season, the model for or echo of the militant branches of the major religions, which because of assertiveness and unwillingness to listen to alternatives are often in control of matters of state.

Things of Caesar and Things of God

What Douglas MacArthur did in Japan to separate religion and state, an absolutely essential condition for democracy as Jefferson realized, we ourselves are endeavoring to reverse as seen in some religious groups attempting to influence the government in the direction of an interventionist foreign policy. Is this a function of a pastor of the Scriptures, or are the Congress, the president, and the leadership of the armed forces sufficiently prepared to bang the drums for war by themselves, a position we inevitably expect in times of crisis and perhaps sometimes welcome in the cause of justice? Should a pastor serve the role of cheerleader for governments or as the conscience of any given government? We might also expect a clergy that would question militant attitudes and solutions and remind us of the possibility that perhaps Jesus was not merely chattering with the admonishment to "Render therefore unto Caesar the things that are Caesar's and unto God the things that are God's." Neither would it hurt us to be reminded frequently by those of the cloth to first get the logs out of our own eyes.

Like Christ after them, the Old Testament prophets stood on the outside of the king's government looking in and acted as its conscience. It's hard for a prophet to be objective when he eats at the king's table. Billy Graham said as much after Watergate. Considering the tendency of all governments to gain power and to hold it, the spirit of overagainstness is always in short supply and even in democracies a little suspect since the party out of power too often complains of the state of things primarily for that reason.

While Jesus made clear the necessity of keeping distinctions clear between the things of Caesar and those of God, he did not, in all candor, help us much on the definition of "things" any more than *Webster's* does 2,000 years later. The word, we learn, can mean "a matter of concern," "state of affairs," "situation," "event," "circumstances," "deed," "act of accomplishment," "individual quality," "fact," "idea" or "entity," "and "inanimate object," among many other "things." A look at *Cruden's Concordance* will reveal that all of Scripture is not much more helpful on narrowing the precise meaning of this elusive word, as there are more than 1,000 uses of it in a bewildering variety of ways, more references to it than to "God" or to "Holy"! Without definition, Emerson probably provided some of the best insight into "things of Caesar" with his remark that "things are in the saddle and ride mankind."

Even Jesus does not say that all the things of Caesar are bad but only, by implication, that they are not divine. While none of us can speak with certainty on what "things" belong to God, we can probably be safe in saying that there were many symbols of power sacred to the Roman emperors that were not ipso facto holy in the sight of God. Sports are things of Caesar as well as things of Zeus, Apollo, and the television networks, and, we suspect, good things much of the time or good or bad things depending on point of view—that of a bored and bemused Roman plutocrat looking down from a box seat on the life-and-death struggle in the arena below or that of the one in the fray who knows at some point he is going to lose and pay with his life. Contests were more civilized and hence much better "things" in Greece where the citizens—not in the name of Zeus but, as Edith Hamilton says, in the name of "pity"—rejected the bloody atrocities of the Roman spectacles. It might be asked what things are not of God since all created things are holy, at least according to Chardin and Whitman.

Sports thus are holy things, good things, or bad things depending on philosophical and ethical perspective and certainly on who is winning and who is losing. Sports in any locale are much like the weather. Some days are good and some are bad, but the weather is probably easier to predict, though forecasting in both sports and meteorology have become major industries, sports primarily in the service of gambling. As far as we know, we have not as yet started betting on the weather as has been proposed by some experts regarding foreign policy. According to apologists, sports do not have to be "things of God" as defined in literate traditions to qualify as a religion. All they have to do is exhibit certain myths and rituals much like those of our ancestors in games and gatherings in response to their own "pantheon of powers."

The Stadium as Cathedral and the Cross as Totem Pole

What things are "good," "bad," or of "God" we are not qualified to define, but we feel obligated to raise questions about the implications of sanctifying combative and territorial sports in modern America as symbolized on the book jacket of *From Season to Season*, which displays a cross atop a football stadium or perhaps a stadium-church. On a lower section of the stadium, there is an entry gate suggestive of an altar reached by an aisle of steps or a stairway to glory. Beyond the triumphant cross high in the sky, eastern no doubt, streams of light beam divine approval. In between the beams of glorification, though, streaks of gray suggest that rapture may still be a while off and that some uncertainties remain. All that is missing is a picture of Jerry Falwell at the altar gate, dressed in referee's attire with arms opened wide in keeping with his love of sports, seeing no more incongruity in a cross on a stadium than in congratulating sports champions from the pulpit. Billy Graham said he never saw a stadium he didn't like, but we are betting that for all his love of stadia and sports, he would be unsettled by a cross erected on top of one. The only other place we can think of where the cross and the coliseum regularly come together is in the "procession of the cross" at the beginning of Holy Week in Rome. Traditionally it is led by the Pope around the coliseum as a ritual celebrating the triumph of Christ over Apollo, god of games, especially the bloody ones that went on within the stadium.

In the thinking of some sports apologists, the stadium itself becomes so much like a cathedral that nothing seems more appropriate to adorn it than a cross. The description of Miller-McLemore, inspired by Elaide, of this house of worship and the sacred ground it encloses becomes an encomium in its reverential tone and style:

> Space also acquires sacred importance in the life of *Homo religiosus*, according to Eliade. The center of the world, represented by shrines, temples, and cathedrals and conceived of as an organized cosmos unto itself, becomes preeminently the zone of the sacred. The construction of the football stadium itself resembles an

organizing self-sustaining cosmos. At the farthest concentric circle arise walkways for spectators. Next, beside each entrance ramp to the center arena, are the necessities of life: food stands, restrooms, first aid, police, and ushers. Moving inside, the space becomes increasingly narrowed and focused until all eyes move to the nave, the middle of the playing field, where the referee and opposing team captains stand for the coin toss at the beginning of the game—the first symbolic act of fate. The intricate patterns of...line markings, the regular plots at both ends, and above all, the sacred space in the air marked by the two goal posts give the central space further meaning and "reality." Within the infinite reaches of the universe, the competition is carefully measured out and centered around a small segment of reality. When the ball leaves these boundaries, the sacred time of the game stops. Fans who have rushed onto this special territory in the excitement of the crowd in the last seconds of victory know the awesome quality of the space which only minutes earlier excluded them from its playing surface.[10]

Other parallels come to mind. In the stadium as cathedral the referee becomes the priest or minister wearing a uniform of black and white stripes, a "zebra" as he is called in sporting circles, perhaps "a holy zebra." His function, in fact, is much like the person of the cloth, to identify transgressions and assign fair and just penalties. In some ways he is like God or gods since he controls the clock of "sacred" time and has the power to eject participants and even coaches if they do not play by the rules—the power, that is, of excommunication. Many other parallels exist between stadium and church or sports and religion, and even more connections are easily imagined like a huge banner hanging from the cross proclaiming that "Touchdowns without Faith are Dead."

Above the stadium, the cross, one could infer, offers a seal of approval for at least the intent of what goes on between the goalposts, which holds little or nothing in common with what went on in the shadows of crude wooden crosses that lined the roads outside of Rome or Jerusalem, whether those upon them were criminals, apostles, or a messiah, a scene as different from a ball game as one could imagine. There were no stadium seats at Golgotha, only standing room on the hard blood-soaked ground amid the

---

[10] Price, 18-19.

bleached bones of former players in the game of life. The referee didn't wear striped shirts or blow whistles but behind heavy armor enforced the rules of his game by sharp retorts with spear or sword.

Theologians have written much about "the play of God" and even the "Crucifixion as Play." To be sure, it may be conceived as play in the form of tragedy, but it is much more difficult, if not impossible, to regard it as play in the form of sport. To the faithful in Christianity, the idea of the cross is a symbol of suffering and sacrifice that points toward the promise of an empty tomb, symbolically or actually. That promise is not based upon victory over others in contests but on a much more important premise, that loss in the name of love is gain and compassion, not conquest, points the way to what is sought. Apologists think this traditional form of faith can coexist with a religion of sports. Perhaps it can; perhaps not, another question we wish to examine in more detail later.

There is a significant irony in the cross on a book jacket as far as the main thesis in the book is concerned—that sports, and especially football, is a religion in and of itself with or without the power of the cross. Of course, the cross could represent a "traditional" religion, which Price recommends without much ado and almost sotto voce in addition to the religion of sports signified by the stadium, a suggestion that football and Christianity, contrary to the grumbling of nitpickers, are in essence unified or can be in sacred purpose. Scripture does not give us much of an idea about how to regard stadia since the term is not even used therein as is the case with "sacred." With stadia, though, we are not exactly talking about "adiaphora," things indifferent, especially when they become cathedrals during games and gathering places for crowds of believers of one kind or another, as different as they may be.

The problem with the cross on the front and back of *From Season to Season* is that, as always, it tends to be taken as a symbol of the holy, as in the case of the cross on the Bible, reflecting both the idea of the numinous and that of dark dread or fear. Yet, it also represents something else, as does the cross on the Bible—a literate or literary tradition. The idea of Jesus dominates the jacket of *From Season to Season*, but certainly not the text. Here Eliade is king with his emphasis on the distinctions throughout history between the sacred and the profane. Can one judge a book by its cover? Not in this case.

The cover seems designed to attract FCA and AIA enthusiasts, but once inside the text they would not find much talk concerning the times of the apostles but rather of ages long before those years when humans worshiped gods of games and the sun and, before that, sacred trees, animals, mushrooms, and mistletoe. There does not appear to be any writing on the cross or icons, but in its location it takes on the significance of a totem pole. One easily imagines all the logos of teams in the conference attached to it, plus the animal or reptile names of the teams. In *From Season to Season,* there is much valuable discussion about religion in its broadest sense but not religion as most Christian athletes would know it, which is not to say they would not broaden their minds by reading it and have a better understanding of religion in its enormous complexity.

It is not fashionable to say so in a time when the idea of love has been reduced to a semiconscious self-indulgence instead of an abundant embracing of creation and its inhabitants (often seen in figures like Mother Teresa), but it might well be that fear of the Lord, the beginning of wisdom, might have the same effect as the power of great love. Fear of the Lord (and the resulting wisdom) brings the shock of recognizing humility and is the main lesson, according to Ben Franklin, that both Socrates and Jesus tried to teach us. As for stadia where Billy Graham and other evangelists frequently preached, they are not inherently sinful places in spite of the awful things done in them to humans and animals as in the Roman empire and in spite of the spirit of discrimination celebrated in them under the Nazi regime and even for much of our own history.

Neither are they, at least in our view, symbols of the decline of civilization as Toynbee believed, signifying a profanation of the masses wherever they proliferate, the settings for bread and circuses. If televised autopsies and executions are already available, even on the playing fields of Afghanistan, it seems to some only a matter of time in our culture until some criminal or perhaps notorious traitor is dispatched in the death chamber during the television half-time show and then before we know it appearing in live action on the 50-yard line as cheers ascend and corporations scramble for prime advertising opportunities. Even Saint Augustine briefly succumbed to the blood lust of the arena and all the madness and excitement that went with it. Yes, Saint Augustine was briefly a sports fan—until the one he addresses as "Thou" plucked him away and with "merciful hand" taught him not "to repose confidence in himself."[11]

---

[11] *The Confessions of St. Augustine,* trans. J. C. Pilkington (Cleveland: Fine Editions Press) 90–91.

Thus stadia should never become "shrines" where "sacred" rites are performed in "sacred" time. To suggest that they are is a retreat into pagan mythology in the electronic age and also into a loss of faith in the belief that the visible word in the age of print could help make us free. No matter how tolerant we try to be, either as liberals or conservatives or both at once, there is something about a huge cross atop a football stadium that, traditionally anyway, is as fundamentally incongruous, to use a metaphor of Melville in *Billy Budd*, as "a rifle upon the altar at Christmas."

There is also indirectly a type of exclusivity hinted at here. Is the implication that only Christianity is compatible with the religion of sports? Are we to imagine a "Star of David" atop the stadium on the other side? Or a Crescent? If these symbols are implied or if what is said or implied about the religion of sports has exclusive connections to traditional Christianity, then our recommendation is to take down all such symbols from the stadium or in other words desanctify sports altogether and then, who knows, war too. Then we might begin to see how much all religions have in common.

Another mood is implied on the jacket of *From Season to Season*, and we are almost reluctant to mention it out of concern for being branded iconoclasts. There is something perhaps deliberately humorous about a large conspicuous cross over a football stadium, something absurd and Romanesque about the idea of stadium stairs serving as a route both for concessionaires plying products to a shouting congregation during "transcendent" play on the field and for penitents to a new life. It is not so much the satire of irony but the humor of a trick, literally trick photography, intended to provoke and stimulate discussion about an age when selling "sacred" objects and shooting "nonbelievers" have become sacrosanct in various creeds around the world. Behind this provocative scene, it is hard not to believe that the tongue was not at least halfway to the cheek for all involved. In fact, if some humor in the book jacket is not intended by the illustrator, editor, and publisher, then we may have bigger problems than we can even imagine, the absence not only of a sense of humor but of humility as well, a feature Flannery O'Connor in *Mystery and Manners* could not find in any national character. Neither can we.

As for the darkened stairs on the cover, we might remember that, like Jacob's Ladder, they lead both ways, and the distance between the lessons of the cross silhouetted against the gray, fall sky and the action taking place on the gridiron at ground level is not as easy to traverse as some might seem to imagine. It could be argued that a book by one of us, Higgs's *God in the*

Stadium: Sports and Religion in America, also has a cross on the cover, and
therefore any criticism from this corner in that regard is a case of the pot
calling the kettle black. That book, however, has an entirely different thesis
from that of *From Season to Season*. Price points this out, calling Higgs's
treatment of the relationship between sports and religion "trenchant," a fair
and probably accurate assessment in line with the announcement of the
publisher with its release: "a stinging indictment of the sports-religion-
media-education complex."

The cover, thus, of the Higgs book suggests incongruity of the cross at
athletic contests, as shown in the background by a basketball player jump-
shooting and a runner carrying the pigskin. Higgs acknowledges that sports
have become more and more like a "religion," but he is not pleased with the
situation. The argument in the Higgs book is for a wider separation of sports
and church or a "turning-well" between them (*eutrapelia*), which makes the
presence of the cross on that book's cover highly incongruous in terms of
the content and indicative of a "disconnect" between modern American
sports and religion. In *From Season to Season*, the cross is a welcome sign
from the Big Guy in the Sky to the Big Game and a symbol of the felicitous
integration of two religions, that of sports and that of any traditional
Christian denomination.

Our games, it can be argued, are different from the brutalities that went
on in Roman stadia across the empire, though some of our own stadia are
proudly named after the famous structure in Rome. Further, when Billy
Graham appears in an American stadium, followers and admirers, including
all modern presidents, are likely to agree that he is doing the same thing the
Pope does at Easter in Rome, helping make sure that the spirit of Christ
governs our lives and that money is never a temptation as it often seems to
be in professional and college sports. Perhaps the dark, foreboding cross, a
bit slender and not in the least rugged, is seen towering above the stadium
both on the front and back covers of *From Season to Season* not so much to
give the impression that everything in the text is sanctified, but to suggest
that the spirit of the cross is indeed in the stadium and all is right with the
world—or at least that not much is wrong with it, especially with our games,
as some are likely to argue.

Indeed it might be that things are all right like they are, and then again
maybe they aren't. In light of the "If" books of the nineteenth century such
as *If Jesus Came to Boston* or *If Jesus Came to Chicago* and the current
questions in the news as to what kind of vehicle Jesus would drive and what

he would eat, we might imagine what he might say in regard to a cross over a stadium. Schweitzer, in *Search for the Historical Jesus* has said we cannot bring Jesus into our own time, but since that has become a favorite pastime or game, let us play it too in regard to either the Super Bowl, the World Series, or the Final Four. Our guess is that Jesus would say pretty much what he always said: "Feed my sheep and love one another."

We acknowledge that often sports "work" as they should, perhaps even most of the time, when competition is waged without hate or rancor and when winners do not gloat either inwardly or outwardly. Sports work when losers accept the results and go on with their lives, realizing, as winners should, that the outcome of games are of little or no significance except for the coaches and administrators who exaggerate their importance to the point of absurdity in the interest of profit, their own egos, and those of the fans.

A Cross Speaks: "The Dream of the Rood"

There is another game we might play: what the *cross* itself might say if it could speak as it does in the classic Old English poem, "The Dream of the Rood" (the cross), dating to the late seventh or early eighth century, as it carries out its awful duty and fate in service of its master:

> I had endured on that hill
> much of cruel fates. I saw the God of hosts
> severely stretched out. Shades of night had
> covered with clouds the Lord's corpse,
> the bright radiance; shades went forth
> dark under the sky. All creation mourned,
> bewailed the king's fall; Christ was on the cross....
> Behold, the Lord of the kingdom of heavens, the Guardian of heaven's
>   kingdom,
> ennobled me then over the trees of the forest
> just as he, almighty God, for the sake of all men
> honored his mother also, Mary herself,
> over all womankind.[12]

Just as in the poem Mary is singled out and blessed among women, so is the tree from which the cross is fashioned made special among trees.

---

[12] "The Dream of the Rood," trans. Alexander M. Bruce, http://www.flsouthern.edu/eng/abruce/rood/ROODTEXT/MODERN~1.htm, March 2, 2004.

Clearly while the cross is perhaps the most familiar symbol of holiness in Christendom, it is not the only one, Mary and child being another. In the rest of the world there are many more symbols still, often at war for many reasons but they always include, "a failure to communicate." Often we cannot explain to ourselves what our symbols mean to us or the meanings of the different varieties of the same symbol, including that of the cross, which is available in many shapes, sizes, designs, and meanings and visible just about everywhere—hanging diamond-studded from ears of home-run sluggers, pressed on rock-and-roll T-shirts, and adorning book covers.

As soon as we got used to "Touchdown Jesus" on the campus at Notre Dame, something else came along—the idea of the cross shedding rays of grace on the gridiron. For those who have traveled in France, statues of Christ at country crossroads are commonplace, but a cross over a football field is an idea difficult for Protestants of a certain age to grasp. We are all the more challenged to imagine what the cross itself would say in the modern world considering its growing number of uses, but before venturing into that theological minefield we want to say a few more things about the cross in general and some of its other uses. Just as there have been many images of Jesus in the last couple of millennia as seen in *Jesus through the Centuries: His Place in the History of Culture* by Jeroslav Pelikan, so there have been many varieties of the cross.[13]

When the "Old English Rood" is decorated with silver and gold, it becomes a different kind of cross with perhaps a different meaning. The bejeweled cross in turn is a different symbol from the Iron Cross of the Nazis and the flaming cross of the Ku Klux Klan, and they are all different from the Red Cross. Then there are Christians who refrain from wearing a cross at all since it might be regarded as a conspicuous display of one's own faith or virtue, which they feel should be shown and not announced. The cross, like people who make them, wear them, and kneel before them, can take on many masks or faces and can be displayed anywhere, on a mountainside in Southern Appalachia or on the jacket of a book about sports as an American religion. It can mean anything to anybody, whether worn or not, from the call toward a holy life to a symbol of worldly power and conquest and even to a midnight murder in the back country of the South in the cause of racial purity.

---

[13] See, for example, the entry for "cross" in J. E. Cirlot, *A Dictionary of Symbols*, trans. Jack Sage (New York: Philosophical Library, 1962).

Focusing on the Cross: Sacred Honor or Holy Meditation

As mentioned, athletes can be articulate dissidents and as capable of divergent thinking as anyone else, but as athletes they appear far more often in the role of symbol of the current hierarchy of power, sometimes famously, as in the case of Reinhard Heydrich, an avid supporter of the cult of Nazi athletics, himself an aspiring athlete in fencing. He was commissioned by Hermann Goering to find a "solution to the Jewish question" and was referred to as the "blond beast," "Hanging Heydrich," and "the Butcher of Prague." Heydrich was a wizard of evil of modern times. For his efforts he won the Iron Cross second class and first class, and after his assassination by Czech Nationalists in 1942 Hitler conferred on him the highest order of the Cross. It is interesting that as crosses become engraved and decorated, they can easily enter into a hierarchy of sacred systems that are notoriously evil.

One is tempted to say that the simpler the cross or the idea of the cross, the more democratic it is, but caution is necessary. "The Old Rugged Cross" was written by George Bennard (1913) and is generally regarded as one of the most popular of all twentieth-century hymns. Even more popular is "Amazing Grace" (1829). It should be remembered that in the lyrics, the old rugged cross will someday be exchanged for a "crown," suggesting that the cross is to be endured to gain a reward. Still, after whatever qualifications one might want to register in the interest of semiotics and linguistic deconstruction of the word "crown," it stands in stark contrast to the "trophies" in the refrain. "Amazing Grace," on the other hand, is not something to be pursued or won but rather experienced and appreciated even though undeserved. The reward in the "Old Rugged Cross" is to be earned through a type of endurance, not for winning but for finishing the race; that which is bestowed in "Amazing Grace" is neither reward nor prize but a gift, freely bestowed and humbly received.

Crosses, it seems, should not cost a lot of money as replicas of Nazi crosses often do, confirming our opinion that the sacred sells, no matter how evil or good, and never the holy, which is beyond good and evil and also beyond the idea of money. Its function is not to elevate or humiliate us but to make us aware of our total dependence upon it for everything that lives and has being. It is ironic and instructional that a wooden marker finally adorned the grave of Heydrich following the downward course of the war after 1942.

Preoccupied with killing and awards and medals for killing as in all military institutions, even those committed to defense of democracy, Heydrich had no concept of the wholly other in distinct opposition to a contemporary who did, Deitrich Bonhoeffer, widely regarded as a "modern saint." Just as Heydrich was murdered in Prague in 1942, so the Nazis murdered Bonhoeffer in 1945 for his involvement in a plot to kill Hitler. Heydrich was a symbol of the sacredness of the Nazi State, which was ingenious in the manipulation of media. Bonhoeffer, instead of seeking a cross of worldly distinction and power that separated people from one another, reflected upon the cross as a vehicle to the wholeness of life as seen in lines from a poem and excerpts from a letter he wrote in Tegel Prison, 18 July 1944:

> God comes to all human beings in need,
> sates them body and soul with his bread,
> dies the death of the cross for Christians and pagans,
> and forgives them both.
>
> Human beings are called to suffer with God's own suffering caused by the godless world. That is, they must live genuinely in the godless world, and are not permitted to conceal or transfigure its godlessness in some religious fashion. They must live in a "worldly" fashion, and precisely in so doing participate in God's own suffering. They are permitted to live in a "worldly" fashion, that is, they are liberated from all false religious ties and hindrances. Being a Christian does not mean being religious in a certain way, or on the basis of some methodology to make something out of one's self, such as a sinner, penitent, or saint. It means being a human being.....
> "the religious act" is always something partial, while "faith" is something whole, an act of life. Jesus calls us not to a new religion, but to life.[14]

Bonhoeffer did not say that Christianity is the best and highest religion of all or conversely even "the least" of them. What he said was that Christianity was or ought to be "religionless," like the eponym who did not come to change other religions but so all could "have life and have it more

---

[14] Deitrich Bonhoeffer, *Meditations on the Cross*, ed. Manfred Weber, trans. Douglas W. Stott (Louisville: Westminster John Knox Press, 1998) 60–61.

abundantly." What he chose was the holy in all religions instead of establishing a new one with sacred antecedents of preliterate man such as we find in the Church of Sports. It is fine to play sports, even to love sports, but it is no more excusable to be a sports fanatic than a religious one. Both see their own choices as the best, and in religion this inevitably means war as it has throughout history, which is not to say that religion is the only cause of war. The cliché in sports that "winning is the only thing is analogous to belief that one's religion is the only way. Both are destructive, making of sports a religion with only one commandment and of religion a game of competition to be settled ultimately by arms with only one acceptable outcome.

If Christianity became "religionless" as Bonhoeffer hoped, what would be the need for a church? The need would be the same as always: a place of communal worship of a transcendent being in a limitless universe, a place of praise, song, learning and sharing, a place of reflection, and a place of community, perhaps literally communion, a place of nonrational rites. The church would be the same but different. It would understand what Gandhi meant when he said, "God has no religion," and laugh with Mark Twain when he said the same thing in a different way: "What God lacks is convictions—stability of character. He ought to be Presbyterian or a Catholic or *Something*—not try to be everything."[15]

A religionless Christianity might also be ritual-less or at least less ritualistic than at present. Aldus Huxley tells why this might be desirable or at least worthy of consideration in a chapter called "Ritual, Symbol, Sacrament" in *Perennial Philosophy*, but only after this reminder:

> That very large numbers of men and women have an ineradicable desire for rites and ceremonies is clearly demonstrated by the history of religion. Almost all the Hebrew prophets were opposed to ritualism.... And yet, in spite of the fact that what the prophets wrote was regarded as divinely inspired, the Temple at Jerusalem continued to be, for hundreds of years after their time, the center of a religion of rites, ceremonials and blood sacrifice.... What the Jews did in spite of their prophets, Christians have done in spite of Christ. The Christ of the gospels is a preacher and not a dispenser of sacraments and performer of rites; he speaks against vain

---

[15] *Mark Twain Laughing*, Ed. P.M. Zall (Knoxville: Univ. of Tennessee Press, 1985) 79.

repetitions; he insists on the supreme importance of private worship; he has no use for sacrifices and not much use of the Temple. But that did not prevent Christianity from going its own, all too human way. A precisely similar development took place in Buddhism. For the Buddha of the Pali scriptures, ritual was one of the fetters holding back the soul from enlightenment and liberation. Nevertheless, the religion he founded has made full use of ceremonies, vain repetitions and sacramental rites.[16]

Thus Huxley acknowledges that for some the most effective means to spiritual truth are ceremonies and sacramental rites: "It is by immersing themselves in symbols that they can most easily come through to that which is symbolized." The danger of course in the formula of ritual is mistaking the symbols for the source. In a world envisioned by Bonhoeffer, a new power would be awakened by a sense of the holy in contrast to the smugness and self-righteousness of the sacred manqué. Bonhoeffer prophesied a time when "men will be called again to utter the word with such power as will change the world.... Until then the Christian cause will be a silent and hidden affair, but there will be those who pray and do right and wait for God's own time."[17]

Until then, the Christian, Bonhoeffer thinks, must practice what he calls "an *arkandisziplin*" ("secret discipline") and "plunge one's self into the life of a godless world without attempting to gloss over its ungodliness with a veneer of religion or trying to transfigure it. He must live a worldly life and so participate in the suffering of God.... It is not some religious act which makes a Christian what he is, but participation of the suffering of God in the like of this world. This is *metanoia*."[18]

What, then, is the case for a stadium in a "religionless" Christianity? On the surfaces of things it would be the same as always, a place of competition where those who attend may be awed by the miracle of the human body in motion, a place of festival, good cheer, celebration of the good things of life, a place of theater where prehistorical rites associated with war, magic, hunting, and drama are enacted in a spirit of fun and make-believe, not with the deadly seriousness of a cliché that winning ball games

---

[16] Huxley, *The Perennial Philosophy* (New York: Harper and Row, 1970) 269.

[17] Bonhoeffer, *Letters and Papers from Prison* (New York: Macmillan, 1953) 188.

[18] Ibid., 222–23.

is the only thing and without the expectation of the display of public piety before, during, or after the game. The childhood spirit of play would inform our games instead of the "vain strivings" after victory over others that now characterize the militant branches of religions all over the globe.

In honor of the shepherd tradition, we can imagine an alternate setting to that of the stadium. It would be an inclusive, pastoral place with a meadow and a natural stream or pond. There would be no bleachers below or box seats above reflecting the social status of the crowd. Rather than spectators there would be participants engaged in play who would experience events at ground level. Trees, not awnings, would provide shade and fruit, and a clear spring, not vendors, would offer refreshments. If this sounds extreme, like a return to Woodstock, we would say it is not as extreme on the Edenic side of play as the Super Bowl is in the direction of Rome in the glory days of the coliseum.

Would a "religionless Christianity" bring about "religionless" sports?

If the Cross Could Speak Today, Would It?

What would the cross say today if it could speak as in "The Dream of the Rood"? Who can know? There would be as many different responses as people on earth. One possibility might be this: "Even in a crowded place I speak in whispers not shouts. I am not about victory in the world but surrender to a power greater than I, and surrender is always the hardest way. The sword seems more efficient since you can hold it with one hand as with pistols, and nuclear weapons require only a button to push or a key to turn. I am much more complex than your technology. I require the work of shoulders as well as that of both arms and hands, total involvement where unceasing prayer is action in the closet of the mind and heart and in the world without at the same time. Though I am heavier than you can bear, I am lighter than the smallest particle in the universe. I am as much idea as I am wood, and I am forever a paradox. As heavy as I am, it is easier to place me over stadia or three of me on a mountain beside some highway in Appalachia or decorate me in silver and gold and hang me around necks or dangle me from ears or from rear-view mirrors of old cars in order to show your sacred love of me than it is to remember my ordeal and my fate, to hold upon my bloody arms the one who in holy terror died for holy love."

Another possibility is that the cross would say nothing, like Christ in the scene with the Grand Inquisitor in *Brothers Karamazov*, like Job at the end of his trial with God, and indeed like God himself in the 89th Psalm.

Noise at ball games, even when apparently joyful and directed at the Lord, is at best, we suspect, sacred and often profane. The holy, on the other hand, is always hidden and often silent, speaking volumes nevertheless and wonders as well for those who have ears to hear and eyes to see.

We do not hear much about the talking cross. In fact we only know of one—in "The Dream of the Rood." In contrast, conversations with God are all over the place, as are pep rallies for holy wars of one kind or another. It is just as well, Sam Keen might say, that we don't have talking crosses to add to the burden of listening, since in his view we are already drowning in "theospeak." In an effort to keep from overworking the "G--" word, Keen, as we noted, uses the term "Cosmic DNA," and like strands of DNA, the categories of human interaction such as business, politics, religion, sports, and war are intertwined in ways beyond our comprehension and certainly beyond our unraveling.[19] Nor is it clear that it would be good to lay out all these strings of human activity and stretch them side by side at a safe distance from one another. The world might look stranger unplaited than at present in its twisted condition. What might be more desirable than complete separation of these eternal mortal undertakings would be moderate overlap as symbolized by the mandalora, a holy symbol.

It may be that all we can ever do is improve the quality of the relationship between the sacred and the holy since the conjunction of the two in some form may be fixed in nature and by the creator. As Andrew Newberg and others have suggested in *Why God Won't Go Away: Brain Science and the Biology of Belief*, the idea of the holy, like God, is here to stay, reflects the metaphor-making side of the brain. "The Holistic Operator" in the brain allows us to see "the forest in the trees"; the "Reductionist Operator" allows us to see the "trees in the forest." By brilliant metaphors for their purposes at hand, Newberg and others have identified how communication with the holy might work inside our minds in helping us see things in larger context, and the same in case of the function of the sacred, that which focuses on a part to help us understand the nature of the whole.

In the King James Version of Scripture Jesus literally says that "The kingdom of God is within you" (Luke 17:21), though Ryrie in responding to

---

[19] See Keen's "A Time for Silence: On Not Speaking About G--," *Spirituality and Health: The Body/Soul Connection*, <http://www.spiritualityhealth.com/newsh/items/article/item_3478.html> (2 March 2004).

the passagesays a better interpretation is "among you" and that Jesus could not have meant "within you" since "the kingdom certainly was completely unconnected with the Pharisees to whom Jesus was speaking" (17:20). Suffice it to say that in Christianity the kingdom, home of the holy, "is not of this world" (John 18:36); it is wholly other, whether it resides totally in the domain of the spirit or some physical state to come or both, whatever the religion under consideration. Still we know of no way even to discuss the idea of the holy without the use of the brain and the mind and the body. By our reckoning, such an awareness is not evident on talk shows debating the sacred and the secular, and nor is not in the noisy world of sports increasingly described as "holy." Perhaps on matters of God and theology, our best alternative is Silence on the part of all as recommended by Sam Keen, though that is impossible even for Keen no matter how much he substitutes other terms.

The contention in the next chapter is that a religion of sports is not new, as apologists would agree. It dates back to the time of the King of the Wood when god or the gods were seen in nature, to classical Greece when they were seen in sacred statues, especially that of Zeus, to the Middle Ages and Renaissance when they were symbolized by kings and potentates in endless holy wars over land and glory, to the present when the motivating gods are money and fame. Both its history and its fate are inextricably related to war and the types of people on both sides who waged them. We speak of knights, and without knighthood there would never have been the sanctification of battles and the symbols of that combat we call sports—those, that is, of a territorial nature. Such a phenomenon as we now have among us could never have originated in simple play, the play of the shepherd.

Chapter 7

Religion, Sports, and War: The Conflicted History of the Knight and the Shepherd

If the connection between sports and religion in the West, at least in a highly organized fashion, begins with the events in honor of Zeus, the god of games, the disconnection begins with the biblical wrestling match between Jacob and the angel at Peniel. As a result of this contest, Jacob's name is changed to "Israel," which means "wrestler with God," "God's fighter," or "having power with God." When the angel touches Jacob in the hollow of the thigh, Jacob's hip is thenceforth out of joint. He loses one type of power but gains another. J. E. Cirlot says the "thigh" is a symbol of strength, but the strength Jacob acquires comes from trickery. Earlier in the story, his cleverness overcomes his brother's strength. In other contests of the ancient world, the father was overthrown or nature overcome, Zeus overcoming Saturn, and Gilgamesh (with the help of Einkidu) cutting off the head of the fierce Humbaba in the Babylonian epic about 2000 B.C. In the Jewish experience, the encounters patriarchs have with the wholly other are quite different from epic struggles in other lands. The Father wins, asks obedience, and promises protection in return.

That a sport should figure profoundly in the very naming of a non-sporting people (in terms of competition for prizes) is remarkable. So too is the fact that Jacob, a "plain man dwelling in tents" (Gen 25:27) is the one chosen for the holy encounter in contrast to his brother Esau, "a cunning hunter, a man of the field." Jacob too is cunning but more in the way of knowledge than in skill. There is real significance in the description of Jacob's character because it stresses the civilian nature of Israel's patriarchs and skepticism of specialization in arms. Both Jacob and Esau are "country" people, but as "a plain man" Jacob stands in contrast to legions of hunters, athletes, soldiers, and emperors performing some act of glory or conquest. Of course, Jacob isn't portrayed as virtuous but as a master manipulator. It is Esau that is portrayed as honorable.

David as Shepherd, David as Knight

Jehovah likes plain, simple people, even flawed ones like Jacob, and God turns to these in the hour of need. Gideon, for example, was threshing wheat when the Lord called him, this "mighty man of valor," to war against the Midianites. Just as Gideon trimmed down his fighting force to 300 men—"everyone that lappeth the water with his tongue as a dog lappeth"(Judges 7:5)—so David prior to his epic battle with Goliath took off the armor of Saul and the helmet of brass, put aside his sword, and chose the traditional weapons of the shepherd. "And he chose him five smooth stones out of the brook, and put them in a shepherd's bag which he had, even in a scrip; and his sling was in his hand; and he drew near to the Philistine" (1 Sam 17:40).

These stories contain an element of the Cinderella myth of the unlikely hero, but what is more evident is the assertion that there is finally no might without right, no matter how large the army or how strong the soldier, which is the point David makes in his speech to "the champion" of the Philistines: "Thou comest to me with a sword, and with a spear, and with a shield: but I come to thee in the name of the LORD of hosts, the God of the armies of Israel, whom thou has defied. This day the LORD will deliver thee unto my hand; and I will smite thee, and take thine head from thee; and I will give the carcass of the host of the Philistines this day unto the fowls of the air, and to the wild beasts of the earth; that all the earth may know that there is a God in Israel" (1 Sam 17:45–46).

In the joy of victory or the agony of defeat, as suggested by Psalm 89:38–45, the lessons learned, David realized, are the same—the Lord is great, given to strange silence and awful retribution, his wisdom beyond understanding and his power unspeakable. Kingdoms come and go, wars rage and famines spread, but the Lord ruleth from everlasting to everlasting, unimpressed by what mortals esteem and often, it may seem, endure. "He delighteth not in the strength of the / Horse: He taketh not pleasure in the legs of a man. / The Lord taketh pleasure in them that fear / Him, in those that hope in his mercy" (Psalm 147:10–11).

Before the Lord, then, there is only one course of action, one plea as it were, that comes fast upon the heels of the heart-wrenching 89th Psalm: "Who knoweth the power of this anger? / Even according to thy fear, *so* is thy wrath. / So teach us to number our days, that / We may apply our hearts unto wisdom" (Psalm 90:12–13). And then there is the Twenty-third Psalm.

What is exalted in all these passages is the idea of ruler (or future ruler) as shepherd instead of soldier, the wise ruler rather than the arrogant one, one who will (or should) care for his flock instead of seeking personal power and glory through military might and who can resist the temptation to equate victory with vindication/proof of worthiness. With the Lord on his side against Goliath, the young shepherd David was unbeatable, but later when he relied on numbers of warriors as determined by his sinful census, inspired by Satan (with God's permission), catastrophe followed. Displeased with such lack of faith, the Lord decided to smite Israel as he often did. Through Gad, David's seer, poor David was presented these unhappy alternatives: (1) three years of famine, (2) three months to be destroyed before his foes, (3) or three days of the sword of the Lord. David, not wanting to fall into the hands of his enemy, chose instead the punishment of the Lord, which took 70,000 men from Dan to Beersheba. Never was David more a shepherd as in the distress of this moment: "Even I it is that have sinned and done evil indeed; but as for these sheep, what have they done?" (1 Chr 21:17). Whoever can answer Job might also give an answer to David. The three great questions of Job, David, and Jesus constitute the consciousness of sublime religious sensibility before the Wholly Other, the incomprehensible—Job: "Does thou seest as man seest?"; David: "As for these sheep, what have they done?"; Jesus: "My God, My God, why hast thou forsaken me?"

All are questions that one side of creation asks the other side, questions wisdom or compassion asks of power. They are the same questions the downtrodden and oppressed have asked of the powerful for millennia. In other words, "How long, oh Lord, how long?" The Judeo Christian tradition is based not upon absolute certainty but upon compelling questions that dog us like shadows, suggesting that in the darkness they reflect there is a felt reality we cannot deny or know. As a human endeavor, religion is more versatile than sports in that it is possible in religion, and indeed preferable, for people to be joined together in admission of weakness (including moral weakness) rather than strength; seeking salvation rather than attempting to display it, knowing that salvation is a process rather than a destination or a "goal," which, in contrast, is essential for all athletic contests, as is a "record."

Much can be said about benefits stemming from competitive sports. One can call sports a religion, but one cannot deny that sports are forms of contests. When religions become contests, as we see in the world today, war and chaos are inevitable. Even as we write in October 2003, a Malaysian politician laced a speech before a Muslim group with Anti-Semitic comments, and a high-ranking general in the American Army spoke of the leader of Islam as Satan, praising in contrast the Judeo-Christian religion. So it goes, the apparently irresistible urge to be right and mightily right at the same time.

The holy, which rules over all religions and the universe, will have none of this international boasting, as global chaos reveals the lie to all expressions of superior righteousness. Pride is perceived as a virtue by those who are absolutely certain, yet it goes before a fall, the central theme in Greek tragedy and in holy scripture of religions. One group in our society has learned these lessons well. We speak of Alcoholics Anonymous, a group that stresses not certainty of knowledge or pride in achievement but the "spirituality of imperfection," as expressed in a book by that title drawing on the wisdom of the ages from around the world. It is co-authored by Ernest Kurtz and Katherine Ketchum, Kurtz is also the author of one of the most learned treatises in American letters titled *Not God: A History of Alcoholics Anonymous.*[1] The meaning of the title is revealed in the text as the basic credo of that organization—"First of all we had to quit playing God."

At a 1998 debate on the relationship between sports and religion at Kenwood Baptist Church in Cincinnati between the authors of this text and leaders of Athletes in Action (AIA), much of the discussion centered on the differences between the archetypes of the knight and the shepherd as representative symbols in Western culture. When one of the AIA leaders remarked that, since David was both a shepherd and a knight, there was a place for both in any nation or culture, Braswell responded with another question: "When was David closer to God, when he was a knight or when he was a shepherd?" The following silence indicated agreement on one point on the role of sports in our society. We wish to say, though, that the separation between these archetypes is not necessarily total.

Their functions may overlap as in the mandalora, but they are not identical any more than the sacred and the holy are identical. The shepherd can do anything the knight can do, including dying for a genuinely noble cause in a

---

[1] Kurtz, *Not God: A History of Alcoholics Anonymous* (Center City MN: Hazelden, 1979).

just war, except stay permanently armed, especially mentally, so fortified by sacred doctrine, ethnic, national, or religious, that the holy itself is locked out for good. In a later discussion of other differences between the shepherd and the knight as seen in David, Susan Braswell made a key observation: as a shepherd David himself went into combat; as a knight he sent someone else.

Fundamentally, it is our point that the shepherd plays while the knight displays. However, it is acknowledged that, yes, the knight and shepherd within reason can be one and the same person and also that both terms in regard to civilized behavior, in the best sense of the word "civilized," have been abused to the point that might appear to make them meaningless. Stalin, alas, wanted to be thought of as a "shepherd" and Hitler regarded himself as a "knight," when of course both were tyrants of the first rank. Still we believe there is a fundamental difference between the terms that will be productive to explore.

It is interesting to note too that most knights see themselves as shepherds seeking to defend sacred territory, rescue others of the same tribe from harm done by outsiders, or wreak revenge for wrongs done by enemies from other tribes. Even tyrannies, as a friend has observed, at least claim to be democracies—except athletic teams, which are never democracies but aristocracies of talent. Just as nature has provided a reservoir for ferocious names of sports teams, so has knighthood as in Black Knights, Scarlet Knights, Raiders, Warriors, and Pirates. In contrast, one never hears of teams named shepherds, prophets, scientists, star gazers, or the wise ones, all of which would seem to be good choices for purposes of evangelism but not for winning ball games, which becomes crucial in proselytism. Losing teams do not do well in bringing others to the Lord.

Just as the knight and shepherd may be one and the same, so too might the hunter (conqueror) and the shepherd. Thoreau, certainly a shepherd steward of the environment, remarked that the hunter was the best friend of game since he helped keep nature wild. Yet Scripture itself makes clear the differences between these roles of hunting and shepherding. Nimrod, we are told in Genesis, was "a mighty hunter before the LORD." This epithet sounds innocent enough until it is realized Nimrod is the "founder" of Babylon. This is the city that is "invariably outlined in scripture both in type and prophecy as an evil system. It is Nimrod in whom earthly power first appears in history." Hence, "he is the exact opposite of the divine ideal as king—that of shepherd."[2] The metaphor is one of "the great commonplaces" of Scripture as in Ezekiel 34:2: "Woe be to the shepherds of Israel that do not feed themselves; should not the shepherds feed the flocks?" Thomas More used the same metaphor in *Utopia*. See also Ezekiel 34:11–31 wherein the good shepherd is defined through qualities of strength and wisdom that bring "showers of blessings."

The idea of the shepherd represents a breakthrough in human evolution. Man the hunter, like wild animals, lived in constant search of food. With the slow advent of the shepherd came time to sit beside still waters and think on the mystery of sky and earth. Now survival was not the only requirement, and gradually the yearning for wisdom became "the principle thing," at least in theory if not in fact. With the notion of "tending" came the notion of "tenderness," the central quality, as Flannery O'Connor has observed, of Christianity, or what it should be. To this day, we think of the three wise men as shepherds, and it is hard not to think of the star gazers of Mesopotamia as "shepherd" scientists, the kind who look for truth in a spirit of deep humility and wonder in contrast to those under government contracts among developed nations to produce new and improved weapons. To Thoreau, there was a destructive aspect to agriculture in its relation to wildness that he cherished. The problem was not in nature, in the fields, woods, and streams as in what humans did to the holy condition of nature. Just as the fields could yield their naturalness to tools of cultivation, so could the woods to the ax. Thank God, he said, "they can't cut down the clouds."

Archetypes: Power and Action
Versus Stewardship and Learning

Quite obviously the hunter-shepherd distinction is as relevant in our own time as ever, as seen in the debate on the federal budget between those advocating arms (the hunters) and those advocating entitlement programs (shepherds)—the Hawks and Doves. Both sides operate (or claim to) under the banner of strength and wisdom, the hunters claiming that wisdom dictates the necessity of a strong military defense, while the shepherds claim that true defense is a healthy society where "the least of" us are cared for and helped. What else is there to defend? The conflict has been with us since the beginning of civilization as seen below in dichotomies of archetypes familiar to the

---

[2] Merrill F. Unger, *Unger's Bible Dictionary* (Chicago: The Moody Institute of Chicago, 1970), 794–95.

ancients. None of the types is inherently good or bad; everything depends upon the character of the person filling the role. The word "prophet" has a positive connotation for us and the very word "king" arouses suspicion. Conceivably, though, there could be a "good" king surrounded by "false" prophets. The categories are based entirely upon primary functions.

Hunter	Athlete	Soldier King	Apologist
Shepherd	Philosopher	Physician	Prophet

The terms in the top horizontal line of association connote action and power, the second stewardship and learning. Individuals filling the roles of the first group supply, compete, defend, conquer, and administer; those in the second tend, study, heal, warn, and teach. Just as crucial as the differences between the roles are the hidden similarities between the vertical pairs. The shepherd may not have a sword of the hunter or soldier, but he has a staff that he uses to protect his flock. The "hooked staff," says Circlot, "is a pastoral attribute in the Church and a symbol of faith. By virtue of the sigmoid significance of the hook, it stands for divine power, communication and connection; because of its spiral form it is a symbol of creative power."[3] As we will see in the treatment of humor in relation to "humility" and the holy, it is the muse Thalia in Greek mythology who holds a shepherd's staff. The need for balance between the functions is evident in practically every ideal inherited from the ancient world; Wisdom and Strength (*Sapientia et Fortitudo*) as seen in the previous chapter, Sound Mind in a Sound Body (*Mens Sana in Corpore Sano*) Music and Gymnastic, Apollo and the Muses *together*, Well-Turningness (*Eutrapelia*), and *Arete* (Excellence in all things as opposed to sacred isolation of expertise or intellect).

Like the athlete, the philosopher must have discipline and may be regarded in fact as an athlete of the mind. Just as the shepherd is concerned with the strength and health of his flock, so the lover of wisdom must be concerned with the strength and health of the mind and body. The philosopher athlete was an ideal among the Greeks as symbolized by the name Plato, which means "wrestler."

The physician must heal, but he or she must also prevent disease, that is, defend like a good soldier. It seems hardly an accident that the emblem of the medical profession is the caduceus, the wand of Mercury, the god of the roads,

---

[3] *Dictionary of Symbols*, 65.

or a runner, with the staff representing power and the intertwined serpent representing wisdom. At first glance it appears that the task of the soldier is to kill bodies, while that of the physician is to heal them. The man with the sword, the soldier, may stand beside the man with the pen, the philosopher or prophet. The pen, however, is itself a sword. Additionally, both philosopher and prophet have yet another type of weapon, the tongue. Like the king, they too proclaim laws, though often a different set of laws.

Amid almost constant warfare, the metaphor of king as shepherd survived in Israel instead of that of king as hunter, athlete, or warrior, the pattern in other lands and often the pattern in Israel. It became the dominant metaphor of Christianity, Christ the shepherd, which haunts us to this day in spite of the fact that we have made of Christ everything else but a shepherd—soldier, quarterback, and CEO, who, respectively, whether shepherds or not, must depend upon the rifle, the football, and the briefcase. The sorry history of corporate crime in recent years indicates the need for good accounting, which cannot occur without good shepherding, caring as much for employees as for one's self. There appears to be an irony, but maybe not, in that the "occupations" of power and action, war and sports, often seem to provide the best examples of shepherding in the emphasis on cooperation and teamwork and far beyond that the ideal of leaving no one behind in the thick of battle.

There is an irony in this, that if the rest of society in every country performed with the same commitment of duty and sacrifice as the good soldier, we would not need good soldiers. We would still need athletes since we would still want to watch games and play, which, without war, we would have more time to do. Anatole France said he would not want to live in a world without Utopia on the map. Neither would we, knowing full well it is a country none of us will ever see.

Perhaps the greatest symbolic adjustment of the relation between the knight and the shepherd in the history of the world is the order by Harry Truman in 1947 to turn around the head of the American Eagle so that the eagle's head is now toward the olive branches instead of toward the arrows. Henceforth we would, at least in theory, be more like shepherds, our armed forces defending ideals rather than seeking power abroad as in the manner of our late enemies and of knights throughout history, according to scholars. Says Frances Gies in *The Knight in History*, "knights of the Middle Ages fought for profit and killed without mercy, robbed those whom they should have defended, and violated those they should have respected. Many Medieval knights were Rolands; few were Galahads."[4] On this point Barbara Tuchman agrees: "Knights pursued war for glory and practiced it for gain."[5] In the view of some, the U.S. foreign policy has been more interventionist in a "defense" mode than before and during the World War II when we had a war department. There are real differences between the knight and the shepherd, but like the sacred and the holy, they can easily be manipulated for any purpose at hand.

The ideal of king as philosopher also stayed alive in Greece as seen in *The Republic*. Alexander had at least a superficial respect for philosophy as seen in his acknowledged debt to Aristotle and his toleration if not admiration of Diogenes, who despised athletes as much as he did emperors and everything else. A conqueror is a conqueror, but somehow it doesn't surprise us that Alexander was relatively kind to conquered Jews. In spite of the vast difference between them, Jews and Greeks shared a common respect for wisdom. "What has Jerusalem to do with Athens?" Tertullian asked. Just about everything, we would say. Among both peoples were great wrestlers with truth, and from Jerusalem and Athens sprang so much of the little we in the West know about the restraint of power. Rome's greatest contribution may not be in the realms of law, administration, or technology. Finally it may be a negative one, that is, its "greatness," the eternal reminder of the abuse of power symbolized by the coliseum.

Who can argue that it was not the spirit of the coliseum that destroyed the temple in Jerusalem in 70 A.D. in the Roman siege that took, according to Josephus in *Wars*, more than a million Jewish lives and completed the diaspora. When the cross began to be carried around the coliseum during Holy Week, it did not mean the holy spirit had redeemed the unimaginable suffering of the Jews so that such atrocities would never happen again or that the pale Galilean had conquered the combative spirit of man. What it meant was that in its dying days, the empire had conquered the upstart religion just as it had dispersed the old one three centuries before. Jupiter, the high god of the Romans, upon hearing that his child would be wiser than he, swallowed his first wife Metis or Wisdom, thinking in heathen fashion as we still do today that wisdom can be ingested and digested. From his forehead sprang his second wife Minerva, fully grown and, not surprisingly, fully armed.

Contrary to what we are taught in school, Christianity did not bring the death of these gods; instead, in the dominant form it was to take from

---

[4] Gies, *The Knight in History* (New York: Harper and Row, 1984) 207.
[5] *A Distant Mirror: The Calamitous 14th Century* (New York: Knopf, 1978) 84.

Constantine on, it merely provided a new theater for their caprice and cruelty. The spirit of the dethroned eagle of Jupiter comes to roost on top of the cross. With the ascension of the Christian emperor Constantine, who, we are now told, roasted his wife to death in a steam bath,[6] the top part of the cross became a sword and symbol in an earthly arena where tournaments and war flourished together. Other voices, those of "the warriors of God" or the saints, were all too often drowned out by the martial rhetoric and the almost constant din of battle that essentially seems to define human history.

The territorial sports provide ready analogies for patriotism, for the display of flags and the playing of national anthems, for speeches of dedication proclaiming stadia memorials or sacred grounds where crowds may enter into "sacred time" when contests begin. In America the nature of territorial sports and their relation to religion was shaped fundamentally by the institution of knighthood, which did not die with the Middle Ages but only reached fruition at the end of the Renaissance when print began to have an impact on the spread of the knowledge of power. A survey of the coalition of military art, tournaments, and state religions reveals how sport came to be intertwined with knighthood in the tapestry of western culture. The type of god that blends so well with the sporting scene is not *Deus Absconitus,* the hidden god of holiness, but *Deus Revelatus* the revealed god with sacred symbols of warring tribes around the globe.

The great fork in the road in Western history between the way of *Deus Absconditas* and that of *Deus Revelatus* occurred in the Renaissance. Sports figured prominently in the features of both paths, one tending toward the idea of the holy and the other toward the devotion to the sacred. The first deals, perhaps ironically, with the naked mystery of truth as explained by Sir Kenneth Clark in his discussion of the sublime art of Michelangelo:

> The nude figures in Michelangelo's drawings for the *Battle of Cascina* are graceful and perfectly poised as well as strong and resolute. Heroic and athletic energy are one. And it is under the title of "athletes" that we refer to the most famous nudes in all painting, the young men, who represent, we are told, the *animae rationali* (rational soul) of the Prophets on the Sistine ceiling. Whatever their precise intention, it is clear that Michelangelo saw them as mediators

---

[6] Colin Wilson, *A Criminal Record of Mankind* (New York: G. P. Putnam's Sons, 1984) 228.

between the physical and spiritual worlds. Their physical beauty is an image of divine perfection; their alert and vigorous movements were an expression of divine energy. The beautiful bodies of young men, controlled by the forms of Greek idealism, have been so charged with the spirit that *they can enter into the service of Christianity.*[7]

On the other hand was *Deus Revalutus*, the revealed god. The Christianity the Greek models served was very different from that other young men served when they put on armor and entered into the service of *Deus Revalatus*. A problem was that in the late Renaissance, the time of the reformation and counter reformation, God was revealed to different groups in different ways as had been the case during the Crusades. Instead of waning with the Middle Ages, knighthood flourished as never before with the advent of printing and the circulation of books on military art and artillery. In the battle of the books of the period, those calling for meditation and reflection on how to improve one's own life spiritually, such as *In Imitation of Christ* by Thomas à Kempis, were the decided losers in the way of the world.

With knighthood in flower around Europe, the sacred flourished as never before with symbols of pride and self-righteousness wherever one looked, elaborate insignia on swords and heavy armor (in contrast to the nude figures in Michelangelo's art), banners and pennants, and other signs of invidious distinction down to the harness on horses. All were especially evident when strewn on the sacred grounds of battlefields testing one faith against another. We speak of the Renaissance as the revival of art and learning but fail to mention that it was also the rebirth of media and proliferation of barbarism on a scale undreamed of by ancient psychopaths. It may be that in the wake of all the barbarism in the name of revealed gods, the simple shepherd model was the primary casualty.

The modern religion of sports, with roots in deep antiquity, could not have evolved without the legacy of knighthood that refined and codified the ancient rites of war. That legacy institutionalized and sanctified the monstrous rites of preliterate tribes among the many still preliterate warring tribes in the Renaissance and Reformation. The effects are evident in many

---

[7] Sir Kenneth Clark, *The Nude: A Study in Ideal Form* (Garden City: Doubleday, 1956) 274–75, italics added.

ways but mostly in the demands in the religion of sports upon the athlete's time and energy, so extensive that little time is available for private closet meditation on things other than the need for victory.

In *Sport: A Philosophic Inquiry*, Paul Weiss has made important distinctions between sports and war, testimony itself that the differences between them need elucidation centered on the matter of rules. In sports rules are indispensable. In war, if there are any rules to start with, they are easily cast aside. There was a myth that knights respected women and children. Today killing at a distance, anybody or anything in any number, is perfectly acceptable, and even as we write, targeters around the globe blithely prepare for destruction of entire populations, and even, if need be in the interest of some sacred credo, of the planet that the holy itself created.

Violence and the Sacred:
Kudos *and* Thymos *in Sports and War*

Wherever there is sacrifice of humans or animals, wherever there are ritualized fights, contests, or war, there inevitably is the connection Rene Girard reveals in his classic book *Violence and the Sacred*.[8] This theme obviously has not pricked the interest of sports apologists as much as one might think. The connection, it appears, is eternal, at least so far. Most of our holidays are built around that kinship either directly or indirectly—New Year's, Super Sunday (not officially a national holiday but still one in effect), Martin Luther King Day, President's Day, Easter, Memorial Day, July 4, Thanksgiving, Veterans Day, Christmas. April's Fool Day and Halloween, days of tricks, are not holidays but perhaps ought to be. When memories or rituals of sacrifice are not specifically called for, they are added in commemorative events such as marches, patriotic songs, and displays of military strength, often flyovers of military aircraft. Some of our holidays can scarcely be envisioned without sports, New Year's, Super Sunday of course, Memorial Day, July 4, and Thanksgiving.

As to what makes some holidays more sacred than others, the fundamental thesis of Girard might help to explain: "Any phenomenon associated with acts of remembering, commemorating, and perpetuating a unanimity that springs from the murder of a surrogate victim can be termed

---

[8] R. Girard, *Violence and the Sacred*, trans. Patrick Gregory (Baltimore: The Johns Hopkins Press, 1989).

'religious.'"[9] Practically every faith on earth would qualify as "religious" by this definition, and so would nations with celebrated rituals in honor of victims of wars—the change of guard at the Tomb of the Unknown Soldier, for example. We are speaking here of sacred rites, of course, not the quest for the holy, possibly a related endeavor but certainly a different one.

In addition to rituals of commemoration of sacrifice and loss of life, as reflected in the "Star-spangled Banner," there are two other features common to competitive sports, especially the Super Bowl on Super Sunday and football games everywhere that connect to the idea of the sacred: the prize in the contest and the violence inherent in the game, neither of which is examined in significant degree by apologists. Girard shows how essential they are in relation to the creation of the sacred and its preservation:

> In his *Dictionary of Indo-European Institutions* Benveniste translates *kudos* as "talisman of supremacy." It is the fascination of superior violence. Violence strikes men as at once seductive and terrifying; never as a simple means to an end, but as an epiphany. Violence tends to generate unanimity, either in its favor or against it. And violence promotes imbalance, tipping the scales of Destiny one way or another.
>
> Those who possess kudos see their strength multiplied a hundred fold; those deprived of it discover that they are hopelessly handicapped. Kudos passes to the man who strikes the hardest—the victor of the moment. It belongs to the man who manages to convince others, and who believes himself, that his violence is completely irresistible. The opposition then must exert itself to break the spell cast by this conviction and to wrest the kudos from the enemy's grasp.
>
> When the rivalry becomes so intense that it destroys or dispenses all its objects, it turns upon itself, kudos alone becomes the ultimate object. The word is sometimes translated as "glory," but, as Benveniste has remarked, such a translation ignores the magico-religious aspects that are fundamental to the term. ...The spiritual effects of triumphant violence are readily apparent in sexual activity, in games of skill and chance, in athletic matches, and in contests and competitions of all kinds. For the Greeks, the issue of violence

---

[9] Ibid., 315.

carried to its extreme was divinity itself. The epithet *kudros* signifies an attitude of triumphant majesty, a demeanor characteristic of the gods. Man can enjoy this condition only fleetingly, and *always at the expense of other men*. To be a god is to possess kudos forever, unchallenged and unchallengable.

It is the gods who confer kudos on men and the gods who take it away. ...As long as the concept of kudos exists—that is, as long as there exists a prize, eminently desirable and thoroughly abstract, that men strive constantly to wrest from another—there can be no transcendent force capable of restoring peace. What we are witnessing in this struggle for kudos is the decomposition of the divine, brought about by violent reciprocity. When the tide of battle turns against them, Homer's warriors sometimes justify their retreats with remarks like "today Zeus has chosen to bestow kudos on our enemies, perhaps tomorrow he will give it to us." This alternation of kudos is identical to the alternations of tragedies.[10]

What Girard calls the "divine" that is decomposing before our eyes we call the holy, the opposite of "violent reciprocity." In other words, the sacred is literally killing us as we see on the news every day. The holy is as rare as a super nova. We see the remarks of Homer's warriors in relation to Zeus and kudos reflected continually in post-game interviews: "God was on our side today," said Bill Parcells, head coach of New York Giants, following the 1991 Super Bowl victory. So was Zeus. We're not so sure about Jesus in light of a passage in John: "Not as the world giveth, give I unto you" (14:27).

With Girard it is not merely that sport and play are metaphors of war; they are the same but different in degree and both driven by a response to redeem some former loss or to honor members of the tribe lost in the same cause as that of one's team or army. Much like Veblen, he sees the link between sports and war as seamless, but whereas Veblen seems content to focus upon the desire for honorific distinction and conspicuous display as the motivating force for conquest, Girard thinks the real motivation lies elsewhere, which he explains by use of another term meaning "soul, spirit, or anger like the 'anger of Oedipus.'" "When a man possesses *thymos* he possesses an irresistible dynamism. When *thymos* is withdrawn he plunges

---

[10] Ibid., 152–53.

into anguish and despair. *Thymos* is derived from the verb *thuein*, which means to make smoke, to offer sacrifices, to act violently, to run wild."[11]

Thymos, as Girard further explains, is related to the idea of kudos but is something different. "It is not some vulgar trophy or second-rate divinity the adversaries are trying to wrest from each other's grasp, but their very souls, their vital force, their being. Each finds this being reflected in each other's violence, because their mimetic desires have converged on one and the same object." Veblen's theory might explain the smugness of a leisure class society contrasting itself to Have-nots of the world, but it does not begin to explain the rage and hatred the victors often have for the losers or the atrocities committed upon them and often in the spirit of revenge, a spirit of sacrifice in memory of martyrs or of previous defeats. Our symbols of success, conspicuously flaunted on programs such as "Lifestyles of the Rich and Famous," do not by themselves explain the history of skinning defeated opponents, going on long before Apollo's music match with Pan, decapitation, drawing and quartering, stonings and burnings, scalpings, general laying waste, and genocide in colossal proportions, making the twentieth century the most murderous on record. It is not, for example, the visible rewards, kudos, that suicide bombers seek but the desire to give vent to *thymos*.

"Far from subordinating religion to sport and play (as does Huizinga in *Homo Ludens*)," says Girard, "we must subordinate sport and play to religion, and in particular to the sacrificial crisis."[12] Sport and play may seem relatively safe under the auspices of religion as they have been throughout much of history, but that itself is an illusion, Girard maintains. In war, sports, or tournaments, "the arbitrary nature of the prize makes it clear that the contest has no objective other than itself. ...In the case of kudos the reciprocity of the violence is not muted so as to suggest some joust or tourney. Because we see that the prize is worthless, we tend to assume that the contest itself, no matter how perilous, is only a pastime, an event of limited interest to the protagonists, mere sport." Girard corrects this impression by reminding us of *thymos*, the emotion of vengeance in sports or war, the one word that probably comes closer than any other to illustrating the ecstasy of victory and the agony of defeat.

---

[11] Ibid., 154.
[12] Ibid.

Religion, as Girard sees it, is far different from the view of Otto. To Girard it is the ritual of reenactment of violence to redeem the sacrifice of a surrogate victim or victims. It is the religion of knighthood. To Otto, religion is a quest for the Wholly Other and practice of those rituals that might lead to a deeper understanding of it. Broadly speaking, there are only these two types of religion—(1) the religion of the sacred, with rituals built around stories of sacrifice and preparation for engagement in war or sports and (2) the religion of the holy, emphasizing prayer, meditation, cultivation of the land, caring for the sick, and observance of shepherd principles. They are often found side by side in the same denominations, one God with two perceived faces, *Deus Revelatus* and *Deus Absconditus*. In late medieval times the pendulum took a decided swing toward the sacred form. The holy form did not vanish but thenceforth the alliance of church and arms would be taken for granted as they would in competing faiths at the time and later.

Tournaments and War:
Soldiers of Christ and Knights for Christ

A look at the extended efforts of the church in the Middle Ages to mediate between religion, sports, and war illustrate a challenge that remains with us today in bewildering variety. Dissident voices offered alternatives, but the idea of corporate militarism was finally triumphant. The man behind this radical change was Pope Gregory VII, who in the eleventh century reversed the meaning of the term "soldier of Christ," or *Milites Christe*, to that of "knights for Christ." "For centuries the church had stood strictly for peace, in the tradition of St. Martin of Tours: 'I am the soldier of Christ; I am not permitted to fight.' Gregory discarded this pacificist ideology in favor of the 'theory of two swords': the Pope, a representative of St. Peter, held two weapons, a spiritual blade to be drawn by his own hand, and a secular one to be drawn by nobles and knights."[13] This "two-sword" theory of course parallels the "two-heart" theory of knighthood, one heart hard as stone and the other soft as wax, the soft one for the tribe and the hard one for enemies of the tribe just as we see today nearly a millennia later. Gregory went even further by repaying the knights on his side with the greatest gift of all, eternal life in paradise, a promise that reverberates today in the ruins of the Middle East amid the mangled bodies of suicide bombers and their victims.

---

[13] Gies, *The Knight in History* (New York: Harper and Row, 1984) 32–33.

Gregory did more than reverse the meaning of the term "Christian soldier"; he re-sanctified sports as well, for "war was both profession and sport."[14] The tournament, for example, was sports, a mini-war, and preparation for war at the same time. John Marshall Carter's scholarship illustrates not only the enormous influence of the tournament on all levels of society, from the knights who fought in them to the children who emulated them, but also the church's role and motives in condoning this competition. Pope Urban II gave doctrinaire authority to the "Just War" in 1095, and the tournament provided in the form of sport a source of training and encouragement for Crusaders, whose sporting skills would advance the ends of organized Christianity. In this spirit, John XXII re-allowed the tournament in 1316.[15]

Chaucer scholar Terry Jones emphasizes the church's sporadic opposition to tournaments as seen in bans in 1179, 1215, 1228, 1245, and 1313, and again in 1368 in order to illustrate the "cheerful incongruity" between the suggestion that Chaucer's knight has "foughten for oure faith" and the revelation immediately following that it has been "in lystes thries."[16] In the Middle Ages the church apparently served the same purpose as the NCAA in our own, and like the bans of that secular organization, those of the church were ineffectual and not permanent.

Jones shows how ecclesiastics of Chaucer's time assailed the tournament, which certainly casts doubt upon the Christian qualities of Chaucer's knight who had killed eighteen men in all, three in a tournament, the John Smith of his time it appears. Just as the church fathers had excoriated the bouts in the coliseum, so many churchmen of the Middle Ages, including John Wyclif, preached against the tournament.

The church was reluctant to legitimize the individual nature of tournament competition despite its desire for the skilled warriors to which the sport gave rise. The ancient concept of the valiant individual (*preux-homme*) was thus sublimated to the rightworthy man (*prud-homme*), which implied a Christian humility conjoined with skill at arms.[17]

---

[14] Ibid., 31.

[15] John Marshall Carter, *Sports and Pastimes of the Middle Ages* (Columbus GA: A Brentwood University Edition, 1984) 39–40.

[16] Jones, *Chaucer's Knight: The Portrait of a Medieval Mercenary* (New York: Metheun, 1984) 81.

[17] Mark P. O. Morford and Robert Lenarden, *Classic Mythology* (New York: David McKay, 1971) 187.

Terry Jones takes Chaucer's "The Knight's Tale" as an example of the church's ironic position on warfare, discouraging it between individuals but sponsoring it on a grand scale. When Theseus intervenes in the princes' duel over the fair Emily, he does not end it but simply enlarges the scale—to a battle between 200 knights on each side.[18] The same incongruities of "the two-sword theory" come down to our time not only among the warring faiths of the world but in the wide embrace of sports by modern churches and the general endorsement of military policies by governments around the world. Ironically, it seems that the only people left with moral outrage are terrorists, either homegrown or from abroad. Today knighthood has been extended to the cult of celebrity ranging from aging rock stars to movie actors.

The Education and Training of the Christian Knight

The ideal of both God and the ancient epic hero was *Sapientia et Fortitudo* (wisdom and strength) as abundantly reflected in the Bible and epic literature, as we have tried to illustrate. It was an ideal that appeared to square well with the two-heart or two-sword philosophy of knighthood. Since God is both wise and strong, then so the knight should be. The catch, though, is that the knight, in seeking to be strong, brought about pride and consequently loss of wisdom. As for the medieval knight, learning counted for little but prowess for everything.

Often poorly educated, the knights were mainly concerned with the show and pomp that accompanied their predominantly military calling. Mental power became equated with physical, so that the aim of the time was not to be wise but to be strong. Tales describing great feats of strength emphasized the importance of this aspect of the knight's education. Pepin the Short, King of France (752–768), earned the respect of the nobles by severing the head of a lion with one blow of his sword, a feat of strength which made up for his lack of stature. Lifting an opponent in full armor above one's head; chinning one's self in full armor, and his horse as well, as a Dutch noble is reported to have done, slicing an adversary and his horse in half, which Godfrey of Bouillon [one of the worthies] is said to have done during the Crusades, were other examples of strength with which minstrels and troubadours kindled the vanity of the knights and thus perpetuated the myth of the

---

[18] Jones, *Chaucer's Knight*, 82.

ascending of physical power. In order to gain the trust and respect of his men, a commander had to be able to mount his horse in full armor without the aid of stirrups. Lame persons or invalids were excluded from official functions, and cripples could not hold the office of judge. This fetish of physical power influenced the lower classes to such an extent that a man was no longer allowed to manage his own affairs without his wife's permission if he was not able to ride a horse or walk three steps....[19]

Henry Adams goes so far as to claim that during the Middle Ages priests were counted as women. Both, for example, were exempt from military service. The attitude that those who were physically weaker, priests and women, were somehow more capable of extreme vice and virtue was further evidence of the destructive two-heart knightly ideal. The "soft" ones had to be protected, but for the violent knight protection was often another name for exploitation and abuse.

To be sure, the various handbooks of chivalry all celebrated a balance of strength and wisdom, but strength in knighthood was not a quality that comes from the hills as in the democratic shepherd ideal but by compliance to an aristocratic code compiled by members of the courtly class.

Invariably strength in the chivalric tradition meant physical strength and worldly success. Says Jan Brockhoff, "The long and arduous training to prepare the knight for his physical duties was obviously not conducive to intellectual pursuits. Eustace Deschamps, the fourteenth-century poet and chronicler, bewailed the fact that in his search for physical prowess, the knight does everything for his body but nothing for his soul. Even during the Middle Ages many amorous knights needed a clerk to record their poetry."[20]

Brockhoff goes on to say "that the education of the young knight was in reality for the most part physical education."[21] How little times have changed, since what was true for knights then is true for many athletes today. Just as colleges today have developed their own curriculum for athletes, so the same thing occurred in the Middle Ages. Petrus Alfonsus (1062–1140) was probably the first to define the aristocratic curriculum by introducing the seven knightly

---

[19] Nicholas J. Moolenijzer, "Our Legacy from the Middle Ages," *Quest*, monograph 11 (December 1968): 35–36.

[20] Brockhoff, "Chivalric Education in the Middle Ages," *Quest*, monograph 11 (December 1968): 27.

[21] Ibid., 27.

arts as parallel to the seven liberal arts—grammar, rhetoric, dialect, arithmetic, geometry, music, and astronomy. The seven arts, described at the beginning of *Mirror of Knights* (1400), are those "which certainly at all times a perfect man will love":

> He must ride well, be fast in and out of the saddle, trot well and canter and turn around and know how to pick something up from the ground.
> The other, that he knows how to swim and dive into the water and knows how to turn and twist on his back and on his belly.
> The third, that he shoots well with crossbows, arm, and handbows; these he may well use against princes and dukes.
> The fourth, that he can climb fast on ladders when necessary, that will be of use in war, in poles and ropes it is also good.
> The fifth art I shall speak of is that he is good in tournament, that he fights and tilts well and is honest and good in the joust.
> The sixth art is wrestling also both fencing and fighting, beat others in the long jump from the left as well as from the right.
> The seventh art: he serves well at the table, knows how to dance, has courtly manners, does not shy away from board games or other things that are proper for him.[22]

Rabelais's *Gargantua* may be regarded as a masterful satire of this entire training program for the knight. The young giant sails through all these "manly sports" almost in order as presented in *Mirror of Knights*, the author obviously having great fun in his grandiose comparisons. A wonderful swimmer, Gargantua "could cross the breadth of the Seine or the Loire at Montscreau, dragging his cloak along in his teeth and holding a book high and dry over the waters, thus renewing the exploit which Plutarch credits Julius Caesar during the Alexandrine War."[23]

Like Milo of Crotena, "the ancient athlete, he could hold a pomegranate so fast in his hand that none could wrest it from him, yet so adroitly that he did not crush it."[24] Rabelais patterns his hero after the worthies of the ancient world, but that he expects us to applaud neither the ancient system nor the

---

[22] Quoted in Brockhoff, "Chivalric Education," 27–28.

[23] *Gargantua, The Complete Works of Rabelais,* trans. Jacques Le Clercq (New York: Modern Library Edition, 1936) 75.

[24] Ibid., 77.

compulsive one of his time is itself a source of humor. In effect, Rabelais is showing how combat training, sports, and play had become obsessive.

Swimming was part of the training for the young Roman soldier and the Greek *ephebe*, but it was rather inconsistent with the idea of heavy armor used by the knight, who was a land warrior and not an amphibian, at least in full gear as Barbara Tuchman reveals in a description of a battle in Flanders between French knights and Flemish workers: "Horses scrambled and fell, knights plunged into the water, a second wave piled upon the first. The Flemish infantry, armed with pikes, speared them like fish, and holding firm against all assault beat back the knights in bloody massacre. Seven hundred gold spurs were stripped from knightly corpses after the battle and hung up in triumphant memorial in the church."[25]

If one strove for physical prowess in all the knightly arts, there was little time for study or reflection because, as is the case for athletes today, the pressures to win are so intense, especially in major college football. Not only are athletes deformed by the athletic experience, as the knights were, but so are their fans who also come to applaud their strength and athletic ability.

What is evident, then, is that at the same time that the church embraced knighthood to combat the infidel, the institution was refining its training, becoming increasingly specialized and divorced from academic learning even as church and nobility praised the ideal of the complete gentleman and all-round man, another situation similar to that of today. There are exceptions, but never have academic standards been lower for athletes and never have we heard so much about the student-athlete and all-round man, ruses to keep colleges from paying athletes for the professional level of work they perform. As everyone knows, college athletes in major programs are neither getting a genuine education nor proper reimbursement for the hard work they are called to do.

The Battle of the Handbooks:
Secular Power Versus Spiritual Discipline

Though the agonal element in the tournament gradually declined in the Renaissance, sports proliferated on all levels throughout society, as *Gargantua* by Rabelais suggests. Chapter 20 alone contains a list of 217 games, including

---

[25] Tuchman, *A Distant Mirror*, 76.

parlor, table games, and open-air sports, all played by the young hero.[26] Strutt's *Sports and Pastimes of the People of England* shows something of the abundance of sports in England at the same time. Much like the situation today, young boys had heroes and usually they were knights.

Knighthood was further institutionalized by an almost endless series of handbooks and guidebooks outlining forms of behavior and courses of action for soldiers and statesmen. Basically these guides were of two kinds, secular and spiritual or, if you will, sacred—the "two-sword theory" again—and war and sports were common to both, on a literal level for the secular guides and symbolically for the spiritual guides. All had to do with the acquisition of power, both temporal and spiritual. Here are a few examples:

Secular Power	Spiritual Power
Johannes Rothe, *Mirror of Knights* (1400)	Thomas à Kempis, *Imitation of Christ* (c.1405–1420)
Count Baldassare Castiglioni, *The Courtier* (1528)	Desiderius Erasmus, *The Enchiridion* (1503)
Niccolo Machiavelli, *The Prince* (1513)	Ignatius Loyola, *Spiritual Exercises* (1522)
Niccolo Machiavelli, *The Art of War* (1520)	William Gurnall, *The Christian in Complete Armour* (1662–1665)
Henry Hexam, *Principles of the Art Military* (1639)	Henry More, *Enchiridion Ethicum* (1690)

There was a virtual army of books on military art, tactics, and drill. Captain Maurice Cockle's *Bibliography of English Military Books up to 1642 and of Contemporary Foreign Works*, published in 1900, gives some idea of the age's preoccupation with military power, including artillery. The flip side of the rediscovery of the past in the Renaissance is seldom mentioned in intellectual history. Along with translations of ancient philosophers came new editions in French, English, and German of such treatises as *Epitoma rei militaris* by Flavius Vegetius Renatus, fourth-century Roman military expert. Vegetius's influential text covered all aspects of military training, from

---

[26] Mikhail Bakhtin, *Rabelais and His World*, trans. Helene Iswolky (Bloomington: Indiana University Press, 1984) 231.

discipline and drill to strategy and tactics and served to transform warfare into a more deadly efficient pursuit than ever before. In *The Pursuit of Power*, William N. McNeil observes in the mercenary character of the armies of the fourteenth century the roots of the modern arms race as military force began to respond to economic factors.[27]

There is yet a third class of guidebooks that also have an indirect bearing upon the history of sports and religion. In this category are such works as *The Schoolmaster* (1570) by Roger Ascham. Though the focus is upon education, this book was in the spirit of Castiglioni's *The Courtier* (1529). They were books for gentlemen, and ultimately the gentlemen's principle business in the Renaissance was killing; books on how to conduct this activity were, as pointed out, released as fast as terrorist manuals in the twentieth century. This is not to deny that the soft side of the *ideal* of the knight has not had a civilizing effect over the centuries as some scholars, including Huizinga, in *The Waning of the Middle Ages,* have argued. What is claimed is that the gentleness of the knight has been negligible compared to the violent and arrogant legacy he has bequeathed to the world.

If we consider expressions of these two basic types of power, secular and spiritual, as represented, say, by *Mirror of Knights* and *Imitation of Christ*, it becomes obvious that the archetypal representatives are Caesar and Christ or Apollo and Christ. Nietzsche will try to combine these two incongruous models into his superman who would, he said, have "the courage of Caesar and the heart of Christ." Why he couldn't have spoken of the courage of Christ as well as compassion is puzzling, courage being the principle virtue of the knight, especially of the Knight Templar. Note that while Christ stood his ground, he didn't try to take ground, the main objective in territorial sports. Long ago the knight usurped courage and limited its presence to the battlefield so that it would be unthinkable for someone to exhibit it elsewhere, say at home or in a business. Like modern politicians, Nietzsche didn't want to be considered what we call "wimpy," and Caesar is always a good name to invoke when one wants to show how virile one is. Hitler, also a believer in the two-heart theory, perverted Nietzsche's philosophy of the superman, but it was a philosophy susceptible to perversion to start with, hovering on the edges of cruelty, waiting as it were for a mad man to distort it completely.

---

[27] McNeil, *The Pursuit of Power: Technology, Armed Force, and Society "Since" A.D. 1000* (Chicago: University of Chicago Press, 1982) 69–70.

Though it may properly be defined as history, Caesar's *Commentaries* is also a "how-to" book on the strategy and tactics of war and lies behind the mind-set of the power seekers such as Machiavelli, who in the *Art of War* glorifies everything Roman, down to the use of sports. Machiavelli would, like the Romans, have his soldiers learn "to run and to wrestle, to leap, to endure exertion in armor heavier than the common sort, and to shoot with the cross bow and to swim."[28] Machiavelli would also have several disciples, the Kaisers, for example, who were named for Caesar. Other writers after Nietzsche have in effect applauded aristocratic institutions, especially chivalry, as a restraint against war and excesses of love, among them Denis de Rougemont.

Chivalry was a form of romantic escape at the same time as a brake applied to instinct. The detailed formality of war was devised to check the violent impulses of feudal blood, even as the cult of chastity among the troubadours was intended to check the erotic excitement of the twelfth century. "Two attitudes to life were formed, so to speak, side by side in the medieval mind—one, pious and ascetic, attracted all moral sentiment; the other, spurred on by a sensuality given over to the devil, went to the opposite extreme. According as one or the other was in the ascendant, there arose a saint or a sinner; but on the whole they balanced one another, though not without now and then a wide swing of the scales."[29]

How de Rougemont, citing Huizinga, can claim a balance in the later Middle Ages between love—either *eros* or *agape* or both—and war strikes one as odd. There may well have been parity in a number of handbooks on love and war or spiritual power and secular, but to suggest that love balanced war or that sinners and saints arose in equal number in the Middle Ages is absurd. Often medieval studies in literature in the universities are so romanticized, like those of Henry Adams, for example, that we rarely get a realistic view of the age such as that of Barbara Tuchman in *A Distant Mirror*.

The same is true of the Renaissance, which we are always told was a period of great awakening of reason, art, and scholarship. Indeed it was, but it was also one of the bloodiest periods in the history of Western civilization when Martin Luther advocated burning synagogues, Thomas More heretics, as one historian has been brave enough to remind us, and virtual open season was

---

[28] Machiavelli, *The Chief Works and Others*. 3 vols., trans. Allan Gilbert (Durham: Duke University Press, 1965) 2:606–607.

[29] Denis de Rougement, *Love in the Western World*, trans. Montgomery Belgion (New York: Harcourt & Brace, 1940) 247–48.

announced on helpless women called "witches" and New World Indians, to say nothing of the slave trade out of Africa. If the Renaissance was a rebirth of humane learning, it was also an explosion in the techniques of power, control, manipulation, and terror, all maintained by rules of war and exercises and contests of the knights and princes behind a facade of Christian courtliness and gentility. It was the best of times and the worst of times.

In the spiritual group of handbooks an attitude of a different sort from that of the power group is at work. Here the influence is the metaphors of Paul and Augustine as in *Enchiridion or Manual to Laurentius Concerning Faith, Hope, and Charity*. "Enchiridion" is a Greek word meaning "handbook," and Augustine's, beginning in the celebration of wisdom, is the model for several later Enchiridions, though something changed by the time Erasmus wrote his. Erasmus wanted to project a vision of an "inward religion" based upon "the ethical implications of the philosophy of Christ,"[30] but the imagery he used was "militant." His book thus became a *Manual of a Christian Knight*. "It was a *pugiunculus*, a dagger; a *gladiolus*, a small blade, not too cumbersome or too ineffectual to do any good. If people thought it necessary to arm themselves physically against the danger of highwaymen, was it not even more essential to arm the mind and spirit to cope with the real difficulties of everyday Christian living?"[31]

Erasmus the Christian humanist was talking about a soldier *of* Christ rather than a soldier *for* Christ, but even the metaphors did something to the message, at least in the eyes of Ignatius Loyola, author of *Spiritual Exercises*. Loyola read Erasmus's *Christian Knight* and was impressed by it initially, but he eventually settled on *Imitation of Christ* by Thomas à Kempis as his spiritual guide, deciding that Erasmus's manual was "calculated to quench little by little the fervor of piety in the souls of the readers."[32] The *Imitation* was, like the gospels, an everlasting well of love and truth. Nevertheless, the *Exercises* became a severe regimen, a "terrifying programme of flesh and blood."[33] Though physically as well as spiritually and intellectually demanding, the order was at odds with the notion of worldly power and its trappings, including courtly display and success in sports. The Jesuit schools

---

[30] Raymond Himelick, trans. and ed., *The Enchiridian of Erasmus* (Bloomington: Indiana University Press, 1963) 15.

[31] Ibid., 13–14.

[32] Henri Joly, *St. Ignatius of Loyola*, trans. Mildred Partridge (1899; New York: AMS Press, 1976) 70.

[33] Ibid., 68.

today may boast great athletic teams, but this was not the wish of the founding fathers. Just as Loyola rejected "courtly exercises"—that is, the tradition of Castiglione—so his most famous student, Francis Xavier, who had won distinction in university sports, would atone, after taking the spiritual exercises for the first time, "for the vanity of his athleticism."[34]

By the late Middle Ages and early Renaissance, military and athletic metaphors of the Bible—for example, "the helmet of salvation" and "wrestler for God"—had become so widespread in the religious handbooks and guides that they seem almost like training manuals for particular sports rather than spiritual instruction for all. Note the belligerent tone and detail in "How True Wrestlers Should Manage Their Combat" in William Gurnall's *The Christian in Complete Armour*. The "Directions" apply to "saints" who engage in "continual wrestling" here on earth.

> First. Look thou *goest not into the field without thy second*. My meaning is, engage God by prayer to stand at thy back…. Did the Ephraimites take it ill, that Gideon called them not into the field, and may not God much more? Thou hast more valour than Moses, who would not stir without God, no, though he sent an angel for his lieutenant. Thou art wiser than Jacob, who to overcome Esau, now marching up, turns from him, and falls upon God; he knew if he could wrestle with God, he might trust God to deal with his brother. Engage God and the back-door is shut, no enemy can come behind thee, yea thine enemy shall fall before thee. God turn the counsel of Ahithophel into foolishness, saith David. Heaven sayeth Amen to his prayer, and the wretch hangs himself.
>
> Second. Be very careful of *giving thine enemy hand-hold*. Wrestlers strive to fasten upon some part or other, which gives them advantage more easily to throw their adversary; to prevent which, they used—1. To lay aside their garments; 2. To anoint their bodies….
>
> Third. Improve the *advantage, thou settest at any time, wisely*. Sometimes the Christian hath his enemy on the hip, yea, on the ground, can set his foot on the very neck of his pride, and throw away his unbelief, as a thing absurd and unreasonable. Now, as a wise wrestler, fall with all thy might upon thine enemy. Though men think it foul play

---

[34] James Broderick, Society of Jesus, *The Origin of the Jesuits* (1940; Westport CT: Greenwood Press, 1971) 43.

to strike when his adversary is down, yet do not thou so compliment with sin, as to let it breathe or rise. Take heed thou beest not charged of God, as once Ahab, for letting go his enemy now in thy hands, when God had appointed to destruction. Learn a little wisdom of the serpent's brood, who, when they had Christ under foot, never thought they had him sure enough, no, not when dead; and therefore both seal and watch his grave. Thus do thou, to hinder the resurrection of thy sin, seal it down with stronger purposes, solemn covenants, and watch it by a wakeful circumspect walking.[35]

Any Renaissance knight who could read would find the directions suitable wisdom for actual combat.

What happened is that the athletic and martial metaphors that seemed to work for the apostles and saints did not work for later generations, or rather they worked so well that the spiritual message the metaphors were supposed to convey was lost altogether, a situation that carries a message in itself. The "enemy," that is, the pride or evil within one's self, the log in our own eye, became the other, an opponent in war or sports. Bereft of analogy, the "enchiridions" became martial manuals not unlike the guides for secular power. The Puritan colonel William Barriffe, author of *Militarie Discipline,* placed the following text on his title page: "Psalms 144:1. 'Blessed be the Lord My strength which teacheth my hands to warre and my fingers to fight.'"[36] The Christian religion had thus become not the way to peace through wisdom but the justification of war waged through strength. Against such confusion, *The Imitation of Christ* stood out like a majestic oak, unadorned except for its theme of simple goodness and faith. Like Augustine's *Enchiridion,* there was not an athletic or martial metaphor in it, both writers avoiding, perhaps deliberately, the misreading to which analogies of armor and wrestling can easily lead.

The church itself was split over the idea of the Crusades as an ideology, and opposition from several factions, including humanistic thinkers, helped bring about their demise or rather change in configuration. Substantial opposition began as early as the Second Crusade and gained momentum with each new expedition, spreading through all levels of society, from troubadours

---

[35] *The Christian in Complete Armour: A Treatise of the Saints War Against the Devil, 1662–1665* (Edinburgh: The Banner of Trust Faith, 1987) 120–21.

[36] See psalms 14:1

to politicians to mystics. The latter called into question the foundation of warfare in evangelism and proposed instead peaceful missions—to convert rather than kill the infidel, an idea that soon gained a backing comparable to that of the Crusades.[37]

The ideology of Crusades, though, did not fade away as much as enter into another form of adventure. The great explorations, Prawer says, were certainly not exclusively missionary, but religious zeal played more of a role than window dressing in this revolutionary phase of history.

Before the end of the world all prophecies have to be fulfilled; the Gospels need to be diffused all over the world and the Holy City of Jerusalem has to be given back to the Christian Church." This was not written by a mystic or a would-be prophet of the Middle Ages; it was written by Christopher Columbus, the Italian navigator in the Service of Their Majesties, the Most Catholic Kings of Spain, after the discovery of the New World. His caravels carried white sails with red crosses, and on the deck of one of the ships was a converted Jew, Luis de Torres, as an interpreter of Arabic.[38]

Further, while sailing westward and expanding the distances between the Christian world and the Holy Land, Columbus noted in his shipboard ledger, "I propose to your majesties that all the profit to be derived from my enterprise should be used for the recovery of Jerusalem."[39] Here was the one of the great discoverers who even in the words of the distinguished historian Samuel Eliot Morison initiated a policy that "resulted in complete genocide."[40]

The saintly Las Casas gives a bleaker picture, being an eyewitness and making no effort to excuse the atrocities of the conquerors. When Columbus arrived in Hispaniola in 1508, "there were 60,000 people living on this island, including the Indians; so that from 1494 to 1508, over three million people had perished from the war, slavery and mines. Who in future generations will believe this? I myself am writing it as a knowledgeable eyewitness can hardly believe it."[41] There is no mention of this in history books for children, only that

---

[37] Joshua Prawer, *The World of the Crusaders* (New York: Quadrangle Books, 1972) 150.

[38] Ibid., 147.

[39] Dawer, 152.

[40] Morison, quoted in Howard Zinn, *A People's History of the United States* (New York: Harper and Row, 1980) 7.

[41] Las Casas, quoted in Zinn, *A People's History*, 7.

Columbus was a great hero. We learn in such long-revered accounts as those of Washington Irving that Columbus was a brave fighter, a bold seaman, an expert swimmer, that he grew up in a culture of almost total war where piracy itself was almost legal, that seagoing expeditions called out "the chivalrous nobleman, the soldier of fortune, the hardy corsair, the desperate adventurer, the mercenary partisan,"[42] all of whom Columbus knew and with whom he sailed.

The argument is made that there would have been no voyages without such restless and daring spirits; perhaps, but they were odd companions of "the prince of peace." Even if the acknowledgment is made that they were needed for the "advancement" of history, it seems clear that the same kind are not needed now. Such was the situation in Europe at the time of the settling of the New World. In different guise, the knight was more powerful than ever. Instead of bringing about his demise, gunpowder gave him added strength, which he would use with lasting effect in the Americas from Mexico to New England. Columbus may have been the first European knight in the New World, but he was not the last. The old world pattern was set in the new.

---

[42] Irving, *The Life and Voyages of Christopher Columbus*, 2 vols. (Philadelphia: Lippincott, 1872) 1:19.

Chapter 8

The Religion of Sports and that Old-time Religion: In the Steps of Mircea Eliade

One key to understanding the trust placed in the religious value of sports by several apologists lies in the work of Mircea Eliade. "Most of the essays in *From Season to Season"*, says Joseph Price, "reflect and acknowledge a conceptual kinship with the perspective found in *The Sacred and the Profane* and *The Myth of Eternal Return or Cosmos and History.* The core of their arguments resides in Eliade's recognition that many forms of contemporary secular rituals manifest fundamental religious proclivities of human beings and reflect the sacred rites and myths of previous, religiously oriented cultures."[1]

The representative essay in regard to Eliade is that of Bonnie Miller-McLemore, who finds common ground between the culture of modern football and the remnants of primitive societies as noted in Eliade's works mentioned above but also in *Patterns in Comparative Religion, Myth and Reality,* and *Rites and Symbols of Initiation.* "Ancient non-literate societies," Miller-McLemore writes, "regarded games as dramatic reenactments of cosmic struggles. Spectators and players adopted important religious roles." Citing *From Ritual to Record* by Allen Guttmann, she continues, "From the Timbria Indians of Brazil to the Mayans and Aztecs of South America to the Athenians in the *early* [italics added for later discussion] Olympian Games,

---

[1] Joseph Price, ed., *From Season to Season: Sports as American Religion* (Macon GA: Mercer University Press, 1999) 6.

persons have envisioned sports as played ceremoniously for the gods to secure favors, prolong life, expel evil, and so forth."[2]

Drawing upon Eliade's distinctions between myth and history and his discussion of sacred time and sacred place, Miller-McLemore argues thus: "camouflaged beneath the more obvious aspects of spectacle and sport," American football "embodies the ongoing power and survival of myth and ritual in popular culture." This is true whether one wins or loses, she concludes. "Winning does not simply mean crushing the opponent. It signifies conquering fate and quieting adversaries stronger than opposing teams. Losing tests and trains the spiritual capacity to adjust to the limits of life, while still retaining hope in the face of finitude."[3]

The religion here described is not so much pagan, when distinctions had already arisen between city and country, as that of primitive man in a constant state of nature, a condition still evident in every grunt and groan on the line of scrimmage in football games and in a staggering number of attendant rituals by witnessing fans down to and including team names, always drawn from nature or war. Among the rituals are the losing coaches, perfect examples of the scapegoat, the *pharakos* (from the Greek meaning "poison"), as from season to season we watch them with tails between their legs head out of town, often the object of contempt.

The yoke of coaches as scapegoats reminds us of the various punishments for transgressions sanctioned among various nationalities and tribes as outlined in Scripture: crucifixion, stoning, hanging, death by sword or spear or beheading, hanging, burning alive, and strangling. "Cutting off" is a term that alumni boards sometimes seem to have adopted in pressing for the firing of winless coaches as with the authority and righteousness of the almighty: "When God is introduced as saying in respect to any person, 'I will cut him off from the people,' the expression means some event in divine providence which shall eventually terminate the life of that person's family (See 1 Kings 14:10; 21–21; 2 Kings 9:8). "Capital penalties" were merely for "absolute" "capital crimes," striking or reviling a parent, blasphemy, Sabbath-breaking, witchcraft, adultery, unchastity, rape, incestuous and unnatural connections, Man-stealing and Idolatry.[4]

---

[2] Price, 115.
[3] Price, 132.
[4] Unger, 902-903

Coaches should always keep an eye on athletic councils to see who among them are talking about the need for capital punishment and returning to the religious values of yesteryear. If such "capital penalties" should return, there is one capital crime that would be added to all the rest in a culture such as ours, that of losing ball games. Since modern sports seem to have so much to recommend them in terms of religion and since they reflect previous religious practices of tribal folks, one must wonder why more is not written about the horrors of cruel and unusual punishment for offenders in days of old. If these penalties were sanctioned under law, we can only imagine what the punishment was like for enemies defeated in combat. One wonders too why, in the interest of ethics, more questions aren't raised by sports apologists as to where civilizing influences came from to mitigate such horrors as stonings and being burned alive. That would be a nod, though, to conscious literary traditions from all lands with their many emphases upon restraint of power and compassion and wisdom.

Every sporting contest, in more respects than we might at first be willing to admit, is a battle for King of the Wood (or Hill), a struggle to see who among combatants is the most fecund, who can protect the "sacred" territory of our zones of defense in combative sports against the audacity of upstarts or familiar foes, that is, rival tribes. Such tribes keep returning year after year across state lines to wrest from us titles and honors that are, we feel, rightfully ours, a struggle to see who can "bring rain" and "good crops" and who must be banished as scapegoat from any territory of drought. The "NCAA Rules" for these contests may give the appearance of civilization, but beneath the veneer lies an eternal struggle on the part of athletes and coaches that is simply, from the athlete's point of view, "cosmic" in its import. To lose is to die symbolically, while resurrection becomes identified with the unexpected victory. Where winning means so much, *kudos* and *thymos*, we can be sure, are hard at work in individuals and teams.

When games are serious enough, as they often are, laughter is permitted only in the dressing room or boardroom of the victors. Such laughter comes in the form of animal delight in winning and in ridicule of defeated opponents, whether they are athletes, politicians, or business people. Those who lose or "die symbolically" lick wounds and deal with humiliation as best they can. Since obviously we haven't been witness to the aftermath of every contest and struggle, we could be wrong in our portrayal of these scenes, but to echo Charles Barkley, "we doubt it."

To get a glimpse of the violence behind this life and death heritage as it connects with rituals of antiquity, the reader should look at these words in the index of *The New Golden Bough*: "initiation," "sacrifice," and "scape-goat." Note the variety of these torturous rites among our beloved ancestors from all parts of the world. "Among the Australian tribes it was a common practice to knock out one or more of the boy's front teeth at those ceremonies of initiation to which every male member had to submit before they could enjoy the rites and privileges of a full grown man."[5] Until the development of the face guard, injuries to teeth and face were common in American football.

We are not denying parallels between ancient myth and modern sports but raising a question as to why the latter can still be called a religion. Such a religion does not really involve praying at midfield on one's knees, as questionable as that is in the teachings of Jesus (Matthew 6:6) but going back to the jungle on all fours as we see to one degree or another in football in every play. Football is not as violent as the frontier "Rough and Tumble," governed as the game is by rules enforced by officials, but maiming for life still occurs regularly. To be sure, football with all its dangers, maybe especially because of its dangers, can be fun to watch, but the natural theatricality of the game does not qualify it for a religion of common sense any more than does a holy war. Good football may take place in "Miller Time," which is not the same as holy time. We can't turn well from one to the other without some sense of distinction between them that apologists seem intent on removing.

No one can play football for long without thinking about sacrifice of time, study, and even health. Sacrifice is a theme common to sports and religion and one that might have been developed more fully in support of the basic theses in apologetic texts. At issue is the price of belonging to a group, and loss of teeth or even broken limbs may seem worthy sacrifices in that endeavor, however irrational the tradeoff might appear to non-combatants. While safety has improved steadily and dramatically in football, the term "sports medicine" reflects a significant degree of danger in all sports as well as an unquenchable compulsion by mortals to keep on competing. We are in agreement that rites of initiation, for better or worse, are part of an enduring myth of belonging, but we do not see the need to classify sports as a religion

---

[5] *The New Golden Bough: A New Abridgement of the Classic Work of Sir James George Frazer*, ed. Theodore H. Gaster (New York: New American Library, 1964) 62.

for that reason or for other similarities noted. Such parallels compliment neither modern sports nor religion.

Neither do we think sports should be an ally of traditional religion with crosses above stadia and public prayer on the sidelines or even applause for victors in Sunday morning services. Rather each should be a check upon the other and both a check upon war, offering alternatives in play and diplomacy to armed conflict. Just as conventional religion should be a check upon sports, so sports can be a check upon religion against the tendency toward an overplus of piety, spirituality, and withdrawal from the physical world. What is needed in sports, religion, and politics is a commonsense arrangement of checks and balances as in democratic government between the legislative, judicial, and executive branches. Otherwise, sports, religion, and politics become "occupations" of a leisure class, each supporting the worst features of the other in the form of invidious distinction.

Today women too participate widely in territorial sports—soccer, lacrosse, and even boxing, among other contests—but among sports apologists there seems to be little consideration of rites of passage for women in athletics, reflected abundantly, as well as other themes, in *Crossing Boundaries: An International Anthology of Women's Experiences in Sport* edited by Susan Bandy and Anne Darden. We suspect that the rites of passage for women in sports are becoming more like those of men, as vastly different as they were in antiquity. These changes probably represent a step forward in terms of gender equity, though puzzles remain in some instances in the directions of cultural transformation. Why, for instance, has boxing by women become a televised sport when common sense, to say nothing of basic human values, tells us men should be giving it up? It may well be the most brutal and senseless of all contests whether practiced by men or women. Perhaps women will, as is often true in the workplace, have to become twice the knights men are to get half the credit.

Today sports constitute a major means for rites of passages for boys and, increasingly, for girls as well. In earlier times this purpose was served and symbolized by the hunt as in Faulkner's *The Bear*. The need for some kind of initiation rites dies hard, as sensational news stories regularly confirm, and whether that need rides in our genes or in inherited myths or both is still unknown. In any event, modern rituals of initiation in traditional religion, as seen in christenings, confirmations, baptisms, and the like, are decidedly less violent than those in sports, especially football. In both religion and sports, rituals of initiation have to do with surrender of the individual and acceptance by a congregation or a team, but in sports the seeking of victory of other groups or tribes is part of the package to bring pride to the team. In conventional religion this too, unfortunately, is sometimes the case when display of virtue replaces the humility all religions profess but do not always practice.

In her comparative treatment of ancient rites and modern football, Miller-McLemore makes little or no mention of the gory details of the competitions and ceremonies of our prehistoric forebears; we get little insight into the violence of archaic games. Had she been more explicit in cataloging barbaric habits of initiations and propitiations in considering ancient rites as religious in nature, it would not have mattered, according to Price, since cruel and unusual forms of rituals are not a critical concern in what is or what is not a religion. "It should be noted that not all religions adopt and encourage humanistic, pacifistic and compassionate values; so the critique of sports on that grounds that they promote violence, bodily abuse, and an aggressive competitive spirit does not, of itself, separate sports from established religious traditions."[6]

It is not our task to fill in the bloody details, but one may state with certainty from the advantage of hindsight that if the habits of burning animals and witches, disemboweling, hanging, stabbing, and stoning are religious in nature, then religion is something we ought to endeavor to cast aside, which some argue we ought to do anyway considering the other forms of violence that still go on in the name of various gods.

It is no wonder that apologists see the need for dual faith of a traditional religion, one based on print and ideas, that might help place the universal compulsion to win in some kind of ethical perspective, a rapport, if one is possible between the sporting spirit and the holy spirit. The restraining wisdom of the holy spirit has, according to Scripture, been present in the cosmos from the beginning though not articulated until the literate phase of human history. It is a quality brought to human attention by an emerging cosmic consciousness as opposed to self-consciousness and simple consciousness of primitives and of animals, which sports, especially territorial sports, furiously reflect in the desire of participants to win. The religion of sports, though making use of all the technologies of the modern world from sports medicine to self-help psychology, Eastern meditation, and traditional Christianity through team chaplains, is a primitive religion of the

---

[6] Price, 228.

first rank but very different from that of Primitive Baptists. In fact, the Religion of Sports makes the Primitive Baptists seem avant-garde, which, considering their reliance on the written Gospel as Good *News*, they are.

Since the subject here is religion and sports, it is not unfair to remind ourselves that boxing was the favorite sport of Adolph Hitler as he enthusiastically reports in *Mein Kampf*, the book designed literally to replace the Bible, as Shirer points out in citing articles from the "National Reich Church" in his epic study, *The Rise and Fall of the Third Reich*:

> The National Church demands immediate cessation of the publishing and dissemination of the Bible in Germany....
>
> The National Church declares that to it, and therefore to the German nation, it has been decided that the Fuehrer's *Mein Kampf* is the greatest of all documents. It...not only contains the greatest but it embodies the purest and truest ethics for the present and future life of our nation.
>
> The National Church will clear away from its altars all crucifixes, Bibles, and pictures of saints. The national Reich Church is determined to exterminate irrevocably...the strange and foreign Christian faiths imported into Germany in the ill-omened year of 800.
>
> On the altars there must be nothing but *Mein Kampf* (to the German nation and therefore to God the most *sacred* book).[7]

The experience of the twentieth century tells us we should be careful what gods of ancient times we import or recognize and elevate to divine status. We need to remember the tragic consequences that can occur when reversions to the oldest gods, invariably war gods, are invoked to displace other gods that preach and teach kinder and gentler ways of dealing with each other. In *From Season to Season* some pains are taken to insure that such will not occur as seen in the recommendation for two religions, the religion of sports *and* a conventional faith, a subject examined later in this text. Also, on the jacket of *From Season to Season* the cross stands triumphant over the stadium, supposedly a repudiation of the outrages recommended in the last and consummate point, number 30, of the Reich

---

[7] William L. Shirer, *The Rise and Fall of the Third Reich* (New York: Simon and Schuster, 1960) 332, italics added.

Church: "On the day of its foundation, the Christian Cross must be removed from all churches, cathedrals, and chapels…and it must be superceded by the only unconquerable symbol, the swastika."[8] Over the millennia the swastika has stood for many things, but since World War II its meanings have been sharply reduced. To what extent a cross over a stadium or indeed over a church can become a swastika in meaning each may judge.

Among apologists, comparative references are always back to nature or to the ancient past. Snake handling as a religion, we are told, is a recent practice in America, though mentioned in Scripture. No one knows how old it really is, but our guess is that in the old days it would seem a ritual of safety compared to the alleged decapitation practices in tribal ball games in Mesoamerica. When in the 1940s we listened to Roy Acuff sing "Give Me that Old-time Religion" on the Grand Ole Opry, in our thinking we didn't go much beyond the religion of our grandparents, which, we are confident, would have been the case with Roy. We can't remember hearing that song in church but did hear scores of hymns such as "In the Garden," a place different from the stadium or the gym.

If we thought about it much at all, we knew that religion had to be at least as old as the Bible, but Roy Acuff made the old seem almost like new, at least as recent as our grandparents. Many of us were not convinced that snake handling was a religion, and no one ever dreamed, considering the general opposition to Sunday sports, that in only a few decades the Tennessee Titans would be playing in the state capitol on Sunday afternoons. Most astounding of all, we would be informed that these were actually religious services as was snake handling and even, it was becoming clear, the beheading rites of Mayan Warriors.

The Religion of Sports:
Revival or NRMs (New Religious Movements) or Both?

Suddenly in the last decades of the twentieth century, everything seemed to qualify as a religion. With an avalanche of NRMs (New Religious Movements), William James's classic, *The Varieties of Religious Experience*, began to seem narrow-minded in comparison.[9] One begins to

---

[8] Ibid., 332–33.

[9] For a discussion of the proliferation of contemporary religious themes in light of the heritage of William James, see Charles Taylor, *Varieties of Religion Today: William James Revisited* (Cambridge: Harvard University Press, 2002).

wonder when nearly everything becomes a religion what happens to religion itself and even the idea of the sacred, to say nothing of the holy and, as far as that goes, the idea of the secular and profane. The great value in comprehensive definitions, and we must admit in doctrines—indeed doctrines and definitions are almost synonymous—is that they lead us not into certainty but into comparisons and contrasts between our own views and those of others and perhaps into higher degrees of tolerance. We may come to realize how our own religious perspectives might have been warped and as damaging to others as ritual decapitation, as seen for example in the churches' promotion and practice of institutionalized racism for centuries. There are many ways besides decapitation to rob others of their lives.

Our evaluation of sports in terms of the holy may seem old-timey and out of touch with current reality, but we would bet that every NRM makes some claim not only to sacredness but to holiness as well, claims of distinctiveness in ritual and belief designed to get in touch with the ground of all being, whether called the holy or some other name. Certainly this is the pattern in the religion of sports, which apologists claim is both sacred and holy. As a reminder, our argument is that while sports may be sacred in terms of being set apart, they are not holy. Again, this is not saying that sports are not good things, or that they are up to no good. We are saying that they are not holy in nature, theory, or practice. An athlete may have a holy experience during practice or games, but so can an overweight computer specialist with carpal tunnel in both wrists sipping coffee and staring blankly at a monitor. Only the "occupation" of religion has assumed the utterly awesome responsibility of leading us to the holy, which traditionally is why one is *called* to the profession. No one for purely rational reasons would ever undertake such a challenge.

Sports, from our perspective, should not be viewed as another NRM. If they are a religion, which we doubt, then they are probably the oldest on earth, a point that apologists are intent upon making us remember. It is doubtful, though, whether or not the Religion of Sports could have flourished as they have without the freedom of assembly, speech, and choice of religion that America has allowed in the relative success of the Civil Rights Movement. There are, though, differences between the Religion of Sports and some other NRMs.

While fetishism and superstition abound in the Religion of Sports, there is little or no New Age theorizing, at least at the doctrinal level now being refined by apologists. Instead, it asks for us to recognize its virtues and powers in what has been around and before us all our lives. All we can say is that all things that are good are not holy, and all that is holy does not, from human perspective, appear to be good such as acts of God, occasional reminders that we are never in control as much as we think we are. Yet, ironically perhaps, we are in control of more than we realize since, unless our eyes deceive us, most of the bad things in the world are not caused by weather but by ourselves. In the words of a displaced tenant in *The Grapes of Wrath*, feeling helpless before invisible forces called "The Monster," "It's not like lightning or earthquakes. We've got a bad thing made by men, and by God that's something we can change."[10]

Miller-McLemore says that Eliade "does not give a precise definition of religion. Nor does he need to." Neither does Miller-McLemore offer a precise definition. Some of the other contributors to *From Season to Season* do feel the need in their essays to operate under working definitions. This is especially true in the essay by James Mathisen, "American Sport as *Folk* Religion" (italics added). What is called "churchly religion" is not the subject but myths informing religion and sports. Tom Faulkner in "A Puckish Reflection on Religion in Canada" draws upon *The Invisible Religion* by Thomas Luckman, who "understands religion to be what humans do when they are being fully human," a perspective close to that of Bonhoeffer and the Dali Lama and to that of preacher Jim Casey in *The Grapes of Wrath*: "There ain't no sin and there ain't no virtue. There's just stuff people do and it's all part of the same thing. And some of the things folks do is nice, and some ain't nice, but that's as far as any man got a right to say."[11]

Sports are "just stuff people do," and sometimes hockey is "nice," a thing of grace and beauty, and sometimes it "ain't nice," a brawl on ice. Hockey, like other territorial sports, allows us either as players or fans to become fully human, to indulge ourselves in a wide range of exhilarating emotions. Within a limited, partisan context, a contest is set aside in time and place, hence sacred by definition of apologists, by cost in the case of professional games, and mostly by ability since relatively few are capable of playing even varsity sports in high school let alone at the professional level.

Sports can help make us fully human, but to be fully human, is still to be severely lacking from the perspective of the divine. Games occur in

---

[10] John Steinbeck, *The Grapes of Wrath* (New York: Viking Press, 1966) 33.
[11] Ibid., 19.

leisure class settings pitting one club against another to determine standings, to stimulate excitement and vicarious participation of fans, and to promote gambling, among other goals. While they stir a whirlwind of feelings within us, all games are what might be called in theology "adiaphora," "things indifferent," neither good nor bad. That they matter so much to us relates to what poet Don Johnson calls the "paradox of inconsequence." Sports matter so much to many of us that they have a powerful influence upon all aspects of our lives, yet there is a certain truth that, according to Veblen, they bear no more relation to culture than a bullfight to agriculture.

Sports qua sports have comic potentiality but are forever isolated from the tragic mode. They may serve as comic relief from the tragic, as troops playing baseball in breaks in the Civil War or troops in Iraq passing the football. Alien to sports, the idea of tragedy is awakened by great sorrow, a sense of loss and helplessness, which is why the holy is inextricably connected to it in the same way the sacred is connected to war. Inherent in sacred thought is the concept of pride, honor, memory, and always, one suspects, a hint of revenge. Dependent on tragedy, the holy vision is one of acceptance, surrender, and atonement that comes after great suffering under real conditions, like the effort of the Oakies of the Great Depression as opposed to the theatrical conditions of sports. Listen again to Jim Casey as he speaks about the "most unreligious thing" he ever thought: "I figgered about the Holy Sperit and the Jesus road. I figgered, 'Why do we gotta hang it on God or Jesus? Maybe,' I figgered, 'maybe it's all men and all women we love; maybe that's the Holy Sperit—the human sperit—the whole shebang. Maybe all men got one big soul ever'body's a part of.' Now I sat there thinkin' it, an' all of a sudden—knew it. I knew it so deep down that it was true and I still know it."[12] Since Steinbeck's novel came out before World War II, one wonders if Bonhoeffer might have read it and been influenced in the direction of a "religionless Christianity." There was, though, abundant evidence before him from primary sources, from in fact the eponym of the faith.

Like the rest of us, hockey players and all athletes in other sports suffer individually, and of necessity they come to some resolution about the mystery of pain and the matter of faith, or they ignore the question entirely. Individually athletes may be paragons of holiness for all we know, but it is not the purpose of sports to lead players into that state. Often the holy seems

---

[12] Ibid., 20.

to emerge in moments of great trials, as Paul in his role of persecutor, fictional Jim Casey in the throes of the Depression, Bonhoeffer in prison. To be sure, the holy can descend at any time and any place, but the arena or ball court seems an unlikely spot to land since by their nature they are exempt from the idea of tragedy no matter how much some fans whine and complain about coaches and won-lost records.

In addition to myths propitiating power, there is in all religions a wisdom literature based not on struggle for conquest but upon acceptance, peace, understanding, tolerance, and rest; in the Judeo-Christian heritage we find it from the Twenty-Third Psalm to the Beatitudes. It remains to be seen what will happen to the connection between sports and religion, but our argument would be that sports will be saner and healthier when we move further from the ancient myths we *unconsciously* follow in our cultural patterns of sports and give more attention to the *conscious* wisdom of restraint that, in contrast to addictive habits, allows us the freedom to live life more fully with good cheer.

We have made progress in sports in one important way in the form of sublimation. Generally, we do not kill losers (or winners) as in pagan times, but we still require sacrifices of all kinds for our tribal teams, asking athletes in effect to waive or at least delay an education and to play while hurt, and firing losing coaches when they don't "produce" as if they were farmers under contract. In point of fact, some coaches are in a sense like farmers, just as many college football teams are now "farm" teams for the pros as minor league baseball teams have always been for big league teams with the difference being that the big league football teams do not help fund their farm teams in colleges and universities.

Owing to the breadth of definitions and sometimes none at all in the case of Eliade on "religion," a question arises: is there any public contest that is not *religious*, including races by housewives through supermarkets to see who can pick the most groceries off the shelf in a limited time or competitions to see who can stay under water longer without breathing? The record for the underwater endeavor is now more than eight minutes.

Even more amazing than holding one's breath is the dry land contest among world-class eaters to determine who can devour the most hot dogs in a limited amount of time. Once this feat, perhaps an extreme sport, would have been branded as gluttony, a major sin, but now we give prizes to champions in the field, present them with championship belts, and listen to how they train as they go around the world from one ritualistic display of digestive greatness to another before television audiences.

Once Kafka could write a fabulous story, "The Hunger Artist," who put on amazing displays of fasting, a show to be sure, but one that would hardly attract our attention in an age when competitors gulp several pounds of hotdogs in minutes. In looks, some of these magnificent devourers or perhaps plain jesters remind us of the smiling Buddha—amazingly the champion looks as thin as a string bean—just as the "Hunger Artist" reminds us of the Christ but again only in looks to show that fasting can be as much a competition and display of pseudo virtue as any other sacred practice. This point is well made in *The Desert Fathers* by Helen Waddell as she distinguishes between the real and the imitative of those, who like the desert prophets before them, returned to the wilderness to keep faith alive.

Essentially the same point is made by Otto, who says that of the many people he has observed who claim to holiness, only two percent seem to him to be authentic, a comment unrelated to forms of faith or denominations or certainly not based upon them. On a similar theme, only a few attain *Cosmic Consciousness*, the title of Richard Bucke's famous work. We have long been confused about what is sport and what is not, but now sports apologists have confused us more by raising questions about what is a religion; we would not be surprised to see a subtitle under the next edition of *Guinness Book of Records* that proclaimed *Amazing Feats in Religion and Sports*.

The possibilities for religious significance keep proliferating under the auspices of Eliade's discourse and include the ambition for corporate achievement, the mass flight to suburbia, and obsessive consumer frenzy. According to Miller-McLemore, "he might have expanded his analysis today to include the current craze about physical fitness, the appeal of therapy and self-help literature, the voyeuristic viewing of television court dramas and talk shows, and perhaps, the mania about football."[13]

What we stand to lose is not so much what is called traditional religion but further loss of distinction between human categories of religion, business, sports, and war so that one day, as tribalization grows, they may be as indistinguishable as in the earliest rites of primitive man. Indeed they already share a common language of sacred self-glorification. One listens almost in vain from any quarter for some clue of the sense of the holy that

---

[13] Price, 121.

requires humility instead of the sacred dictates of corporate takeovers, interventionist wars, and suicide bombings.

With so much sacredness everywhere in everything, especially in our wars, one wonders if the Lord's Prayer has not already been fulfilled. The daily news reminds us otherwise, including the sporting news, showing fan rage at ball games, which we can be sure was also well-known to our forebears in their many rituals to confront evil and to please their gods.

The Religion of the Olympic Games: Old and New

Sports as a religion has support not only from academe but also from the popular press. Says Frank Deford in "The Saga of Sport,"

> ...from *early on and everywhere* [italics added for later discussion], major sporting events were linked to religious ceremony, if only because fun and games—and, all too often, the ugliest blood sport—would attract worshipers to the duller prayer worlds. At Olympia it was the huge statue of Zeus, not the stadium, that was one of the Seven Wonders of the World. Early Mesoamericans saw in their ball games reenactments of conflicts between the sun and the moon. And not all that much changes, does it? Baron Pierre de Coubertin, who inspired the recreation of the Olympics in 1896, declared: "For me sport is a religion with church, dogma, ritual."[14]

Several noted students of ancient sports, however, see no connection between religion and the *origin* of sport in ancient Greece. Classic scholar David Young makes key distinctions easily overlooked in the association of early Greek sports and religion:

> Homeric games set in heroic times are sometimes joined to a funeral celebration but not to religion. In historical times, the games themselves were firmly attached to religious festivals (cf. *Iliad* 22.159f.), but that says nothing of their origin. Most experienced students of Greek athletics discount a religious or ritual origin for Greek athletics and warn against exaggerating the association of athletics with religion (Patrucco, pp. 28, 33, Harris 1972, pp.16 f.).

---

[14] Deford, "Let the Games Begin," *National Geographic* 190/1 (July 1996): 46.

Gardiner flatly states, "There is no ground for attributing any religious significance to the games themselves. The fact is that Greek athletic sports, though closely associated with religion, are in their origin independent and secular" (*History and Remains of Olympia* [Oxford, 1925], p.67). On this point Gardiner seems to have the early evidence on his side.[15]

With these distinctions and qualifications in mind, Young does say in his main text that the ancient Greeks differ from all other peoples in that they "institutionalized these questions (surrounding children at play) as serious matters for adults, hiring poets and artists to immortalize what others fearfully relegated to the separate, inconsequential world of children. And the Greeks did not merely remove these things from the realm of child-play; they boldly placed them in the basic categories of religion, politics, and business."[16] In other words, in *historic, literate, even literary times*, the Greeks made sports the final corner of the four "occupations" of a leisure-class society, as defined by Thorstein Veblen, that is, politics or government, warfare, religion, and sports. To be sure, all these institutions were satirized by one Greek writer or another, but the coalition of categories held as it has everywhere since, in the Roman empire, during the crusades of the Middle Ages, the struggle for power among the Atlantic and Mediterranean peoples, the endless Indian wars and our own civil war, and the long world wars of our last century.

What all this means is that the "sacred" became not a special quality eminent in nature as in the case of prehistoric man but a *manipulative* quality *created* by the state for purposes of conquest, defense, and entertainment. In nature and in the world of plants and animals, the idea of the sacred, as Joseph Campbell has observed, was everywhere as was the acceptance of the idea of sacrifice.

In prehistory, tribal rites, no matter where they took place, were no doubt based on the efficacy of results, an "innocent" practice in spite of the blood shed in sacrifice and war and passed on through generations by word of mouth, while *in literate history* they became *conscious* enactments narrated orally but also recorded in writing for future generations on the

---

[15] Young, *The Olympic Myth of Greek Amateur Athletics* (Chicago: Ares Publishers, 1984) 172.

[16] Ibid., 172–73.

advisability or perhaps necessity of aligning sports with the other structures of power in the state, namely religion and patriotism or preparation for war. So it was near the beginning of the idea of the city-state, so it is now, and perhaps it ever shall be since tribes are here to stay.

Even our hymns or hymnals are divided between the sacred and the holy with patriotism the determining factor. The sacred, by our under-standing, is part of a symbol of one's culture plus an effort to link that culture to the holy, as in hymns such as "God Bless America" in contrast, say, to "Holy, Holy, Holy" or "How Great Thou Art." If the idea of the holy were removed from church hymnals, none would be bigger than a pamphlet, and those remaining would, using America as an example, reflect patriotic themes—"My Country Tis of Thee," "God Bless Our Native Land," "America the Beautiful," and "The Star-spangled Banner." None would be out of place, like the National Anthem required at the Super Bowl, where the intent is to clothe a mere game in robes of patriotism and religion.

At its best, patriotism, according to Joseph Conrad at the beginning of *Under Western Eyes*, is among "the noblest aspirations of humanity" along with "the desire of freedom, the love of justice, the sense of pity, and even the fidelity of simple minds," the very opposite of "the lusts of hate and fear, the inseparable companions of an uneasy despotism." At worst, patriotism is, in the opinion of Dr. Johnson, "the last refuge of the scoundrel, as stated according to Boswell on April 7, 1775." We are not advocating removal of sacred hymns from any hymnal wherever they remain but merely observing a difference with holy ones. It can be argued that sacred and holy hymns overlap, to which we would respond by saying that this may be true with the provision that the degree of overlap will not depend on how many times or where a sacred song is sung, say "God Bless America," but upon the amount of wisdom, justice, and freedom America exhibits day to day, the kind of great ideals to which Conrad refers.

In the "Conclusion" of Walden Thoreau made another distinction between these two types of patriotism: "Every man is the lord of a realm beside which the earthly empire of the Czar is but a petty state, a hummock left by the ice. Yet some can be patriotic who have no self-respect, and sacrifice the greater to the less. They love the soil which makes their graves, but have no sympathy with the spirit which may still animate their clay. Patriotism is a maggot in their heads."

Whatever the degree of relationship between sports and religion in ancient Greece before the beginning of the Olympics in 776 B.C. or afterward, more than two and one-half millennia later Baron Pierre de Coubertin left no doubt where he stood on the matter and boldly made a modern dogma out of the ancient games. As high priest of the revival of the pagan sports, he performed a *hieros gamos* (sacred wedding) out of *paideia,* the ideals of Greek culture, a new old religion based not so much on the "holy spirit" of Scripture but on the sporting spirit.

To Coubertin as reflected in what might be called his Olympic Bull, "sport is a religion with church, dogma, ritual," and sports apologists offer a "hearty amen." They might add that the Olympics is only one branch in the UCOS (the Universal Church of Sports), which has as many denominations—football, baseball, hockey, etc.—as Protestant evangelism. They would say that the term "Sportianity," coined a few years ago by Frank Deford to describe rampant Muscular Christianity, is too outdated and even inaccurate, that sports, thank you very much, is a religion that can stand on its own two feet without the old-timey ideas like love your neighbor as yourself, which, if taken seriously, plays havoc with the will to win. While all branches of UCOS are loaded with myth and ritual, dogma has not yet been fully developed in all of them. The implication is that we should not fear nor doubt the universal triumph of the UCOS, which through athletic competition, civilized rules of governance, and good sportsmanship will at last bring about a world of peace and cooperation that warring religions of the old faiths could never achieve. There are still problems with matters of funding, but those too will be resolved.

The "religious" qualities identified in sports are often those inherent in the contests or more correctly *inherited* from preliterate tribal cultures and reflected in patterns of rituals, including uniforms and masks, and fan behavior, which may have changed less than we think over the last several thousand years as seen in the painted faces at any high-profile competition such as the "Final Four." These features are not matters of litany or responsive readings in the usual sense of "churchly" services but responses to magnificent physical performance, sporting rituals instead of verbal ones, rituals of any kind being enactments of myths as Lord Raglan in *The Hero* and Joseph Campbell in *The Hero With a Thousand Faces* have both observed. While not the same level of quality as those Gregorian priestly orders, faithful sports fans also sing and perform their own "chants" such as "Push 'em back! Push 'em back! Way back." Such rituals, we can be sure, are connected to heroic rites of passage, roles celebrating seasons and preparations for war or remembrances of war, and sacrifice as reflected in the playing of national anthems (especially at the Olympics) and the passing of the colors.

In these sporting acts or rather enactments of the myths of war, defense of territory, and glorification of tribes, students of antiquity see not only ancient patterns of culture but universal and eternal ones as common as the weather, hence reality itself, and they pronounce it good much in the manner of Coubertin. Miller-McLemore herself quotes the Baron with apparent approval: "Coubertin...sees modern athletics as 'an impassioned soaring': The 'deep play' of the (Olympic) games, the ultimate sporting event, resolves paradoxes and occasions the 'revelation of higher order, non-contradictory truths.'"[17] Here in effect is the philosophy of *citius, altius, fortius* (faster, higher, stronger), to some a dubious philosophy owing to its accessibility to elitist regimes, especially the Nazi Regime who made it their credo. It is the religion of Apollo, the Sun God, a religion of glory, and how well it can coexist with religions of grace has been the principal focus of theological debate in Christendom for two millennia.

These "non-contradictory truths" of the Baron based, we assume, on the indisputable evidence of victory and defeat do not, for better or worse, appear to resolve spiritual contradictions such as those, for example, discussed by G. K. Chesterton in *Paradoxes of Christianity*. Dealing with irony and paradox is a far more complicated matter than keeping score or counting medals by country after Olympic games. The religion of print thrives on irony and subtlety; the religion of sports demands resolution, the elevation of the winners. In the Christian tradition the central ideals are faith, hope, and charity, whereas in the religion of sports, especially in the denomination known as Olympics, they are the true, the good, and the beautiful, as seen in the lyrics of the Olympic Hymn first played at the 1908 Olympics in London.

Immortal Spirit of antiquity, father of the true, the good, and the beautiful, descend, appear, shed over us thy light, upon this ground, and under this sky, first witness to thy glory.

Give light and vitality to these noble games: Throw imperishable floral crowns to the victors in the running, wrestling, and discus, and with thy light animate hearts of steel! In thy light, plains, mountains, and seas shine in roseate hue and form a vast

---

[17] Price, 122.

temple to which the nations throng to adore thee, *O immortal Spirit of antiquity.*[18]

The Olympics, sometimes pharmaceutically enhanced, have become a spectacle, whether sacred or not, but this may not be as bad for the religion of sports as some might think. Just as the stadium spectacle of Billy Graham has brought apparent converts to Christianity by the tens of thousands, maybe millions, so too may the sporting spectacle bring spectators to embrace the sacred in monumental events like the Olympics and the Super Bowl. John J. MacAloon, author of *This Great Symbol* cited above, observes that "a sports event should not be lumped under any single rubric, whether ritual, game, festival, or spectacle. All four genres are intimately connected to one another on all levels."[19] In modern culture, though "spectacle," according to MacAloon and as interpreted by Miller-McLemore,

has triumphed over the other three genres of sport, festival, ritual and game—as the dominant genre in the Olympian Games and in general. However, the decline of ritual, festival, and game does not mean their demise. In fact the festival may serve as a recruiting device, dissembling suspicion toward "mere ritual" and luring the proudly uncommitted. So those who believe that they come to watch a secular spectacle are drawn unknowingly into an experience of ritual renewal and reformulation. Football may embody what MacAloon predicted: "A ramified performance type" would emerge as a sort of servo-mechanism or "meta-genre" that would integrate festival, ritual, and play. Beneath the guise of spectacle, football continues to foster ritual, festival, and play. Sacred forces are evoked, and social and spiritual transformations effected.[20]

The problem with the rationale here is that all the terms used, except perhaps "play" and maybe even "it," are value free—"ritual," "festival,"

---

[18] Quoted in John J. MacAloon, *This Great Symbol: Pierre de Coubertin and the Origins of the Modern Olympic Games* (Chicago: University of Chicago Press, 1984) 215. The steel metaphor used by Coubertin was also a favorite of Hitler, Lenin, and Carnegie. See Robert J. Higgs, *God in the Stadium: Sports and Religion in America* (University Press of Kentucky, 1995) 172, which is not to suggest identical philosophies between them. However, the steel metaphor, perfect for knighthood, stands in sharp contrast to the agricultural metaphors used by Christ the shepherd.

[19] Ibid., 134.

[20] Price, 132.

"sacred forces," and "social and spiritual transformation." These could as well describe the celebrations of the Nazi Olympics as an Easter egg hunt in a church in the wildwood. They're like the tofu of religiosity taking on the flavor of the sponsoring organization. Ethics cannot enter fully into the picture of any festival until some understanding of what is being celebrated is identified. In Easter egg hunts, the goals are joy and surprise in the minds of children; in the Olympics it is sometimes difficult to see that the same two qualities, joy and surprise, are also the objects of the competition in light of "isms" involved—commercialism, nationalism, monumentalism, and professionalism, which once was barred—and doping.

After Coubertin, the latter-day prophet of the religion of sports, evangelical apologists for sports such as Jerry Falwell appeared, in addition to organizations such as FCA and Athletes in Action, to say nothing of a growing number of theologians who bless the competition as forms of transcendence, a way of celebrating individual gifts, natural or divine, and a way of holding society together. There are here and there murmurs of doubt about it as in Bill Baker's *If Christ Came to the Olympics*. On the other hand, it can be said that just as every religion needs martyrs, so they need doubters, backsliders, and even heretics. As has been the case with conventional religions, as the church of the Olympics continues to grow in influence, so will doubters and maybe even heretics. Those who create new religions face enormous challenges even in success as they continue to grow in visibility and influence on television and as network executives look about them and say, "Hey, we really are doing something good since the ball parks where we carry our cameras are sacred!"

In any event, we should know something about the effects of heresy in new religions and old. As Hans Kung in *The Church* has observed, "There is nothing to be gained here by passing self-righteous judgment on the past. A century of concentration camps and gas chambers has no cause to despise the centuries of the stake and the rack."[21] It can be argued that many if not most human atrocities, even those more recent ones of the concentration camps and gas chambers, have been conducted in the name of state religions. To what extent a religion of sports tends to become that of the state each may judge. It is not, though, a question to be dismissed as irrelevant or preposterous.

---

[21] H. Kung, *The Church* (Garden City: Doubleday, 1976) 326–27.

Speaking of what John Updike called the "forgotten slaughters of history," it must be said that whatever level of deity the Baron attained appears superior to that of Theodosius I, an early Christian emperor who banished the Olympics as forms of pagan idolatry. That was not all he did: "In 390 A.D. when the governor of Thessalonia was lynched by a circus mob for his punishment of a brutal but favorite charioteer, Theodosius ordered the people of the city to be invited into the circus and there massacred. At least 7,000 were put to death. The subsequent humiliation of Theodosius I and his submission of the penance demanded by St. Ambrose for the massacre was regarded by the church as one of its greatest victories over the temporal power."[22]

"The Byzantine emperor Theodosius II (A.D. 408–450) apparently didn't even like the idea of the Olympics since in A.D. 426 he ordered the destruction of the temples of Olympia, including that of Zeus. The letter of Saint Ambrose to Theodosius I is a masterpiece of divine rhetoric on the need for penance and the moral supremacy of the church, but here too things get complicated since not all popes have been any more moral than have Christian emperors.[23] On the matter of papal infallibility, some Protestants have responded with absolute certainty on their own with the doctrine of biblical inerrancy.

In the view of some, the path the church took after its triumph over a despotic Christian emperor was not a cause for unreflective celebration since, in Ambrose's words, "Christ was now at the head of legions," another Caesar, as it were, but a sacred one—*Christi Militant* instead of the holy shepherd as depicted in Scripture—in the lives of prophets and saints and in Christian art early and late. Even today we worship the "*Prince* of Peace," and at Christmas we sing "King of Kings" not "Shepherd of Shepherds." Deny it as we may, we are linguistically all royalists, even as we profess to worship one born in a manger. A similar example of the victory of the church but within a specific locale is enacted annually at Easter, as

---

[22] "Theodosius I," *Funk and Wagnall's*, vol. 30 (New York: Unicorn Publishers, 1952), vol. 32.

[23] Letter of St. Ambrose, based on H. De Romestin, trans. in Library of Nicene and Post Nicene Fathers, 2d series, vol. 10 (New York: 1896) 450–53, <www.fordham.edu/halsall/source/ambrose-let51.html> (2 March 2004).

For additional commentary on the face-off between Ambrose and Theodosius, see http://www.jesusneverexisted.com/theodosius.html (March 2, 2004).

mentioned, in a candlelit procession around the coliseum, led by the Pope, to illustrate the triumph of Christ over the horrors that once occurred therein.

The "sacred" in the reckoning of sports apologists includes sacred turf of university stadia such as that of Shields-Watkins Field in Neyland Stadium in Knoxville, the third largest in the country, as well as the knightly combat that occurs in this domain, all part, we are now told, of a secular faith and a popular religion. To be sure, the correlation is strong enough in East Tennessee to provoke a satire of the possibility of a new religion of sports and to suggest humorously the need for definitions about what is really meant by a religion. A cartoon a few years back in the *Knoxville Sentinel* shows a fan at a University of Tennessee football game wearing a baseball cap with a banner in hand. The caption reads, "Statistics show that Baptists are the largest single denomination in Tennessee. I guess that depends on what you call a religion."

In archaic cultures, the themes of war and religion, the spirit of play, and the power structure of the tribe were intertwined into a seamless whole, and the same is true in an age of television in spite of technology that can take us to the moon. In 1968, for example, when the Billy Graham Crusade came to Shields-Watkins Field in Republican East Tennessee, Richard Nixon appeared on the platform with the famous evangelist to endorse and sanctify the war in Viet Nam. Whether or not that was the purpose of either Nixon or Graham or Henry Kissinger, who arranged the meeting, each may judge, but one question is raised about the enormity of such gatherings—their inevitable alliance with patriotism in whatever form in whatever country. Veblen's take, rightly or wrongly, on that scene in Knoxville, would have been that it was a confirmation of his thesis, that the alliance of sports, government, warfare, and religion constitutes the four "occupations" of a predatory culture and leisure class. Such concerns seem beyond the scope or interest of the study of apologists, but when sports are defined as a religion in and of themselves, it seems legitimate to expect some treatment, however limited, of the implication of that correlation with other highly structured "occupations" in society such as government and war, regardless of country.

A Reminder from the Hollers:
Things that Are Good and Things that Are of God

Religion as entertainment has been a familiar scene in America since the Second Great Revival on the Tennessee-Kentucky Frontier in the early decades of the nineteenth century. Billy Sunday mastered the craft of showmanship, and it is truly regrettable that he came along when he did, else we could still be enjoying reruns and marveling at his histrionic talents. Abraham Lincoln said he liked preachers who looked like they were fighting bees when they delivered their messages. From all reports, Sunday, a major league ball player, fit that bill and more too. On the same night that Sunday died in 1935, as if by providential succession, Billy Graham gave his life to Christ. Graham too stressed the necessity for salvation not in the style of the frontier ministry but in the calm, cool delivery that both television and urban life required. The numbers of conversions, as presented by Oprah on her show, are testimony to his success, but not everyone has been converted to Graham's manner. Brother Buell Kazee, a native of Magoffin, Kentucky, and an old-time Baptist, tells why he is concerned about "big" productions such as the Graham Crusades and similar programs.

I take the position that we are in the day of the "light stuff." I don't think the depth of spiritual life in the churches today is very noticeable.... I could have played the banjo in church...but I would have put myself in the position of mixing banjo-playing with...church work. Of course that is what is happening right now. There's Johnny Cash on Billy Graham's program the other night just whooping it up, you know, and telling all about what all the "Lord meant to him" and playing in Las Vegas in the last six months. I just don't see how you can mix it...like that.

The "Crusade" has taken people *away* from the church, away from the interest in church life.... They're drawing the money from the churches, the church members, to those "big" things. There isn't a man or a woman who can appear on Billy Graham's program who hasn't been a great "success" *in the world*. That is to say, his success in the world qualifies him to appear on the crusade program. He has to be a headliner in the world. They had a fellow who was the world's champion yo-yo artist on this program in Lexington.... Now I've preached fifty-seven years, and my witness, beside his, wouldn't be worth two cents.... And this is, as I see it, pure sham. Because most of the people who are dedicated to Christ in the real sense wouldn't have any time for any of that other stuff.[24]

The "religion" practiced in Neyland Stadium is, according to apologists, both ancient and new, ever present in contests for all time, while that of Brother Kazee, though it be called old, is also eternally new to followers but in a different way. "Religion is popular now," says Kazee.

It's good business and good entertainment, but it's shallow, nothing rugged about the Old Cross now. Well it's got some good things in it and a lot of gospel. But, there's a lot of difference between "good" and that which is "from God." Keep that in mind. A Christian must never ask "Is it Good?" He must ask "Is it from God?" That's where the Christian's life is centered, and he must become absorbed with the goodness of the world as if it were the godliness of the Lord....

But you understand, the Devil's not mean, he's not got a forked tail and horns; he's a god, he's a counterfeit god, he's going to be as much like god as he can without being God.... The Devil's got more religion going on than the Lord has, and it's a "good" religion, it has humanitarianism in it, it has morality in it, it's got all the marks that we are looking for as good in it. But godliness...that's something else.... You see, good honest people are deceived by Satan: it isn't the fellow who's not honest. He's working on very religious people.... That's where he's working. But the deception lies in the Devil getting them to believe something other than the word of God. You have to be guided by *that word*.[25]

Later we will argue with reference to testimony of religious mystics and scientists both that the "word" itself is not really a word but a silent vehicle pointing to the divine spirit itself, the source of all creativity. In the

[24] Kazee, quoted in Loyal Jones, "Old-time Baptist and Mainline Christianity," *Appalachia Inside Out: A Sequel to Voices from the Hills*, vol. 2, ed. Robert J. Higgs, Ambrose N. Manning, and Jim Wayne Miller (Knoxville: University of Tennessee Press, 1995) 411. For a fuller treatment of these issues, see Jones, *Faith and Meaning in the Southern Uplands* (Urbana: University of Illinois Press, 1999).
[25] Ibid., 412.

world of the human, we are daily drowning in media that allows us to talk to ourselves in an epidemic of somambulism. In the minority world of interplay of spirit between the human and the divine, or the seeker and the Sought, know that to be awake is to be alive. We know nothing and need nothing that the holy does not already know. All our so-called creations are discoveries and rearrangements of what was already waiting for the pure and humble in heart and mind to draw forth onto common ground.

Almost like a corporate whistle blower, Brother Kazee in the hollers of Appalachia brings up an aspect of the similarity of modern sports and religion generally overlooked, the staged packaging of "sacred" time and events, not just for purposes of "salvation" in the case of evangelical telecasts but for purposes of entertainment and business in the case of both sports and religion, in other words the perpetuation of prominence and political power.

Loyal Jones notes that the old-time Baptists are not against involvement in the world on a personal basis but only as a church. He points out, among other examples, that "it was Ollie Combs, a member of the Old Regular Baptist Church, who sat down in front of and stopped the bulldozers trying to strip her land, who was carried off to jail, and who later testified before the Kentucky legislature to bring in the first strong strip-mine regulations in Kentucky. This bill was called the 'Widow Combs Bill.'"[26]

The question raised by Brother Kazee as to whether a work is Good or of God goes to the heart of the conflict in Western civilization between Christianity and Hellenism. Apologists do not see any ineluctable problem, since both together would form dual religions that would coexist in the new Religion of Sports. Without a doubt, Brother Kazee's traditional faith is a religion, but so, apologists would argue, is that of the Olympics. Perhaps, but it must be admitted by apologists that the Olympic hymn represents a faith far different from that reflected in "Whispering Hope," which is not to say that the Olympic hymn has no good in it and that "Whispering Hope" is always sung by the godly.

There is "good" in the Olympic hymn but also the potential for bad as is the case in everything human, including the spiritual hymns we sing. In "Whispering Hope," the emphasis is not upon the good, the true, and the beautiful or upon the "spirit of antiquity" but upon the idea of "love" and the idea of the eternal. What the Olympic hymn does represent, though, is not

---

[26] Jones, "Old-time Baptist and Mainline Christianity," 413.

mentioned in the text—that is, it is an expression of the "sacred" as was the ancient Olympic site distinguished by the huge statue of Zeus. This is not to say that the spirit of the Olympics is either fascist or communist, but the central metaphor in it is the same beloved by both Hitler and Lenin, and that is "steel."

The Olympics, as a denomination of the modern religion of sports, is a religion of actions, works, living art, a struggle for worldly glory and for records. The rites or performances require display, a theater of acts celebrating the miracle of the human body in motion and the excellence of physical effort few of us can even imagine. Other than in tributes to the athletes, the odes of Pindar and others at the ancient Olympics and accounts by announcers and sports writers in our own time, it is not a religion of the word or words. In modern times, competition in literary and dramatic presentations have had limited appeal, like a poetry reading on Friday afternoon before a championship high school football game. In conventional religion, the emphasis is not on works or public glory but on "revealed" or holy words and inner grace.

Can grace within, which comes from total surrender to the Wholly Other, and glory without, which comes from total commitment in training for worldly recognition, coexist? Are they like peanut butter and jelly or like oil and water? Can athletics, like poetry, also reflect knowledge of the soul, even of the holy? In the imagination of the certain artists, we have to admit to this possibility. First, though, we have to look at the workings of the holy spirit in the lives of selected people in an effort to see how it relates to the minds and souls of mortals. Then we will be in a better position to evaluate its effects in art and in ethics, always, it appears, two concomitants of the holy in relation to the world of sports.

Chapter 9

Varieties of Mystical Experiences:
Old and New

Just as victory can be confused with virtue and the beautiful with the good, as in ancient Greece and modern America, so too can the enthusiasm of some television evangelists be confused with the holy. Sports have been assimilated into religious causes and now even pronounced a religion themselves because of the values they presumably promote—discipline, teamwork, and sacrifice, which are also highly valued in business, education, and war. In addition, they have in the last several years provided the milieu for a wide variety of psychic phenomena, accounts of which are growing into nothing less than a sacred corpus of writings in the Religion of Sports.

In their book, *In the Zone: Transcendent Experience in Sports*, Michael Murphy and Rhea A. White, according to the jacket advertisement, "recount moments of illumination and ecstasy, out-of-body experiences, altered perceptions of time and space, and exceptional feats of strength and endurance spanning almost the entire spectrum of sports and physical adventure, including football, basketball, tennis, sailing, mountain climbing, parachuting, and running."[1] The authors also include a bibliography of more than 1,500 stories of these "astounding occurrences" and "draw striking parallels between these uncanny experiences and those of mystics and yogis to show how the religious heritage of both East and West provide a basis for understanding spiritual experiences arrived at through physical activity." Their effort, we suspect, is much like comparing the Samurai Warrior to a Buddhist Monk and, while worthy and helpful, may leave significant room for difference between the two kinds of mysticism.

---

[1] Murphy and White, *In the Zone: Transcendent Experience in Sports* (New York: Penguin Books, 1995).

In the Zone is a revision of an earlier work by Murphy and White called *The Psychic Side of Sports: Extraordinary Stories from the Spiritual Underground of Sports*, a title that requires attention as far as the terms "psychic" and "spiritual" are concerned. Though "psychic" comes from the Greek word *psyche* for "soul," it has taken on a meaning somewhat removed from the idea of the soul as generally perceived in most religions. For better or worse, "psychics" as mediums are not called upon in most churches, especially in the South, to demonstrate powers of healing or learned examples of ecumenical wisdom gained from a passionate pursuit of gnosis either within or outside the established church. Still there remains considerable overlap between the definitions of *soul*, "the immaterial essence, animating principle, or actuating cause of an individual life, the spiritual principle embodied in human beings, all rational and spiritual beings, or the universe," and the definition of the adjective *psychic*: "lying outside the sphere of physical science or knowledge, immaterial, moral, or spiritual in origin or force."

Most of the phenomena identified by Murphy and White lie within the "hidden dimension of sports" in contrast to ritualistic displays of faith as witnessed in pre- and post-game prayer at outdoor games and in miraculous indoor feats, for example, by those who practice "Karate for Christ" or other martial arts. Televangelism is challenged to keep up with all the advances in spiritual power in the physical realm but holds its own with stunning exhibitions such as those of Benny Hinn, who with a mere command and flick of the wrist can precipitate others falling down or into the arms of assistants until the stage looks like the last act of a Shakespearean tragedy (or an unsuccessful goal line stand). Not even "the Greatest" (Muhammad Ali) had such power with so little effort. Not to fear, though, for in the Hinn show, the power that fells folks through Benny can with another command make them arise again healed and whole. We have never heard of Benny, unlike Jesus, advising anyone who has been healed not to tell about his or her experience with Hinn.

As marvelous as this talent is, it pales beside the healing at a distance regularly practiced over the tube. Jesus, disadvantaged by the absence of television in his life, never, as far as we know, attempted this except through the "comforter" or "Holy Spirit." It is interesting that what we can't see, like the "comforter" within, makes perfect sense, whereas what we see with our eyes, especially in the media, does not make sense. While we are doubtful about healing by remote control, as opposed to the idea of "touching," we have no doubt about killing at a distance, which has been perfected in the twentieth century; we can see the evidence every day in our media.

An "occupation" is defined as "an activity in which one engages," and between the ones in which we all engage—education, government, military service or other kinds of service, play, sports, religion, and work—there ought to be in the interest of all a sane and healthy interaction for which the mandalora might serve as a symbol. There are, however, limits to overlap, and we are dangerously close to those undefined barriers in our occupations, especially in the world of entertainment, sports, and religion. Kareem Abdul Jabar commented on the danger in the NBA when he said that professional basketball was becoming like professional wrestling.

Recently Cox News Service in Atlanta pointed to the limits following the stunt of Joe Horn, receiver for the New Orleans Saints, who, after scoring a touchdown in a game on 14 December 2003 against New York Giants, used his cell phone to call and make sure his family was watching, resulting in a fine of $30,000 from the league office. Previous acts of end-zone celebrations by sports celebrities, as noted by the Cox reporter, include the Ickey Woods touchdown shuffle, the Mark Gastineau sack dance, and the Dirty Bird dance by Jamal Anderson. "Gone and forgotten is the warning from Paul Brown, legendary Cleveland Browns Coach, who advised his players: When you score a touchdown, act as if you have been there before. Just give the ball to the ref and score another one."[2] The writer leaves us with a choice—go completely toward entertainment and let players break into song and dance after every first down, or put an end to such foolishness by fining the millionaires $100,000 for every dance step taken.

A heritage of another kind that helped pave the way for the conspicuous display of success, minor when compared to that of corporate executives, is the kneeling prayer of thanks in the end zone, which creates problems on the other end of the spectrum of play. In American sports it dates back to the late nineteenth century to "Mr. Football," Amos Alanzo Stagg, who coached a team called the "Christians" for the School of Christian Workers, later Springfield College, and who, as a pitcher for Yale in the 1880s, prayed (privately) before every pitch that he might do his best. Danny Wuerffel, former quarterback at Florida, prayed publicly with his hands after every (completed) pass.

---

[2] "Pro Football Clowns Ruin Game, Sport with Foolishness," *Johnson City* (TN) *Press*, 18 December 2003, 6A.

The names of teams in connection with religion are intriguing. The teams of Elon College of North Carolina are known as "Fighting Christians," but it is interesting that while teams readily adopt names from the world of nature, from tribes, and from the tradition of war to show ferocity and other primal values—indeed how "bad" they can be on the field—there are names that are unthinkable, almost taboo. We have teams named "Kings" and "Warriors" and "Knights" but no "Servants" or "Shepherds" or "Apostles" and certainly not "Lambs," a metaphor that, with shepherd, lies at the soul of Christianity. The same holds true for a term that all genuinely religious people apply to themselves, "Sinners," redeemed Sinners perhaps but still "Sinners." We think nothing of naming a team "Saints" but never "Sinners," a situation that might well revive interest in the idea of sin owing to the ambiguities and ironies that nickname might create. It would then be interesting to see whether "Sinners" would pray in the end zone or dance or both and also how announcers in the broadcast booth might react to such an individual or even a team. One can almost hear Deion Sanders or Terry Bradshaw turning to colleagues in the broadcast booth and asking, "What do you guys think the Sinners will do in this situation? Punt first or pray first?"

Team names are meant to be humorous, but there are limits as seen in the controversy following a football tournament in a Muslim football league in Irvine, California, when some teams chose names such as "Intifada," "Soldiers of Allah," and "Mujahideen." In response to the outcry, the league posted an open letter on the Internet apologizing "if anyone took offense to what was intended to simply be a positive outlet for Muslim youth." "The organizer of the tournament, 18-year-old Sabih Khan, said, "I don't understand it all. They are just words," pointing to professional teams such as the Washington Redskins, a nickname deemed offensive by some American Indian groups. The names of "Soldiers of Allah" and "Mujahideen" were changed, but the Internet letter defended the use of the word "intifada," citing the Palestinian movement. "While normally our team names appear innocent and humorous, the seriousness of our games too often keeps the fun and play at bay regardless of names."[3]

For the first time in history, we have reports of mystical experiences during play by individuals who bear such nicknames as Gophers, Wolverines, Pirates, and the like. We jest in part, never closing any possibility to the

---

[3] Chelsea J. Carter, "Soldiers of Alah on the Gridiron," <http://aolsvc.news.aol.com/news/article> (28 December 2003), 2.

interaction of individuals and the holy, regardless of situation, but we will stick by our argument that as an "occupation," sports, in spite of the talk of transcendence surrounding them, remain worldly things. In fact, sports are deluged by worldly things, but good things if managed by common sense and good will, bad things if not, as in all other human affairs. The extraordinary things that occur in them in the flow of performance are admittedly "uncanny," that is, "*seeming* to have a supernatural character or origin, that is, eerie and mysterious." It is a definition close to "magic," "an extraordinary power or influence *seemingly* from a supernatural source" (italics added). The terms "seeming" and "seemingly" are significant in the relation of sports and magic to the idea of the supernatural, suggesting the idea of "illusion," from "in-lusio" (beginning a game).

To be sure, the psychic phenomena the athlete experiences are "real" and unforgettable to him or her, but, we suspect, illusory as far as penetrating a reality beyond the body that mystics traditionally have sought and even attained, a thing utterly "inconceivable," which is a long distance even beyond the "uncanny." For glimpses into what Eliade called the "non-human cosmos" beyond time and space and matter, even beyond eternity, it would be foolish to rule out entirely the agonic moments of athletes in the heat of competition. Still, the betting is better, we think, upon the seeking mind and the feeling heart, both hungering and thirsting after knowledge of the infinite. For all we know, athletes might be more successful in this undertaking than the rest of us both on the field and off, but on the field gaining such a gift of insight is not their purpose or at least not the purpose of their teams, which is, as has been the case for millennia, to win visible prizes of their culture, usually rings, trophies, money, and applause that lingers, if only for a short while.

There are parallels between the spiritual experiences arrived at through physical activity and those reached through sitting still, but the differences are worth noting or at least suggesting. For the most part, the defining term for the athlete in a mystical state is "ultimacy" achieved at the height of performance. For the mystic surrendering the self to a higher power, the applicable term is "intimacy" with a consciousness that, even when encountered, remains beyond all human comprehension, leaving in the seeker not a memory of elation to be sought again and again but an unspeakable sense of awe and sometimes terror that opens the door to worship, gratitude (in the sense of belonging), and joy. The distinction between "ultimacy" and "intimacy" will be examined in the following chapter. Here we wish to examine "spirit" in at least two of its forms, the sporting spirit and the holy spirit.

The Thing Called "Spirit":
Monism or Dualism or Both?

Both televised sports and televised religion depend upon converts or fans, and both stress the power of "spirit." Teams get "psyched" up for the big dramatic moment, as do sinners before the altar call, and both invite victory dances whether in the end zone or the sanctuary. It is no wonder that prayer precedes games so frequently, in the dressing rooms if not on the sidelines, and no wonder either that so many sermons and services, especially those on television, seem like pep rallies. In Protestant theology and in modern sports, the spirit moveth and maketh anew. To be "born again" means not a retreat into contemplative life of meditation but a call to action, perhaps even a run for political office.

What *is* this thing called "spirit"? We are not sure humans can ever fully know. Certainly we don't. Again we turn to the dictionary for even an attempt at understanding. Of the fourteen meanings in *Webster's*, we cite the first four: "(1) An animating or vital principle held to give life to physical organisms; (2) a supernatural being or essence as Holy Spirit or Soul; an often malevolent being that is bodiless but can become visible, ghost, a malevolent being that enters and possesses a human being; (3) temper or disposition of mind or outlook especially when vigorous or animated, the immaterial intelligent or sentient part of a person; and (4) the activating or essential principle influencing a person, an inclination, impulse, or tendency of a specialized kind."

As vague and ambiguous as these definitions are, we understand that the spirit is something primal, that which moves, as the spirit in Genesis that moved over "the face of the deep." According to the law of inertia, matter is that which is at rest or remains at rest until acted upon by an outside force, but we also learn from physics that matter always generates a force or action that is opposite and equal. Similarly, spirit appears to have at least two sides, one that is animating and vital and one that is malevolent and capable of possessing a human being, perhaps what Flannery O'Connor meant by the term "malign intelligence."

The association of "spirit," "sport," and "art" through the ages does not surprise us in light of Robert Pirsig's comment in *Lila: An Inquiry into Morals* about the value associated with the "rt" morpheme in Proto-Indo-European languages as also seen in such words as "arithmetic," "worth," "rite," "ritual," "right" (handed) and "right" (correct), and "aristocrat." Also in the list of derived terms is *Arete*, the Greek name for excellence or quality as developed in *Zen and The Art of Motorcycle Maintenance*. Later the hero of the novels, Phaedrus, "discovered that even though the Hebrews were from 'across the river' and not part of the Proto-Indo European group, they had a similar term, *arhetton*, which meant 'the One' and which was considered so sacred it was not allowed to be spoken."[4] In the history of religions there are objects so sacred they can't be touched, places so sacred they can't be entered, times so sacred that all other activity stops in their honor, so there are words so sacred that they cannot even be uttered. Pirsig uses the word "sacred" in this context, which is appropriate, but we would add that every sacred object, place, time, and word, if sacred in its best sense, is a symbol of the holy, a version of the thing and not the thing itself.

In *Zen and the Art of Motorcycle Maintenance*, the key idea Pirsig examines in Western civilization is *Arete*, which he translates as "quality" and "excellence" and equates with such concepts as God, the Latin *Virtu*, and the Hindu *Dharma*. We have been tempted to add "holy" to Pirsig's distinguished list of synonyms for "quality," for certainly it is at home in such company. Yet we cannot, for the holy, while, like wisdom, is both consort and servant of the Almighty, is "less" than quality, *if* quality is the same as God. At the human level, the idea of the holy, in spite of widespread semantic abuse, still seems more distinguished than quality, which unfortunately has attained the same yawning commonplace in our culture as "leadership." Both "leadership" and "quality" have been co-opted by the establishments of power around the world for purposes of control as in "quality control" in industry and in governments' manipulation of news and numbers. The same fate may await the idea of the holy as little by little it is appropriated for political propaganda by all sides claiming superior righteousness.

Emerson said that everywhere he looked he saw dualism, but he contemplated a monism. "One spirit," he said, "animates all." Michael Novak, perhaps the bishop of sports apologists, seems to agree when he writes,

> The root of human dissatisfaction and restlessness goes as deep into the spirit as any human drive—deeper than any other drive. It is the human spirit. Nothing stills it. Nothing fulfills it. It is not a need like a hunger, a thirst, or an itch, for such needs are easily satisfied. It is a

---

[4] *Lila: An Inquiry into Morals* (New York: Bantam Books, 1991) 379.

need even greater than sex; orgasmic satisfaction does not quiet it. "Desire" is the word by which coaches call it. A driveness. Distorted, the drive for perfection can propel an ugly and considerably less than perfect human development. True, straight, and well-targeted, it soars like an arrow toward the proper beauty of mankind.[5]

The use of the term "proper beauty" is intriguing. "Beauty" is a term popular in the religion of sports and understandably since sports are unquestionably forms of art. Almost extinct in our culture is the old Judeo-Early Christian skepticism of the pagan idolization of "beauty," considering its easy and almost inevitable confusion with goodness such as we see everywhere in the modern world.

Because "spirit" is emphasized so much in present society—school spirit, sporting spirit, community spirit, national spirit (or patriotism), martial spirit, and holy spirit—without any effort to distinguish between its different forms, it is necessary to talk about a kindred concept, that of "soul." The list of meanings for "soul" is considerably shorter than that for "spirit," but in the interest of equality we will cite the first five from *Webster*, repeating in part one definition offered above: "(1) The immaterial essence, animating principle, or cause of an individual life; (2) the spiritual principle embodied in human beings, all traditional and spiritual beings, or the universe; (3) a person's total self; (4) an active or essential part, a moving spirit or leader; (5) man's moral or emotional nature, the quality that arouses emotion and sentiment, spiritual or moral force or fervor."

While the meanings of the two terms have become confused, faint differences remain, retaining much of their earliest distinctions, between, for example, the Egyptian *Knu* (spirit) and *Ba* (soul) and especially between the Greek *Pneuma* and *Psyche*. *Pneuma* is "breath," an animating force or life-giving principle. *Psyche*, on the other hand, suggests personality since Psyche was in Greek myth the personification of the soul. Spirit may come first in the nature and creation of life, but soul is the purpose it serves. Joseph Campbell might well be pointing to such differences when he says man is the servant of life but woman is life itself. According to *Webster's Unabridged*, "*spirit* often denoted the vital principle of the body as something inferior to *soul*." This is no attempt on our part to stir up strife in the world of gender, for surely in all

---

[5] Novak, *The Joy of Sports: End Zones, Bases, Baskets, Balls, and the Consecration of the American Spirit* (New York: Basic Books, 1976) 27.

individuals and in culture spirit and soul are essential for each other. This, in fact, was Whitman's primary message—that the body, vehicle of the spirit, was not greater than the soul nor the soul greater than the body. He was also one of the first, perhaps the first major American poet, to sing of the equality of women in all things, especially in terms of body (spirit) and soul.

The distinctions between *Pneuma* and *Psyche* help shed light on another dichotomy in the world of religion, particularly in Christianity—the prophetic and the mystical. *Pneuma* represents the basic principles of a prophetic religion, *Psyche* of a mystical one. The God of the prophetic religion is the "revealed God (*Deus revelatus*), the ever-active God (*Deus Semper Agens*)," while that of the "mystical piety is the hidden God (*Deus Absconditus*), the God always at rest (*Deus Semper Quietus*)." The prophetic tradition may best be summed up in the words of "Onward Christian Soldiers," the mystical by "Take Time to Be Holy." Hans Kung, drawing upon the work of Friedrich Heiler, differentiates further between them:

> The basic attitude of mystical piety is "passive, quietist, resigned, contemplative.... The mystic aims at the extinction of the emotional and volitional life, for the delight of ecstasy can be purchased only at the price of killing the will to live.... The mystic is one who renounces, resigns, is at peace."
>
> The basic attitude of prophetic piety is "active, challenging, desiring.... In prophetic experience, the emotions blaze up, the will to live asserts itself, triumphs in external defeat, and defies death and annihilation. Born of a tenacious will to live, faith, immovable confidence, reliance and trust firm as a rock, bold, adventurous hope breaks forth at last out of the bosom of tribulation and despair.... The prophet is a fighter who ever struggles upwards from doubt to assurance, from tormenting uncertainty to absolute security of life, from despondency to fresh courage of soul, from fear to hope, from a depressing consciousness of guilt to the blessed experience of grace and salvation."[6]

This prophetic tradition, more than the mystical, has characterized Protestant evangelism and on occasion made its denominations resemble

---

[6] Kung, *Does God Exist? An Answer for Today*, trans. Edward Quinn (New York: Vintage Books, 1975) 605.

competing secular teams in basketball, bowling, or softball, often generating confusion about what is important in church leagues. Prophetic piety was evident in the acrobatic exercises and preaching in the campgrounds on the American frontier, and in modern sports it finds a natural ally for its cause, the conversion of the world through the preaching of the word. However, while prophetic piety emphasizes energy, will, and action, it is not divorced from the mystical piety since the conversion act itself is a mystical experience, a still point, the lighting of the holy spirit in the heart. After the still point comes the call for action to bring others into the fold. Several Catholic orders are noted for spiritual discipline, mystical experiences that, however, commit or recommit the exercitant for service in the world. Thus for both Protestants and Catholics the prophetic and the mystical function are like diastole and systole, the infusion of the spirit and its diffusion in the world through the ones transformed.

Granted that prophetic and mystical expressions of faith are inseparable—that the relation between them is always proportional in emphasis favoring one at the expense, so to speak, of the other—we are saying that for purposes of distinction the goal of the former is *ultimacy*, as in transformation of the world through unceasing devotion to a calling and a cause, that of the latter *intimacy,* the seeking of a deeper knowledge of a personal God through private meditation and prayer. The Religion of Sports is a form of prophetic piety both in uses of athletes and athletics for purposes of proselytism in an age of television and in the publication of psychic/spiritual phenomena in sports that is intended to serve notice that athletics can provide the same type of "uncanny experience" as those of mystics and yogis in the religious heritage of the world.

We thus have two criteria for the religion of sports fulfilled: over-whelming evidence of prophecy as seen in sports as a symbol of triumphalism and the compelling argument that athletics are a means of transcendence even as the athlete is competing for a material prize. All that is needed is a history or a theodicy that scholars and theologians are beginning to provide by claiming, rightly, that sports are as old as religion, both means of preliterate folks of propitiating the gods and warding off evil, that they are no more destructive, or even not as much, as religions have been, that they are a lot more fun than going to church as should be evident in numerical comparisons of participants in one or the other. As is clear by now, our view is a skeptical one of the claim that sports are a religion on any or all of these grounds. Here though, at least for purposes of arguments, we will register our dissent against the similarities claimed by apologists between the mysticism in sports and that arrived at by those who were not participating in games when the mysticism occurred.

The crux of the problem in defining "spirit" lies in one's attitude toward the holy, that which has traditionally distinguished religion from all other human endeavors. It will become clear when we remind ourselves what the holy is, or has been, that sports, as different as they are from work and labor, scarcely qualify as an "occupation" for that distinction and perhaps not even for the designation "sacred," which is not to devalue them in the least. There is nothing wrong with the secular unless divine claims are made in its behalf or, oppositely, if it is perceived by adherents as "the only thing." It may be that the "secular" is all there is, but, true or not, the arrogance in such an attitude, matched only by narrow self-righteousness of some religions and by the cliché in sports that winning ball games is the only thing, indicates ignorance is also alive in the world. Beloved family farms or city parks are secular, not sacred or holy, but cherished nonetheless, and examples are endless.

The holy, as we shall see, is "Something" else, supranatural, transcendent, mysterious, awful, sublime, beautiful, wholly other, and as overpowering in wrath and energy as in love and joy. "Love," says one of the mystics, "is nothing else than quenched wrath."[7] That the Wholly Other exists, we moderns—riddled as we are by behaviorism, dogmatism, commercialism, materialism, patriotism of all nations and endless chatter on television—genuinely doubt, but the words of mystics themselves haunt us and suggest otherwise. Otto provides numerous instances of the encounter with the holy in *The Idea of the Holy*, which has a chapter on the "numinous," a chief feature of the holy in both the Old and New Testaments, as does *Mysticism: East and West*, but as illustration of the power of such an experience we would like to turn to an American, Jonathan Edwards, who tells what happened in his own words:

> Once as I rode out into the woods for my health in 1737, having alighted from my horse in a retired place, as my manner commonly has been, to walk for divine contemplation and prayer, I had a view that for me was extraordinary, of the glory of the Son of God, as Mediator between God and man, and his wonderful, great, full, pure and sweet

---

[7] Otto, *The Idea of the Holy: An Inquiry into the Non-Rational Factor in the Idea of the Divine and Its Relation to the Rational*, ed. John W. Harvey (New York: Oxford University Press, 1958), 24.

grace and love, and meek and gentle condescension. This grace that appeared so calm and sweet, appeared also great above the heavens. The person of Christ appeared ineffably excellent, with an excellency great enough to swallow up all thought and conception—which continued as near as I can judge, about an hour; which kept me the greater part of the time in a flood of tears, and weeping aloud. I felt an ardency of soul to be what I know not otherwise how to express, emptied and annihilated; to lie in the dust, and to be full of Christ alone: to love him with a holy and pure love; to trust in him; to live upon him; to serve and follow him; to be perfectly sanctified and made pure, with a divine and heavenly purity. I have, several, other times had views very much of the same nature, and which have had the same effects.[8]

Here, clearly, are the characteristics of the holy, the numinous and overpowering aspect of the experience, the transcendent and supernatural quality, and the weeping of the beholder of the vision. Such an instance is not apt to occur either in sports or play, since both serve different ends than those of the spiritual quest engaged in by Edwards. His own mystical experience was a taste (a confirmation) of what he already believed, which, in the view of the America that rejected him and his theology, "was too narrow and medieval," in the words of Robert D. Richardson , biographer of Emerson and Thoreau. It is probably safe to say that Edwards has the distinction of being the most versatile of all Protestant ministers in the new world. He was, it might be said, the "complete believer" in his book of the same name as opposed to Hoffer's term "True Believer," which carries a judgment that Edwards in his greatness as minister and philosopher does not deserve.

Keenly aware of his own sins yet totally dedicated in the missionary tasks he laid out for himself, Edwards was both evangelist and mystic, a believer in a God that was both revealed and hidden. He saw no conflict between them but a complete interdependence as he did in the rational use of the mind, as in philosophy, and the intuitive or nonrational, as in meditation and prayer, and even in the workings of nature and the lessons of Scripture, a correlation that still awaits revival in modern fundamentalism that is awash in the world of mammon. Says Edwards's biographer George Marsden, "The question of

---

[8] Edwards, *Selected Writings of Jonathan Edwards*, ed. Harold P. Simpson (New York: Frederick Ungar, 1970).

biblical authority, Edwards was convinced, could not be entirely settled apart from the work of the Holy Spirit, who would give people the spiritual sense intuitively to see the beauty of the truth it contained."[9]

It is tragic that Edwards's work, especially his work in philosophy such as *Freedom of the Will,* is rarely taught in American universities at any level. The conservative canard about God being banished from the schools now grates and bores, wrongheaded and misinformed in many ways, but in the case of Edwards it would be justified, especially in the colleges. Unfortunately, many religious conservatives have not heard of him and have no idea what he wrote or thought even though it would be hard to find a more conservative Christian voice in all of American history. One thing we know for sure on which Edwards would differ from many fundamental Christians is that he would see in the madness of modern sports an idolatry that might possibly make him faint with shock and disbelief, his final words before passing out, "I told you so!"

Certainly Edwards's mysticism was of a different order from that of his perhaps equally famous contemporary, Benjamin Franklin, a Pythagorean with a different vision of the cosmos from that of Edwards as suggested by his epitaph, which he wrote at age twenty-two and never changed:

The Body
Of Ben Franklin
Printer
Like the Cover of an Old Book
Its Contents Torn Out
And Stript of its Lettering and Gilding
Lies Here, Food for Worms.
But the Work Shall Not be Lost
For It Will (As He Believed) Appear Once More
In a New and More Elegant Edition
Revised and Corrected By
The Author[10]

Both Franklin and Edwards, as different as they were in temperament and philosophy, show us what an investment of mind may be required for

---

[9] Marsden, *Jonathan Edwards: A Life* (New Haven: Yale University Press, 2003) 480.

[10] See Koestler, "The Mysticism of Franklin," 685–86. *Act of Creation: A Study of the Concious and Un-Concious Processes of Humor, Scientific Discovery, and Art* (New York: MacMillan Company, 1964), 685-86.

transcendent experience of some kind, which is not to say that investment of sweat cannot also fetch wonder, as, for example, the moving account of Mike Spino in "Running as a Spiritual Experience." Says Spino,

> My running was a pouring feeling. The final horn sounded. I kept on running. I could have run and run. Perhaps I had experienced a physiological change, but whatever, it was magic. I came to the side of the road and gazed, with a sort of bewilderment, at my friends. I sat on the side of the road and cried tears of joy and sorrow. Joy at being alive; sorrow for a vague feeling of temporalness, and the knowledge of the impossibility of giving this feeling to anyone.[11]

The argument here is not to deny such narratives and certainly not to devalue them but to put the mysticism of sports in context with other kinds and to suggest contrasts where appropriate. Sometimes the contrast, judging from reports, cannot be made. Spino's experience, for example, even though he admits to the possibility of physiological stimulation and the similarity to magic, seems to exhibit several features of a holy encounter such as that of Edwards—the sense of joy and sorrow, tears, and the flood of a new understanding of self and the world. In *The Idea of the Holy*, Otto identifies features common to all forms of mysticism and the one quality that elevates one kind of mysticism over others:

> ...essentially mysticism is the stressing to a very high degree, indeed the overstressing, of the non-rational or supra-rational elements in religion; and it is only intelligible when so understood. The various phases and factors of the non-rational may receive varying emphasis, and the type of mysticism will differ according as some or others fall into the background. What we have been analyzing, however, is a feature that recurs in all forms of mysticism everywhere, and it is nothing but the "creature-consciousness" stressed to the utmost and to excess, the expression meaning, if we may repeat the contrast already made, not "feeling of our createdness" but "feeling of our

---

[11] Spino, "Running as a Spiritual Experience," in *The Sporting Spirit: Athletes in Literature and Life*, ed. Robert J. Higgs and Neil D. Isaacs (New York: Harcourt Brace Jovanovich, 1977) 135. Also see the case of Roger Bannister and the mystical in running in Allen Guttmann, *From Ritual to Record: The Nature of Modern Sports* (New York: Columbia University Press, 1978) 1–4.

creaturehood," that is, the consciousness of the littleness of every creature in face of that which is above all creatures.

A characteristic common to all types of mysticism is *Identification*, in different degrees of completeness, of the personal self with the transcendent Reality.... "Identification" alone, however, is not enough for mysticism; it must be identification with the Something that is at once absolutely supreme in power and reality and wholly non-rational. And it is among the mystics that we most encounter this element of religious consciousness.[12]

The Challenge of Identification:
Who or What Is that "Something"?

The "Identification" of the Other or rather with the Other, that is, the transcendent reality, takes many forms or goes by many names. In the passage from Jonathan Edwards cited above, the One, not surprisingly, is Christ. Often in descriptions of mystical states the reference is to God or God's Spirit. Otto refers to chapter 3, "The Reality of the Unseen," in *Varieties of Religious Experience* by William James for further evidence of his thesis of "Identification," that for instance of a clergyman who wrote,

> I remember the night, and almost the very spot on the hilltop.
> Where my soul opened out as it were to the infinite, and there was a
> rushing together of the two worlds, the inner and the outer. It was deep
> calling unto deep.... I stood alone with him who had made me, and all
> the beauty of the world, and love, and sorrow, and even temptation. I
> did not seek Him, but felt the perfect unison of my spirit with His. The
> ordinary sense of things around me faded. For the moment nothing but
> an ineffable joy and exultation remained.... The darkness held a
> presence that was all the more felt because it was not seen. I could not
> any more have doubted that *He* was there than that I was. Indeed I felt
> that myself to be, if possible, the less real of the two.[13]

James also refers to a memorandum in the letters of James Russell Lowell where the "Something" is identified as God: "I had a revelation last

---

[12] Otto, *The Idea of the Holy*, 22.

[13] Ibid., 22–23, referencing William James, *Varieties of Religious Experience: A Study in Human Nature* (New York: Collier Books, 1961) 68–69.

Friday evening. I was at Mary's, and happening to say something of the presence of spirits…Mr. Putnam entered into an argument with me on spiritual matters. As I was speaking, the whole system rose up before me like a vague destiny looming from the Abyss. I never before so clearly felt the spirit of God in me and around me. The whole room seemed to me full of God. The air seemed to waver to and fro with the presence of *something* I knew not what. I spoke with the calmness and clearness of a prophet."[14]

The Wholly Other may be a spirit or place or both, but definitely "Something" other than us yet also part of us, as Thoreau writes in "A Week on the Concord and Merrimack Rivers": "I see, smell, taste, hear, feel that everlasting *Something* to which we are allied, at once our maker, our abode, our destiny, our very Selves; the one historic truth, the most remarkable fact which can become the distinct and uninvited subject of our thought, the actual glory of the universe; the only fact which a human being cannot avoid recognizing, or in some way forget or dispense with."[15] Throughout his works, Thoreau unashamedly talks about "God," who, he says in *Walden*, will see that "we do not lack company." The "everlasting Something" he mentions could be about as close as he comes to describing attributes of God, "the one historic truth," "the most remarkable fact," "the actual glory of the universe," "the one fact which we cannot avoid recognizing, or in some way forget or dispense with." In Thoreau's view we are part of that "Something" but distinct from it the way any child is distinct from parents.

The Psychic Side of Sports by Michael Murphy and Rhea White and *In the Zone,* the revised edition, contain compelling testimony of many athletes that at first glance would lead one to think both sports and play have been underrated throughout history as far as mystical experiences are concerned. Perhaps they have, and perhaps George Leonard, author of *The Ultimate Athlete*, is also right when he says,

> Pressing us up against the limits of physical exertion and mental acuity, leading us up to the edge of the precipice separating life from death, sports may open the door to infinite realms of perception and being. Having no tradition of mystical experience, no adequate mode of discourse on the subject, no preparatory rites, the athlete might refuse

---

[14] James, *Varieties of Religious Experience*, 68, italics added.
[15] Thoreau, "A Week on the Concord and Merrimack Rivers," *Thoreau: Walden and Other Writings*, ed. Joseph W. Krutch (New York: Bantam Books) 66.

to enter. But the athletic experience is a powerful one, and it may thrust the athlete, in spite of fear and resistance, past the point of no return, into a place of awe and terror.[16]

Leonard knows that mystical states can be dangerous, a wise qualification he would see no need to make unless he were convinced of the authenticity of the psychic narratives of athletes. Neither do we doubt their authenticity. We do, though, have reservations about the apparent ease with which parallels are drawn between the cases of the "uncanny" in sports and the "inconceivable" long associated with the mystical heritage from around the world as seen in such works as *Cosmic Consciousness* by Richard Bucke, *Mysticism East and West* and *The Idea of the Holy* by Otto, and *Varieties of Religious Experience* by William James. To be sure, the language of athletes "in the zone" or maybe even transcending the zone is convincing and often extremely spiritual in tone, almost evangelical, as in the testimony of former basketball player and teacher of physical education Patsy Neal in her book *Sport and Identity*:

> There are moments of glory that go beyond the human expectation, beyond the physical and emotional ability of the individual. *Something* unexplainable takes over and breathes life into the known life. One stands on the threshold of miracles that one cannot create voluntarily…. Call it a state of grace, or an act of faith, or an act of God. It is there and the impossible becomes possible…. The athlete goes beyond herself; she transcends the natural. She touches a piece of heaven and becomes the recipient of power from an unknown source.
>
> The power goes beyond that which can be defined as physical or mental. The performance almost becomes a holy place—where spiritual awakening seems to take place. The individual becomes swept up in the action around her—she almost floats through the performance, drawing on forces, drawing on forces she has never previously been aware of.[17]

---

[16] Leonard, quoted in Murphy and White, *The Psychic Side of Sports* (Reading MA: Addison-Wesley, 1978) 133–34.

[17] Neal, *Sport and Identity*, quoted in Murphy and White, *In the Zone*, 28, italics added.

There again is that recurring term in mysticism, that "Something" or "something other" that in Neal's case takes over and "breathes life into the known life."

Continuing with reference to Neal's "spiritual awakening," Murphy and White in the following lead into what they regard as corroborative evidence from Otto in *The Idea of the Holy*.

> The athlete many times finds that things go beyond what he understands, and what he knows should happen logically. The German theologian Rudolph Otto described the human encounter with the awesome aspect of the sacred—with "that which is alien to us, uncomprehended and unexplained…that which is quite beyond the sphere of the usual, the intelligible, and the familiar, which therefore falls quite outside the limits of the 'canny' and is contrasted with it, filling the mind with blank wonder and astonishment" and a "consciousness of the absolute superiority or supremacy of a power" beyond one's self. Thus the athlete knows that being in perfect control of the football, or the puck, or the bat may be a matter more of grace than of will, and that one can only do it by letting it happen, by letting *something else* take over. And it is the awareness of and closeness to that *something else* that can lead to terror. Otto calls it the emotion of a creature, submerged and overwhelmed by its own nothingness in contrast to that which is supreme above all creatures.[18]

We wish to mention several matters in this passage from *In the Zone*. First, notice again the ongoing reference to the "something" or "something else" that takes over. Emerson expresses the same idea in his advice to live life free and with abandon, using a sporting metaphor, "be a football to chance." This too is what Bobby Bare would have us do as in his song "Drop Kick Me Jesus through the Goal Posts of Life." There seems little doubt that, just as Otto says, in all mystical experiences there is that "something," that transcendent reality that the personal self must confront, deal with, or dismiss.

Murphy and White say Otto is dealing "with the awesome aspect of the sacred," which though, is *literally not the case* From one end of Otto's book to the other, *the focus is upon the holy*, which is a different phenomenon from the sacred. It is as if sports apologists are in a conspiracy to keep from

---

[18] Murphy and White, *In the Zone*, 29, italics added.

acknowledging that Otto is investigating the idea of the holy. What is ironic is that among intellectuals and scholars, the idea of the sacred is esteemed more than the holy as is often the case with fundamentalists. Only the poets seem to applaud the holy. That the terms sacred and holy are interchangeable is a common but misleading assumption. The holy is "uncomprehended" and "unexpected." The sacred, from the pyramids to the Washington monument to Yankee Stadium, belongs to the commonplace. We know how to get to the sacred and what to do when we get there—perform some kind of ritual, tour the pyramids and take pictures, climb the Washington Monument, yell or boo in Yankee Stadium, or matter-of-factly take communion at the Methodist church. The essence of the sacred is routine that helps shape reality but not in a dramatic way unless the holy enters the scene of the sacred by surprise, itself a mystery. The events Murphy and White describe do not occur with every play in football or with every pitch in baseball. The sacred is the ordinary; the holy the extraordinary.

By speaking of the mystical in sports as holy, Murphy and White could have advanced their argument with more persuasion and been forgiven for the try, yet it, their argument, would still need qualification as we shall see in a discussion of the examples below from the world of sports and from the rich neglected heritage of mystics. It is important to remember that there is a difference between athletes having mystical experiences, if indeed the things happening to them are mystical, and mystics who have had what to most of us are extraordinary experiences on a regular basis. We are not trying to be cynical or make an iron law out of "the division of labor" when we say mystics do mysticism just as athletes do athletics, but there is some truth to the statement.

As Leonard says, though, "the athletic experience is a powerful one" and not easily discounted, if at all. Sometimes it is interwoven with conventional religious imagery and symbols, which makes analysis even more challenging, as in Neal's narration about her participation in the free-throw championship at a national AAU basketball tournament when she was a freshman in college. Having been too nervous during opening rounds to do as well as she knew she could, she prayed for help the night before the last round and after falling asleep she dreamed: "I was shooting the free-throws, and each time the ball fell through the goal, the net would change to the image of Christ. It was as though I was flowing into the basket instead of the ball. I felt endless, unhampered...and in some way I was connected to the image of Christ that kept flowing into the basket. The sensation was that of transcending *everything*. I was more than I was. I was a particle flowing into all of life."[19]

Murphy and White report that Neal won the championship, missing only two baskets out of fifty. "As a result of this and related experiences," Neal says, "I know God exists, regardless of the name we give Him, or the way we describe the way he works." Murphy and White seem to realize that the incident is ripe for criticism, even satire: "To find union with Christ shooting baskets!" To their credit, they attempt to spike such criticism with the following quotation from Saint Francis de Sales: "God requires a faithful fulfillment of the merest trifle given us to do, rather than the most ardent aspiration to things to which we are not called."[20] With no efforts on the part of authors to deceive, mystical stories from the world of sports are often cast in such a way that to doubt any aspect of them is to reflect a lack of faith in a transcendent being by the doubter.

Sports may indeed lead us into "infinite realms of perception and being," but the track record on spiritual exercises and meditation is already well established in both East and West. We do not wish to shut the door on spiritual possibilities of sports, but we will continue to play devil's advocate by arguing that the psychic experiences recorded by most athletes are really no more "uncanny" than, say, the phenomenon of synchronicity or coincidence investigated by Jung, and certainly not of a holy order. The same appears to be true of the amazing feats of strength such as that recounted in *The Psychic Side of Sports* by champion Russian weightlifter Yuri Vlasov:

> At the peak of tremendous and victorious effort…while the blood is pounding in your head, all suddenly becomes quiet within you. Everything seems clearer and whiter than ever before, as if great spotlights had been turned on.
>
> At that moment you have the conviction that you contain all the power in the world, that you are capable of everything, that you have wings. There is no more precious moment in life than this, the white moment, *and you will work very hard for years just to taste it again*.[21]

---

[19] Quoted in Murphy and White, *The Psychic Side of Sports*, 32.
[20] Ibid.
[21] Ibid., 127.

Just prior to this passage, Murphy and White quote a passage from Eckhart in which the mystic says, "no one can experience the birth of God in the soul without a mighty effort," and then they go on to say that this is "not unlike" the praise of discipline that comes from Vlasov. The praise of discipline may be similar, but the results achieved are worlds apart. What Vlasov achieves is the nature mysticism of primitive man, romantic poets, and, we would add, usually that of other athletes. "In such rare moments," says Otto, "the individual is all being, all strength, all joy, all desire, all pain in all things, inseparably." Rare as this moment is, it is the lowest stage of mysticism and a far cry from that of the Eckhart, as Otto explains in *Mysticism East and West*:

> The unbridgeable gulf set between Eckhart's mysticism and nature mysticism is that [in nature mysticism] the divine One is reached and experienced in the essence and joy of nature, while for Eckhart the very opposite holds true. He views things and the essence of things from the standpoint of the significance and value of the divine, in absolute contrast to nature. This is a spiritual, not a natural nor an aesthetic valuation.... Sankara and Eckhart seek the illimitable as spirit, as knowledge, as consciousness....[22]

The word "knowledge" is the key here. In religious tradition, some compassionate fruit must fall from the spiritual encounter with the Other as in the case of Jacob, Rumi, Saint Teresa of Avila, Paul, and Las Casas, to name only a few who have been seized by the holy.

Billie Jean King, to her credit, is probably closer to the truth of an experience such as that of Vlasov in describing her own emotions during play and after. She wanted "lots and lots of money" and to "hear the fans hoot and holler so she'd know they cared." Of her feelings after a perfect shot, she says, "My heart pounds, my eyes get damp, and my ears feel like they're wriggling, but it's also just totally peaceful. It's almost just like having an orgasm—it's exactly like that."[23] Having an orgasm may be different from "the white moment" but not as different as both are from the encounter with the holy as related by religious mystics through the ages in all climes and conditions. It

---

[22] Otto, *Mysticism East and West*, 93–94.

[23] King, quoted in Robert Lipsyte, *Sports World: An American Dreamland* (New York: Quadrangle, 1975) 280.

might appear that we are being too skeptical of the mysticism in sports but not as much, we would venture to say, as Otto concerning the validity of the mystical experience in religions.

The Dancer and the Dance and the
Player and the Play:
Nature Mysticism or Divine?

In the case of the uncanny in sports, it is not so much a matter of authenticity of the cases as of category and comparison with other forms of mysticism. For instance, we believe Gerardus Van der Leeuw sees a nature mysticism almost sexual or erotic in primitive rituals. When the masked dancer becomes one with "the being that is represented by him," Van der Leeuw calls it "a new path to the *other*, the holy."[24] This may be a good illustration among primitive societies of the complete overlap of vehicle (the dancer) and tenor (the Other) so that a holy *identification* ensues. Still, when dancer and creator of dance are one, that union is not necessarily reflective of the idea of a Wholly Other as envisioned by mystics in more recent stages of human consciousness. It may well be the same nature mysticism that Robert E. Neale praises so highly. "The sacred," he says, is "never encountered purely as power.... The sacred is present in a stone, tree, star, or building; in a leader, murderer, secret society, or conquering tribe." It is, he says, always evident in *"powerful form."*[25]

Judging from testimony, *the sacred may always be present in powerful form,* one of the problems in worshiping objects or having beliefs in visible gods, *but the holy does not require visible form such as a dancer or athlete to make its presence known.* The word or whisper still works. This may be the chief difference between the sacred and the holy. There are powerful accounts in which the "wholly other" is anything but form and shape. Says a master, "therefore it is (rightly) called a word. But what it was, was hidden from me (an inconceivable idea). Therefore, it is said: 'It comes in a whisper, in a silence, to reveal itself.' It appeared and was yet hidden."[26]

---

[24] Van der Leeuw, *Sacred and Profane Beauty: The Holy in Art*, trans. David E. Green (New York: Holt, Rinehart, and Winston, 1963) 19.

[25] Neale, *In Praise of Play: Toward a Psychology of Religion* (New York: Harper and Row, 1970).

[26] Otto, *Mysticism East and West*, 43.

What are the implications of the difference between nature mysticism and the kind Otto speaks of as "divine"? Quite possibly it is the difference between expansion of ego on the one hand and retreat of self before the infinitude of the Other. It is the difference between ecstasy of power (or maybe even drunkenness of power) at the limits of physical excellence and the reverential awe of the surrendered self. The mysticism of the Nazis was a nature mysticism in which adherents sought more and more power in the name of their *power form* (Hitler) but knew nothing of simple humility.

"Whoever truly serves beauty serves God," says Gerardus Van der Leeuw.[27] While the word "truly" can help defend the statement against several charges, it should be remarked that beauty comes in many strange packages; the parade, the games, and even the dance are forms of sacred beauty and action, but they are not always forms of virtue. In fact, more often than not, they are expressions of pride rather than of humility that results following a head-on encounter with the holy. Van der Leeuw convincingly cites several sources, not just Gnostic, in which dance is taken as "the movement of God."[28] Catherine Cleveland, though, seems to enter a cautionary note in her description of "holy dancing" during the "Second Great Awakening," drawing upon firsthand accounts:

> Rev. Mr. Lyle reported that he saw several young women leaping most nimbly at Point Pleasant in 1803. A young girl sprang a dozen times nearly two feet from the ground notwithstanding she was held by the hands.... The dancing is described as a gentle, not ungraceful, movement, with little variety in the step to the accompaniment of a lively tune. Some of those subject to visions declared that as they entered upon the heavenly scenes their whole soul and body were perfumed with a peculiar fragrance, which rendered everything mortal disagreeable or unsavory. Under the influence of this singular perfume, which seemed to answer the scriptural notion of the smell of Christ's garments from the ivory palaces and all the powders of the merchant, "they would swoon away three or four times a day, recover, rise and dance round with incarnate and elevated springs."[29]

---

[27] *Sacred and Profane Beauty*, 19.

[28] Ibid.

[29] Cleveland, *The Great Revival in the West, 1791–1805* (Chicago: University of Chicago, 1916) 102–103.

Of course dancing as religious ecstasy was not a new phenomenon in the nineteenth century. The whirling dervishes of Kona, Turkey, dating back to the thirteenth century when they were founded by the great philosopher and poet Mevlana Celaleddin Rumi, seem notable examples of the way art and religion can work in unison in the creation of a sacred or holy ritual as the case may be. One of us having witnessed the dervishes in Kona, we wish to grant them their claim that in their dance they are in communication between heaven and earth as symbolized by the use of palms in receiving grace from above and imparting the same to our planet. Yes, it is a sacred performance and a compelling one, though a certain streak of skepticism remains about its holiness when we consider that the dervishes are getting paid, not unlike the professional athletes having uncanny moments and making money in the process. While there is nothing wrong in payment for professional excellence in dance and athletics, the question remains: can we make money at what we do and talk with God at the same time? Perhaps; perhaps not. Possibly the holy requires "time out" from whatever zone we might be in before beginning a conversation. Nonetheless, Catherine Cleveland contends that throughout Christian history, dancing emerges periodically as an almost uncontrollable and visionary expression.[30]

We do not wish to discredit dancing or the use of the body as a way of worship. David danced before the ark of the covenant. Dance is expressive of joy and could even have a place again in ritual worship but we would suggest as a vehicle rather than vehicle and tenor both. The danger always is mistaking the movement for the mover, the symbol for the thing symbolized. Keeping that distinction in mind requires consciousness. Henry James has said that in the novel, "incident is character"; in the case of God, this observation is certainly open to doubt. One should, in arriving at a fuller picture, consider not merely the spirit that "moves" us physically in dance or play or emotionally in response to art but also the spirit that has "spoken" directly to the "chosen" among us over the ages in exalted states of the soul. God is not just a choreographer but a speaker as well—and much else needless to say.

Belief in the sanctification of action, the glorification of bodily movement, helps devalue the written and spoken word in our society, especially among athletes and many others who can read but who choose not to. The confusion of nature with the divine has been one of the crucial problems of our times, and sports theorists have not shed a great deal of light

---

[30] Ibid., 104–105.

upon that all-important distinction, though they have rushed in to show similarities in such numbers as to make play theology a new cult. On the one hand, the ordinary person is caught between the alignment of muscular Christians and sports apologists such as Bobby Bowden, Jerry Falwell, Michael Novak, Charles Prebish, and on the other hand, the celebrants of play such as David Miller, Robert Neale, Sam Keen, and Jurgen Moltmann. We ordinary folk don't know whether to watch the Super Bowl or jog. If we want to worship or have contact with the divine, it might be best to do neither but to go into a nearby closet and pray in the manner of one's choosing, including Emerson's idea of praying as the contemplation of facts from the highest point of view, or to take a walk in the nearest woods. What might get confused in all these schools are joy and pleasure, themes we earlier discussed but would now like to reflect on again in connection with mysticism.

In our age of material girls and boys, the distinctions are so blurred that one does not settle for pleasure in sex or in a bottle of Bud, but must have "joy" instead, a religious transfiguration. For example, much has been written in recent years, as mentioned earlier, on the joy of sports and the joy of sex, both being titles of books, as well as *More Joy of Sex* and everywhere we look we see what appears to be more joy of sports, which apparently is only available to winners or in winning traditions. What has happened is that joy, traditionally a religious term, has been appropriated by writers in the secular realm in order to elevate, if not sanctify, activities that in themselves were always considered worldly and pleasurable. Sex, however, has been used as a means of nature mysticism as much as sports, and religious claims have been made for both that would have astonished the most liberal of saints.

Pleasure and joy have often been used indiscriminately, but the difference between them, until recently, has been clear. Pleasure derives from expansion or indulgence of the self in sports, play, sex, fantasy, eating, drinking, etc.; joy, by contrast, comes from relation with or worship of the Other, from giving due homage and praise, and on rare occasions from encounter with the holy. Pleasure, if carried to excess, is sinful, hence invariably predictable, which is why the church has always made provisions for pleasure. Joy, however, is always a surprise and comes, so the mystics tell us, after great effort—spiritual effort as opposed to physical, though asceticism may be a factor in both. So may bodily movement, proponents of "flow" and "zone" theories may remind us. Those who trust the "flow" and "zone" methods of mystical experiences may reiterate to us, and rightly so, that Eckhart has "dancing shoes" as well as an "inward organ."

In mystical experiences, an element of surprise is so common that it ceases to be surprising, a reminder that foreknowledge of action of the holy is unavailable. Even what passes for joy may be deceptive, as Loyola learned from instructions on discernment coming from Christ via St. Catherine of Siena. Says Christ to the saint, "If you ask me how you are to recognize what comes from the devil and what comes from me, I answer that this is the sign for your guidance—if the idea comes from the devil, the soul receives all at once a feeling of lively joy; but the longer the state lasts, the more the joy diminishes, and leaves you in weariness, confusion and darkness—But if the soul is visited by me, the Eternal Truth, it is, at the outset, seized with holy fear and subsequently receives gladness, sweet prudence, and the desire for virtue."[31] The test is not so much in the nature of the original encounter, not in the spirit, but in the fruits thereof and even the lastingness of that fruit.

As yet there have not been too many instances of seizures of holy fear on the playing field. Until there are more reports of the same, the mysticism of sports and play will need to be regarded with a skeptical eye as well as all shouts of "joy" coming from the stadium or playground. Joy claimed from sports should be compared (or contrasted) with that mentioned by the scientist Pascal in describing his famous "night of fire":

> In the year of the Lord, 1654, Monday, November 23, from 10:30 p.m. until half past twelve, fire.
> God of Abraham, God of Isaac, God of Jacob; not of the philosophers and the scholars. Certainty. Certainty. Certainty. Feeling. Joy. Peace.
> Joy! Joy! Tears of Joy![32]

The distinction between joy and pleasure could not be more clear, even by implication, than in Aquinas's commentary on Aristotle's *Nicomachean Ethics*: "As man needs from time to time to rest and leave off bodily labors, so also his mind from time to time must relax from its intense concentration on serious pursuits: This comes about through play.... Those who go to excess in

---

[31] Henri Joly, *St. Ignatius of Loyola*, trans. Mildred Partridge (New York: AMS Press, 1976) 16.
[32] Pascal, quoted in de Riencourt, *The Eye of Shiva: Eastern Mysticism and Science* (New york: William Morow, 1980), 157.

merrymaking…are not softened by the pleasure of play."[33] Once again, as the church fathers have taught, rest relaxes the body; play (in moderation) the mind and soul. Hence play is a pleasure, but hardly a joy that may belong to another order. There is only one disconcerting aspect of Pascal's revelation and that is in the chant of "Certainty. Certainty. Certainty." From surveying the current scene, it appears to us that many who have never even heard of mysticism are every bit as certain in their beliefs as Pascal was after his famous "night of fire." One thing seems certain about certainty—sooner or later those who are "certain" are at war, pulling into the conflict with them those who may have all kinds of doubts about endeavors at hand.

The Play of God in the Mystical Event

There is, admittedly, little doubt that play is closer to the idea of the holy than is sports competition. One cannot imagine God competing, at least as men do, while play seems a fitting activity as David Miller argues in quoting Eckhart:

> This play was played eternally before all natures. As it is written in the Book of Wisdom, "Prior to creatures, in the eternal now, I have played before the Father in an eternal stillness." The Son has eternally been playing before the Father as the Father has before the Son. The playing of the twain is the Holy Ghost in whom they both disport themselves and he disports himself in both. Sport and players are the same. Their nature proceeding in itself. "God is a fountain flowing into itself," as St. Dionysius says.[34]

Eckhart, Miller believes, has achieved the view of God as a player, which is what human beings and the church both need to do, he argues. This is a compelling argument, but there are qualifications we would like to register. It should be noted that while Eckhart sees trinity at play, he himself is *still*. True, the experience he has is not, as Otto says, "a work," but it is something other than "experience," the term most often used in description that is loaded in

---

[33] Quoted in Hugo Rahner, *Man at Play*, trans. Brian Battershaw and Edward Quinn (New York: Herder and Herder, 1972) 99. For more on the comparison and contrast of pleasure and joy, see chapter 3 in Mihaly Csikszentmihalyi, *Flow: The Psychology of Optimal Experience* (New York: Harper and Row, 1999).

[34] Miller, *Toward a Theology of Play* (New York: World, 1979) 158.

favor of the idea of play. Mysticism, especially that of the high order of
Eckhart and Sankara, however, is as much a matter of vision as experience, as
Otto claims in *Mysticism East and West*.

> The real knowledge is that which (Sankara) calls "one's own
> vision"—darsanam. This vision for him, as knowledge for Eckhart, is
> not a matter of "having visions." It is rather an awareness of identity
> with Brahma, and that as an "intuitus," a dawning of insight, our own
> clear-sighted realization of that which the scriptures taught. This
> awareness cannot be "produced," we cannot reason it out. It is not a
> "work." It comes or does not come independently of our will. It must
> be seen. The way may be prepared by the words of the Vedas and by
> meditation (*pratyaya*) on them, but in the end it must be our own
> vision. It dawns like an apercu (Goethe) and as soon as it is perceived,
> the Vedas becomes superfluous. Study and reflection then cease....[35]

Just as study and reflection cease, so too does play, both of the mind and
the body. "When the confusing play of ideas (Chittam) has come to rest and he,
thus, through himself, through the purified 'inward organ' apprehends the
Highest, which is wholly spirit, essentially light, then he wins through to
joy."[36] Jacob Boehme makes the same point when he says, "Blessed are thou
therefore if thou canst stand still from self-thinking and self-willing, and canst
stop the wheel of thy imagination and senses."[37]

The message is clear: God may be at play, but play may not necessarily
be the way to know him. Worship, meditation, and study may still be the safest
ways, all of which imply a focused attention or perhaps a relaxed state of
concentration. To know God, God the player, if play theorists prefer, it may
well be necessary to sit still as the psalmist advised—or at least walk slowly
like Thoreau, sauntering to the holy land with each step taken.

Well before William James, Otto, and Carl Jung, Thoreau was saying
the same things as they about the ways of knowing and relating to the Other.
As a mystic, which he claimed to be, he was constantly seeking the
inexplicable delight he found in the presence of the "everlasting Something"
on his daily "saunters," as he remarks in his essay "Walking":

[35] Otto, *Mysticism East and West*, 51.
[36] Ibid., 52.
[37] De Riencourt, , 113.

I have met with but one or two persons in the course of my life who understood the art of Walking, that is, of taking walks—who had a genius, so to speak, for which word is beautifully derived "from idle people who roved about the country, in the Middle Ages, and asked charity, under pretense of going *à la Sainte-Terrer*," to the Holy Land, till the children exclaimed, "There goes a Sainte-Terrer," a Saunterer, a Holy-Lander. They who never go to the Holy Land in their walks, as they pretend, are indeed mere idlers and vagabonds; but they who do go there are saunterers in the good sense, such as I mean. Some, however, would derive the word from sans terre without land or a home, which, therefore, in the good sense, will mean, having no particular home, but equally at home everywhere. For this is the secret of successful sauntering. He who sits still in a house all the time may be the greatest vagrant of all; but the saunterer, in the good sense, is no more vagrant than the meandering river, which is all the while sedulously seeking the shortest course to the sea. But I prefer the first, which, indeed, is the most probable derivation. For every walk is a sort of crusade, preached by some Peter the Hermit in us, to go forth and reconquer this Holy Land from the hands of the Infidels.[38]

As in the writing of Edwards and throughout *Walden*, the holy is equated with awakening. "So we saunter toward the Holy Land," Thoreau concludes in "Walking," "till one day the sun shall shine more brightly than ever he has done, shall perchance shine into our minds and hearts, and light up our whole lives with a great awakening light, so warm and serene and golden as on a bank-side in Autumn."[39] The holy may be experienced directly, but there is a real question as to whether or not it can be effectively related to others without the use of metaphor. Logic and doctrine need not apply for that challenge. The holy land is everywhere at once, and if we are to ever know it, we must be still, even still inside, though he might be walking or running, the idea, perhaps, of "rest most busy."

---

[38] Thoreau, "Walking," *The Natural History Essays*, intro. Robert Sattelmeyer (Salt Lake City: Gibbs-Smith Publisher, 1980) 93–94.

[39] Ibid., 135–36.

If we are to sit still in wonder before the play of God, play being only *one* characteristic, when is there justification for play among ourselves? When the mind and soul need rest and pleasure. A splendid example of man at play may be seen in Dr. Samuel Johnson, who once set himself rolling down a grassy hill like "a great laughing brown ball," in the words of Heywood Hale Broun in *Tumultous Merriment*, one of Johnson's definitions of "sport", and at the bottom "arose hay-streaked and refreshed."

Play also refreshed Thoreau, the refreshment being evident in his *Journal* of his own fox chase.

> Suddenly looking down the river, I saw a fox some sixty rods off making across the hills on my left. As the snow lay five inches deep, he made but slow progress, but it was no impediment to me. So yielding to the instinct of the chase, I tossed my head aloft, and bounded away, snuffing the air like a foxhound, and spurning the world and human society at each bound. It seemed the woods rang with the hunter's horn, and Diana and all the satyrs joined in the chase and cheered me on. Olympian and Elean youths were waving palms on the hills. In the meantime, I gained rapidly on the fox, but he showed a remarkable presence of mind, for instead of keeping up the face of the hill, which was steep and unwooded in that part, he kept along the slope in the direction of the forest, though he lost ground by it. Notwithstanding his fright, he took no step which was not beautiful. The course on his part was a series of most graceful curves. When he doubled, I wheeled and cut him off, bounding with fresh vigor, Antaeus-like recovering my strength each time I touched the snow. Having got near enough for a fair view, just as he was slipping into the wood, I gracefully yielded him the palm.[40]

In spite of Thoreau's references to cheering of the gods and goddesses, all pagan, he did not intend this experience to be regarded as divine. Divinity he sought in his hours of contemplation as he walked or sat perfectly still in his doorway and as he "sauntered." Neither did Dr. Johnson confuse play with meditation. To him worship was a separate category. Man was an animal who played, but he was also "a worshiping animal." He could hardly do both at the same time. In any event, both men are examples of the forgotten virtue of

---

[40] "The Journal," *Thoreau: Walden & Other Writings*, 424.

eutrapelia as described by Hugo Rahner in *Man at Play*. Both could "turn" from play to seriousness with relative ease, but both would have been bewildered by the call for a "theology of play." To them, religion meant worship or meditation, the reward of which was joy.

Thoreau, perhaps better than his church-going neighbors, after 1841 when he ceased attending church, knew the real meaning of the old Westminster Catechism: "The chief end of man is to worship God and enjoy Him forever." Thoreau loved the wild (nature) no less than the good (divine), but he would never have confused the two or mixed them up into what Miller calls *spoudogeloios*, the absence of distinction, being as he was a transcendentalist instead of, like Emerson, a believer in immanence. Neither, of course, would Dr. Johnson, who was not even enamored of the wild as was Thoreau. For Thoreau, the universe was not created "in jest." He was a great humorist but no more a worshiper of humor than he was of sports or play. Humor, irony, and paradox, as we shall see, are ways of keeping us humble and distinct from the Other, whose purposes cannot be limited to all that is meant by either jest or seriousness or any other human qualification one might want to employ.

The problem with the theses of Miller, Neale, Van der Leeuw, and others lies in their praise of celebration of the "original unity" of religion and dance and their lament over the essential breakup of unity. Dissolution of primitive or pagan unity is simply an evolutionary law of life, a prerequisite for deeper unities in which the encounter with the Other is based not upon physical experience alone but consciousness as well. The problem of our times is not so much that we have lost touch with the rhythms of our bodies, but that we have lost faith in intellectual or spiritual possibilities such as, for example, those pointed out by Chardin in *The Future of Man*. To lament the original unity of functions is to reduce God to immanence where he can be anything or to reduce him altogether as did Henry Adams, the most famous lamenter on the death of unity in his *Education*. It is also to diminish or ignore the rich and powerful accounts of the many mystics who have not only felt the presence of God, but "seen" "Him" with their "inward organ."

Another who achieved *eutrapelia* is Loren Eiseley, a spiritual descendent of Thoreau who also had an encounter with a fox, one that was, we suspect, truly holy, but that also needs to be put in perspective lest it be assumed that the encounter was experience only, devoid of vision, and hence a justification for belief in immanence.

On one of his many excursions in the natural world, Eiseley came upon a young fox under the timbers of a foundered boat. The fox "innocently" placed a chicken bone in his mouth and shook it at the author invitingly while placing his forepaws appealingly together. "Gravely," Eiseley did likewise with a whiter bone, facing the fox and arranging his own forepaws appropriately. "Round and round," he says, "we tumbled for one ecstatic moment." For Eiseley, it was the gravest, most meaningful act he would ever accomplish, leading him to a view of the universe "as it begins for all things. It was, in reality, a child's universe, a tiny and laughing universe."[41]

Here on the surface appears justification for the play theology of Miller, Neale, and others, but again modification is required. Certainly the incident could never have happened without a playful attitude on the part of the author. Neither could it have happened without the intellectual curiosity of a poet and scientist. It is this intellectual content that the play theologians overlook in their talk of psychic harmony and "seeing" with the whole body. Mysticism, in spite of the new emphasis on body knowledge, has always included a significant mental aspect that is not equivalent to an aspect of formal education. Eiseley did indeed experience something, shuffling around on all fours with a bone in his mouth with the innocent fox, but he also *beheld* something. God may be in the universe in other words but is also above it and breathing through its pores, an idea best expressed by the term "panentheism," which means God is both immanent and transcendent.[42] The universe may be "a laughing universe," but it is also much more than that as is the Other who remakes it forever.

Perhaps this explains why so many mystics, though not all, have been individuals of soaring passion and intellect, not in the normal sense of "being educated" but in the sense of seeking and caring: St. Paul, St. Augustine, St. Ignatius, Pascal, Jonathan Edwards, Walt Whitman, and perhaps most notably, Sankara and Eckhart. On this matter, Otto is clear in *Mysticism East and West*:

> The special character of both masters is that of an intellectual and not of an emotional mysticism...theirs is a knowledge which is to be translated into a comprehensible doctrine with all the aids of proof, scholarly presentation and keen dialectic. Indeed, we are confronted with an almost unbelievable spectacle: both these heralds of the absolutely non-rational, inconceivable, and incomprehensible Godhead which escapes all definition and before which "words and

---

[41] Eiseley, *The Unexpected Universe* (New York: Harcourt Brace Jovanovich, 1969) 210.

[42] See William J. Wolf, *Thoreau, Mystic, Prophet, Ecologist* (Philadelphia: United Church Press, 1974) 172–73.

understanding recoil," become the most critical theorists, the strictest of scholastics, and create a language and dogma of rigid formulas.[43]

Unfortunately, Otto says in a footnote, the followers of Sankara become rationalistic and dialectic until "feeling is almost crushed out," a familiar story in the history of religions.[44]

Sports may be considered a type of tribal or natural religion in the manner of Michael Novak in *The Joy of Sports*, but what gets shortchanged in such religion is consciousness itself. The individual is called upon to surrender the ego, individual consciousness that is, to the group. He or she is asked to become a "fan" and to take up all the totemic practices fandom entails, such as getting "the spirit" or "fever" and painting one's face. We once met a Clemson fan with little tiger paws on her eyeglasses, and she told us of someone else who had them on their molars—a "Tiger grin," which is close to the spirit of sport but not the holy spirit as traditionally perceived. For all we know, every Clemson fan the world over may throughout the fall weeks dwell in the holy spirit by means of the rituals chosen for that purpose, but on Saturdays they may dwell in another kind of spirit, which is quite all right as long as it stays within the boundaries of human law and its nature understood and appreciated for what it is—a means of play while watching sports, which contain an element of play yet are different in essence from it and from religion and the holy.

---

[43] Otto, *Mysticism East and West*, 48–49.
[44] Ibid., 49.

Chapter 10

The Holy and the "Flow": Ultimacy Versus Intimacy

Football weekends and tailgate parties started on the American frontier with the covered wagon at the camp meeting and, in spite of all excesses, they have quietly enjoyed the blessing of the church ever since. The spirits of the fruit, however, are quite different from the fruit of the spirit, though on the frontier it was sometimes difficult to tell the difference. The more our sporting system moves toward machinery, away from the natural spontaneity of frontier play, the more applause the fans are apt to register, drunk or sober. The well-oiled machine, especially in football, is the goal toward which coaches work and the metaphor they frequently employ.

How is it, then, that mystical experiences among athletes have proliferated as our games have become increasingly organized and mechanical, shedding the exuberance of frontier sports for the serious, rigid discipline necessary for victory in our obsessive society? Says Charles Prebish, who teaches religion at Penn State, "My work with athletes convinces me completely that ultimate experience occurs regularly in sport."[1] We want to emphasize the word *completely*, for it is a favorite term of Prebish. "For me," he says, "it is not just a parallel that is emerging between sports and religion, but rather a *complete identity. Sport is religion* for growing numbers of Americans, and this is no product of simply facile reasoning or wishful thinking."[2] Other terms that proliferate in Prebish's writing are *ultimate* and *total*. There is no mandalora here but total overlap. Here is the same type of certainty often visible on television that daily brings us news from heaven.

---

[1] Prebish, *Religion and Sport: The Meeting of the Sacred and Profane* (Westport CT: Greenwood Press, 1993) 68.

[2] Ibid., 62.

We cannot bring ourselves to agree with Prebish, one of the founding fathers of the religion of sports, even after granting him his definition: Religion is the experience of "ultimate reality" that radically changes the individual.[3] The main questions here are (a) What is ultimate reality? and (b) What is the nature of the change in the individual undergoing the transformation? Is war a religion since VA hospitals are full of people who have been radically changed in their combat experiences? In traditional religions there are degrees of mysticism, and even the language of the highest order, at least in the West, tends to suggest a vision of God as well as an experience of God, as de Riencourt points out. In other words, as awesome and terrifying as the mystical encounter may be, before which "words and understanding recoil," there is far more spiritual energy beyond human grasp, so much that we cannot imagine it and would be overwhelmed if allowed much more than a glimpse. This is not to say there is no ground to our being, but only that we are naïve to talk so glibly about its nature and accessibility. Thoreau warned us about this naïveté near the end of *Walden*: "There is a solid bottom everywhere. We read that the traveler asked the boy before him if the swamp had a hard bottom. The boy replied that it had. But presently the traveler's horse sank in up to the girths, and he observed to the boy, 'I thought you said this bog had a hard bottom.' 'So it has,' answered the latter, 'but you have not got half way to it yet.'"

On the Nature of Prizes and Gifts: Two Types of Athletae Dei

As the issue of spirit relates to the religion of sports, the question is this: Do the sporting spirit and the Holy Spirit have a common source? We suspect that they do, which is not to say that they are the same nature. Rather, it might be said that they are the same but different (*eadem sed aliter*). What determines the difference is the "taste" in the mind and soul, what one wants or needs for fulfillment as perceived by self, which determines the direction of the human quest and the intensity of it and the commitment to it. One writer, John P. Sisk, has summarized the similarities and differences between the two in his discussion of asceticism, which some regard as a natural ally of sports as well as of rigorous spiritual discipline:

> Helen Waddell writes in *The Desert Fathers* that "asceticism had not traveled far from the *ascesis*, the training of the athlete, and the fathers themselves to their contemporary biographers are the *athletae*

---

[3] Ibid., 139.

Dei, "the athletes of God." Austerity was not an end in itself, however it was cultivated. Waddell quotes Dorotheus the Theban's ancient formula, "I kill my body for it kills me." To the Fathers the killing of the body meant the liberation of spirit for holy living and holy dying; to the Greek Olympic athlete it meant a triumphant return home and possibly a celebration by Pindar; to the Green Bay Packers, Vince Lombardi's ascetics, it meant two Super Bowls.[4]

Fundamentally, the Desert Fathers, those adjudged sincere, as opposed to those showing off, were seeking invisible prizes; professional athletes visible ones. Paul and any number of ancient writers knew that the key to all human activity lay in the nature of prizes. He and others admired the training and dedication of the athlete who was exemplary even in pursuit of an earthly prize. How much greater should be the dedication of those that sought an everlasting one? The spirit within, it appears, is not absolutely set upon one course of action but is flexible, depending upon our human choosing and the commitment we bring to the choices we make regarding rewards.

The athlete, no matter how skilled and talented, is always one of us, seeking recognition in this world in addition to whatever virtues of another kind he or she might possess. In essence, there is no difference between the drive of an NFL team to win a third Super Bowl and that of academic institution to break records in endowment through alumni giving and market investment in order to maintain traditions of excellence. In a capitalistic society, both are "sacred" endeavors but, as far as we can see, unrelated to the holy. This is not to inveigh against capitalism in order to elevate socialism or communism or monarchy. All are things of Caesar, which Jesus did not indict outright but suggested they are not things of God—not evil things necessarily but by no means holy, as, we suspect, fewer things are than we normally imagine.

In the halls of academe, "publish or perish" is the sacred credo and every bit as destructive as the athletic department's "winning is the only thing." Both axioms reveal how fragmented and unholy our schools have become, not in relation to the doctrines of churches but in relation to common sense. Both "publish or perish" and "winning is the only thing" are warped, the definition of heresy, in relation to the idea of the whole person that universities ought to endeavor to produce rather than technicians of the body or the mind. Both

---

[4] "Hot Sporting Blood," *Intellectual Digest* 4 (November 1973): 46–47.

mottos use the spirit within us as a means to an end, the world of prizes—sports by getting us "all fired up" and academics by lighting within us "the lamp of learning."

The idea of "awakening" the soul to the pleasures of play, as opposed to the delirium of winning, and the joys of discovery, as opposed to being the brightest bulb in the class, now seems like a sentimental anachronism from the unenlightened past. Education has become a matter of competition for cultural prizes rather than common pursuit of discovery of the gifts within the soul and in the mind of God, the idea that motivated Einstein and other geniuses over the ages. We have much respect for the idea of "edification" as presented in Scripture, the notion of "living stones" working together to build a "great spiritual temple of God" (Eph 2:20–22; 1 Pet 2:5), but temples are at best sacred, the structures of others' "symbols of faith" that we often tear down in order to build up our own.

What we cannot tear down is the earth on which all temples sit, the earth of the holy, not the holy itself but work of the holy, which provides us with another metaphor for education: "digging down" rather than building up. In the right spirit, both may be the same thing, if the spiritual temples we seek to build are not primarily for purposes of displaying our moral superiority. Such an attitude is perhaps a worse sin than display of superior intellect and athletic talent, and our private schools, colleges, and universities, even those with a religious affiliation, are not always sterling examples of humility or concern for the overall good of society in that regard. Whether we are talking about body, mind, or soul, these examples of invidious pride now become a virtue instead of the unpardonable sin. They are all around us and nowhere so visible as in religious institutions that claim to have all the answers.

In the endeavor to compare and contrast different branches of spiritual energy, that serving self-gratification and its opposite that seeks to enlighten the soul, we can be well instructed by the models identified and described by Shirl J. Hoffman in his essay, "Nimrod, Nephilim, and the *Athletae Dei*." Drawing on Kenneth Vaux's article "How Do I Love Me?" Hoffman observes that Nimrod's warriors "through sheer exercise of power...bend or break another's body to feed, fuel or gratify oneself, one's clan or nation. He is the god of violence and terrorism, the god of unwarranted aggression on another.... The Nephilim cult of bodily perfection is humans seeking to be gods by exploiting science and technology."[5]

There are two types of *athletae dei* ("athletes of God") as envisioned by Hoffman. He distinguishes between the ancient ones in the fourth century A.D. who went to the desert to meditate and find God and modern players who seek God in natural places. His comparisons and contrasts are instructive. "In their insistence on solitude and isolation, the ancient *athletai dei* underestimated the power of religious contemplation to 'draw the widest range of human activity within its hallowing orbit'...the ability of one to gather unto himself solitude at the center of furious physical activity. The modern *athletai dei*, unlike their spiritual forefathers seems intuitively to have recognized the possibility of this 'rest most busy,' the untapped potential of sport as a contemplative experience."[6]

For Hoffman, sport as a religious experience is not centered on what we call "territorial sports" with their heavy baggage of primitive rites. Says Hoffman, "Sport as a religious experience, if it can be a religious experience, is sport in the desert so to speak, sport on the playground and in the backyards, where the environment encourages the soul to play itself into the body rather than forcing it to maintain a healthy distance. Sport for religious experience is side-by-side non-contact sport, not face-to-face contact sport, because it must if to be successful, afford the body the same dignity it affords the soul."[7]

No argument is made here, we must keep insisting, that athletes of whatever degree of skill cannot experience the holy either in running alone or even in face-to-face sports. The position taken is that the aim in territorial sports is not knowledge of or experience of the holy. Teams in these sports seek a public victory over nature or others, a cultural prize. After all these millennia, the fact probably remains that one seeking salvation of the soul gains a victory not over others but over self and the world, a spiritual gift. Evidence of the cults of Nimrod and Nephilim is all around us, and we have paid them perhaps the highest worldly tribute of all by establishing an ongoing comic opera in their honor called professional wrestling. Concerning the struggle in every mind and soul over the definitions of prizes, or the difference between prizes and gifts, it might be argued that here too "winning is the only thing," but that is not what the cliché means in business, sports, and war. It

---

[5] Hoffman, *Sport and Religion*, ed. Shirl J. Hoffman (Champaign: Human Kinetics, 1992) 281–82.

[6] Ibid., 284.

[7] Ibid.

means, just as it says, victory over competitors or over external nature, often resulting in a sacred honor. Victory of the soul over ego or self or both or of hope over sorrow, if ever achieved or even if sought, is without public fanfare or even knowledge as Emily Dickinson makes clear.

> To fight aloud, is very brave—
> But *gallanter*, I know,
> Who charge within the bosom,
> The Cavalry of Woe.

> Who win, and nations do not see,
> Who falls, and none observe,
> Whose dying eyes no Country
> Regards with patriot love.

> We trust in plumed procession,
> For such the Angels go,
> Rank after Rank, with even feet
> And Uniforms of Snow.

Here is an inner scene of private struggle where cameras and commentators cannot go—but only the poet.

One may define any religion as he or she wishes, but in spite of parallels between sports and religion as conventionally perceived, the distinctions are not insignificant. The holy spirit and the sporting spirit may not always be incompatible, but they are certainly not synonymous, and in territorial sports, face-to-face sports such as football, they may approach the soul from opposite directions. In side-by-side sports such as golf, the congruence between them would seem to have a better chance. In pure play, whatever the sport, the holy itself seems like one of the players, extending blessings and reminding us of our humanness as in "Golf and Other Courses" by Barbara Smith.[8] Once, however, we establish complicated criteria for winning or losing in any game with elaborate rules, costly prizes, and the like, what Caillois calls "ludus" or "gratuitous difficulty," the holy, as if ashamed of all the human contrivance,

---

[8] Smith, "Golf and Other Courses," *Aethlon: The Journal of Sport Literature* 8/2 (Spring 1991): 138.

makes its exit, leaving the scene to the sacred and secular with little difference between them.

The Self and the Wholly Other

What appears to be going on in the world of mysticism are two distinct approaches to the Wholly Other that are much alike but different, that of getting in the flow or the zone and that of sitting still, the difference between the methods of West and East as interpreted by Amaury de Reincourt in *The Eye of Shiva: Eastern Mysticism and Western Science*.

The fundamental problem of Eastern consciousness is to bring about the *identification* of the Self with the Ultimate Subject.... Whereas the fundamental problem of Western consciousness is one of *relation* between sharply distinct entities, the objectified human soul and an equally objectified God Almighty perceived as an external *Deus ex Machina* or, better still, as the *totalier aliter*, the "Wholly Other," the Supreme Object.

In historical terms, the basic divergence between East and West became manifest in Mesopotamia in the second millennium B.C. when the divine and human realms, hitherto fused together, split away from one another. The king or ruler lost his inherent divinity and became the humble servant priest of a transcendent, and no longer immanent deity. The problem now became one of relationship between man and an external god, rather than identification with it, in the Eastern fashion. The objectifying trend, religiously anticipating the forthcoming Greek philosophizing one, started in Babylonia under Semitic auspices. The increasing transcendence of the Almighty, the growing distance separating gods and men culminated in the Bible.... But nowhere in pre-biblical Babylonian religious literature is there any reference to the mystical impulse, to the existence of a Divine essence within man; the divine is wholly and completely transcendent, never immanent. The gods dwell in the sky or underground, never in the hearts of men—in Sumero-Babylonian cuneiform script, the sign for a deity was a star....

In the east, ultimately there is no objectified Godhead, no supreme Lord that exists in and for itself, no cosmic creator of the universe, no permanent external divinity nor imperishable soul that is more than a convenient and wholly temporary symbolic prop: the godhead is your own, deep concealed unindividualized and transpersonal Self. And not beyond death, in some distant heaven or other, but right here and now.... The West's Ultimate goal is to know *about* and to relate to the Ultimate Object, the East's to identify with and *be* the Ultimate Subject. The following parable may help to illustrate the contrast: let us imagine a crossroads with one sign on the right pointing to heaven and another on the left pointing to "lectures on heaven"; the Easterner would turn right and go straight to heaven, while the Westerner would turn left and attend the lectures.[9]

Herein lies a clue, perhaps, for a better understanding of the difference between two types of religious expression in sports. The god of prayers before battle and ball games would appear to be the god of transcendence, the Ultimate Object or Wholly Other. The god athletes and dancers may experience in the flow or in the zone, regardless of creedal affiliation, would seem to be a god that is immanent. Perhaps these are two sides of the same god, a god reflected in the idea of panentheism, a god in the world and beyond it. In accounts of mystics, though, one cannot, judging from accounts, keep from noting an emphasis upon either intensity of experience or vision. Among some, Eckhart for example, it seems likely that both occur to a remarkable degree.

"In the Flow" and "In the Zone":
Wind Tunnel to Ultimacy

Granted, there may be an ultimate reality somewhere, but we doubt if it is as uniform and handy as Prebish and other sports apologists make it appear. Few of the great mystics found it so accessible, attainable, or recoverable. Since in the religion of sports the main concern is neither with conventional ethics nor ritualized verbal worship of a transcendent being, it does not have anything remotely resembling the Ten Commandments or the Beatitudes. In the religion of sports, much emphasis is placed upon the "flow experience," which Mihaly Csikszentmihalyi defines as "the state in which people are so involved in an activity that nothing else seems to matter; the experience itself is so enjoyable that people will do it at a great cost, for the sheer sake of doing it.... Players and spectators cease to act in terms of common sense and concentrate instead in the peculiar activity of

---

[9] De Reincourt, *The Eye of Shiva: Eastern Mysticism and Western Science* (New York: William Morrow, 1980), 62-65.

the game.... Such flow activities have as their primary function the provision of enjoyable experiences."[10]

Like the word "holy," "flow" is difficult to pin down, but we infer that Thoreau, a climber as well as a world-class walker, might have been in the "flow" on Mount Katahdin, the highest point in Maine. It is, one imagines, the same type of sublimity reflected on camera by Colin Rowe on the heights of the world, nature photography being in his words an "action sport." One of the most impressive aspects of Csikszentmihalyi's book is that it he makes no effort to equate "flow" with holiness as apologists do for sports. "The flow experience," he says, "like everything else, is not 'good' in an absolute sense. It is good only in that it has the potential to make life more rich, intense and meaningful."[11]

The idea of flow does, though, lend itself readily to the spirit of the Olympics, which de Coubertin regarded as a religion. Even here, to his credit, the author of *Flow* registers a faint caution: "The Latin motto of the Olympic games—*citius, altius, fortius*—is a good, but incomplete summary of how the body can experience flow. It encompasses the rationale of all sports, which is to do something better than it has ever been done before. The purest form of athletics, and sports in general, is to break through the limitations of what the body can accomplish."[12] Csikszentmihalyi scattered literally good ideas upon the wind and apologists gathered them in and adopted them, not as a rationale for sports but as a rationale for a Religion of Sports—a huge difference.

There is a great irony in the use of "flow" theory as a foundational principle for the religion of sports. Used or exploited in modern culture as a motivational concept in improving sales for businesses and winning ball games, flow has deep, even quintessential roots in the history of the holy. Its use in Scripture deals with the giving and taking of the Lord (see the word in *Unger's Bible Dictionary*) including giving of the holy spirit in the red-letter verse of John 7:38: "He that believeth on me, as the scripture hath said, out of his belly shall flow rivers of living waters." It is a passage replete with metaphors that must be grasped for understanding within or without the Christian tradition since the dilemma it points to is common to every

---

[10] Csikszentmihalyi, *Flow: The Psychology of Optimal Experience* (New York: Harper and Row, 1990) 46. See also Susan Jackson and Csikszentmihalyi, *Flow, Keys to Optimal Experience and Performance* (Champaign: Human Kinetics, 1999).

[11] Ibid.

[12] Ibid., 96.

religion, the struggle between holy spirit and mammon. "Belly," according to Ryrie, refers to "innermost being," and the Old Testament reference, he says, is "probably" to Isaiah 55:1: "Ho, every one that thirsteth come ye to the waters, and he that hath no money; come ye, buy, and eat; yea come, buy wine and milk without money and without price."

The second verse continues in the same poetic vein, the chief way of speaking the truth in any religion or philosophy: "Wherefore do ye spend money for that which is not bread? And your labor for that which satisfieth not? Hearken diligently unto me, and eat yea that which is good, and let your soul delight itself in fatness." Peanut butter and jelly is certainly that which is good, but how appropriately the metaphor justifies sports and religion remains to be seen.

The connection between "flow" and "holy" is old. Recall Eckhart's citation of the statement of Saint Dionysus, "God is a fountain flowing into itself." Traditionally and in every use of the word in Scripture, "flow" appears as a verb! Today we have made a noun out of it just as we have taken two very fine verbs, educate and communicate, and made departments out of them, even colleges, even cabinet departments. We deemphasize flow's long association with the holy spirit and opened it up for commercial possibilities so that we could make money in sports and business and still be holy at the same time.

Even today, flow can be a good thing though less and less, from our perspective, a holy thing. Admittedly, there are many kinds of flow and some seem more decent than others. The idea of flow often involves crowds whose behavior throughout history is questionable, as people who have studied them, like Elias Canetti, remind us. Yet there is something democratic about the idea of flow since anyone can get psyched up, take on enthusiasm, and get on a team of one kind or another and with energy start a new life on one's own. Flow theory seems to suggest that if we can't walk, run, race, or climb, we may choose to sit still and know, also mastered by Thoreau. If we prefer and if freedom allows, we can join a sports team or follow one so we can see on some sort of regular basis the beauty of performance of the human body and so we can feel a sense of exhilaration from belonging to something in particular, something set apart, distinguishable, maybe even distinguished, yet not necessarily holy. A key word in the idea of flow seems to be "experience" and, if we're fortunate, the experience of awe and wonder of being itself.

Rational assessment of flow remains important since it is a nonrational phenomenon, whether holy or not. Some scholars have described flow as the outpouring of the sense of divine love and the blossoming awareness of the holiness even of nature, but they agree that it is a different type of experience from that stimulated by extreme action in football or climbing a challenging mountain. In a discussion of flow in sports, the idea of effects of the sacred is always present; in Jonathan Edwards it never is. His key word is "holy," which is used more times in three pages of *A Personal Narrative* than sacred is in the entire canon of sports apologists. Words fail to describe the distance we have come in our thinking on religion from that of Jonathan Edwards and his efforts to inaugurate a "Great Awakening" in the 1740s. How could Edwards possibly comprehend that on the same continent there would come a time when theologians would describe a religion of sports and then applaud it?

Flow seems a marvelous thing yet is quite different from the idea of the holy, seeming much closer to the idea of the "Force" of Luke Skywalker and as discussed by Joseph Campbell in *The Power of Myth* than to the enthusiasm of a gathering of sales staff at Amway or Wal-Mart. Void of ethical content without context, flow could aid the efforts of a Saturday afternoon athlete in his quest for heroism or the maligned intentions of a zealous Gestapo interrogator torturing suspects of sabotage against the state.

Compelling evidence of the transforming power of flow comes from Phil Jackson, former coach of the Chicago Bulls, son of Pentecostal ministers, and student of Zen Buddhism. The secret of playing basketball well, he says, is "*not* thinking: a Buddhist sense of being aware of what everyone on the court is doing and responding to, interacting with, and directing the flow of the game, precisely by *not* thinking." Jackson is also quoted to this effect: "Even for those who don't consider themselves 'spiritual in a conventional sense, (the process of) creating a successful team—whether it's an NBA champion or a record-setting sales force—is essentially a spiritual act.... It requires the individuals involved to surrender their self-interest for the greater good so that the whole adds up to more than the sum of the parts."[13] For Chicago the flow worked like magic, and the surface parallels between departure and return to the Bulls seem more evidence of Deion Sanders's claim that sports and religion go together like peanut butter and jelly. According to Joseph Price, "The fervent fans of the Bulls, in yearning for the second-coming of Michael Jordan during his hiatus from the team, made their way to the United Center, home of the

---

[13] Price, 225.

Bulls, and prayed at the foot of Jordan's statue—a shrine to his transcending the court, his being 'Air Jordan.'"[14]

We used the term "magic" above deliberately to distinguish between it and religion much in the manner of Sir James George Frazer, who in *The Golden Bough*, as Prebish points out, "maintained that magic was concerned with natural forces while religion concerned itself with the supernatural. Religion was utilized when magic produced less than satisfactory answers. Further, religion assumed either of two essential forms: animism or ancestor worship"[15] A good case could be made that what Prebish calls sports, considering our adoption of creature names from the natural world and the animalistic fervor of players and fans, remains closer to what appears as transcendence in sports by players and fans may well be a form of lingering animism, at least in part.[16]

To be sure, Jordan and the Bulls represent a perfect illustration of the idea of the flow and of another idea dear to the hearts of apologists, that of "ultimacy," which is made to appear as a synonym of the holy. The Bulls may have been magicians on the court, but to apologists the idea of magic is not strong enough. According to Charles Prebish, the transformative power of sports involves "redemption as well as rebirth into a new type of reality, separated from ordinary reality by its sense of being permeated with ultimacy and holiness, with beauty and freedom." This cheering section may have started with Prebish, but it is growing in number and in distinction. Michael Novak, for example, believes that "sports partake of the divine because they foster glorious abstractions: Being, beauty, truth, excellence, transcendence—these words, grown in the soil of play, wither in the sand of work. Art, prayer, worship, love, civilization: these thrive in the field of play."[17] Joseph Price concluded that sporting activity is indeed a route to the holy never announced in the front office, and the highest experience one might be able to attain in this world. "The ultimacy or holiness of the religious experience derives from its location, not in a remote realm of transcendence, but in a sense of alterity generated by the freedom and

---

[14] Ibid., 225.

[15] *Religion and Sport: The Meaning of Sacred and Profane* (Westpart: Greenwood Press, 1993), 5-6.

[16] See *The New Golden Bough: A New Abridgement of the Classic Work of Sir James George Frazer*, ed. Theodore H. Gaster (New York: New American Library, 1964) 496–97.

[17] Novak, *The Joy of Sports: End Zones, Bases, Baskets, Balls, and the Consecration of the American Spirit* (New York: Basic Books, 1976) xii.

beauty of the sports activity itself."[18] Perhaps this might be the case, but in keeping with our thesis this is not the purpose of sports. If it should occur that holiness is made an advertised goal of sports, then at last, perhaps too late, we will realize what Kierkegaard meant by his observation that when Church, that is, the Church of Sports, is triumphant, Christianity will be dead. So too will all the other forms of faith with which we are familiar. We will have television, but mentally and spiritually we will be back at Nemi.

Sitting Still with the Holy: The Case for Intimacy

In conventional faith mysticism is best described by "intimacy," especially in the conversion experience. Emphasis in this ritual is upon privacy, surrender, stillness, and humility. Ultimacy, in contrast, suggests competition or struggle and actual triumph over others or nature. One is tempted to ask how one could ever know what the ultimate experience is until one has died, but the same question we acknowledge might be asked about intimacy. We don't know what a representative fight song might be for the expression of ultimacy—perhaps that of the Michigan Wolverines, "Hail to the Victors"—but the one best expressive of the idea of intimacy may well be "In the Garden." These songs also reflect the two symbols of being and doing in Western civilization, that of the knight and that of the shepherd earlier discussed.

In making such claims about "ultimate" experience being available in sporting competition, sports apologists have not presented competing evidence on the idea of the holy since Otto's classic is rarely mentioned in the discussions. This is not to say that the flow in the hands of Phil Jackson is not a thing of beauty and power and joy for him, his team at the time, and spectators. We appreciate the paradox that in the flow, "knowing" can occur by "*not* thinking," and we understand ultimacy in the Bulls' remarkable achievement in the NBA and in the sense that Michael Jordan, like Gilgamesh, will not come again. Perhaps Michael was "ultimate" but is now retired. We need to keep in mind that ultimacy occurs in a lot of places outside stadia or gymnasia and in a lot of different ways, we imagine, as in childbirth for the mother and often on the battlefield and everywhere else that trauma and shock occur. It is also a claim that might be made by certain bars or houses of prostitution. One could make an argument that it is a value-free value.

---

[18] Price, *From Season to Season*, 223.

The biggest problem with the word "ultimacy" is linguistic. Simply put, "ultimacy" is not even the ultimate, since the word "penultimate" penetrates every aspect of our culture, as super-sized as we have become. There is even a book called *The Penultimate Truth* by science fiction writer P. K. Dick about World War III, one reviewer saying that it is "as full of muscle, teeth, and flashing surprises as an alligator pool," a sort of penultimate praise. There is even among us the phrase "super ultimate," but we don't know if it is more or less ultimate than "penultimate," only that there is a "Super Ultimate Body Fat Monitor and Scale" that is "not for athletes."

The flow in sports is an example of what Otto calls "nature mysticism," the "absolute" opposite of the kind experienced by Eckhart, as cited by Otto. In the nature mysticism, joy appears to be the reward, which, since we have said it is generally different from pleasure, would appear to be the highest boon possible. As wonderful as joy is, it is not the pinnacle of mystical achievement or the only supreme reward in human terms. In the divine kind of mysticism, the priceless pearl is consciousness and insight and knowledge of being. Joy combines with consciousness for a divine unity of vision and experience, what might be described as living atonement or at-one-ment. Such a state might be called the "ultimate intimacy," and it is debatable whether any mortal has achieved such union this side of the grave. What is reassuring is that the evidence of "Something Other" is among us, in the language of science fiction an "alien" to many of us yet one, being within, we can't search for with either telescopes or spaceships.

In intimacy, the question of mergence with the Other does not seem to apply. Instead, the goal is nearness or closeness. Intimacy is a state of being intimate (adj.), "intrinsic, essential, from the Latin *intimus* or innermost, belonging to or characterizing one's deepest nature, marked by very close association, contact, or familiarity..., friendship developing through long association, suggesting informal warmth." Note the differences between the two ideas. Ultimacy is a quality of the state of being ultimate, from the Latin *ultimus*, fartherest, last, final, superlative of (assumed) Latin *Ulter* situated beyond, most remote in space and time, finally reckoned.

In Western civilization the idea of ultimacy has played a major role in shaping culture and religion, even including the idea of subduing the earth and others to build a more perfect society, either a New Jerusalem or Utopia, whatever the case may be. Though we pray for the kingdom to come on earth, we know that almighty powers and wisdom are beyond us. God and the holy both are wholly other. According to de Riencourt,

Mysticism is the same the world over, in the East and in the West; but whereas the East bases its metaphysical insights upon it, the West has refused to do so.... Meister Eckhart did feel that he had become divine, and Pope John XXII condemned him for teaching that Man and God had a common divinity.... In the East there can be no such surrender since the philosophical premises that make such a capitulation in the West do not exist.... Thus, time and again, the Western mystic is warned not to let himself be carried away by the subjective illusion of his own potential divinity, warned that there can be no divine incarnation in man—save in the one and only case of Jesus for the Christians—and that his rapturous experience is actually a "vision" of an objectified, transcendent and forever separate Almighty God, rather than a "fusion" with it.[19]

Surrender in mystical experiences is a matter of to whom or to what depending on the tradition of one's faith, but intimacy appears to be a quality central to both East and West as in the works of Thomas Merton, who draws upon both traditions. A book by the Cistercian Monk Thomas Keating, *Intimacy with God*, is proof, as Jung noted, that whatever jewels of meditation can be found in the East are also in the house of the West. A recent book with a similar title is *Developing Intimacy with God: An Eight-week Prayer Guide Based on The Spiritual Exercises of St. Ignatius* by Alexander Aronis, a Baptist minister.[20]

What makes Aronis's book different is that it is structured for Protestants as well as Catholics or indeed anyone. Of course, "spiritual exercises" have always been available for those outside the Catholic faith, but "developing intimacy" is designed to widen the availability of the same essential message with the blessings of Jesuit priests, including one who led Aronis through the "exercises." The book has also received high praise from Protestant ministers.

The simple method of the book is old. Instead of letting thoughts ramble through our head at will, which may work well for many, the emphasis is upon focused attention on scenes from Scripture in an effort not to change the mind but to change the heart, *metanoia*, the intent of *Imitation*

---

[19] De Reincourt, *The Eye of Shiva*, 75–77.
[20] Available through amazon.com. as are works of Merton and Keating.

of Christ by Thomas a Kempis and the *Spiritual Exercises*. Reason cannot drive out troubling spirits or addictions. As Jung contends, only a spirit can drive out spirit.

As rationally structured as the book is with suggestions for prayer times and meditation, it is also poetic as texts often are in this particular tradition. Spiritual truths are drawn from scenes of ordinary things—"the plow, the seed, the yoke, the salt, the light, the leaven, the door, the coin, the jewel, the fire and many more," as stated by Elton Trueblood in *The Humor of Christ*.[21] The words lead the individual seeker to the biblical scene in Scripture, more or less serving as guide, and then leave the seeker and the scene together for personal reflection and symbolic thinking, the kind that occurs beyond the realm of language in what we generally call the unconscious. According to William Faulkner, *Absalom, Absalom,* "memory knows before knowing remembers" so that the means of a deeper knowing become a matter of digging in the detritus within, personal and cosmic, to find the lode of the spirit and to make it conscious.

In the "flow experience," it is not clear what the "Wholly Other" really is since a sense of materiality is always present, often one's own body and the bodies of others. The flow experience in sports seems close to the idea of Maslow's "peak experience," which Joseph Campbell describes in response to Bill Moyers's question on that subject:

> When I was running at Columbia, I ran a couple of races that were just beautiful. During the second race, I knew I was going to win even though there was no reason for me to know this, because I was touched off as anchor in the relay with the leading runner thirty yards ahead of me. But I just knew, and it was my peak experience. Nobody could beat me that day. That's being in full form and really knowing it. I don't think I have ever done anything in my life as competently as I ran those two races—it was the experience of really being at my full and doing a perfect job.[22]

Moyers, as if things were not already complicated enough, asks Campbell to tell what James Joyce meant by the term "epiphany," to which Campbell responds,

---

[21] *The Humor of Christ* (New York: Harper & Row, 1964), 42.
[22] *The Power of Myth*, 220.

Now that's something else. Joyce's formula for the aesthetic experience is that it does not want to move you to want to possess the object. A work of art that moves you to possess the object depicted, he calls pornography. Nor does the aesthetic experience move you to criticize and reject the object—such art he calls didactic, or social criticism in art. The aesthetic experience is the simple beholding of the object. Joyce says that you put a frame around it and see it first as one thing, and that, in seeing it as one thing, you then become aware of the relationship of part to part, each part to the whole, and the whole to each to the parts. This is the essential aesthetic factor—rhythm, the harmonious rhythm of relationships. And when a fortunate rhythm has been struck by the artist, you experience a radiance. You are held in aesthetic arrest. That is the epiphany. And that is what might in religious terms be thought of as the all-informing Christ principle coming through.[23]

The difference between an aesthetic experience and what Joyce calls pornography is much like that between a young boy pretending to be Michael Jordan while playing basketball in the backyard with friends and a teenager or adult killing someone for their Michael Jordan shoes, sacred objects or fetishes, which further substantiates the argument that money itself is sacred, though certainly not holy.

In the mysticism of the holy encounter, the world as we know it seems insignificant or perhaps even nonexistent. Rumi writes, "If you want what visible reality can give, you're an employee. If you want the unseen world, you're not living your truth. Both wishes are foolish, but you will be forgiven for forgetting what you really want is love's confusing joy. 'Lo I am with you always' means when you look for God, God is in the look of your eyes, in the thought of your looking, nearer to you than yourself...."[24]

In the holy encounter neither the aesthetic object nor motion is required. The "Wholly Other" is not a thing, yet it is *not* "nothing" as a master cited by Otto in *Mysticism East and West* suggests: "Therefore it is rightly called a word. But what it was, was hidden from me (an

---

[23] Ibid, 220.

[24] Michael Braswell, John Fuller, Bo Lozoff, *Correction, Peacemaking, and Restorative Justice*, (Cincinnati: Anderson Publishing Company, 2001) 24.

inconceivable idea). Therefore, it is said. It comes in a whisper, in a silence, to reveal itself. It appeared and yet was hidden."[25] It is acknowledged that in all kinds of mysticism there is undoubtedly a high degree of "knowing" and "joy," but one major difference between the mysticism of Eckhart and that of the "flow" or "peak experience" is that the last two kinds seem to take place in this world, in the United Center in Chicago or on the track at Columbia.

In the kind of mysticism of Eckhart, the special moment seems to occur in what might be called "the subliminal self," raising the possibility that though we live in time and space, there is a greater milieu in which time and space are subsumed, a realm perhaps of mind and spirit that is all around us and in which we move and have our being and yet know not. In the divine mysticism, this world is a mere launching platform for the seeker. Indeed as bodies we all have to be somewhere during our brief lives and deaths, but in religious mysticism place is insignificant compared to timelessness and "spacelessness" of the spiritual journey. To repeat for emphasis from *Mysticism East and West*: The mysticism of Eckhart "is a spiritual, *not a natural nor an aesthetic valuation*…. Sankara and Eckhart seek the illimitable as spirit, as *knowledge, as consciousness*…."[26]

As in appendix 1 in *Mysticism*, "Chrysostom on the Inconceivable in God," the idea that something other than us without form or shape could precede the universe itself seems preposterous, yet a poet scientist, Loren Eiseley, has expressed the same idea in this striking way: "Before time was or act existed, imagination grew in the dark." In any event, we can accept the mysticism of the flow now co-opted by the religion of sports, but we are not ready to assign a crown to it as a superior or equal replacement for the holy encounter as reported by the select (or elect) over the ages in and out of various religions.

Price claims that the holiness of religious experience derives from "its location, not in the realm of transcendence." He means an experience closer to the sacred where materiality is always present as in *Sacred Hoops*, the title of the book by Phil Jackson. The flow of "Air Jordan," perfect perhaps in form and beauty, may be a good example of "epiphany," an aesthetic experience Joseph Campbell described in such a way with regard to art.[27]

---

[25] Otto, *Mysticism East and West*, 43.
[26] Ibid., 93–94, italics added.
[27] Ibid., 220.

The art of sports, in fact, may prove to be one of its lasting virtues and greatest attributes. *Living art* as seen in Jordan indeed has something in common with the *living god*, but to deify Jordan and other athletes and celebrities and icons of pop culture is to celebrate the sacred to such an extent that the idea of the holy begins to appear absurd and even irrelevant in a culture given over to competitive athletics and games of every kind, including the ones going on at the stock market and in corporate boardrooms. Such an idea or experience of "living" reflects modern culture's obsession with living "for" the moment rather than living "in" the timeless moment.

Instead of location being the main consideration for the spiritual quest, as apologists argue, we would say that attitude of the mind and heart count for more, whether the seeker or player is sitting still, walking in private, or getting in flow with others. The holy requires surrender in contrast to the sacred, which is invoked for victory over others. Distinctions between mystical states are not easy to make, but even if we say that mystical moments in sports are also epiphanies ("beholding" or seeing) they remain *peak experiences* which is not to diminish their value. Campbell himself says, "My own peak experiences, the one I knew were peak experiences after I had them, all came in athletics."[28] It is clear though that he does not feel that "peak experiences" and "epiphanies" are identical, one based primarily upon experience, even performance, and the other upon seeing or vision.

The differences between the flow and the holy encounter are analogous to two literary theories of Ernest Hemingway, who wrote so much about sports, and of Joseph Conrad. Hemingway believed the writer's job was to capture the experience of an event so that the reader would feel a part of it, similar to the idea of participation in the flow. For Conrad, as he writes in the preface of *The Niger of the Narcissus*, the function of the writer is to make the reader "see," perhaps to make the reader laugh, perhaps to cry, but above all to make us *see*. See what? Conrad does not answer, and neither does the holy mystic any more than Jesus does when the Grand Inquisitor in *The Brothers Karamazov* asks him why he didn't turn the stone into bread, only smiling in response. What is it that the great mystics *see*? That is the part "before which words recoil and understanding cannot penetrate." That

---

[28] Ibid, 220.

is a matter of faith, that "something" somewhere is more than worthy of our seeing and knowing.

Comparing the Incomparable: Mystical Experiences in and out of Sports

Partly as a review and partly as a way of distinguishing between phenomena of the "flow" and the "zone" on the one hand and holy encounters on the other, we wish to share the basic qualities of what might be called mystical experience as identified by William James in his classic, *Varieties of Religious Experience.*[29] For the qualities in their entirety, see James's lecture 16, "Mysticism." Here we supply only a few comments on each distinguishing feature.

(1) *Ineffability*. The subject of it (the experience) immediately says that it defies expression, that no adequate report of its contents can be given in words. It follows from this that its quality must be directly experienced; it cannot be imparted or transferred to others.

(2) *Noetic quality*. "Although so similar to states of feeling, mystical states seem to those who experience them to be also states of knowledge. They are states of insight into depths of truth unplumbed by the discursive intellect. They are illuminations, revelations, full of significance and importance…and as a rule they carry with them a curious sense of authority for a lifetime.

(3) *Transiency*. "Mystical states cannot be sustained for long. Except in rare instances, half an hour, or at most an hour or two, seems to be the limit beyond which they fade into the light of common day.

(4) *Passivity*. "Although the oncoming mystical states may be facilitated by preliminary voluntary operations, as by fixing the attention, or going through certain bodily performances, or in other ways which manuals of mysticism prescribe; yet when the characteristic sort of consciousness once has set in, the mystic feels as if his own will were in abeyance, and indeed sometimes as if he were grasped and held by a superior power."

Considering Shirl Hoffman's commentary on those mystical states resulting from a "rest most busy" and other qualities common to both the mysticism of sports and that not directly associated with sports, we can say there is no clear line of distinction between them except as suggested by

---

[29] William James, *Varieties of Religious Experience: A Study in Human Nature* (New York: Collier Books, 1961), 299-300.

Otto between nature mysticism and what he calls the mysticism of the
intellect and what we call holy encounters. To be sure, body and mind figure
in both kinds, though in strikingly different proportions, and the same can be
said of the relationship between feeling and knowledge in all. No one can
speak with certainty on such matters, but the mysticism occurring in sports
does not seem to approach in power, depth, scope, or cosmic consciousness
that, say, of Abraham, Sankara, Eckhart, or Pascal, as remarkable as those
athletic experiences often appear to be.

Perhaps the best phrase to use by way of summary is to say that all
mystical occurrences in sporting milieus, churches, deserts, woods, prisons,
living rooms, or wherever are the same but different (*eadem sed aliter*) with
some, to echo Orwell, decidedly more different from others. Some of those
differences might be grasped between the psychic/spiritual events now
regularly occurring in sports and the more sedentary ones recorded over the
ages as suggested below, keeping in mind that overlap between the two as in
the symbol of the mandalora is always present.

Mysticism of the Religion of Sports		Holy Encounters
Getting in the flow/zone	**Requirement for the Mystical State**	Being still/Being quiet
Motion or "Rest most busy"	**Activity in State**	Receptiveness
Competition with others/self	**Relation to Others**	Solitude
Performance/ Victory	**Triggering Event(s)**	Surrender
Sense of Ultimacy in self	**Feelings During State**	Intimacy with the Other
Spiritual Experience	**Lasting Effects**	*Moral Vision*
Desire to Repeat it		Once is Enough

As an example of what might be regarded as a classic case of the holy
encounter, we have selected the following instance from the many presented
in *Varieties of Religious Experiences* by William James. The narrator,
Richard M. Bucke, author of *Cosmic Consciousness*, has catalogued the
evolution of intellectual and spiritual consciousness from Moses and
Buddha through Jesus, Saint Paul, and Mohammed to Walt Whitman.

I had spent the evening in a great city, with two friends, reading and discussing poetry and philosophy. We parted at midnight. I had a long drive in a hansom to my lodging. My friend, deeply under the influence of the ideas, images, and emotions called up by the reading and talk, was calm and peaceful. *I was in a state of quiet, almost passive enjoyment, not actually thinking, but letting ideas, images, and emotions flow of themselves, as it were, through my mind.* All at once, without warning of any kind, I found myself wrapped in a flame-colored cloud. For an instant I thought of fire. An immense conflagration somewhere close by in that great city; the next, I knew that the fire was within myself. Directly afterward there came upon me a sense of exultation, of immense joyousness accompanied or immediately followed by an intellectual illumination impossible to describe. Among other things, I did not merely come to believe, but I saw that the universe is not composed by dead matter, but is, on the contrary, a living Presence. I became conscious in myself of eternal life. It was not a conviction that I would have eternal life, but a consciousness that I possessed eternal life then; I saw that all men are immortal, that the cosmic order is such that without any peradventure all things work together for the good of each and all; that the foundation principle of the world, of all worlds, is love; and that the happiness of each and all is absolutely certain. The vision lasted a few seconds and was gone; but the memory of it and the sense of reality of what it taught has remained during the quarter of a century which has since elapsed. I knew that what the vision showed was true, I had attained to a point of view from which I saw that it must be true. That view, that conviction, I may say that consciousness, has never, even during periods of deepest depression, been lost.[30]

Note in the italicized portion above several similarities to the flow of the Bulls games as described by Phil Jackson, including the emphasis on "not thinking." Both cases are impressive, but there is a major distinction. The flow in the case of Richard Bucke is inside him; that of the Bulls is in a public arena and on television. Further, the products of each kind of flow are different in the extreme—for the Bulls, a record and a statue of Jordan, and

---

[30] Ibid., 314. Italics added.

for Bucke, an abiding interest in the phenomenon that led him to write a book for the ages on human consciousness, though admittedly a minor achievement compared to an NBA championship.

In Western Christendom, neither the early church nor medieval nor Protestant church has quite known what to do about "bodily exercises." In Timothy it is said that they "profiteth little," yet Paul drew from the madness of sports around him an illustration of commitments he would like to see in the followers of Christ as they sought prizes of another kind. In the Middle Ages, as we have seen, the church fluctuated in positions on knightly tournaments. In the nineteenth century there was a wide range of opinions in Protestant churches about the role of the ministry in helping to bring on the "exercises" at the frontier camp meetings in the South and Midwest. All of these, rightly or wrongly, were called "holy," as questionable as some of them seem today—holy barking, holy dancing, holy falling, holy jerks, and holy whining.

Indeed, all of these make the psychic occurrences in modern sports seem tame in comparison, especially the exercise called "holy jerks." One observer, quoted by Catherine Cleaveland, described the one afflicted by the jerks at a camp meeting as follows:

> He must necessarily go as he was stimulated, whether with a violent dash to the ground and bounce from place to place like a foot-ball, or hop around with head, limb, and trunk, twitching in every direction, as if they must inevitably fly asunder.... By this strange operation the human frame was commonly so transformed and disfigured as to lose every trace of its natural appearance. Sometimes the head would be twitched right and left to a half round with such velocity that not a feature would be discovered, but the face appear as much behind as before, and in a quick progressive jerk it would seem as if the persons were transmuted into some other species or creature.[31]

To some, such results were the measure of effective preaching, but opinion was divided. Considering that out of the second great revival on the frontier there evolved not only modern churches but hospitals and great universities created by them, one understands the meaning that the Lord

---

[31] The Great Revival in the West, 1797–1805 (University of Chicago Press, 1916) 99.

works in mysterious ways his wonders to perform. On the frontier it is impossible to imagine the great revival without the exercises of which the jerks were only one. James B. Finley, the celebrated Methodist circuit rider, considered himself a free thinker until, by his own account, he witnessed a scene of "holy falling" at the vast Cane Ridge Revival in 1801.

> After some time I returned to the scene of the excitement, the waves of which, if possible, had risen still higher. The same awfulness of feeling came over me. I stepped up to a log, where I could have a better view of the surging sea of humanity. The scene that then presented itself to me was indescribable. At one time I saw at least five hundred swept down in a moment as if a battery of a thousand guns had been opened upon them, and then followed shrieks and shouts that rent the very heavens.... I fled for the woods a second time and wished I had staid at home.[32]

Here is an episode that qualifies to the letter Otto's for criteria for the holy in contrast to many, if not most, we have read about in modern sports.

On the Wonders of Mystical Experiences:
The Responses of Jesus and Buddha

In the days ahead as the religion of sports continues to press its claim for entitlement of the holy, with supporting evidence from the transcendent experience of athletes in the thick of competition, the established church will find it necessary to make some kind of accommodation, official or otherwise, to the new kid on Church Street who just looks like a new kid. He is in fact a mutant older than millennia. The suggestion we would offer to orthodoxy, for which there is always a case just as there is for heresy, is that mystical experiences might well be overrated inside the church and out. At best they are vehicles to truth, not the tenor of truth itself, which in its totality is always beyond us, as is the holy.

Longfellow powerfully makes this point in "The Legend Beautiful" in *Tales of the Wayside Inn*. Amid a vision of Christ, a monk hears the ringing of a convent bell, which signals the arrival of the poor in search for food. His dilemma is this:

---

[32] Quoted in Charles A. Johnson, *The Frontier Camp Meeting: Religious Harvest Time* (Dallas: Southern Methodist University Press, 1955) 64–65.

Should he stay or should he go?
Should he leave the poor to wait
Hungry at the convent gate,
Till the vision passed away?
Should he slight his radiant guest...
For a crowd of ragged, bestial
Beggars ...?
Lines 58–62, 64–65

Reluctantly the monk decides to go and feed them, and when he does he sees them in a new light. When he returns to his cell, to his joy the vision is still there, with, to Longfellow, a clear moral, and to the reader as well: "And he [the monk] felt his bosom burn, / Comprehending all the meaning, / When the Blessed Vision said, 'Hadst thou stayed, I must have fled.'"[33]

Just as Otto stressed, the holy encounter and the ethical are two sides of the same holy spirit, with how we treat one another being more important even than encounters with the Other. Each person with whom we come into contact is an invitation to enlarge the union. "Through 'each other' we come nearer to the 'Other.'"[34] We may not all have transcendent experiences, but we can all recognize, respect, and perhaps, as demonstrated by extraordinary individuals, love others as ourselves. In other words, what is of significance is not the great light we might see or experience in a mystical state, but the simple wisdom anyone can act on such as "Feed my sheep" that alleviate suffering and bring grace to the soul of the provider and the one who receives help.

Sports are about the chosen ones, those who are able to make the team—the fit, the able, and the talented. All religions at their best are about caring for the unchosen, the rejects, those who don't qualify for any team. At their worst, religions are like sports, business, universities, and politics, more interested in counting sheep than in feeding them, more interested in sales, enrollment figures, and votes. The emphasis is upon expanding flocks rather than attending to the lost sheep. In such a climate, emphasis is placed

---

[33] Quoted in George Allen Davy, "Three Techniques of Moral Argument and the Short Poems of Longfellow," (M.A. thesis, East Tennessee State University, May 1958), (lines 58-62, 64-65, 125-28).

[34] Michael C. Braswell, *Journey Homeward: Stages Along the Way* (Chicago: Franciscan Herald Press, 1990) 66.

on "growing churches" while the homeless go unfed. Unfortunately, such folks can't seem to "make the cut." Their sanctuary becomes the street. As promotion gimmicks, though, all modern institutions make appeals based upon how much they care for the individual, which is true—but only for the individual who qualifies for admission to "the club" or "the team." The real Jesus and the real Buddha are not victors seeking glory but only love directed at the least of these. They too are the wretched of the earth.

The wretched do not even qualify for the designation of "walk-on," but sports do point to the longing in each of us for the "underdog" against the "favorite," exemplified by the movie *Seabiscuit*. There are wonderful metaphors and examples of spirit all through the world of sports, but all too often they are overshadowed by the cliché "winning is the only thing," as if in mere conquest all questions were resolved, as if getting a diploma signaled the end of education rather than the beginning of a search for wisdom.

Finally, in regard to mysticism of any kind there are reminders and warnings:

> What Would Buddha Do About New Age Gurus?
> Psychic powers and wonders are not to be revealed.
> Anyone who reveals such powers openly is doing wrong.
> *Vinaya Cullavagga 5. 8.2*
> Many gurus in the west try to prove their status by demonstrating psychic powers. Such powers are truly impressive, so if they convince others that they have these abilities, people follow them, as teachers. But having those powers is no guarantee of possessing wisdom. This is why Buddha told his followers not to display such powers. Wisdom, not psychic power, is the mark of a good teacher.... Such powers are like drugs; they are distractions that lead people away from what really matters in life: love and wisdom. Whether we think we have psychic abilities or our teacher possesses them, we are better off turning away from that playground and paying attention to living a wise and loving life. To do that we need to concentrate on using our normal powers—and lots of them.[35]

---

[35] Franz Metcalf, *What Would Buddha do? 101 Answers to Life's Daily Dilemmas*, ed. Ray Riegert (Berkeley: Seastone, 1999) 104.

In the tradition of religions of intimacy, the value of mystical experience lies in the care we give to those in need. Jesus teaches us to be in the world but not of it, and Buddha encourages us to be involved but not attached.

Intimacy with the Other compels us to awaken and become aware of the suffering around us and to do something about it. The quest for ultimacy in sports is by definition centered on the experience of the self as the body transcends the ordinary limits of reality. It is a form of overcoming obstacles or others to merge with the Other; intimacy in contrast is a turning inward in response to the realization of the connection of all things. It is an attitude or feeling essentially at odds not with play or even sports as traditionally perceived but definitely with the idea of a Religion of Sports.

Chapter 11

Ethics, Values, and Excellence: Testing the Spirits

Many religions, if not all, exhibit three familiar features from primitive times to the present: (1) forms of art or icons symbolic of gods and/or governing powers in a particular religion, (2) patterns of behavior or conduct expected of adherents, and (3) rituals for encountering the transcendent world either on a recurring basis or permanently after death. After a fashion, the religion of sports can claim qualification in all three areas. The beauty of sports, the subject of the following chapter, is inarguably a major consideration, though strangely it is not emphasized by apologists as a criterion in consecration, possibly owing to the fact that modern muscular Christianity tends to be Protestant (though not entirely by any means), exhibiting the long-held skepticism of Protestants toward art as a source of idolatry. In traditional muscular Christianity, what Frank DeFord called "Sportianity," the highest value is placed on ethics with athletics being a means or media for witnessing for the Lord on and off the field, which tends to work best for the champions of sports. An athlete, no matter if an indisputable saint, would not in the current climate be effective in proselytism with one losing season after another.

While the previous chapter examined the role of mysticism in religion and sports, this chapter focuses on perhaps the most important issue in sports-as-religion texts, the subject of ethics, a requisite subject in any kind of religion as Otto and his translator John W. Harvey tried to make clear. As mentioned in our chapter three, Otto takes pains to distinguish between the rational and nonrational components in religion and the necessity of each for the other. The interaction of the two spheres of rational and nonrational is also central to the idea of "ethics" as explained succinctly and clearly on the jacket of the 1958 edition of Otto's landmark work, *The Idea of the Holy*:[1]

> Before religion became "morality" touched with "emotion" it was the emotion itself, or a group of emotions, and it still is. Those emotions are, in the translator's summary, "the feeling of the 'uncanny,' the thrill of awe or reverence, the sense of dependence, of impotence, or of nothingness, or again, feelings of religious rapture and exaltation." The author of the present book calls them the non-rational feelings, the sense of the tremendous, the awful, the mysterious, or in a word of his own choosing, the "numinous." Both the author and the translator make it clear that religion must accommodate both the numinous and the ethical.

The "Harmony of Contrasts": The Holy and the Ethical

In the "Translator's Preface," John Harvey states that

> Otto in the first edition of *The Idea of the Holy* in 1917 was definitely *not* opposing the attempt of reverent minds to interpret the divine nature in rational and ethical categories. He was urging, on the contrary, that the rational and the moral is an essential part of what we mean by holy or sacred: only it is not the whole of it. There is an overplus of meaning which is non-rational, but neither in the sense of being *counter* to reason on the one hand nor *above* reason on the other. The two elements, the rational and the non-rational, have to be regarded (in his favorite simile) as the warp and woof of the complete fabric, neither of which can dispense of the other.[2]

Harvey goes on to say that Otto, was the first perhaps to make religious use of the phrase "The Wholly Other," *das ganz Andere*. In doing so, says Harvey, his purpose "is not open to the criticism of exaggerating and isolating the divine transcendent Otherness. God for him is not, so to speak,

---

[1] Rudolph Otto, *The Idea of the Holy: An Inquiry into the Non-Rational Factor in the Idea of the Divine and Its Relation to the Rational*, ed. John W. Harvey (New York: Oxford University Press, 1958)

[2] Harvey in Otto, *The Idea of the Holy*, xvii.

wholly 'wholly other.' That aspect of deity, the mysterious overplus surpassing all that can be clearly understood and appraised is asserted emphatically against any excessive anthropocentric tendency to scale down the Sacred and Holy to the measure of our human reason. But it is an aspect only, one note that has to be preserved in (to use another favorite phrase) the 'harmony of contrasts'. And here it seems to me that his teaching is more wholesome (and may I add, more Christian?) than that of those who would stress exclusively the one note or the other and so oversimplify the harmony into a monotone. Every such one-sided interpretation can only, and must inevitably, provoke its opposite extreme, and indeed we have seen this happen."[3]

To Otto, then, there are two approaches to the Other, the rational or ethical, and the nonrational or the mystical, but neither of them, nor both together, can reveal ultimate knowledge of the Other. Religion thus was a matter of balance, perhaps of "moderation," a New Testament ideal as well as Greek ideal of the fifth century B.C. Says John Harvey,

> Had Otto ever been able to deliver the course of Gifford lectures (in Scotland) upon the religious basis of ethics which he was planning, I think he would have been able to give a final statement to his position on this matter which would have done much to bring together points of view, each based on authentic experience, which cannot fall irreconcilably apart without disaster to religion…. The double note was sounded long ago by Pascal in his *Pensees*, in a passage which is strange Otto did not quote, but which admirably expresses his own attitude: "If one subjects everything to reason our religion will lose its mystery and its supernatural character. If one offends the principles of reason our religion will be absurd and ridiculous…. There are two equally dangerous extremes, to shut reason out and to let nothing else in."[4]

The same dangers await the Religion of Sports. To be sure, it is a religion with plenty of emotion or spirit, often drunkenness of spirit following victory celebrations, but not exactly a spirit that produces or is synonymous with the "fruit of the Spirit" identified in Galatians 5:22–23

---

[3] Ibid, xviii.
[4] Ibid., xviii–xix.

and generally regarded as the goal or goals of virtues by Christians and we dare say most other religions as well: "love, joy, peace, longsuffering, gentleness, goodness, faith, meekness, and temperance." They are not all among the great ideas of pagans, but they are all among the great emotions of humankind everywhere.

To what extent the religion of sports regards these or defines these, or for that matter the contrasting emotions in verses 19 and 20, each may judge as well as the differences, if any, between "the fruit of the spirit" and the fruit of victory in major athletic contests, the Super Bowl for instance. To be sure, sports have tons of rules for competition in games and for behavior off the field as stipulated by governing organizations such as the NCAA and by coaches. This contrasts with simple play, which is generally without written rules, especially where it is imaginative and harmless and where the aim is fun rather than victory over others. It is difficult to talk about the relation between the nonrational and rational in religion and even more difficult to examine those same phenomena in sports. Ethics are every bit as hard to get a handle on as the elusive transcendent spirit called the "flow."

Joseph Price does not make things easier in this regard when he remarks in *From Season to Season*, "A challenge for scholars who pursue a religious studies critique of sports is not to concentrate so much on sports in terms of what is good and bad in an ethical sense, but to identify and classify the values in sports that motivate action of players and interaction with and among faithful fans."[5] With all due respect to Price and other apologists, we cannot merely describe the Religion of Sports in terms of motivations of fans and players since, for one reason, they have already done that much better than we could.

To push the matter of ethics of sports even further away from his approach, Price reminds us, as noted earlier, "that not all religions adopt and encourage humanistic, pacifistic and compassionate values; so the critique of sports on the grounds that they promote violence, bodily abuse, and an aggressive competitive spirit does not, of itself, separate sports from established religious traditions."[6] This is certainly true, since Nazi sports reflected the precepts of the Church of the Third Reich as did the sports of the militant branch of Shinto prior to and during World War II. To reiterate

---

[5] *From Season to Season: Sports as American Religion* (Macon GA: Mercer University Press, 2001) 228.

[6] Ibid.

a point made in our preface, we know of no way to evaluate the Religion of Sports except to look comparatively at qualities of those religions long established.

Just as, according to Price, the worship of God as far as a criterion for all religion, is not required, "a second issue emerges out of ethical concerns about the inculcation and transmission of values. Not all the values (in sports) are negative, as some might want to claim in light of ongoing exposes about athletes' corruption, their appreciation and practice of violence, the cultivation of bodily deformation as a way to achieve success (as with the use of anabolic steroids) and the issue of cheating in order to win at any cost."[7] Fortunately, our general understanding of Price's perception of ethics as discussed here is much the same as defined by *Webster's*: "1. The discipline dealing with what is good and bad and with moral duty and obligation. 2. A set of moral principles and values."

In the interest of trying to find common ground in ethics and in order to play as fairly as possible we have, as announced at the beginning of this text, refrained from exploiting in our argument what might be called the "sins of sports" and concentrated instead on the virtues proclaimed by apologists. While we have no intention of cataloging the obvious ethical lapses in the current sporting scene, we do feel a need to balance the picture of the moral landscape so that the reader will not have to keep tilting his head sideways to get a fair perspective of the good and bad in modern sports. To do this, one does not have to refer to the sensational cases of athletes on trial, who, guilty or innocent, become what the French call "the damned souls," those the ravenous media feed on in both their fame and shame.

Instead, let's look for a moment at one group of high priests behind the Religion of Sports, those who in invidious robes annually lead academic processions but who long ago determined that academics for athletes are a minor matter compared to other uses athletes might serve for the literal enrichment of others. Note what one sports columnist has observed about university administrators jockeying for slots in the most profitable of athletic conferences:

> In the past several months [as of November 2003], there has been a mad scramble by institutions of higher learning to position themselves in athletic conferences to maximize their revenue streams.

---

[7] Ibid.

The levels of absurd rhetoric and naked hypocrisy have been extreme even for the jaded world of American higher education. The beauty of the exercise is that it has exposed yet again the endless greed generated by intercollegiate athletics with the spectacle of university presidents and athletic directors maneuvering their institutions, double dealing with friends and enemies, and flat out lying. The quest for television and bowl football dollars is the holy grail....[8]

If the settings for bowls are "sacred" in place and time, as apologists claim, and if the holy grail is the lure of the dollar, then this question must be asked: Is the religion of sports a religion of money and, if so, does that invalidate it morally? Philosopher Paul Weiss did not think so, claiming that the athlete does not sell his soul by playing for money. Following rules, Weiss believes, is the moral determinant that also defines the major difference in his view between sports and war. "Wars begin with a disagreement precluding the acceptance of rules," which is where sports begins.[9] Unfortunately, rules are often shaped in war and sports by the green elixir—money.

Psychiatrist Arnold Beisser also attaches great importance to rules. The explicit goal of all competition, he says, is to win within the rules. "There is conflict between the naked desire to win and good sportsmanship...the essential conflict in man is selfishness and altruism, 'I' and 'We'.... If we insist that winning is the only thing, this human concern for others will appear in less obvious ways; if we insist that winning doesn't matter, but only how you play, then the killer instinct will emerge in some hidden form."[10]

As in sports, rules are essential for traditional religions, but in contrast to the situation with athletes, money cannot be, or cannot appear to be, an inducement for professionals, that is, preachers entering the ministry. Ministers follow a calling or enter a service for others, while athletes follow a dream of competing with others in public places for prizes, the bigger the better. In this context we are speaking in the abstract and are in no way advancing an argument that individuals cannot, especially at different times in their lives, be

---

[8] Richard C. Crepeau, "Sport and Society for H-Arete," Arete on-line column 14 November 2003, 1.

[9] Weiss, *A Philosophic Inquiry* (Carbondale: Southern Illinois University Press, 1969) 177.

[10] Beisser, *The Madness of Sports*, 2d ed. (Bowie MD: Charles Press, 1977) 153.

both athletes and ministers. We are also well aware that some ministers, like some humans in every occupation, abuse their profession.

In sports, fans as a rule do not worry so much about the size of salaries of athletes as about matters of cheating as in gambling on games and using steroids. In traditional religion, displays of wealth in elaborate churches or by pastors is often viewed as a conflict of interests, if not sinful, though breaking rules in the pursuit of wealth is probably regarded as a bigger sin. As topics of investigation in religious aspects of sports, Price, as noted above, seems to favor the use of the term "values," which helps determine motivations of athletes and fans, over "ethics," which governs behavior. Values have to do with what we want, usually success of one kind or another, while the purpose of ethics is to guide our behavior in pursuit of those values. Ethics is defined in terms of values, but values are not defined by ethics as seen in the fifth definition (among eighteen) of "value" in *Webster's Unabridged*: "Relative worth, importance, or utility, degree of excellence of usefulness, status in a scale of preferences...."

Ethics, Values, and the Great Ideas:
A Morality of Checks and Balances

Just as ethics should be a check on values, so religion, we feel, should be a check on both sports and war instead of an *ally* of either or both. When sports become a religion in and of themselves because of features presumed inherent in them, there is no longer any check to keep them from becoming militaristic just as Apollo, the sun god and god of games, becomes a tyrant when he is separated from his half sisters, the muses of arts, dance, and learning, on either Olympus or Parnassus. When these children of Zeus are together, serenity reigns. When Apollo gets separated from them, he becomes a moral monster, persecuting competitors such as Marysas or Pan, those of other faiths, and burning books and people as well.

Instead of regarding "contests" in stories (written or oral), on stage, in film, on fields and courts of play, and even in courts of law in terms of values, we might do better to learn to consider them in light of the great ideas that surround the holy such as truth, goodness, beauty, liberty, equality, and justice. Note the difference not only between values and ethics but between values and ideas. Values involve a response to ideas. They tend to be local and relative, even tribal, and hence sacred to one group or another as in "Christian Values," "Marxist Values," "Muslim Values,"

"Community Values," and "Family Values," almost always one set of values in conflict with another. Since we want our values to remain constant, but given that they are ever changing—community values in eighteenth-century Boston were different from those of twenty-first century Hollywood—they are always sacred, at least for a while, in contrast to the great ideas that are timeless and coexistent with the holy, inconceivable in regard to origin and duration. Indeed, values and ideas may overlap and often do, but less than we might think if we understood more about the inherent differences between them, especially about the great ideas on which law itself is based as well as religions, which themselves are subject to law in matters of justice.

Regarding justice and players in the game of life—whatever the context—Natalia Ginzburg describes the virtues unobtrusively present in those genuinely seeking to do the right thing: "Not thrift but generosity...not caution but courage...nor shrewdness but frankness and a love of truth; not tact but love for one's neighbor and self-denial; not a desire for success but a desire to be and to know." Concerning justice, she adds, "I think we should be very cautious about providing rewards and punishments.... Often evil deeds go unpunished, at times they are even richly rewarded with success and money." Here is irony that is not humorous, the kind that must be faced and endured stoically or even serenely. Says Ginzburg, "in life we have to expect to be...misinterpreted, and to be victims of injustice; and the only thing that matters is that we do not commit injustice ourselves."[11] Suffering injustice, a synonym for irony, with grace, is akin to the virtues of good sportsmanship and dignity that, according to Albanes and Miller-McLemore, sports can and do teach. These obvious benefits of sports, however, do not make of them a religion that, unless we change the name and meaning of the word, also includes the idea of the holy.

Ethics make up an accepted practicum of conduct in business, commerce, education, the military, religion, and sports to govern behavior and conduct of members in work or play and perhaps during other times as well. In the best sense, ethics are concerned not with visible conformity in conduct but with visible justice and fair play and, ideally, with a good mix of mercy for losers in all categories. Value reflects the desire for excellence

---

[11] Natalia Ginzburg, in Michael Braswell and John Whitehead, "In the Beginning Was the Student: Teaching Peacemaking and Justice Issues," *Crime and Delinquency* 48/2 (April 2002): 344.

and distinction on an individual level, the drive to separate one's self from others, ideally within the rules, for a prize in a public place, the very definition of "athlete" in *Webster's*. The Odes of Pindar do not celebrate ethics but *arête*, the excellence of the victorious athlete in a particular event, which does not mean excellence in all things, a point we still haven't understood in our culture. In other words, victory in any one endeavor is not automatically equatable with virtue, a matter of ethics.

Of the four philosophical disciplines—metaphysics, epistemology, ethics, and aesthetics—the first two, it can be said, deal with the search for truth while ethics and aesthetics involve the quest for the good and the beautiful, respectively. Of these, Robert Pirsig argues in both *Zen and the Art of Motorcycle Maintenance: An Inquiry into Values* and *Lila: An Inquiry into Morals* that the Good is a higher value than truth. This is also the opinion of one of the most noted theologians of the last century, Karl Barth, who once said "that a systematic theologian ought to begin with ethics, that is, with life as it is lived."[12]

The person citing Barth is none other than Michael Novak, who in *The Joy of Sports* thinks that he too has put ethics first when in point of fact he has dealt primarily with every other aspect of religion and philosophy, especially praise of sports. Amid a panegyric celebrating sports, Novak does take time to recommend reforms, "Burkean" instead of "Jacobin," which means that what he finds wrong with sports are primarily peccadilloes amid the glorious gift to humankind of sports. "Sports are our chief civilizing agent. Sports are our most universal art form. Sports tutor us in the basic lived experiences of the humanistic tradition."[13] Sports, Novak says, belong to the "Kingdom of Ends" and not to the "Kingdom of Means." Catherine Albanese is equally generous in her praise of the ethics of sports: "'Hence it is not surprising that our public games have given people a code of conduct for everyday living. If the ball field is a miniature rehearsal for the game of life, it tells us that life is a struggle between contesting forces in which there is a winning and losing side.' It also teaches that 'success (or winning) depends on teamwork' and that in competition, loyalty, fair play, and being a 'good sport' in losing are virtues."[14]

---

[12] Barth, quoted in Michael Novak, *The Joy of Sports: End Zones, Bases, Baskets, Balls, and the Consecration of the American Spirit* (New York: Basic Books, 1976) 342.

[13] Novak, quoted in Price, *From Season to Season*, 228.

[14] Albanese, quoted in Price, *From Season to Season*, 35–36.

All these tributes are resoundingly familiar, reflecting the highly moralistic themes in sports books by the wagonloads for the last century and a half on how sports can make us better citizens, scouts, soldiers, students, Christians, Muslims, Jews, or whoever or whatever. There is much truth in these clichés but not the whole truth as apologists themselves recognize. For instance, James Mathisen, coauthor of *Muscular Christianity: Evangelical Protestants and the Development of American Sports*, sees the notion as naive that sports in and of themselves promote character, a theme essentially unrelated to his excellent essay in *From Season to Season* arguing that American Sport constitutes a "folk religion" in addition to or in contrast to other types of religion by which sports have been identified—"quasi," "civil," "surrogate," and "secular."[15] If we add up all the adjectives by which the religion of sports have been modified, the implication is that sports are a major religion touching every aspect of our lives, which if true should not make us as happy as some apologists seem to be with that possibility.

In the Religion of Sports, relatively little attention, in spite of examples cited, is paid to ethics in a traditional sense. Outside of the need for teamwork, not much is said about duty and moral obligations essential to conventional religions, including obligations not merely to members of one's own tribe but to everyone and especially to the "least" among us, at least in theory or doctrine. To be sure, competition between major religions is immediately evident around the earth, but it is not required for living a good and meaningful life. The religion of sports, in contrast, would wither and die without competition.

What distinguishes religion from sports, business, and war is not aggressive proselytism and militant policies but the opposite, as Thomas Merton speaks of in *Mystics and Zen Masters*:

> The aim of Zen, is...simply the aim of Buddhism itself, "ultimate emancipation from duality." Hence to maintain a concept of authority in which (the limited individual) self of the monk attains to perfection and illumination by remaining face to face with Buddha who perfects and illuminates him from the outside would be to negate the whole meaning of Buddhism. This is why to some Christians Buddhism seems to be atheistic—"pantheistic." Suzuki and his associates claim that it is neither. God is neither affirmed nor

---

[15] Price, 141.

denied by Buddhism, insofar as Buddhists consider such affirmations and denials to be dualistic, therefore irrelevant to the main purpose of Buddhism, which is precisely emancipation from all forms of dualistic thought.... It is an ontological awakening to the ultimate ground of being, or the Buddha which one is.[16]

While numerous athletes practice Zen to get "in the flow" as an aim both of experience and victory, sports by nature, like business and war, are eternally dualistic. Competition is the name of the game, and after the game, numbers are posted, trophies awarded, and sooner or later credit given to whatever god or way was helpful for winners in reaching "ultimacy" or a physical prize or both. Whenever any religion or philosophy connects with sports, business, or war, the intrinsic qualities of that faith or way of living begin to yield to the instrumental aspects so essential to helping mortals get through a day. It is true that the teachings of Jesus have much in common with the Buddha ideal of "living in the timeless moment rather than for it" as seen in such wisdom as "Be in the world but not of it" and "Not as the world gives give I unto you," and in other philosophy contained in *Be Still and Know: Reflections from Living Buddha and Living Christ* by Thich Nhat Hanh.

When, however, we take to the ball field or hardwood court, be we Christians or Buddhists or members of any other faith, our situation becomes that of the priest in the cartoon who lectures young boys that in church league, it is not a matter of whether one wins or loses. "What is the point, then?" asks one of the players. "I forget," admits the priest. In truth, the only way we know to bring about a complete separation between sports and religion, as opposed to play and religion, is to cease one or the other. There are people who refrain from competing in sports for this reason, perhaps more than we might think. The ones we know who have made that choice do continue to play.

It comes as no surprise that in the church of sports the idea of the Good is based upon transcendent *experience* during athletic competition. Etymologically, "experience" is based on roots meaning "to try," "attempt," and "fear," all of which imbue the term with a heroic cast. It is a dynamic quality closely associated, as we have seen, with the idea of "flow." In athletics it requires a performance on the field or court of play and is not

---

[16] Merton, *Mystics and Zen Masters* (New York: Farrar, Strauss, and Giroux, 1986) 282.

analogous to a code of behavior for conduct with impossible demands such
as "love thy neighbor as thyself," which, if followed, would severely
complicate boxing and perhaps all other sports as well and have a more
disastrous effect upon Wall Street and other world markets than attacks by
terrorists. Getting in the "flow" or in the "zone," to repeat, means getting
involved mentally, physically, and spiritually in some sort of "play" either
for autotelic reasons, the joy of the thing itself, or for extrinsic reasons such
as better health, money, fame, or a sense of belonging to team, tribe, or
nation.

The reasoning here in terms of ethics, we infer, is something like this,
which, we acknowledge, makes some sense: If we are going to look for an
inherent good in sports, we have to look at what is intrinsic within them and
not how we align sports to military, patriotic, or religious systems of self-
righteous tribes or prideful nations. What is it that sports offer us in their
essence in contrast to a gratuitous game of survivorship or victory? As far as
we can tell from reading apologists' works, it is participation in "sacred
time," "deep play," and "the flow experience," a subject to which we need
to return in order to deal with the matter of ethics in sports and in other
faiths.

Drawing upon Csikszentmihalyi and cultural theorist John MacAloon,
Miller-McLemore writes,

> The rock climber as well as the football player reaches or
> discovers a state rare in normal life—"flow experience." This
> experience lifts persons out of time and disengages them from
> internal and external clocks. The timing of the "flow" is not quite
> within the best athlete's control. Football requires long periods of
> cognitive planning and physical recuperation as well as bursts of
> intensity. A truly dramatic play that has the power to transform time
> comes only in its own good time. Years of practice and preparation
> can increase but never entirely determine either their advent or their
> frequency. Even the people in Eliade's study of pre-modern societies
> only acquire the escape from time for a relatively brief period and
> never completely.[17]

---

[17] Price, 128.

Let us emphasize that it is not just two or three theologians gathered together arguing the case for a Religion of Sport, but a chorus of them and other talented scholars and formidable sympathizers, if not admitted adherents and even true believers. Further, their views are buttressed here and there in one way or another by such giants of intellect as Mircea Eliade and Johan Huizinga who, if there were such a thing, would be memorialized on the ground floor of a scholarship hall of fame, one in the mythology wing and one in the section on history, or perhaps both in the same room since there may be less difference between mythology and history than commonly assumed. In fact, in reading *From Season to Season* alone one could get the distinct impression that recorded history has not had nearly as much impact upon the nature of our culture, especially our games, as the mythology of prehistory.

In any event, the pioneers in the Religion of Sports provide the language of philosophic speculation that serves modern apologists like responsive readings in the birthing of a canon for a Church of Sports. Since the main concern is neither with conventional ethics nor ritualized verbal worship of a transcendent being, the Church of Sports does not have anything remotely resembling the Ten Commandments to be hung on locker room walls or placed on monuments outside the high school, to say nothing of the new commandment, which could be written on the side of helmets. Such words, though, would bring an end to territorial sports but not, interestingly, an end to play, which under such conditions might well grow in ways we can't imagine.

Since sports always involves winning and losing, and since the flow of one team always creates an ebb for another, both together have value as a symbol of the spirit of Wall Street. Says Price in "The Final Four as Final Judgment," "The format of the Final Four also reveals our delight in a capitalistic sort of competition. It assumes and plays out the myth of the survival of the fittest.... By having a champion determined in an elimination tournament, we can know with certainty who the champion—the surviving conqueror—is, not necessarily (as the defeated hopefuls and favorites might argue) who the best team is."[18]

The term "survival of the fittest" is also used elsewhere in the text. It is, as Marylynne Robinson points out, a phrase coined by Herbert Spencer, the Social Darwinist, "in a work published before the appearance of the *Origin*

---

[18] *From Season to Season,* 180.

of Species and adopted—with acknowledgement of Spencer as the source—in later editions of Darwin's book. There is an apparent tautology in the phrase. Since Darwinism (and of course, Spencerian) fitness is proved by survival, one could as well call the principle at work 'the survivor of the survivors.'"[19] The same can be said of the incredibly imbecilic game called *Survivor*. The currently popular theatrical program of survivor skills enacts ancient myths by design and even staging so that one would have to ask if this competition, sporting in the sense of hunting and fishing and skill in trickery and deception, is also religious in nature or if the tremendous response by such large numbers of viewers is also "religious."

The glorified language celebrating victory in the "Final Four" would not surprise us coming from Social Darwinists whose high priests are, as Robinson shows, Malthus, Nietzsche, and Freud in addition to Darwin himself—not, by the way, in an effort to defend "Creationism." It is surprising, though, that a professor of religious studies finds key metaphors for sports as religion in the theories of Social Darwinism. This language, we suspect, is like the picture of the cross above the stadium—intended to describe the current situation rather than to bless it without reservation and meant to be taken only in the context of sporting competition rather than in life in general. We were never surprised in the old days when church members would proclaim that though their ancestors may have hung by the neck, none ever hung by their tails.

It can be argued, of course, that rules of play and eligibility constitute ethics, but as complicated as all these rules have become, as seen in the guides and bibles of governing organizations in Sports World, they are all limited systems, which is no effort to argue that good eligible players are not good people but merely to place them in perspective. What "Good" could come to either sport or religion by proclaiming similar identities between them? "What is the role of ethics in mythology?" Bill Moyers asks Campbell, who answers as follows: "We spoke of the metaphysical experience in which you realize that you and the other are one. Ethics is a way of teaching you how to live as though you were one with the other. You don't have to have the experience because the doctrine of the religion gives you molds of action that imply a compassionate relationship with the other. It offers an incentive for doing this by teaching you that simply acting in

---

[19] Robinson, *The Death of Adam: Essays on Modern Thought* (New York: Mariner, 1988) 31.

your own self-interest is sin. That is identification with your body."[20] Here is one problem that looms larger for the Religion of Sports than for those involved with traditional kinds of religion. As Paul Weiss has observed in *Sport: A Philosophic Inquiry*, the athlete accepts his body as himself. This should not surprise us, owing to the demands and expectations of those pursuing a career in sports.

This is not to say that athletes have no mind or soul, but at the height of training both must be in the service of the body in matters of concentration, preparation, techniques, and inspiration. If in contests the trained body of the athlete does not win out over other trained bodies, the result for the ego can be cataclysmic, for the athlete in ancient Greece sometimes a cause for suicide. For the rest of us, if we were inclined to associate ourselves so strongly with the body, the tendency toward suicide might be a more frequent problem. Our many other interests of mind or soul tend to push matters of the body to the background until we are confronted with matters of health and have to acknowledge the role of the body in relation to mind and soul just as Socrates advised and saw as essential.

In the relation of the spirit to ethics, we feel safe in saying again that as remarkable as mysticism is in all its forms, it is not more important than ethics. Hitler, we must remember, was a mystic of sorts and had one peak experience after another, visions of the super man, according to reports. The phenomenon of mysticism clearly exists, but those who apparently know it best seem to appreciate it in a context of humility, reflecting loving-kindness of a pure and simple heart. It might be more correct to say that unless the experience softens the heart with fruits of the spirit, it is better that it never happens.

As a rule, the Religion of Sports has an agenda different from these kinds of issues, which is not to say that individual members of the church seeking power, prominence, and transcendent experience in stadia and courts of play are less inclined to shepherd acts than those of us outside this new elitist faith. It is not reassuring, though, that charity in the Religion of Sports is often a public affair as in televised ads for the United Way. Super Sunday has even given rise to "Souper Sunday," a day for feeding the hungry as well as a day of entertaining those in box seats at the stadium. The charity of the professional leagues is anything but anonymous. These groups definitely want us to know how generous they are to others less fortunate.

---

[20] Moyers, *Power of Myth,* ed. Betty Sue Flowers (New York: Doubleday, 1988) 225.

Transformation and Sublimation:
Jung Versus Freud

The Religion of Sports, like all other religions, proclaims to do that which is publicly good. How, though, do we know which spirits to follow toward the good when so many contend daily for our attention? The Religion of Sports may not help us much in this particular search, but we may possibly benefit from a look at how nonrational spirits are rationally selected in "Old-timey" Religion, which is based, at least theologically, on what is called "transformation," change of heart, or the Greek idea of *Metanoia.*

The moral principle by which sports are often justified is called sublimation or ventilation, letting off steam and frustration on the field or in the stands, which would otherwise become manifest in more dangerous ways if not sublimated in culturally approved violence such as found in sports, especially face-to-face violent sports. The idea is as old as Aristotle, who used it in discussion of stage tragedy as Marshall McLuhan reminds us in an endorsement of the theory for our time: "Do not our favorite games provide a release from the monopolistic tyranny of the social machine? In a word, do not Aristotle's ideas of drama as a mimetic reenactment and relief from our besetting pressures apply perfectly to all kinds of games and dance and fun?"[21] Perhaps. McLuhan was referring mainly to dance and play, but the possibility of the benefits of sublimation for contact sports is summed up in one question: "What is wrong with a little good, clean violence?" This question, asked by a theology student at the University of Michigan who was also a varsity football player, provides the title for Ivan Kaye's history of United States college football, *Good Clean Violence.* In many ways this is the fundamental question of sports, especially in the relation of sports to religion.

The great modern champion of transformation is Carl Jung who, long before the modern siege against catharsis, based upon much empirical evidence, expressed his own skepticism in the early thirties.

> In order to mitigate this cramp of conscious, Freud invented the idea of sublimation. Sublimation means nothing less than the alchemist's trick of turning the base into the noble, the bad into the

---

[21] McLuhan, *Understanding Media: The Extensions of Man* (New York: New American Library, 1964) 210.

good, the useless into the useful. Anyone who knew how to do this would be certain of immortal fame. Unfortunately the secret of converting energy without the consumption of a still greater quantity of energy has never yet been discovered by the physicists. Sublimation remains, for the present, a pious wish fulfillment invented for silencing inopportune questions.[22]

The problem, precisely, in Jung's view of the Freudian approach, was that the mind for Freud had become knowable by means of the rational analysis.

He believed in the power of the intellect.... Whenever he could he dethroned the "spirit" as the possessing and repressing agent by reducing it to a "psychological formula." Spirit for him was a "nothing but." In a crucial talk with him I once tried to get him to understand the admonition: "Try the spirits whether they are of God" (1 John 4:1). In vain. Thus fate had to take its course. For one can fall victim to possession if one does not understand why one is possessed. Freud's "psychological formula" is only an apparent substitute for the daemonically vital thing that causes a neurosis. *In reality only the spirit can cast out "spirits," not the intellect, which at best is a mere assistant...scarcely fitted to play the role of an exorcist.*[23]

Jung's effort with Freud "to try the spirits whether they are of God" would be a good question for pious coaches, athletes, administrators, psychiatrists, and ministers to ask themselves concerning school spirit, team spirit, booster spirit, and other highly praised forms of enthusiasm (*en theos*) that they are always whipping up or endorsing. The spirits of God are, again, "the fruits of the spirit": "love, joy, peace, longsuffering, gentleness, goodness, faith, meekness, temperance" (Gal 5:22–23). Who is to say that Freud did not possess these qualities and demonstrate them in his practice, even if he was wrong on catharsis? In defense of Freud, one can appreciate his reluctance to try the spirits whether they are of God when it is observed that some, like Wes Neal, have done precisely that in regard to team spirit and found it to be

---

[22] Jung, *The Spirit in Man, Art, and Literature*, trans. R. F. C. Hull (New York: Pantheon Books, 1966) 37.

[23] Ibid., 48–49, italics added.

entirely divine, just another name for the holy spirit as he reports in *The Handbook of Athletic Perfection*:

> *Team Spirit* will not evolve of itself. We have a guideline from Paul concerning what sort of action you're to take: "Therefore encourage one another, and build up one another, just as you also are doing" (1 Thessalonians 5:11). For instance let's say that one of your football teammates doesn't know how to use an effective stiff arm. As a result, he frequently gets tackled and stopped short of the yards he should be gaining. He needs some instruction. Some of your teammates might be down on him for frequently getting tackled so easily. You take the positive approach of I Thessalonians 5:11. On the sideline, you show him how to employ the stiff arm effectively. You might introduce your desire to help by saying something like, "You've got some good running ability. I think there's one move I can show you that possibly could make you even more effective." In doing this, you're helping him where he has a particular need.[24]

From a Freudian viewpoint, this passage shows what happens when people try the spirits to see if they are of God—they make of God whatever they want, in an almost Jungian transformation. In this case the fruit of the spirit is a stiff arm, which is made to seem as holy as the elevated host; it is a manifestation of the death instinct, but at least no one is killed by the stiff arm since the instinct is sublimated by the effect of the superego. In Nazi Germany, even that veneer of civilization came off, leaving the death instinct to prowl over Europe with the cruel results that we know too well. Freud at least had the intellectual honesty, one could argue in his defense, to see things as they are and to avoid the hocus pocus of what others call "spirit" and the so-called "fruits" thereof. The only answer, therefore, is a world authority such as Freud mentioned to Einstein that would give Thanatos breathing room but never allow him to reign in any country under the guise of religion, his favorite dress, or extreme nationalism—all forms of infantilism that must be held in check. Freud in essence tells Jung not to take too seriously his archetype of the child with its celebrated innocence. Our only hope is maturity, which can only come from the use of reason to see things clearly and to see them as a whole.

---

[24] Wes Neal, *The Handbook of Athletic Perfection* (Prescott AZ: Institute of Athletic Perfection, 1975) 95.

Though the catharsis theory is virtually enshrined in Sports World, it itself is only an emergency measure to justify violence when necessary. As a rule the main emphasis in sports is upon the creation of aggression rather than the alleviation of it, and the most spirited are those the coaches most admire as seen in the following story told by Frank Howard, former football coach at Clemson, quoted by John Madden in *One Knee Equals Two Feet*: "'I know a guy who's so tough,' Frank said with a straight face, 'when he goes to the can, he takes a baseball bat with him. He never knows when he is going to shit a wildcat and he'll have to beat it to death.'" Madden goes on to say:

> Every time I watched Mike Curtis play middle linebacker, I thought about Frank Howard's story. The way Mike ran around, his eyes blazing, I thought, He just might shit a wildcat.
>
> In a 1971 game in Baltimore, the Colts' defensive unit was waiting for the Dolphins to come out of their huddle when a thirty-year-old fan suddenly ran onto the field and grabbed the ball. All the other Colt players stood there stunned, but Mike reacted with a linebacker's instinct. Mike sent the man sprawling with what was described as a "crunching arm block from the rear." Wham, the guy had to be scraped off the field. He was arrested and fined $100 for disorderly conduct, spent a couple of hours in jail, then spent a couple of hours in a hospital being treated for dizziness and a hip injury.
>
> "You shouldn't have hit him so hard, Mike," someone said. "He shouldn't have been on the field," Mike replied.[25]

What football coach does not want a Mike Curtis on the team? We do not know him, and he may be the perfect Christian or Buddhist or whatever else off the field, but on the field his actions did not exactly exemplify the fruit of the spirit as defined by Paul, though they would be acceptable as defined by Wes Neal. It might be argued that Curtis got rid of his violence on the field, which left him to be gentle, kind, loving, patient, and meek off the field, but this does not seem to be the case with Frank Howard's imaginary linebacker who was pent up all the time, even in the can and even, apparently, after using the can, which shows that catharsis doesn't work in some folk tales, anyway.

---

[25] John Madden, *One Knee Equals Two Feet (And Everything Else You Need to Know About Football)* (New York: Random House, 1986) 112–13.

For Freud, sublimation was a way to self-knowledge and self-control; for the modern sports fan, it is a form of repeated entertainment, yelling and cheering year in and year out, from season to season, without ever raising a question as to the value of what is being engaged in and cheered for. Such behavior to Freud would be a sign of neurosis with little relevance to what he meant by catharsis or how he thought it could and should work. Jung did not think the theory worked at all. Why, he would ask, does the self require ventilation over and over like an addiction, some "high" in the form of a drug, sexual experience, sporting event, or public applause? What is the nature of the "return," and what is learned by the "high" one has experienced? Did the experience lead to a commitment to change, a desire to break certain crippling patterns of behavior, or a desire to repeat the event over and over?

Transformation in the Wrong Direction: Myths to Watch Out For

Thus Jung discredited sublimation because it did not address the real issue, the growth and transformation of the self, an idea that has, in contrast to catharsis, almost no application on the modern sports scene, except in a negative way. Some forms of transformation were bad, Jung would grant Freud, and these are everywhere evident in the sports scene of the modern world. A few of these are as listed:

1. *Change of Internal Structure*: One of the most important is the phenomenon of possession: some content, an idea or part of the personality, obtains mastery of the individual for one reason or another.... Every calling or profession, for example, has its own characteristic persona. It is easy to study these things nowadays, when the photographs of public personalities so frequently appear in the press. A certain kind of behavior is forced on them by the world, and professional people endeavor to come up to these expectations. Only, the danger is they become identical to their personas—the professor with his textbook, the tenor with his voice. Then the damage is done; henceforth he lives exclusively against the background of his own biography.... One could say with a little exaggeration, that the persona is that which in reality one is not, but which oneself and others think

one is. In any case the temptation to be what one seems to be is great, because the persona is rewarded in cash.[26]

Obviously, as Jung clearly states, the danger engulfs others besides athletes, but just as clearly athletes in our sporting age manifest the abortive transformations wherein spiritual growth stops with physical accomplishments and they go about the green peas and rubber chicken circuit for the rest of their days, often FCA banquets, saying the same clichés and having trouble symbolically removing the uniforms of earlier days.

   2. *Identification with a Group*: A group experience takes place on a lower level of consciousness than the experience of an individual. This is due to the fact that, when many people gather together to share one common emotion, the total psyche emerging from the group is below the level of the individual psyche.... The psychology of a large crowd inevitably sinks to the level of mob psychology....
   Thus identification with the group is a simple and easy path to follow, but the group experience goes no deeper than the level of one's mind in that state. It does work a change in you but the change does not last. On the contrary you must have continual recourse to mass intoxication in order to consolidate the experience and your belief in it.... Since this is such an easy and convenient way of raising one's personality to a more exalted rank, mankind has always formed groups which made collective experiences of transformation—often of an ecstatic nature—possible. The regressive identification with lower and more primitive states of consciousness is invariably accompanied by a heightened sense of life; hence the quickening effect of regressive identifications with half-animal ancestors in the stone age.[27]

This is the basic principle of bonding and teamwork, school spirit or esprit de corps. It lies behind the booster mentality as reflected in the need for logos and totemic symbols. It could be fun if the whole celebration could be recognized as primitive rituals, like Halloween, and the trappings of religion and nationalism left out of the picture. That we can't do this shows something

---

[26] Jung, *The Structure and Dynamics of the Psyche*, vol. 8 of *The Collected Works of C. J. Jung*, ed. Herbert Read, Michael Fordham, and Gerhard Adler (New York: Pantheon, 1953) 123.
   [27] Ibid., 125–26.

of the old Puritan hostility toward useless play. We say that we love play, but in our bones we still fear it like a plague. Play seeks to break down social hierarchy, but sports both help to stratify society between the chosen and the unchosen and, paradoxically, to bond on almost endless levels—among team members, with student body, alumni, citizens of the country, and then saints and God. Jung saw the principle at work in political movements of the right and the left, both of which draw upon sports to further underscore the seriousness and oppressiveness of their causes.

> 3. *Magical Procedures*: …the rite is used for the express purpose of effecting the transformation. It thus becomes a sort of technique to which one submits oneself. For instance, a man is ill and consequently needs to be "renewed." The renewal must happen to him from the outside, and to bring this about, he is pulled through a hole in the wall at the head of his sick bed, and now he is reborn, or he is given another name and thereby another soul, and the demons no longer recognize him; or he has to pass through a symbolical death; or grotesquely enough, he is pulled through a leathern cow, which devours him, so to speak, in front and then expels him behind; or he undergoes an ablution or baptismal bath and miraculously changes into a semi-divine being with a new character and an altered, metaphysical destiny.[28]

This is the familiar initiation of young hunters such as Faulkner describes in *The Bear,* a ritual that fails, we can infer from the story, unless it teaches the tyro humility as well as pride, a key theme in all of Faulkner. Central to this humility is a deep respect for the "opponent," in this case a bear, symbol of the sublime, and a sense of the connection with all living things. Even the familiar rites in religion such as baptism are construed by some as magical wherein miraculous powers are immediately conferred, including salvation for all time, where what might be called the practical effects of the rites are often overlooked, commitment toward a new life on earth. Yet magic, like sports, resides in a different realm entirely from the holy, which doesn't mean it is not important. The real trick is to turn well from magic and the sacred (and sports) to the religion of transformation, granting all their proper sphere and due respect.

---

[28] Ibid., 129.

What we speak of as the "miraculous"—a phenomenon connected to the magical, the sacred, and the holy and a prominent theme in Otto, Chardin, and theologians such as Walter Wink—is beyond the scope of this study. Whatever else the miraculous is, we believe with Whitman that it can be found in a leaf of grass and that "a mouse is miracle enough to stagger sextillions." Here we use the word "miracle" to define extraordinary events in religious doctrines—the falling of manna, sudden materialization of food, resurrections, ascensions, and the like. But who can say that all these do not also suggest "extraordinary power or influence seemingly from a supernatural force," one definition of magic? The first definition of "miracle" in fact is similar to that of magic, "an extraordinary event manifesting divine intervention in human affairs." Only one major distinction is apparent. Magic is wrought by the power of the "supernatural," miracle by the "divine," a higher state than the "supernatural," which might well be demonic as in "black magic."

If ancient shamans could speak to us, they might say, as would some scholars who have studied them, that they do not quite see the difference between divine and supernatural and that the relation of the supernatural force of evil to the divine is as much a mystery to the Pope as to our prehistoric forebears dancing apotropaically around a sacred tree, which logically makes as much sense as making the sign of the cross to bless adherents, essentially the same rite but different.

Throughout history the supernatural force of evil, whatever its source, is still manifest more in others than in ourselves, children of light that we are. We may well have passed through three stages of consciousness in our evolution, as Frazer claims—the age of magic, the age of religion, and now the age of science—yet from one perspective little if anything in our relation to other groups has changed. Our myths are for the most part what they have always been, stories about ways to propitiate higher powers and to ward off evil.

Sports, Magic, and Religion:
Testing the Efficacy of Sacred Symbols

One of several strengths of *From Season to Season* is an intelligent probing of symbolic aspects of sports. These aspects are so obvious that they are easily overlooked, whether the subject is the mythology of the pitcher's mound or the inestimable value placed on record-breaking home run balls.

In traditional religions we tend to reject the idea of magic, as opposed to the idea of miracles, but that is not true in the religion of sports, where magic, especially sleight of hand, is celebrated and applauded. In other words, think "Magic" Johnson or "Air" Jordan. Clark's law, after Arthur Clark, states that at certain levels in the development of technology it becomes hard to distinguish between science and magic. The same is true in the relation between sports and magic. It might be said that only in religion is there constant resistance to such correlations based upon the endangered distinction between the "wonder-working power" in sports and the "wonder-working power" in religion—the former a natural phenomenon, even supernatural and miraculous, as seen in Johnson and Jordan, in order to win prizes in public places, and the other a divine miracle to soften and change the heart (*metanoia*). This is not to say that athletes cannot possess both types of power, but only that they are not the same.

Indeed there may be a wider gulf between the sporting spirit and the holy spirit than we imagine, and whether both are religious is a matter of tailored definition and opinion. To repeat, the fruit of the Holy Spirit is "love, joy, peace, longsuffering, gentleness, goodness, faith, meakness, temperance" (Gal 5:22-23). This is not to imply that the fruit of the sporting spirit cannot be the same or that they are automatically the nefarious qualities identified in verses 19–21.

However, we do need to ask an honest and sincere question: How do you prepare for an agonic event for months by rigorous training, defeat a worthy opponent in public contest for a worldly prize and glory, and still be an example of "gentleness" and "meekness," to name only a couple of the famous "fruit"? Is this also as difficult to do as a camel going through the "the eye of a needle"? To make matters more complicated, what if the winning athlete in question makes a quarter of a billion dollars per decade? More and more it becomes evident why some apologists advocate the ethical safety net of a traditional religion with its virtues of gentleness and meekness to temper the sporting spirit, often ferocious in its intent to prevail over another, the essence of competition.

Whether one is seeking the fruit of the holy spirit or the prize of the sporting spirit, the "joy" of victory, though a "joy," is, we suspect, quite different from that envisioned by the author of Galatians. This difference comprises one of many issues that go unexamined in our uncritical age, when objects are invariably used in rites to propitiate the power, spiritual or worldly or both, sought by the petitioner in religion or the contestant in sport. Without the chalice of wine and the plate of wafers in the Christian church, there is no essential rite of communion, distantly connected with the ancient hunt and animal sacrifice, the blood of the lamb; in the religion of sport, say the denomination of baseball, there is no rite of propitiation without the contest between batter and pitcher using in their enactments perhaps the oldest objects of play in the history of the world, stick and stone. The secular objects in communion and baseball, though, become "sacred" in different ways.

Both baseball and communion are nonrational, which is different from irrational but not without meaning. The myths of meaning in each, however, move in opposite directions, in communion toward a sense of atonement and in the contest between pitcher and batter toward apotheosis, the subject of the final chapter. In communion the attempt is to gain a peace that passes understanding that will carry over into eternity, or at least to the edge of the grave, while in the struggle between pitcher and batter the goal is to become, as they say in baseball, "one of the immortals."

Is the former a genuine religious act and the latter totally secular without religious significance? Who can say? The pitcher who pitches a shutout or the batter who hits four home runs in one game could be as eligible for communion as anyone else and could make arrangements to have his minister or priest conduct the rite at another time when games are played on Sunday. Communion is an act of surrender to a God of another world, the transcendent and transformational one. The contest between batter and pitcher is a ritual struggle for domination in this world. Thus the purely secular things in the act of communion, the bread and the wine, become sacred in the rite of connecting the communicant with the holy, while secular objects in sports—the baseball, for instance—become sacred with the acquisition of glory by the hitter or pitcher and in the process evolve into a fetish.

The efficacy of sacred symbols is based on faith of the participant. The efficacy of the baseball fetish, especially the home run ball or the record-breaking ball, is based on statistics and numbers. To be sure, there are several other kinds of fetishes in baseball, as well as in the corporate world and in other sports, but the purpose of all, like superstitions to which they are related, is to assist in the creation of luck, enhancement of skill, and concentration of power for the athlete—mysteries all, but with the mundane goal of helping the athlete succeed.

The myths or archetypal patterns that shape our lives are like matter and energy in that they can neither be created nor destroyed, only repeated. If myths are here to stay, our best course of action is to try to see them anew in the fresh light of modern evidence in the daily news as opposed to, or in addition to, those that prompted primitives in various parts of the world to use frogs, toads, hides, skulls, and animals as weather charms or fetishes to bring on rain needed for survival.[29] Fetishes come in all shapes in all times. In "The Fetish and McGwire's Balls" in *From Season to Season*, Paul Christopher Johnson reminds us that the fetish never really went away from our lives, at most merely out of sight, and is a phenomenon far more diverse and with a history much more complex than most of us ever realized:

> Remember that the fetish is a fluid, mediating term, an idea about objects, not an object itself; a mode of action, 'to fetish.' It is not important to determine whether a baseball is or is not a fetish. What is important is that by looking at baseball in terms of the concept of the fetish, we begin to see the fixation on contemporary memorabilia in a new light. In order to understand ourselves 'in history'…it is possible that we require the fetish, the fixation on objects, more than we did half a century ago. More likely it is that we have always relied on objects to stabilize memory and to animate history, suggesting again that Tylor's 'animism' and Frazer's 'sympathetic magic' were not stages of religious evolution but rather stable, persistent modes of human consciousness."
>
> Does the return of the idea of the fetish surprise? Were the decades of post-colonial rehabilitation enough? The rehabilitation is that the fetishes are we, that the fetish never left, and that its return only surprises under the 'common-sense' of Protestant and Enlightenment discourses against the animating power of objects, a six-inning slumber after which we now stand to stretch."[30]

The idea of the return of the fetish is rhetorical since the fetish never left. Whether we are talking about the oral stage of human evolution, the age of print, or the electric age, the fetish is always with us. Here are some other attributes of "this persistent mode of human consciousness:" It is "finally

---

[29] See Gaster, *The New Golden Bough*, 78.

[30] Johnson, "The Fetish and McGuire's Balls," in Price, *From Season to Season*, 95.

not an object but rather a cognitive and existential problem of location. It is about issues relating of the self to time and space. It is about territorialization" as are all features of the religion of sports discussed in this text. "The fetish functions as an ordering, a location where the self is related to time, space, and power. …Fetish may best be viewed as a mode of action rather than a kind of object itself. It is a condensation of social powers onto an object in order to reconfigure them. …The fetish is a wordless metaphor."[31] In terms of the poem "The Pure Good of Theory" by Wallace Stevens, it is both a "thing" and a "version" of some other thing we cannot name. Fetishing is for all time and every clime, but it is made to order for both preliterate and postliterate ages, as we think McLuhan would agree.

By McLuhan's definition, a fetish is a cool medium: "…hot media do not leave so much to be filled in or completed by the audience. Hot media, therefore, are low in participation, and cool media are high in participation or completion by the audience. Naturally, therefore, a hot medium like the radio has very different effects on the user from a cool medium like the telephone."[32] The value of McGwire's balls is something we make up as we go along, creating demand and popular history quite different from the official histories.

Magical transformation is also evident in the aliterate electronic age as demonstrated by the mania of tattoos, as if painting permanent images on the body could make one on the inside what he or she wanted those on the outside to think he or she was. Unfortunately, tattoos are symbols not of a persona but of a shadow within as are painted faces for key territorial games if continued for, we could guess, more than a season after age eighteen.

As an alternative to these essentially primitive types of transformations, Jung offers what he calls "Enlargement of Personality," which may be the best way for positive transformation but which also poses a paradox and a danger. It is a transformation based upon the principle of psychic growth from within:

> We…tend to assume that this increase (of personality) comes only from without, thus justifying the prejudice that one becomes a personality by stuffing into oneself as much as possible from outside…. Richness of mind, however, consists in mental receptivity, not in accumulations of possessions…. Real increase in personality means

---

[31] Ibid., 82–84.
[32] McLuhan, *Understanding Media*, 36.

consciousness of an enlargement that *flows* from inner sources. Without psychic depth we can never be adequately related to the magnitude of our object.... A classic example of enlargement is Nietzsche's encounter with Zarathustra, which made of the critic and aphorist a tragic poet and prophet. Another example is St. Paul, who, on his way to Damascus was suddenly confronted by Christ. True enough it may be that this Christ of St. Paul's would hardly have been possible without the historical Jesus, the apparition of Christ came to St. Paul not from the historical Jesus but from the depths of his own consciousness. ...the man who is inwardly great will know that the long expected friend of his soul, the immortal one, has now really come, "to lead captivity captive," to seize hold of him by whom this immortal had always been confined and held prisoner, and to make his life *flow* into that greater life—or moment of deadliest peril. Nietzsche's prophetic vision of the Tightrope-Walker reveals the awful danger that lies in having a tight-rope walking attitude towards an event that St. Paul gave the most exalted name he could find.[33]

The word *flow* has been italicized to contrast with that celebrated in the religion of sports.

What is the danger in this type of transformation? It is the danger of the cult of the superman, the danger of certainty, the danger of spiritual exclusiveness based on the mystical experience, which is why Freud distrusted such phenomena. Jung too warns against the problems associated with "enlargement," saying that in contrast to the extraordinary experiences of Nietzsche and Paul, there "is no lack of more trivial instances, a list of which could easily be compiled from the clinical history of neurotic patients," another reason why he wanted to try such spirits to see if they were of God.[34] It is not always easy to tell which spirits are from God as the long and torturous history of persecutions for witchcraft and other heresies more than adequately illustrate.

Note that both Zarathustra and Paul used athletic metaphors to express the nature of their vision, Zarathustra that of the tight-rope walker and Paul that of the boxer and runner, yet they seem to be on opposite sides, Paul stressing meekness and Zarathustra disdaining it. In Nietzsche's defense, it needs to be

---

[33] Jung, *Structure and Dynamics*, 120–21.
[34] Ibid., 122.

said that he was discrediting the herd morality and mediocrity, which the church fathers, "athletes of the spirit," also disdained. At stake is the level of consciousness an individual can bear and the nature of that consciousness. One thing we can be sure of is that at the fartherest reaches of consciousness, catharsis does not seem to be relevant. One may or may not like either Paul or Zarathustra, but neither can one imagine endorsing sports as a way of averting more destructive forms of expression. It is not realistic (or fair) to expect sports to build the fruits of the spirit defined by Paul or to develop the philosophic sensitivity of a Zarathustra, but sports do not have to point entirely in the other direction, sublimating energy day after day, year after year, without noticeable enlargement of consciousness on the part of participants.

The same could be said of politicians generally and of Congress in particular. We think it absurd to regard sports as a religion, but on the other hand we don't want to regard them as practical alternatives to crime, which is where the catharsis theory finally places them—"good clean violence." One example of the failure of sublimation is Mike Tyson, who went from a world-class bully and juvenile delinquent to world-champion boxer. Unfortunately the professional persona is not easily maintained in separate quarters. While millions of dollars may buy layers of insulation from the past, sports cannot guarantee safeguards against recidivism any more than religion or education can.

On sublimation and transformation, the jury is still out, if one was ever convened. What we know for certain is that for all of us who are reasonably conscious, life is a continual process of failing and starting over. The aspects of sports and religion and education that recognize this truth are those that truly benefit culture far more than can be done by constant boasting and displaying successes. To paraphrase Will Rogers, we are all losers, just about different things. Blessed are the losers, for we make possible the exercise of faith, hope, and charity in others and ourselves. Soon we will consider one other phenomenon that might increase the chances of effectiveness of both sublimation and transformation, a natural ally, we suspect, of sports, religion, and education, but too little esteemed among them at the present time owing to the super-seriousness with which all seem to regard their missions on earth.

Sacred Stadia and Holy Wilderness:
Different Spirits for Different Places

If there is one holy living thing we are all in contact with on a daily basis, it is the living earth, which is not to equate nature directly with God any more than did Native Americans or Henry David Thoreau. For that matter, the idea of the holy is not identical to the idea of God but a quality of God—the milieu, radiance, or cloak of God. So too it might be said of nature, the handiwork of God but not the thing itself. As is often the case, humor, especially rural or mountain humor, provides the best insight into complex issues of the human condition. In regard to the difference between the sacred and the holy, there is the story of a minister who goes to see a farmer about coming to church and attempts to get on his good side by compliments, noting the sturdy painted buildings, well-kept fences, and abundant fields. "This is really a nice little place you and God have here," the minister said, whereupon the farmer replied, "Yeah, but you should have seen it when God had it all by himself."

We may go to the stadium for all kinds of motives, perhaps most often in hope of a victory, but rarely to be alone and rarely to be quiet. We come to the wilderness by ourselves or at least in small groups to get away from others in search of some Other that we sense but can't name or identify. In the wilderness, the thought of victory or defeat of other humans is the last thing on our minds, and the implicit or explicit approval of others brings no comfort. It will sound strange, but we go to the deep woods because we are lost or even to get lost but at the same time in hopes of finding or recreating ourselves again.

Whatever ethics might be inherent or developed in the world of sports or a religion of sports, they must, it seems, in order to be appreciated or rejected, compared and contrasted with those ethics sought in nature, in wilderness or parks. Both stadia and forests have been imbued with religious significance, but values each inspires are significantly different and matters of personal preference. Still no treatment of the subjects of ethics in sports would seem complete without a brief excursion into those associated with the wilderness.

It may seem unfair toward sports to say the following, but the stadium in history has too often been a symbol of collective barbarism, whereas the wilderness has been a refuge for prophets and a source of inspiration and prophecy. In the language of mysticism, the stadium is made for ultimacy, the wilderness for intimacy, and in the case of Thoreau for holiness. His daily saunters around Concord were at the same time a pilgrimage. The holy land he sought was both in the world and beyond it as suggested in credo in Chapter 18 from *Walden*: "Direct your eye right inward, and you'll find / A thousand regions in your mind / Yet undiscovered. Travel them, and be / Expert in home-cosmography."

Ever the optimist, Thoreau believed knowledge of nature was a path not only to truth but to goodness as well: "There are continents and seas in the moral world to which every man is an isthmus or an inlet." He had a keen and abiding sense of humor and of play but no love of sports, which in his time (1817–1862) were just emerging: "Beneath the games and amusements of mankind," he stated, "there is an unconscious despair." He was daily in touch with the natural world, which, properly viewed, was itself miraculous and at the same time an opening upon the holy and transcendent, providing him a perspective in contrast on the seas of sacredness around him.

"To travel into the wilderness is to go into what one is not," says Holmes Rolston III, an ordained Presbyterian minister who is also known as "the father of environmental ethics," "so that returning to and returning from its natural complement, mind grasps itself. I encounter an *other* of which I have the deepest need. This journey here is an odyssey of the spirit traveling afar to come to itself."[35] In the words of T. S. Eliot's *Four Quartets*, "And the end of all our exploring / Will be to arrive where we started / and know the place for the first time."

There is more to the matter than discovery or rediscovery of the self or soul. There is for all of us a matter of balance. "Society and Solitude" is the title of an essay by Emerson presenting the need for both, a view Thoreau shared, for he was anything but a hermit even during his two years at Walden Pond. Thoreau knew well what Holmes Rolston, one of his spiritual descendents, also knows,

> To seek absolute solitude is therefore suicidal, for the exiled self disintegrates. But there is a relative solitude that is essential for personal integration—a separateness complementary to human community, its polar opposite. Nature does not define humans in

---

[35] Rolston, *Philosophy Gone Wild: Environmental Ethics* (Buffalo: Prometheus Books, 1989) 225, italics added.

order that they may be cultured, but neither can humans depend upon society wholly to make us human. Each must finish himself.... But distance is essential for this individuation. So, paradoxically, unless one can come by a lakeside...and let physical distance loosen the hold of society upon him, he cannot find space and sanity within which to establish and maintain the boundaries of the self. Without such space there is no togetherness—merely fusion and homogeneity. Alone we cannot be human, Yet we cannot be human until we are alone....

We live collectively, but each of us must distinguish himself—not over against his fellow, but among them. When rightly reciprocal with society, the creative individual is its growing edge. Therefore, that community stagnates which suppresses solitude. Hence the wilderness is as important as the university. All real living is on the frontier....[36]

The frontier has always been defined as the line between civilization and unknown territory, terra incognita. The frontier may also be the defined between the sacred and the holy, between that which lies behind and that which lies ahead in the land of settlements, between that which has been safely ensconced in doctrine by rational explanation and the habit of ritual, and that which can only be imagined in metaphor.

In closing this chapter on ethics and values, it is worthwhile, we hope, to note the possible relation between Thoreau's love of wilderness (or wildness) with social action and cultural influence. It might be difficult to prove that his philosophy of nonviolence was a direct result of his daily involvement with nature, yet his life illustrates Otto's idea of the holy in regard to the rational and the nonrational, which may also be viewed in light of the theological concept *panentheism*, God above and within, neither one or the other completely but both at once. It was coined in Europe, says William J. Wolf, in the early part of the nineteenth century but is "a theology as old as St. Paul (1 Corinthians 15:25) and as modern as Teilhard de Chardin."[37]

Thoreau, says Wolf, gave striking testimony to the idea even before he knew it had a name: "Emerson chose the consistent alternative, the complete

---

[36] Rolston, 228-29.

[37] *Thoreau: Mystic, Prophet, Ecologist* (Philadelphia: United Church Press, 1974) 172.

immanence of God, or pantheism. Thoreau, on the other hand, kept the transcendence of God but brought God so intimately into the world that most thought him a pantheist. Note the retention, however, or transcendence in the following: 'By usurer's craft...we strive to retain and increase the divinity in us, when infinitely the greater part of divinity is out of us'."[38] This theology—common with slight variation to Saint Paul, Thoreau, William James, Otto, Jung, and Chardin—linked nature to the holy, the world of the senses to the world of ideas, as good poetry always does. As Wolf observes, Thoreau's knowledge of the Bible was extensive. There are in his works, Wolf points out, more than 500 references to Scripture, 116 to Matthew alone, and his perhaps singular view of the New Testament in "A Week on the Concord and Merrimack Rivers" is a rare reminder of the challenge it presents to those who profess to live by it.

> I know of no book that has so few readers. There is none so truly strange, and heretical, and unpopular.... "Seek first the kingdom of heaven." "Lay not for yourselves treasures on earth." "If thou wilt be perfect go and sell that which thou hast, and give to the poor, and thou shall have treasure in heaven." "For what is a man profited, if he shall gain the whole world, and lose his own soul? Or what shall a man give in exchange for his soul." Think on this Yankees.... They never *were* read, they never *were* heard. Let but one of these sentences be rightly read from any pulpit in the land, and there would not be one stone of that meeting house upon another."[39]

For Thoreau, nature was a creation of God, but he was not easily impressed by the creations of man, especially those regarded as sacrosanct such as slavery, which defenders justified using the Bible. Yet the North had no need to feel self-righteous since in his view it was in bondage to the machine. It is bad to have a Southern overseer, he said, but worse to have a Northern one. The state, he felt, was an instrument of power devoid of wisdom and mainly concerned with the acquisition of territory as in the Mexican War. He loved the earth and could love a nation if its "sacred laws" were just and if he "should chance to meet with such." The "Higher Laws,"

---

[38] Ibid.
[39] Thoreau, Quoted in Randall Stewart, 55.

the title of a chapter in *Walden*, were in another realm from those of the state, and these he elected to obey.

Perhaps the most troubling thing of all about the Religion of Sports is that it has immunized itself to the vexing issues of the ages such as those mentioned above. There are many spirits in the world of sports—animal spirits, spirits of place, spirits of the past, and the sporting spirit itself. If sports are a new religion, by what authority, tradition, and method will the priests in charge check and judge the contending spirits within it? What are the goals of ethics in modern sports—indoctrination, edification, education—especially if they are a religion as claimed? What are the methods by which the goals will be approached—sublimation, transformation, both, or neither? With increasing sanctification, sports will sooner or later have to become responsible for matters other than winning games.

Chapter 12

The Statue of Zeus and *Creation of Adam:* Athletic Art as Sacred and Holy

Let us, then, ask again, what is the holy? And let us turn once more to Otto to refresh our thinking about the essence of the holy, however vague in understanding it may be to us, though not so vague that we do not hear it mentioned almost daily in connection to self-righteous violence, to nationalism, or as a modifier for expletives.

> Holiness"—"the holy"—is a category of interpretation and valuation peculiar to the sphere of religion. It is, indeed, applied by transference to another sphere—that of ethics—but it is not itself derived from this. While it is complex, it contains a quite specific element or "moment," which sets it apart from "the rational"…and which remains inexpressible…—or ineffable—in the sense that it completely eludes apprehension in terms of concepts. The same thing is true (to take a quite different region of experience) of the category of the beautiful.[1]

This distinction between the holy and the beautiful is crucial. In theory, sports belong to the realm of the beautiful, play the natural, and religion to the sublime or holy. There is overlap between all categories, but they do not mix as facilely as we often assume. There is, too, another source of wisdom different from that gained at the altar or playing field, and that of course is reason, itself

---

[1] *The Idea of the Holy*, trans. John W. Harvey (New York: Oxford University Press 1958) 5.

a type of mysticism dating back to the Pythagoreans and extending down through Albert Einstein, as discussed in Koestler's *Act of Creation*. Otto himself says the holy may "be developed into something beautiful and pure and glorious," but this is not the holy thing itself, which is "wholly other," that which, no matter how approached, either by reason or intuition, causes "blank wonder, an astonishment that strikes us dumb, amazement absolute."[2]

Increasingly sports are seen as forms of living art often breathtaking in their beauty. In the evolution of sports, art replaced nature as an expression of the sacred associated with them. The harmony of strength and beauty as reflected in statuary lay at the soul of the Greek athletic ideal with its seamless ties to almost every aspect of Greek culture and religion. It is also a symbol associated with the God of the Old Testament even as Jehovah is contrasted with the "false gods" in other places. "For all the gods of nations are idols: but the LORD made the heavens. Honor and majesty are before him: strength and beauty are in his sanctuary" (Ps 96:6).

Note that "the LORD" created "nature" (heavens), but "idols," created by man, are "artificial," one of the older meanings of art. To Emerson art was "nature passed through the alembic of mind." Thus into the relation between nature and art, which derives from nature, Emerson poses perhaps the most puzzling phenomenon of all, the mind of man that cannot create even a speck of dust, yet is capable of rearranging matter to produce marvels in science and every kind of art imaginable, from what might be judged holy to the profane depending largely on point of view. We forget that all art is "dumb" but not necessarily a "dumb idol," a distinction that depends upon criticism, whether of literature or of other art, as Northrop Frye explains:

> Physics is an organized body of knowledge about nature, and a student of it says he is learning physics, not nature. Art, like nature, has to be distinguished from the systematic study of it, which is criticism. It is therefore impossible to "learn literature": one learns about it in a certain way, but what one learns, transitively, is the criticism of literature. Similarly, the difficulty often felt in "teaching literature" arises from the fact that it cannot be done: the criticism of literature is all that can be directly taught. Literature is not a subject of study, but an object of study.... Criticism is to art what history is

---

[2] Ibid, 26.

to action and philosophy to wisdom: a verbal imitation of a human productive power that in itself does not speak."[3]

Keats's "Grecian Urn" is a classic example. In this chapter, we will endeavor to distinguish between athletic art that is sacred and that which is holy, humbly keeping in mind that such a task is far beyond our powers without the aid of criticism more perceptive than our own.

Strength and Beauty:
The Athletic Ideal

Strength and beauty may be in the "sanctuary" of Jehovah, but that ideal of Greek athletics appears far more prominent in the domain of Zeus. We have to adopt some caution in the celebration of beauty either in the Old Testament or in Greek philosophy. Its use in Psalms is probably quite different from the prominence given to it in the art and culture of classical Greece. In statuary of that time, as E. Norman Gardiner, Sir Kenneth Clark, and others have pointed out, beauty was conjoined with the ideal of the good to form a composite ideal of *kalo kagathos* or "good beauty," an ideal still highly prized in sentimental fashion in beauty queens, who present their qualifications for virtue by brief responses to questions on ethical and moral issues, and in film stars who as heroes are often handsome and on the "good side" in the struggle with evil people usually seen as un-American in one way or another. In earlier days, this display of morality was called "front porch" virtue, but one could say it might rightly be called "contestant virtue."

For Jews and early Christians, external beauty was not even a quality to be expected in the coming messiah as stated in Isaiah. There is a kind of obvious sense to such a description. If the messiah were handsome and possessed of extraordinary beauty, the focus would be on him rather than the one who sent him. He was to be a seeker rather than a looker as in good-looking. When we think about it, we should not be surprised that of the "six great ideas" identified by Adler in his book by that name, beauty is the only one not mentioned in our great national documents so essential to democracy.

---

[3] Frye, *Anatomy of Criticism: Four Essays by Northrop Frye* (New York: Atheneum, 1967) 11–12.

Constantly glorified in a commercial culture, beauty is the sine qua non of sacred sites of all kinds—religious, political, and athletic, as in a player demonstrating beautiful running on videotapes in museums of all professional football teams and many major college teams so that past glory can be summoned forth for touring fans, some 40,000 annually at the Bear Bryant Museum in Tuscaloosa, by the mere push of a button. In good athletics there is always the attraction of physical beauty but also of strength as seen in the importance of rankings and the shibboleth that "winning is the only thing," qualities of power that call for eternal vigilance in the cause of other ideas such as truth, goodness, liberty, equality, and justice.

The claim of Adler that the six great ideas belong principally to Greece of the fifth century B.C. is questionable since even a quick ramble through any concordance shows their abounding presence in Scripture, most notably in the use of the first of each set of three of the great ideas in the sentence, "And ye shall know the truth, and the truth shall make you free" (John 8:32, KJV) There is no mention here of either beauty or strength, both visible features of the Greek athletic ideal and the practical ideal in advertising in American business culture. Because of the inner quality of that ideal, *aidos*, the ideal of strength and beauty is not eternally at odds with the truth and freedom espoused by Socrates and Jesus, but it is by no means identical.

Just as, since the time of Constantine, the "inner stream" of Christianity based on love and meditation has been replaced by an outward stream based on conflicting doctrines and worldly conquest, as argued by Jacob Needleman in *Lost Christianity*, so the subtle essence of the Greek athletic ideal, *aidos*, that which is "stolen by secret gain," has also been lost. As a competitive ideal, it was different from that of early Christians, but who can say it had nothing in common with it, especially in regard to the corrosive effects of money?

Jehovah, after wiping out numerous "false gods," had to realize that Zeus was no ordinary god but a persistent competitor. What made Zeus so formidable was not that he was the head of a pantheon of powers, "President and CEO" we might say in this age of inflated terminology, but that he himself was the "God of Games." This meant, among much else, that Zeus and his sporting ways would be a constant temptation not only to Jews but later to Christians and eventually to those of other faiths. Zeus knew what buttons to push to get our attention, and he did that while Jehovah looked on in astonishment, amazed that any self-respecting god would endorse and promote such activities of narcissism and self-glorification, especially in the nude.

Zeus appealed not only to his own kind but to the children of Israel, and the games he sponsored, instead of being reviled by the Apostle Paul, were so popular and instructive in discipline that Paul used them as "vehicles" to promote the "tenor" of his own newfound religion. He did this so effectively that even Billy Graham thought Paul was a sports fan like Billy himself, indeed like nearly all of us, Jew and Gentile alike. Up to some point, there is nothing wrong in what Billy Graham, Jerry Falwell, Pat Robertson, and indeed Western Christendom did in embracing games and athletics as a means of proselytism to the Christian cause, or any religion doing the same for its cause. Jerry Falwell, in justifying his approach in this regard, has said that what appeals most to young people are "sports and music," apparently without realizing that this is essentially a pagan ideal known as "music and gymnastic." Even this seems all right and by no means invalidates any Christian principle.

Where modern Protestantism, especially televangelism, has gone astray is not in embracing things of the body such as competitive athletics and competitive cosmetics, immediately evident on any program on televangelism in the makeup and hairstyles of proselytizers, but in dismissal of things of the mind, specifically the philosophy of Greece. As if disdaining the searching intellect, televangelists opted for a few sacred clichés and jumped in bed with the media of sports and the doctrine of success, also known as the "bitch goddess" in the words of William James. The tradition of private meditation, as Jung observed, is one of the precious jewels in the house of Christianity, but that feature of faith wandered to other arms, often Oriental, so that now amid the endless sermonizing on television it seems almost heretical when in fact it is thoroughly scriptural and what Jesus himself practiced. Since philosophy, like spiritual meditation, is ill-suited for an age of television, it too has been delivered walking papers by the apostles of television, barely surviving in a few isolated courses in universities.

In looking at sports as a religion, as argued by leading apologists, all of whom are academics or intellectuals, we see even more irony. Traditionally what has made human rituals at least appear religious is the pursuit of the holy and an abiding preoccupation with ethics or the philosophy valued by adherents, the "beliefs" held by members of a group or at least espoused by them as guiding principles of behavior and conduct. In the religion of sports, we do not have much of either. Instead we have the celebration of the "sacred" and of something called the "flow." The only thing left of ancient Greece in this religion is the ancient Olympics. There is little or no mention of the endless discussion about gods in the philosophy of Greece, which is foundational to all subsequent philosophy in the Western world. Any "holiness" that occurs on the ball field or court comes about not through meditation, at least not from sitting still in an isolated place, but through the flow of the game and the transcendent experiences of individual players.

The televangelists led the way in sanctifying modern sports, and now come the apologists saying that sports is not just like a religion but actually a religion, *a complete identity*. If so, we repeat, it is a religion of power and beauty, of Mars and Venus, in America the first religion ever to be sponsored by Viagra and Budweiser. (But don't be surprised if it is not the last.) Perhaps the next step might be to suggest that it is the greatest of religions. The religion of sports flies into the face of Old Jehovah, and while Zeus smiles on it, there are other sides to Zeus that apologists and most churches and universities neglect or ignore. Ironically, Zeus may give one thumbs-up to the new religion, but the other one might well be turned down.

Gods Seen and Unseen: Zeus and Jehovah

As any encyclopedia or handbook will reveal, Zeus is a god of astonishing versatility: "As the supreme god, with his home on Mount Olympus, he was known as *Zeus Olympius*. As the god of victory, both in war and in athletic contests, he was called *Nicephoros* ("victory-bringing") and *Soter* ("preserver"). As the god of good faith, he was *Zeus Pistios*, as the god of council, *Zeus Boulaios*; and as god of assemblies of court, *Zeus Agoraios*. As the head of a clan, he was *Zeus Phratrios*, and as head of the state, Zeus *Polieu* or *Basileus* As head of the whole *Hellenic* nation, he was Zeus *Hellenios*, and as liberator of the Greeks from the Persian yoke, he was *Zeus Eleutherios.*"[4]

Like Zeus, Jehovah as God also went by "Jehovah, or Yahweh, as one of the Old Testament names for God. The early Hebrews thought of him as their own God. But after the time of Moses, especially under great Prophets such as Samuel, Yahweh was recognized as the universal God, the Father of all men, the source of righteousness. Psalmists often used the name 'Elohim,' but the name Jehovah had a deeper significance as Redeemer.

---

[4] "Zeus," *Funk and Wagnall's*, vol. 36, 1952.

Many Jews avoid pronouncing the divine name by using the term *Adonai*, meaning *the Lord*."[5] In this discussion we will use the word "Jehovah" since he was (and is!) a contemporary of Zeus. In the Olympics or anywhere sports have become a religion, Zeus, we can be sure, is the one being honored, not Jehovah whose beauty is of another kind than that nakedly celebrated in public view.

In *The Power of Myth* Joseph Campbell calls both Zeus and Jehovah "gods of the Thunderbolt," but there are major differences between them as Walter Kaufmann makes clear in his introduction to Martin Buber's *I and Thou*. Not surprisingly, the "sacred," a central theme in the Buber's book and in Kaufmann's introduction, requires comment since it varies considerably from that presented by apologists in their view of sacred time and place in stadia. There is too a straightforward indictment of what we are doing here, talking about God, which, as bad as that might be, is not as bad as the fighting over God now occurring in one form or another in various places around the globe as seen in the work of Karen Armstrong and in direct violation of Whitman's advice, "Argue not concerning God."

Note the power in Kaufmann's commentary, "The sacred is here and now"; it is everywhere.

The only God worth talking about is a God that cannot be kept. The only God worth talking about is a God that cannot be talked about. God is no object of discourse, knowledge or even experience. He cannot be spoken of, but he can be spoken to; he cannot be seen but he can be listened to. The only possible relationship with God is to address him and to be addressed by him, here and now in the timeless present. For him the Hebrew name of God, the Tetragrammaton (YHVH), means he is present. *Er ist da* might be translated: He is there, but in this context it would be more nearly right to say, He is here.

Where? After Auschwitz and Nagasaki, where? We look around and do not see him. But he is not to be seen. Never. Those who have claimed to see him did not see him.[6]

---

[5] "Jehovah," Louis L. Mann, *World Book Encyclopedia*, vol. 11 (1970).

[6] W. Kaufmann, introduction to Martin Buber's *I and Thou*, trans. Walter Kaufmann (New York: Charles Scribner's Sons, 1970) 30.

Note too Kaufmann's distinctions between the ancient Greeks and Hebrews, in a sense *the* question of the ages, the visibility/invisibility of God. This is certainly the major theme of this chapter since it relates directly to the emergence of a God of Games, Zeus, who is so strikingly different from YHVH, the one who abhors graven images, golden calves, and golden statues both.

> The Greeks were an eminently visual people. They gloried in the visual arts. Homer's epics abound in visual detail; and they created tragedy and comedy, adding new dimensions to visual arts.
>
> The Hebrews were not so visual and actually entertained a prohibition against the visual arts. Neither did they have tragedies or comedies. The one book of the Bible that has sometimes been called a tragedy, Job, was clearly not intended for, and actually precluded, any visual representation.
>
> The Greeks visualized their gods and represented them in marble and in beautiful vase paintings. They also brought them on stage.
>
> The Hebrews did not visualize their God and expressly forbade attempts to make of him an object, any object. Their God was not to be seen. He was to be heard and listened to. He was not an it but an I—or a You.[7]

The distinctions Jung makes in *Answer to Job* between the same two gods is also helpful. Jehovah, he says,

> Had proved himself to be jealous defender of morality and was especially sensitive in regard to justice. He had always to be praised as "just," which, it seemed, was very important to him. Thanks to this circumstance or peculiarity of his, he had a *distinct personality....* His jealous and irritable nature, prying mistrustfully into the faithless hearts of men and exploring their secret thoughts, compelled a personal relationship between himself and man, who could not help but feel personally called by him. That was the essential difference between Yahweh and the all-ruling Father Zeus, who in a benevolent and somewhat detached manner allowed the

---

[7] Ibid., 30.

economy of the universe to roll along on its accustomed courses and punished only those who were disorderly. He did not moralize but ruled purely instinctively. He did not demand anything more from human beings than the sacrifices due him; he did not want to do anything *with* human beings because he had no plans for them. Father Zeus is certainly a figure but not a personality. Yahweh, on the other hand, was interested in man. Human beings were a matter of first-rate importance to him, urgently and personally. Zeus too could throw thunderbolts about but only at hopelessly disordered individuals. Against mankind as a whole he had no objections—but then they did not interest him all that much. Yahweh, however, could get inordinately excited about man as a species and men as individuals if they did not behave as he desired or expected, without ever considering that in his omnipotence he could easily have created something better than these bad earthenware pots.[8]

Another difference between these two deities, and not absolute since there are so many sides to both, is in the attitude toward winning and losing. Zeus judges on outcomes while Jehovah judges on good intentions sincerely acted upon, an idea reflected in Paul's idea of "finishing the race" rather than winning the race. For Zeus, winning is the only thing. For Jehovah, what we call "success" is meaningless in his eyes since he and he alone defines it. For Zeus, we are only accountable if we lose in the games of the world, accountable to alumni and to the media; for Jehovah, we are more accountable if we win. Jehovah is clearly the god in the famous couplet by Grantland Rice: "For when the one great scorer comes to mark against your name, / He writes not that you won or lost but how you played the game."[9]

Since the 1950s and the advent of televised games and evangelism, both of them committed to the doctrine of success that has little to do with either the spirit of sports or of religion but primarily with money, Rice's words have fallen into the status of "classic corn" as *Time* called it. The opposite attitude, that winning is the only thing, was gradually turned into a national dogma by the likes of Leo Durocher, Vince Lombardi, Bear Bryant,

---

[8] Jung, *Answer to Job, The Collected Works of C. J. Jung*, vol. 2, Bollingen Series 20, trans. R. F. C. Hull (Princeton: Princeton University Press, 1973) 8.

[9] These are the last two lines of the poem titled "Alumnus Football," which, says Rice, in *The Tumult and the Shouting*, he wrote "back in the gloaming." The complete poem appears in *Only the Brave* (New York: A. S. Barnes, 1954).

and others with applause from televangelists. A single metaphor of Rice catches the entire spirit of sports much better than the ecstasy of victory and the agony of defeat—his idea of "the uphill heart."

In spite of his versatility and popularity, the Greek philosophers and dramatists laughed Zeus off stage, while, Jehovah endured,. as Jung argues in *Answer to Job*. In the book of Job, the nature of Jehovah and his relation to humankind is so powerful and mysterious that neither laughter nor tears can make that relation go away.

Thus, the reasoning goes, the Wholly Other descended to earth in suffering, something inconceivable to Zeus who is always something other than human but not wholly other, which would have to include the mystery of a god who suffers. Prometheus, the fire giver who is highly esteemed among humanists, is a god who suffers greatly but as punishment by Zeus for bringing knowledge to man. In the Jesus story, the crucifixion is not regarded as a punishment by believers but as a sacrifice to the idea of love over hate, though it's still a mystery as to why an omnipotent and all-loving god would crucify himself in the form of his son as testimony to truth's innocence. Almost all religions deal with relations between fathers and sons, which Oedipal theories still cannot penetrate.

If Zeus is no longer on stage, he is still behind the curtain pulling strings and especially behind the television cameras taking endless pictures of athletes and actors so they may be seen of men and by as many as possible. When he is seen only as the "God of Games," he appears as a god of limited interests, but his virtues are many though known mainly to scholars. Without Zeus and his many children, the campuses of the world would, for better or worse, probably look different since the college stadium would not be nearly as large and perhaps not present at all. Missing also would be the campus theater, and this is only the beginning of the tabulation of the losses in our culture without the heritage of Zeus.

What we tend to forget is that many-sided Zeus, like Jehovah when the situation demanded, is also the father of trickery, as seen in the versatile ingenuity of Hermes, Zeus's son by Maia, the oldest and comeliest of the seven Pleiades. With Apollo and Heracles, Hermes presided over athletic contests, and his statues were common sights in the stadia and gymnasia of Athens. For Nike, the goddess of victory, Zeus reserves a special place, holding her in his right hand. Like any number of fathers today, Zeus, rightly or wrongly, made sure that all his children—Apollo, Heracles, Hermes, and Nike—were athletes.

As the trickster, Hermes is the god of the curveball and head fake now practiced in business as much as in the world of sports. As the father of Hermes, Zeus pulled a fast one that Jehovah is still trying to deal with, knowing that something is wrong with making a religion of games either in 700 B.C. or A.D. 2000, but not knowing quite what to do about it. One can imagine Jehovah with furrowed brow listening atop Sinai, site of the revealed word, to the haughty laughter of Zeus reaching his ears from Olympia, the place where men scandalously worshiped not by listening to the voice above them, ahead of them, behind them, and within them but by magnificently performing in the nude in pursuit of victory and an ideal of excellence called *Arete*. To be sure, Jehovah was not opposed to sports either as a means of defense for the state or as competition, but what is at issue is a matter of degree and the moment when idolatry begins. Evidence of the undying spirit of play and the hell that ensues when sports become a religion or the power symbol of a state religion is contained within the pages of *Children and Play in the Holocaust* by George Eisen. The text, with abounding evidence, convincingly proves the otherwise unthinkable claim on the jacket.

More than a million Jewish children died during the Holocaust from starvation, disease, exposure, and murder. As one Warsaw ghetto diarist wrote, "The streets resounded with the futile screams of children dying of hunger. They whine, beg, sing, lament, and tremble in the cold, without underwear, without clothes, without shoes...tired of living at age five." Yet alongside these grim scenes, children also laughed, played games, sang, and danced. In the ghettos and camps parents and civic leaders—often risking severe retribution—made makeshift playgrounds, organized games and sporting activities, coordinated concerts and theatrical performances. Although Holocaust children engaged in the universal play of most children, they also devised games that reflected the unique horrors of their world, such as "Blockade," "Going through the Gate," and "Gas Chamber."[10]

---

[10] George Eisen, *Children and Play in the Holocaust* (Amherst: University of Massachusetts Press, 1988). On the history of Jewish sports and play, see H. A. Harris, *Greek Athletics and the Jews* (Cardiff: University of Wales Press, 1976) and *Physical Education and Sports in the Jewish History and Culture*, Proceedings of International Seminars in 1973

In addition to the fear of idolatry, there were other reasons why some nations rejected competitive athletics, especially as practiced by the Greeks as David Young explains:

> The ancient Persians had no athletics, and were mystified by the Greek games. A Persian sought only certain and immediate gain. To train when there was a chance to lose the prize was something he could not comprehend. The Romans adopted almost every other aspect of Greek culture as their own. But they held aloof from Greek competitive athletics. It was probably a matter of pride. No Roman could stand the risk of losing such an individual test, of looking inferior in public. To do it in full view of one's enemies would have made the Roman blood run cold.[11]

Two Wonders of the World:
A Sacred Statue and a Holy Painting

Like the medals for the modern Olympic victors, gold is *the* symbol of Zeus as seen in the statue of him in the temple at Olympia, one of the Seven Wonders of the ancient world, situated in a sacred grove between two rivers at Olympia on the west coast of modern Greece. A paraphrase of the description of the wonder by Pausanias, a Greek traveler writing in the first century, follows:

> Within this temple the statue of the supreme god sat upon an intricately carved cedar wood throne that was decorated with mythical scenes of lesser gods and heroes rendered in gold, ebony, and precious stones. In his left hand Zeus carried a scepter made of a multicolored alloy of rare metals; crowned with an eagle's head, it symbolized his rule over the earth. His extended right hand supported a life-size statue of Nike, the goddess of victory, and the stool beneath his feet was upheld by two impressive gold lions. His

---

and 1977 (Israel: Wingate Institute for Physical Education and Sport). See also Steven A. Reiss, ed. *Sports and the American Jew* (Syracuse University Press, 1998).

   [11] Young, *The Olympic Myth of Greek Amateur Athletics* (Chicago: Ares Publishers, 1984) 173.

hair, beard, and drapery were made of gold, and his unclothed flesh—head, hands and feet—was rendered in burnished ivory. To keep the ivory from cracking, the god had to be regularly anointed with olive oil, which was collected in a shallow pool beneath his feet. Over 40 feet in height, Zeus was too large to fit in the temple if he stood up—a curious fact to ancient commentators, who thought of the temple as Zeus's actual home.

According to Dion Chrysostom, Greek Rhetorician and Philosopher, in the first century, A.D., "If anyone who is heavy laden should stand before this statue, he would forget all his griefs and troubles of this mortal life.[12]

The history of the statue of Zeus seems to provide further evidence that originally religion was not directly connected with the Olympic games since this "Wonder" wasn't created until some three and half centuries after their official beginning.

The first dictionary example of sacred as in "sacred tree" in this definition is telling, since before the age of human architecture all sacred sites could not be *set apart* from nature but were *set in nature*—around a tree, under the shadow of a mountain, or, significantly, as we will suggest, in caves. It was also believed to exist in certain plants and animals with extraordinary power or meaning as in the "sacred mushroom" and the "sacred baboon."

The significance of the difference between sacred sites set in nature and those gloriously set apart from it for religious purposes such as the Statue of Zeus at Olympia in the "Golden Age" of Greece and the Sistine Chapel in Rome in the Renaissance can scarcely be overemphasized in terms of the ideas of changing relationships between gods and men. In the fashion of genius, Michelangelo eclectically drew upon both Old Testament stories and upon classic athletic art. Without the ancient Olympics there might well have been no athletic art. Without athletic art there might have been no Renaissance, when the moral qualities associated with the Greek concept of the beautiful body entered "the service of Christianity," in the words of Sir Kenneth Clark, who observed further that "the Greek confidence in the body...expresses above all their sense of human wholeness. Nothing that

---

[12] Pausanias, "The Statue of Zeus at Olympia," <http://www.amazeingart.com/2_amaze/mazes/statue_zeus.l.gif> (2 March 2004).

related to the whole man could be isolated or evaded; and this serious awareness of how much was implied in physical beauty saved them from the twin evils of sensuality and aestheticism."[13]

In Clark's view, the statue of the "The Athlete Walking" by Polykleitos represents "a set of values in which restraint, balance, modesty, proportion, and many others would be applied equally in the ethical and aesthetic sphere.... We should not hesitate to pronounce before his work the word 'moral,' that vague, but not altogether meaningless, word which rumbles in the neighborhood of the nude until the academies of the nineteenth century."[14] Thus, for the Greeks, true beauty reflected an ethos, but the ideal was fragile even in stone and certainly elusive. "The *Heremes* of Praxiteles," according to Clark, represents "the last triumph of the Greek idea of wholeness; physical beauty is one with strength, grace, gentleness, and benevolence. For the rest of the course we witness, in antique art, the fragmentation of the perfect man, and the human body becomes either very graceful or very muscular or merely animal."[15]

In the Renaissance that idea of physical whole was resurrected, as Clark explains:

> Several of the athletes of the Sistine are derived from antique originals, notably the two earliest which are in poses that have come down to us in gems. In these there remains the same basic rhythm of movement that first appeared in the *Diskobolus* of Myron, but already there is a sense of urgency expressed in every inflection of the outline, in every transition of modeling, which the Greeks would have considered fretful and undignified. In spite of the movement, the *Diskobolos* exists entirely in the physical present; the Michelangelo athletes are struggling toward some bodiless future which may perhaps be a past—
>
> *L'anima, della carne ancor vestita,*
> *Con esso e gia piu volte aciesa a Dio.*
> [Your soul already, still clothed in its flesh,

---

[13] Sir Kenneth Clark, *The Nude: A Study in Ideal Form* (Garden City: Doubleday, 1956) 49.

[14] Ibid., 69–70.

[15] Ibid., 77–79.

Repeatedly has risen with it to God].[16]

In addition to everything else he did, Michelangelo wrote some three hundred sonnets.

Clark makes the same point about the comparison and contrast between the athletic art of the Renaissance and the classical models even more powerfully and more concisely in his discussion of the *Creation of Adam.* As mentioned, the same sculptor, Pheidias, who according to tradition created the statue of Zeus, also sculpted the reclining *Dionysus from Parthenon* (c. 435 B.C.), which served as the model for Adam in Michelangelo's Sistine masterpiece, though with a huge difference as Clark reminds us: "*The Dionysus,* in its timeless world, obeys an inner law of harmony; the *Adam* gazes out to some superior power that will give him no rest."[17] Clark's genius of insight into these matters is to art criticism what Michelangelo's genius of insight is to art itself.

In the contrast between Novak's insatiable "driveness" and the expression on the face of Adam we can glimpse, as we can in few other places, the distinction between the human spirit and the holy spirit, which is written all over Adam's face. Instead of "resolving paradoxes," as sports in the view of Miller-McLemore and others have the power to do, religion or religious art almost blatantly makes use of irony and paradox. In Adam's face there is no "driveness" at all, not a look of agony immediately after a strenuous competition but a reflection of adoration, peace, surrender. He does not even bother to lift the forefinger on his left hand to touch the forefinger of the right hand of God. He does not want to "be" God but to be able to "enjoy him forever," much like a good Presbyterian regardless of what the will of the Wholly Other might be for him. We feel that nowhere else in the world is the separation between humankind and the divine so profoundly illustrated as in the space between the forefinger on the left hand of Adam and the right hand of God. Nowhere else is love between God and man so divinely rendered in art.

Why is this irony? Because Michelangelo has, as Clark observes, "after Greek models, given him [Adam] the body of one of the most active of all human types, the body of the athlete." Moreover, he has painted on Adam's

---

[16] Ibid., 275. Bracketed is a translation of "Li Poesia di Michelangelo Buonarroti," <http://www.ucsu.colorado.edu/~Spauldia/poems.html> (30 October 2003).

[17] Ibid., 102.

face (even from the side!) that quality of "aidos," the central trait of the athletic ideal of Greece, which among other things conveys the virtues of reverence, modesty, and honor that might well be called a look of holiness. Here we see the almost perfect blending of Hebraic myth and Greek art. It is as if Michelangelo got Zeus and Jehovah to shake hands, leaving as testimony of the truce a supreme epiphany into the nature of things worthy of the gods themselves.

Other truths are suggested—one, for instance, that the "driveness" Novak finds behind athletics may be closer to a need to eat, drink, scratch, and have sex than the need to worship a superior being. The purpose of athletics is to win a prize in a public place; the purpose of athletic art is, like all other kinds of art, to make us see, perhaps on occasion even to see the holy. Athletics, as stated earlier, may offer fine examples of living art that makes us see the beautiful, which is a by-product of the aim of sports and remarkably preserved in a variety of genres of art, including sports photography, but for great art, beauty is only one side of the picture. The other side is the sublime, and the two together present us with the sense of the holy as Otto himself observes and as Michelangelo demonstrates for the ages.

"Adam," unlike the "Discus Thrower" and the "Athlete Walking," is not poised for any action or motion but in the moment only, and perhaps for the moment only, at rest in body and soul. Indeed Adam's face is a *picture* of "soul," the state when the spirit is at peace with some higher power, whatever that power has in store for him. Adam was waiting and receptive to the touch of the divine. Deep within us all, acknowledged or not, is a burning question, as Jung well knew: Am I connected to something infinite or not? It is a question that cannot be answered by food, sex, drink, scratching, or sports (all things of this world) but by reflection upon mysteries of the transcendent. Put another or even better way, it is the question of Hillel, a Jewish Rabbi and teacher reputed to have exercised a great influence on Jesus, as quoted in Kaufmann's prologue to *I and Thou*: "If I am only for myself, what am I? And if not now, when?"[18]

It can be argued of course that being still, at rest, silent, and centered in meditation upon the idea or image of a superior being is only one form of worship, that shouting and clapping and jumping and singing in congregations where such might be encouraged are also expressions of

---

[18] Kaufmann, prologue to Martin Buber's *I and Thou, 48.*

worship and joy. Who can argue that they are not? We know too that these types of emotional displays can be seen and heard in stadia following scoring against an opposing team, but then we would say that they are rendered unto Zeus as a way of thanking him for turning events in the contest in one's favor.

All joyful noise is not of the same genre, and that sent heavenward from the sidelines, we would argue, is meant for the benefit and amusement of the God of Games. It can still be called "religious" if one would like, and while by no means automatically a bad religion, it is an entirely different religion from that Michelangelo tried to capture in painting, poetry, and sculpture. Here we don't mean simply Catholic religion alone, but a religion where athletics are a *means* to elucidate the themes of strength and beauty, sacrifice, sorrow, and resurrection in a religion already a millennium and a half old and not a means to a worldly prize in peace or war. Zeus's religion touched all sides of community life; it was still centered on athletics as ours, increasingly, is tending to be.

In Michelangelo the athlete is a prominent and essential figure, but he is not the center of attention. Instead he is a symbol reminding us of a God who is not merely up there but is also ahead of us and even behind us, a God not so interested in man's works or achievement either in sports or business but in man's devotion to him alone. After all these centuries, the perspective is still startling. Jehovah is very much alive, but Zeus is gaining in influence in a world where winning is said to be everything, which judging from appearances may well be the case, though this does not make such a philosophy the right one or best one. Regardless, apologists for sports make Zeus smile, even as our scene creates another furrow in the brow of old cantankerous Jehovah, who has all the time in the universe and whose ways are unsearchable and therefore unpredictable, which doomsday prognosticators seem to have forgotten.

An Athletic Culture in Crisis:
Athens, Fifth Century B.C.

Indeed the fortune of the spirit of Zeus has varied inversely with that of his temple and the graven image of him that created awe in all who saw it. After the Olympic games were banned in A.D. 391 by the emperor Theodosius I as pagan practices, the temple of Zeus was closed and in A.D. 426 Theodosius II gave the order for its destruction. "The statue may have perished then or been carried off to Constantinople, to be lost in the great fire that engulfed that city in A.D. 475."[19]

Obviously it's a tough road for a pagan god who is also the "God of Games," a god of illusions in many ways, the word "illusion" coming from *in-lusio*, which means "beginning a game" (see *Man, Play and Games* by Roger Caillois). There is not only the Jewish/Christian God to contend with but megalomaniacal Roman emperors and natural catastrophes called the "acts of God," a phrase that would make you suspicious if, as a thinking statue, you reflected on the warning that there would be no other gods before Jehovah!

Poor Zeus. He has had a hard time of it through the millennia, and the irony is that he always represented more than his statue of gold and ivory would suggest. Even in the totality of his being, however, he is a very different god from Jehovah. There is another irony in the history of Greek culture: the statue of Zeus was erected around the same time the great writers were beginning to ridicule much of what he stood for, though not all of it. Black and white situations are hard to find in cultural or religious history. Euripides (480–406 B.C.) was one of those who looked with skepticism and disdain upon the games, but in his plays there is an ambiguity about Zeus and all the pantheon of the gods as remarked by Werner Jaeger in volume 1 of *Paideia*:

> The relentless criticism to which his characters subject the gods accompanies all tragic action throughout his dramas, but it is only a subordinate motif. In that respect he is in a direct line of criticism which starts with Xenophanes' attacks on the Homeric and Hesiodic myths of the gods, and leads to Plato. The paradox, however, is that the same critical attitude which led both Xenophanes and Plato to denounce the myths as false and immoral obtrudes, in Euripides, into the dramatic representation of these myths, and constantly destroys the illusion which the drama is intended to create. He denies the existence and power of the gods, but at the same time he presents the gods as real and powerful forces in his plays.... He criticizes not only the gods, but the whole of mythology, insofar as it was

---

[19] "The Statue of Zeus at Olympia." http://www.amazingart.com/4_thebook/chpt2.html 6/10/2004

considered by the Greeks to be an ideal world which should inspire mankind to imitation and admiration.[20]

Note the following heartbreaking example from the speech of Hecuba that Jaeger uses to illustrate this ambiguity on the part of characters toward the gods, Zeus in particular: "Thou, earth's support, enthroned on the earth, / Whoever thou mayest be, hard to discover, / Zeus, be thou nature's law or the mind of man, / I pray to thee: for by a noiseless course / Thou guidest human fate in righteousness." "The woman who speaks like this," says Jaeger, "has ceased to believe in the old deities. Her tormented heart, incapable in its agony of abandoning the search for some meaning in the chaos of life, prays to a vison of the first cause set up by philosophers in the place of the vanished gods—as if her prayer could be heard by someone or something in universal space."[21]

Today, we find ourselves in the same dilemma that Euripides and others experienced in the fifth century B.C. when, on the one hand, the Temple of Zeus was being erected, and on the other, writers were calling for a new vision of the gods. It is like hearing hourly reports on threats of bioterrorism and watching a new museum go up in honor of Billy Graham, a sacred site, even as his son Franklin speaks of Islam as "a very evil and wicked religion." If Christianity changes significantly, we can be sure that sports will change accordingly, for even if sports are a religion in and of themselves, they are shaped profoundly by the current rituals and beliefs of traditional religions around them. The tail of religion, owing to the untapped power of good or bad within it, can still wag the growing dog of sports one way or the other.

In significant ways, our current crisis of faith is the reverse of what the Greek intellectuals and writers faced in the fifth century B.C. in order to separate the many powers and attributes of Zeus so his qualities of mind could be embraced even as his intoxication with sports could be lampooned at the height of his glory, as we shall see. With us, the situation is backward; the arts and the humanities are in eclipse while our love of sports accelerates. Sanctifying sports and calling them a religion does not bode well for either a golden age of thought and art or even a mini renaissance,

---

[20] Jaeger, *Archaic Greece: The Mind of Athens*, vol. 1 of *Paideia: The Ideals of Greek Culture*, 2d ed., trans. Gilbert Highet (New York: Oxford University Press, 1945).
[21] Ibid., 350 -51.

for a renaissance is a time when the miracle of the mind is recognized and celebrated as well as the miracle of the body, and both in their combined potential. It can also be, as indeed was the case with the big one in Europe, a time of unspeakable barbarism.

We must acknowledge that any admirer of Zeus, secret or otherwise, would be within his or her rights to say something like this: "There is a lot more to Zeus than a marvelous statue that was banged around for several hundred years. Yes, he is eternally the God of Games, but he knows the struggle of the spirit and mind in the quest for meaning as well. Yes, he has a different agenda from that of Jehovah, but he is more of an opponent than an enemy, an old one to be sure and more honorable than some have given him credit for being."

A look at the index of the *Paideia* volumes shows how integral Zeus, especially as an irritating stimulus to contending perspectives, was to the vast range of great ideas that emerged from ancient Greek culture. Mortimer Adler, as mentioned, reduced these to six ideas by which we live—Truth, Goodness, and Beauty—and those by which we judge—Liberty, Equality, and Justice. He also cites Mark Twain, who quipped that "the ancients stole all our ideas."[22] Emerson remarked that Zeus hates those who do too much, a criticism that seems applicable to Zeus himself until one remembers that he is as much a god as the jealous Jehovah, guarding closely certain prerogatives he is loathe to yield to others.

As the Roman god Jupiter, Zeus is listed in Bible dictionaries, as one more in the long line of some forty false gods with whom the invisible Jehovah/God, eternally beleaguered by rivals with graven images, has to compete, a matter more difficult than confronting, say, the cult of Baal. As "false gods" go, or as any gods go, Jupiter-Zeus comes off well, even sharing several qualities with the stern and rigorous Jehovah in the language of biblical scholarship. The Canaanites had their ideas of what was sacred, and so did the Romans: "Just as the calends (1st) of each month are sacred to Juno, so the ides (13th or 15th), which are full moon days, are sacred to Jupiter. He controls all weather, sends the lightning and rain, was the giver of wine, the decider of battles and giver of victory, watches over justice and truth, and is therefore the most ancient and most important god of oaths."

"Jupiter is mentioned in Acts 14:12, 13, where it is recorded that the people of Lycaonia cried: 'The gods are come down to us in the likeness of

---

[22] Quoted in Adler, *Six Great Ideas* (New York: Collier MacMillan, 1981), 17-18.

men. And they called Barnabas, Jupiter, and Paul, Mercurius, because he was the chief speaker.' Barnabas was probably identified with Jupiter because of his majestic appearance. Paul was identified with Mercury because he was the god of eloquence."[23]

The statue of Zeus is gone, but his spirit thrives. Today he remains the god of sports, stage, screen, and television, especially network sports and the Olympics. As CEO of the financial structures of the world, Zeus is where the money is, and where the money is, mainstream religion also lurks, under whatever name it may use. We can't imagine this world without Zeus because, whatever else he may be, he is the god of striving for notice in this world. He can be a decent god, but he would be a better one if he didn't believe so strongly that winning games in this world is the only thing, something he has never convinced Jehovah/God to accept.

Can Zeus and Jehovah/God live happily together in this world along with gods of other faiths? Apologists and Deion Sanders seem to think they can, that sports can be a common ground for providing such an opportunity much in the manner of Baron de Coubertin. We remain skeptical, but we are not opposed to the possibility as an article of faith. There are enough parallels and counter influences between *Paideia and Early Christianity,* the title of a slim but important volume by Jaeger, to dismiss the idea entirely and no doubt also several parallels between *Paideia* and other faiths.

Examples of art in connection with the sacred occurred as far back as thirty thousand years ago in the rude cave paintings hunters designed for animals they held sacred. Likewise, the sacredness of Zeus and the Olympic games can now only be imagined by the aid of surviving art and in the art of words. In the right hands, such as those of Pindar (522–443 B.C.) and translator Richmond Lattimore, we can easily imagine the scene at the Olympics when prayers for victory were common.

Michelangelo adds to the sacredness of the Sistine Chapel, but his art is so magnificent that it could also be described as holy, a dimension beyond the sacred. Having said this, we must point out that Northrop Frye is right when he says that art, from the walls of the ancient caves to the statue of Zeus to that of the chapel in the Sistine, never improves. Only our critical understanding of art improves, assuming critical intelligence, such as that of Sir Kenneth Clark, continues on the world scene. What we understand about the role of art in connection with the sport or sports and religion is that it

---

[23] *Unger's Bible Dictionary,* 415-16.

serves the twin purposes of memory and meaning, reminding us of the need and value of enacting rites to propitiate the gods or fill us with awe necessary for worship.

It should be noted that all of the sacred sites mentioned above exist "inside" the hunting caves, the Temple of Zeus, and the Sistine Chapel, the last two shrines "caves above grounds," so to speak. Coliseums have such a different mission and history from caves that it strikes one as absurd that they could be considered sacred in any way, especially during athletic contests. Caves in contrast housed the treasures of our earliest art, which may still outlast treasures like the Sistine and have already outlasted the statue of Zeus.

Where, though, we might ask, is the art in stadia that might help establish them as sacred sites in addition to the reasons already indicated by apologists, special time and sacred ground? Stadia can be aesthetically pleasing, but their architecture, no matter how striking, is not the art we go to see in these sacred places (if sacred they are). The art we seek and find is in the performances of the players, the miraculous beauty of the human body, at its best a thing of beauty and a joy forever. The "commingling" of sport, art of the body, and the human spirit driving them both clearly reminds one of any number of rites of previous, religiously-oriented cultures. They are, we believe, good things, which means they can also be bad things.

The more sports lose their special character, their sense of innocent abandon and even raucous fun, the more religion loses some of its sobriety of thought and purpose, especially if it should become a game, that is, an illusion. In a time when categories are vanishing and blending into each other in meaningless ways, it is worth considering the maintenance of distinctions of the different types of rites we practice in our days and their different but similar purposes—to help us find the good life at the ball fields and playgrounds and elsewhere.

If we keep plying Zeus with honors, the next thing we know someone will want to rebuild his statue, which we think would be a mistake at least in the eyes of Jehovah. In this age of monumentalism, we already spend more on the extravagant settings for the Olympic games than the Greeks did with their ancient Wonder and maybe as much for sacred half-time celebrations at the Super Bowl. We already have a 42-foot statue of Athena in the Parthenon in Nashville (the original also created by Pheidias) without becoming any wiser as a result thereof, as Jehovah would likely say while the magnificent passages about his beloved wisdom go widely unread in the electronic age. A creation of a modern version of the statue of Zeus might bring sorrow to Jehovah's heart since he could not help but see it as an obsession he thought we had outgrown or at least put in rational perspective.

Perhaps worse than what Jehovah would suffer from the re-erection of such a statue would be the deleterious effect upon Zeus himself. A giant statue of him in New York, say, at the opening of the 2012 Olympics would suggest that Zeus was just a God of Games and nothing more, when in fact he was always far more than that. We could learn more about him if we didn't look at him in one light only, and the same is true of Jehovah. All of our problems relate to seeing, what the ancient Jews and Greeks both called vision—without which we perish.

Thus Speaks Zeus: God of Media

It may be that Jehovah at last has been revealed as too narrow in his view of graven images, as he himself might conclude by looking at the image of his magnificence on the ceiling of the Sistine Chapel. We have no idea what God thinks outside of passages in Scripture, and those are open to endless debate, but since conversations with God have become a popular genre on television (as illustrated by Andy Rooney and Pat Robertson), since questions of what Jesus would drive, eat, and wear are daily before us, and since Emerson in "the Divinity School Address" pronounced with the resonance of a dogma that "God speaketh, not spake," we are taking a smaller liberty of imagining what a pagan god, Zeus, might say about his mighty competitor over the ages:

"I am so tired of Jehovah getting all the credit for everything when my contributions are scarcely mentioned. I'll admit I am sort of a god manqué since I didn't make the world. Jehovah did that for reasons known only to him, but I am sure I have better judgment about some things that ought to go into it than he does—for one thing athletics and for another athletic art. Without me there would never have been either, and what thanks do I get? Even at ball games Big J gets all the praise, though he secretly disdains just about all of it he sees. I love the Super Bowl and World Series and especially the Olympics, but not one in a thousand knows that save for me people would not have these wonders to enjoy. If Big J had his way, we would all be lying down in green pastures beside still waters counting sheep grazing on the hillside to make sure, as Little J wanted, that all are present and accounted for, especially the lambs. Not me. I love that look of agony in the face of the athlete at the moment of exhaustion.

"Unless I totally misread the fallen world that Big J allowed to happen, there have to be winners and losers. Not many people ever realize it, but that was one of the reasons for the original Olympics, to allow men to compete in some way other than war and under orderly conditions. Battlefields are such a mess, and the number I have seen are legion. Oh, I'm not bothered by it morally and all that rot, just aesthetically, which is why I love sports.

"I am so weary of being ignored. Take Michelangelo, for instance. What would he have amounted to without me? From me he got technique, and what did he do? He turned around and applied his skills to themes from the old book of Big J and the new one about his only begotten son, Little J. It is the same way with Mike's poetry. If he wasn't sculpting or painting, he was writing verse in honor of Big J and Little J as if I had nothing to do with the odes of Pindar honoring me. I can read Mike's mind like a book, for he is as much my child as he is Big J's.

"He got taken in by all the stuff about sorrow. Loss I can understand, even pain, for both those can be overcome, but this anguish and grief of the so-called soul is beyond me. Yet there he is, the greatest genius of all time buying right into it in his *Pieta* and worse by his *Self-Pieta* with angels now coming to his rescue or probably he would say to his redemption. Once that kind of stuff is in the world, it never leaves.

"Now there is a *Boxing Pieta* with a boxer sitting on the canvas and obviously the loser. That scene anyone can understand, but here the compassion stuff rushes in with the referee trying to lift him to his feet, and who is that referee? None other than the boxer himself and his helping hands symbols of angels within. Oh, it's original all right, but you can see in it the same kind of Christian schizophrenia that plagued Mike all his life. More of the endless stunts of Jehovah trying to get everybody to think there is always an invisible world in addition to the one we see so clearly. Here is the big difference between me and Big J. I am the god of the outside world; after all the evidence against him, he keeps insisting that the only true reality is inside. Give me a break.

"I notice now that sports are recognized as a religion. Well, take note of what goes on. Instead of erecting a big statue of me outside the stadium, they put a cross up on top of it! Neither Big J nor Little J approves of such a thing, and neither do I but for different reasons. I don't like crosses. They too are always proclaiming some mystery. What I favor are scepters. I would love to have little statues of me and all my offspring scattered throughout the land just as it was in the good old days in Athens before all these playwrights and philosophers started diminishing me. If I had one motto to share with humans who aspire to scepters and divinity, it would be this—beware of prophets, poets, playwrights, philosophers, and some preachers who either can't hold a regular job or who don't even want one.

"I guess I am like Jehovah in one respect in that it's the little things that get me. Let's take a backward state like Tennessee in the land called America, itself abysmally provincial. In the state capitol of Tennessee, they erected a building called 'The Parthenon,' which at first filled me with joy because I thought it meant that there would be at last be statues of me all over town and maybe a big one, especially since that town came to be called the 'Athens of the South.' Alas, they filled that magnificent replica with statuary I inspired, and not too long ago they placed a 42-foot statue of Athena for all to come and gawk over. They honored my child Athena, who sprang not from my loins but from my head, but not a word was said about me and to add to the insult they made her statue 2 feet taller than the old one of me in Greece that Christian emperors had a frenzy over and tore down and tried to sell, predictably.

"It is the same way with Nike, who originally I held in my right hand. Now her swoosh is everywhere while my thunderbolt is relegated to a logo on helmets here and there, often it seems on those of losing teams. In Nashville there was one indignity after another. Nashville is also noted as a center for the publication of religious texts and never a mention about me except for some occasional putdown in a footnote about the chief god of pagans. It is also known as 'Music City USA' and the 'Home of the Grand Ole Opry,' which at first I thought about encouraging since I have an ear for music and have been known to promote it. Alas again, I bet that half the songs are in praise of 'Little J,' who is always pictured as the friend of the little man and the down and out. Notice how the inner person themes even enter into their music" 'Are You Drinkin' with Me, Jesus?' and 'Her Teeth Were Stained but Her Heart was Pure.'

"It is itself an irony that my heritage is most visible in Tennessee, called 'the most interesting state,' not 'the craziest state,' which California owns and will not relinquish. By the way, I was pleased that Arnold became governor of that state, but I wait for thanks from him for what I did for him as god of the body. Anyway, to return to Tennessee. Just as I am the source of the art in the Parthenon in Nashville, so I am for the R. Tait McKenzie Collection at the University in Knoxville, a big country town with a decent university as American universities go. A former president of that school once spent $165,000 on a tailgate party which makes him my kind of guy, for I am the father of boosters as well as much else. Jehovah can't stand boosters, which is another irony since most of them honor him instead of me.

"Americans suspect great art as the work of Satan, another who will hog all the credit he can gain. As for me, I have ignored him and happily so, since he spends all his time dogging Jehovah. He is a perfect nuisance and doesn't have the sense to just go off and die. Why Big J doesn't squash him once and for all I'll never understand.

"By the way, it is I who am the father of comedy siring Thalia by Mnemosyne (memory) and it is interesting to note, and something in which I take considerable pride, that it was I who taught athletics and comedy to the Jews right under the very nose of Jehovah, and they excelled at both as all people can if they will loosen up. Jehovah himself, the original Puritan, sees nothing funny and never laughs except to laugh last after wiping out some challenger to his domain.

"Another irony, which by the way is something I invented. At the University of Tennessee I have for several years been needling authorities to build the biggest stadium in the country, for I love stadia, and they are attempting to do that. As many as 110,000 attended the game with South Carolina, but, as I expected, there was never a cheer for me from the sidelines, and prayers I picked up on from both sides were headed toward You Know Who. It never fails, but as I say, it's always the little things that hurt most. I never expected to be honored by a huge throng by any town in the Bible Belt, but I would have appreciated a kind word of thanks for the patronage I have provided for athletic art such as that within short walking distance from the stadium at the university. People think that I am merely the god of jocks who themselves pay me no attention but direct their attention to Big J who doesn't care a whit about what they are asking for. I imagine he does little more than yawn. I am the one who could really provide help on such a thing for it is I who has always been the god of victory (*Zeus Nicephoros*).

"In a nutshell, just what is the difference between me and the one across the river? He believes in *mystery* and wants everyone else to believe in such a thing, the impenetrable vapor around the thing he calls the holy, which itself is like a billowy cloak of light and dark with which he surrounds himself. He remains hidden in the shadows. On the other hand you don't have to look hard to find me. I don't believe for a minute that there is a so-called 'inner man,' a holy spirit and all that.

"I love a parade, the spotlight even better. I believe in power but quality too, doing things right which involves victory in the things of the world, for that is all we have. That is why I place so much worth on technique, art, competition, worth and honor of achievement, certification, qualification, arête, without which the thing called culture falls apart, people driving buses or airplanes who don't know how or are trying to win in sports without devoting every last ounce of energy to that purpose.

"It is not an accident that I too am a god of the sun, a god of gold who sees in victory of one kind or another the only happiness we can ever know, the happiness of getting a good job so you people can afford those gold coins and sacred jewelry you like to dress up with on Sunday morning. Jehovah these many centuries keeps insisting that the mystery lies in the absurd faith that what people experience here is not all there is to it, whether one wins a Gold Medal at eighteen or dies in a car wreck caused by a drunken driver. I am the real truth and the light. What we are born into and what we win or lose is the whole ball of wax. There is a majesty in such truth that my adversary has never acknowledged. He and those who follow after him use the idea of mystery to stay in power, which is a trick practiced by governments and, I must confess, by me, for I know there is no mystery except as lies in the contest about who will win. So does the one over the river, but he cannot afford to give up the illusions of that game. I too have abided insufferable indignities and I too have had enough.

People who rave at ball games know I am the supreme god, but I am wanting to hear it from their own mouths. I too have thunderbolts and a quiver as big as the horizon over which the sun rises and sets. I have not used one since Libon asked me what I thought of the temple he had built in honor of me 2,500 years ago. Then I flashed a big one with thunder out of a cloudless sky to display my approval and gratitude. What I have seen since then by Christian worshipers of Big J is destruction of my temple, banishment from my homeland, and endless apostasy while I continue to inspire all who call on me in the name of art and athletics. I am, as far as gratitude goes, like a pariah in the modern world. I am the God of all media, and who is the one always honored on that media? You know who! He is a trickster all right. He knows as well as I that the medium is the message.

"Although you may pretend that I am Jehovah, my real name is Zeus. I am tired of your misspelling it. It is spelled with a Z not a J! As far as I am concerned, 'the first shall be first.' So let the games begin."[24]

---

[24] The *Boxing Pieta* to which Zeus refers is the work of the late Joe Brown, sculptor in residence at Princeton University for many years. The formal name of the piece is *Pieta, 1944*, and a photograph of it appears in *Joe Brown: Retrospective Catalogue, 1932–1966*. Sir Kenneth Clark has said that "the Christian acceptance of the unfortunate body has permitted the Christian privilege of a soul. The conventional nudes based on classic originals could bear no burden of thought or inner life without losing their formal completeness" (*The Nude,* 441). Brown's *Pieta* is an exception, reflecting both the strength of the classical world and the compassion of the Judaic-Christian, a rare achievement. The "R. Tait McKenzie Collection" mentioned by Zeus is officially known as "The Joseph B. Wolffe Collection," housed in the physical education building on the campus of the University of Tennessee, the efforts of Andrew J. Kozar, author of *R. Tait McKenzie: The Sculptor of Athletes* (Knoxville: University of Tennessee Press, 1975). One of the pieces in the collection, "Invictus," shows a boxer on one knee taking the count. The model is Joe Brown, himself a boxer at one time, another illustration of the athlete bearing the burden of an inner life.

Chapter 13

Humor and the Eternal Triangle: Mind, Sports, and Religion

By way of review, we have provided working distinctions between the sacred and the holy, looked at the relation between wisdom and the holy in Scripture and at the role of the media in determining our attitudes toward the sacred, briefly examined the role of sacred knighthood in relation to war, and compared and contrasted the Religion of Sports with conventional religion in terms of spiritual experiences, ethics, and aesthetics or the idea of beauty. In this and the following chapter we wish to look at this new-old religion in light of the phenomenon of humor, which derives from the Greek *hygros* (wet) and the Latin *humere* (to be moist) and is akin to the Old Norse *vokr* (damp). It should not surprise us that the word "humble" has a similar etymology from the Latin *humilis* (low) and *humos* (earth) and akin to the Greek *chthon* (earth), nor that the muse of humor, Thalia, carries a shepherd's staff, an agrarian and spiritual symbol. The prefixes of "humor" and "humble" more than hint at connections with the word "human" and "humility," the quality the holy seems intent on bringing about within us before coming for a visit or as a result of a visit.

As we have seen, the holy may overpower us, awe us, inspire us by the transcendent beauty of music or other art, remind us of lapses or spiritual obligations to ourselves, others, and the earth, and, we strongly suspect, make us laugh at ourselves when we pretend to be more than we are. Humor, the play of the mind, is itself no more inherently divine than sports, the play of the body, yet both as forms of media may serve purposes of the divine. This is not to say we think it's all right to develop religions around either one. Indeed, humor is abused the same way sports often are by reinforcing prejudice of various sorts and making it an end in itself, when the vehicle runs riot and destroys the tenor of the whole or holy.

Just as we have to guard against the idea that "winning is the only thing," so we have do the same in the case of "laughing is the only thing," especially laughing at others. When humor turns serious, it becomes cynical, from the Greek *kynikos* (like a dog), instead of making us "skeptical," from the Greek *skeptikos* (thoughtful) or *skeptesthai* (to look, consider). Unlike the humor of cynicism, the humor of skepticism does not tell us what to believe, but it can suggest what might not be good about our actions. As Emerson remarked in his essay "Montaigne; or the Skeptic," skepticism keeps to the middle way, a potential ally for either doubt or faith. Humor can lean to either side, in the case of Flannery O'Connor toward faith, as argued by Thomas F. Gossett.

> In many writers, humor is associated with a skeptical attitude toward life, but in Flannery O'Connor humor sprang not from skepticism but from faith. I do not mean a generalized faith but faith specifically in the Christian religion. This faith was obvious and the fact that it was often not obvious to other people she saw sometimes as a mistaken judgment but more often as a willful perversity. This perversity was, in her writings and in her life, associated with the idea of comedy. Its most frequent form occurs in the life and philosophy of a person who has raised up some idea to an importance which it does not deserve but which nonetheless prevents a person from seeing life with what she regarded as the wholeness of Christian faith. The fact that the person who makes this mistake is often an intellectual was, for her, one of the chief sources of her comedy. In her fiction, a person can know a great deal and still fail to recognize a truth so obvious that it is instantly apparent, sometimes, to persons who are not blessed with either much intellect or much education. "We are all ignorant," Will Rogers once said, "except about different things." It is this ignorance that can occur in the most surprising places and in the most surprising people which is a chief source of the humor of Flannery O'Connor.[1]

---

[1] Thomas F. Gossett, "Flannery O'Connor's Humor with a Serious Purpose," *Studies in American Humor* <http://www.compedit.com/flannery_o'conner.htm> (2 March 2004).

To O'Connor, humor was helpful, perhaps indispensable, in showing the human displacement from some "center," which we see occurring in most of her stories and in others and ourselves. She would have agreed, we wager, with this opinion of Hugo Rahner: "The inner essence of humor lies, no matter how heretical this may seem, in the strength of religious disposition; for what humor does is to note how far all earthly and human things fall short of the measure of God."[2] Indeed we are all "characters," some in stories, some not, some in jail, some not but not necessarily "free" on that account. Humor may be limited in suggesting what the holy is but quite helpful in telling us what it is not.

The title of Gossett's essay, "Flannery O'Connor's Humor with a Serious Purpose," is intriguing. It suggests that normally the serious is a higher order than the playful, but at the same time, as in a paradox, it more than hints at the basic theme that runs through *Homo Ludens* by Huizinga regarding the essentialness of the playful: the playful can be serious, but the serious can't be playful. The intertwining of the playful or humorous and the serious appears to be a key feature of the holy, and when we elevate one part to the exclusion of the other we make one attitude toward life sacred and the other profane, as the Puritans did with their attitude toward fun, according to H. L. Mencken in his celebrated definition of Puritanism, "the haunting fear that somewhere, somebody might be happy."[3]

There is, though, a trap in the other direction as well—first of all, identifying what is serious and what is playful and elevating one or the other to the level of sacredness, a tricky and dangerous undertaking. In spite of appearances, at least in Huizinga's view, war is playful, or play at its brutal worst—the abandonment of comity, civility, and rules—and the peaceful is serious—dependent upon a "pledge," the roots of which are virtually synonymous with "play," Old English "*plega*" and Middle French "*plege*" respectively. Playing "in peace" is a higher, creative play than the destructive play of war, dependent upon mutual caring by all concerned. In other words, we have made of war a sacred game, which is why its awful consequences are not evident to us unless we are directly involved.

Let's put the matter this way—the best play and perhaps the only pure play is "fair play," which war or politics never are. For us in "developed

---

[2] Rahner, *Man at Play*, trans. Brian Battershaw and Edward Quinn (New York: Herder and Herder, 1972) 35.

[3] Mencken, *The Vintage Mencken*, ed. Alistair Cooke (New York: Alfred A Knopf, 1955) 233.

countries" with resources and power, we continue to play our sacred games in which victory remains the only acceptable outcome. For many of the underdeveloped countries, war remains the primary thing, even though winning is rarely an outcome of any consequence in a continuous dance of despair. Sports may be "fair play" in regard to closely regulated and enforced rules, but they must be judged, as war must be, in terms of cost and nature of the prizes for which they are undertaken. Sports, thus, especially sports in the schools, must be considered not only in terms of fair play during contests but balanced *in context* of the whole of students' lives.

What literally needs to come into play in academe especially pertaining to demands between mind and body, the playful and the serious, is the classical ideal of *Eutrapelia*, "well-turningness" between one endeavor and another as discussed in Rahner's *Man at Play*. We must recognize that there are at least two sides to everything, not only to football games and war but even to the darkest events central to our religions—in Christianity the crucifixion itself. If Christ is in heaven where the faithful will also go, then Golgotha appears to be part of a comedy, which means that in the end everything is joyfully resolved. If Christ is eternally on the cross, then it is a tragedy, though either view can offer truths by which to live.

In the manner of the ancient Greeks, we tend to see life in a polarized fashion, either as tragedy or comedy. The same is true of Christianity, which has popularized a host of dichotomies with wide fill-in-the-blanks for individuals or groups: Good (American) and Bad (communists), Saved (the baptized) and Unsaved (unbaptized), Sacred (stadia and churches) and Profane (bars and houses of ill repute). The same type of polarization and simplification is readily visible in other religions as well, keeping war between faiths not merely an option but a likelihood.

The world, we are discovering, is not so simple. It is not simply polarized but amazingly diversified in every area of consideration and complicated beyond our imagination as suggested by Sam Keen's metaphor that God is in our DNA. We are seeing too that the old labels such as tragedy and comedy are not running side by side as in two lanes around a track but intertwining constantly every moment of our lives, filling us with a sense of irony, confusion, wonder, stark terror, and sometimes abounding joy—all fleeting aspects of the human condition. In *Telling the Truth: The Gospel as Tragedy, Comedy, and Fairy Tale,* Frederick Buechner puts the familiar "as" to good work in literary genres. He aims to illuminate one inconceivable story haunting the chambers of the soul—three fixes or lines, as in celestial navigation, that are needed for determination of one's location and course.

Buechner moves in a different direction and manner from that of the sports apologists. He takes the familiar genres of literature and uses them as vehicles to view the tenor of the Gospels, assuming on intuition, if nothing else, that their worth is undeniable, which calls for constant review and rethinking. The sports apologists use our familiar games as vehicles to try to convince us that the vehicles themselves are of worth not as aids in understanding but as religious in and of themselves. Buechner tries to shed more light on the mystery of the Gospels. Sports apologists, on the other hand, try to sanctify our games by referring to traditions far older than the written Gospels and, from our perspective, more mystifying but less mysterious since they reflect merely struggle for power with others and with nature, but not a struggle within the individual soul as in the Gospels, a struggle every minute of every day, or as Thoreau says in "Higher Laws "in *Walden*, "there is never an instant's truce between vice and virtue."

One thing is for sure in exegesis these days—the word "as," both preposition and conjunction, is having its finest hour, its versatility unquestioned. It stands outside the ornate mansion of theology and literary criticism like (or as) a faithful steed waiting to carry any argument as far as possible into the heart of mystery and to return again for assessment of discovery, if any. We have become so fascinated by the use of "as" that we want to use it in our final chapters. Specifically, we would like to regard humor, sports, and religion *as* an eternal triangle that, ideally, would be balanced much like truth, beauty, and goodness, with each serving as a check on the others. Unfortunately, over the years this harmony has not frequently prevailed; humor is often pushed aside by a serious alliance between sports and religion in a super serious enterprise of one kind or another as we see in ancient Greece, Medieval and Renaissance Europe, on the American frontier in the nineteenth century, and in the present.

Before illustrating the abundant presence of the triangle in history, we first want to demonstrate the connection, often ironic, between humor and religion, not just one religion but many if not all. It is a kinship not often assumed in contrast to sports and humor, which have much in common since both are supposed to be fun and both forms of play. Similarly sports and religion have been courting one another for the last few thousand years, from time to time even engaging in sacred matrimony in different lands—ancient Greece, Mesoamerica, Medieval Europe, and modern

America as apologists remind us. Religion and sports find common ground in the realm of transcendent experiences, in expression of beauty, and in ethics, as different as these positions are between them in terms of holy and sacred, as we have tried to show. The question of the relation between humor and religion is not so apparent. It is analogous to Tertullian's question as to what Jerusalem has to do with Athens. In both cases we would answer, "just about everything."

The Ecumenicalism of Humor

The ad on the back cover of Elton Trueblood's book *The Humor of Christ* bears testimony to the content: "Christ employed humor for the sake of truth and many of his teachings, when seen in this light, become brilliantly clear for the first time. Irony, satire, paradox, even laughter itself help clarify Christ's famous parables and important events in his life."[4]

Since the idea of prizes presented in public places is central to ritual in sports, as well as in business, education, the military, and even in religion, it is appropriate to cite the passages dealing with conspicuous goodness, which are also illustrative, in Trueblood's view, of Christ's use of irony. Jesus mentions the well-known practice of men who wish to advertise their piety or their benevolence and rejects this as totally unworthy. "'Beware,' He says, 'of practicing your piety before men in order to be seen of them' (Matt. 6:1). In regard to philanthropy He rejects, in our terms, the *bronze plaque*. 'Thus, when you give alms, sound no trumpet before you, as the hypocrites do in the synagogues and in the streets, that they may be praised by men' (Matt. 6:2). All this is very clear, very straightforward, and not really funny. It is too sad to be funny, as we all know when we examine our own practice by this elevated standard. The sentence seems to bring the discussion to an end *but it doesn't*, and therein lies the humorous twist. The punch is topped by the added line, 'They have their reward.' This says volumes and it is profoundly amusing. Watch out for what you want, He seems to say, for you are very likely to get it." The same irony applies to those who try to look sad in order to display their piety (Matt. 6–16). They have their reward; *they succeed!*[5] Like junk food for the soul, it may taste good for the moment but doesn't last or satisfy the deepest needs within.

---

[4] Trueblood, *The Humor of Christ* (New York: Harper and Row, 1975).
[5] Ibid., 58.

One of the methods of humor Jesus used, says Trueblood, was the "preposterous" as in the metaphor of the difficulty a camel would have going through the eye of a needle. In regard to the problem of riches and salvation of the soul, he wanted to say something memorable, which fell on deaf ears then and now.

> For humorous purposes this is evidently the same camel swallowed by the Pharisee when he carefully rejected the gnat. That the listeners failed to see the epigram about the needle's eye as a violent metaphor is shown by their question, "Then who can be saved?" (Mark 10:26).
>
> By making the statement in such an exaggerated form, termed by Chesterton the *giantesque*, Christ made sure that it was memorable, whereas a prosy qualified statement certainly have been forgotten. The device is mirrored in our conventional Texas story, which no ones believes literally, but which everyone remembers.[6]

The same genius of Jesus for use of the preposterous is seen in the metaphors about the log in the eye of the beholder and the speck in the eye of his neighbor[7]. Trueblood wrote *The Humor of Christ* after being inspired by his four-year old son. As the child's parents read the boy part of Matthew 7, the little boy began to laugh.[8] Children naturally love metaphors, even of wild association of images; our education seems purposely designed to kill that instinct so that the vast majority who graduate from high schools and colleges, following long indoctrination of academic jargon and rational thinking, have one thing in common—an aversion to poetry and symbolic thinking. The poet James Dickey said that we had sentenced language to the utilitarian, and James Still told us that around universities one listened in vain for a memorable metaphor, so saturated have we become with jargon in all the things we study with such seriousness in the halls of academe, not to mention in business meetings of the churches and in churchly meetings of corporations.

The use of the "preposterous" by Christ, says Trueblood, was essential. He "had a revolutionary message to give and he knew that he could not make himself understood by speaking mildly. He said that, following John, 'the good

---

[6] Ibid., 47–48.
[7] Ibid., 1.
[8] Ibid., 48.

news of the kingdom of God is preached, and every one enters it violently'
(Luke 16:16) We do not know all that he meant by 'violently,' but we know
that there was an element of 'violence' in His speech, a feature that comes
down to us today even after the toning down on the part of the reporters" (48).
One is immediately reminded of the serious humor or humorous seriousness in
Flannery O'Connor's fiction, especially the novel *The Violent Bear It Away*,
whose title she took from a verse in Matthew: "From the days of John the
Baptist, until now, the kingdom of Heaven suffereth violence, and the violent
bear it way" (11:12). Whatever the meaning of violent in the New Testament
or in O'Connor, it would appear related to the idea of radical, even final,
choice, a breaking through to something new. It does not appear to be related
to the idea of shock and awe as in modern journalism and weaponry, but to the
shock of recognition of one's actual condition in the cosmos.

Humor in Scripture is not limited to the New Testament. In examining
laughter, Frederick Buechner writes,

> Sarah was never going to see ninety again, and Abraham had
> already hit one hundred, and when the angel told them that the stork
> was on the way at last, they both of them almost collapsed. Abraham
> laughed "till he fell on his face" (Gen. 17.7), and Sarah stood cackling
> behind the tent door so the angel wouldn't think she was being rude as
> the tears streamed down her cheeks. When the baby finally came, they
> even called him "Laughter"—which is what Isaac means in
> Hebrew—because obviously no other name would do.
>
> Laughter gets mixed up with all sorts of things in the Bible and in
> the world too, things like sneering, irony, making fun of, and beating
> the competition hollow.
>
> It's the crazy parrot-squawks that issue out of David as he spins
> like a top in front of the Ark (II Samuel 6:16–21).... It's what Jesus
> means when he stands in that crowd of cripples and loners and odd-
> balls and factory rejects and says, "Blessed are you that weep now, for
> you shall laugh" (Luke 6:21).
>
> Sarah and her husband had had plenty of hard knocks in their
> time, and there were plenty more of them to come, but at that moment
> when the angel told them they'd better start dipping into their old age
> pensions for cash to build a nursery, the reason they laughed was that it

suddenly dawned on them that the wildest dreams they had ever had hadn't been half wild enough (Gen. 17, 18, 21).[9]

If anyone in Scripture can testify to the variety of modes the holy uses in dealing with mortals, it is Abraham. In the two encounters with the "Other" cited in this text, he is struck down to the earth, reduced to "dust and ashes," and later reduced to uncontrollable laughter of surprise and joy and overwhelming absurdity as in *Webster's*—"having no rational or orderly relationship to man's life." Fear and joy are familiar extremes of holy encounters that mystics have often noted. The way Buechner uses "wild" is intriguing and has more significance for the future of the race than we might expect. It is, we suggest, another name for the holy or one side of the holy with which we have largely lost touch.

When Thoreau said that "in wildness lies the hope of the world," he could just as easily have said "in the holy lies the hope of the world." He sought the holy every day in his saunterings and in his climb on Mount Katahdin. "I love the wild no less than the good," he said, which was his way of acknowledging the place of ethics, but without the wild there may be no good of any lasting worth. In his *Journal* he writes, "Bless the Lord, O my soul, bless Him for wildness, for crows that will not alight within gunshot and bless Him for hens, too, that croak or cackle in the yard."[10]

The wildness of celebrating fans following sports victories is not the same as that sought by Thoreau. Instead, it is a form of pseudo wildness or, as Thoreau would say, more evidence of the unconscious despair beneath the games and amusements of mankind. Abraham encountered the "real deal," real terror and real fun. Spectacles on television are illusions, a word from *illusio,* "the state or fact of being intellectually deceived or misled." Again, what we see is incredible and irrational, while what we read about Abraham is credible and nonrational, though meaningful. The laughter of Abraham and Sarah is a surprise to them, a response to the totally unexpected. The laughter on reality shows is always expected, not a response but a reaction. Humor in its highest form makes us "see," perhaps to make us laugh, as in the stories above from the Old and New Testaments; in its lowest form it simply makes us laugh, if

---

[9] Buechner, *Peculiar Treasures: A Biblical Who's Who* (San Francisco: Harper and Row, 1997) 152–53.

[10] *Thoreau: Walden and Other Writings, ed.* Knutch (New York: Banter Books, 1965) 427.

at all. Consider the following examples from faiths other than Christian and Jewish that make us "see" and laugh:

Buddhism: A young female disciple undertook to develop the meditation of loving-kindness. Sitting in her small room, she would fill her heart with loving-kindness for all beings, yet each day as she went to bazaar to gather her food, she would find her loving-kindness sorely tested by one shopkeeper who would daily subject her to unwelcome caresses. One day she could stand no more and began to chase the shopkeeper down the road with her upraised umbrella. To her mortification she passed her teacher standing on the side of the road observing this spectacle. Shame-faced she went to stand before him expecting to be rebuked for her anger.

"What you should do," her teacher kindly advised her, "is to fill your heart with loving-kindness, and with as much mindfulness as you can muster, hit this unruly fellow over the head with your umbrella."[11]

Hindu: When the guru sat down to worship each evening, the Ashram cat would get in the way and distract the worshipers. So he ordered that the cat be tied during evening worship.

After the guru died, the cat continued to be tied during evening worship. And when the cat expired, another cat was brought to the Ashram so that it could be tied during evening worship.

Centuries later learned treatises were written by the guru's scholarly disciples on the liturgical significance of tying up a cat while worship is performed.[12]

Islamic: The following is attributed to Nasreddin Hodja.

One day four boys approached Hodja and gave him a bagful of walnuts.

"Hodja, we can't divide these walnuts among us evenly. So would you help us, please?"

Hodja asked, "Do you want God's way of distribution or mortal's way?"

---

[11] *Stories of the Spirit, Stories of the Heart*, ed. Christina Feldman and Jack Kornfield (San Francisco: Harper, 1991) 297.

[12] Ibid., 249.

"God's way," the children answered.

Hodja opened the bag and gave two handfuls of walnuts to one child, one handful to the other, only two walnuts to the third child and none to the fourth.

"What kind of distribution is this?" the children asked, baffled.

"Well, this is God's way," he answered. "He gives some people a lot, some people a little and nothing to others. If you had asked for mortal's way I would have given the same amount to everybody."[13]

The Eternal Triangle in Classical Greece and the Renaissance

Sometimes humor has been part of the problem, creating laughter at the misery of others. Thalia, muse of comedy, is always tempted to abuse her art in a world in conflict, but, like her sister muses, she is a figure of serenity and good will. When occasion demands, she is a fighter, though armed only with comedy, dance, wit, and a sense of festival. If humor is a check on sports and religion, so sports and religion are a restraint on humor. Melpomene, muse of tragedy, is a reminder to Thalia that not everything in life is song, dance, and fun. Not surprisingly, she carries a sword and like Thalia wears a mask. Polyhymnia, muse of sacred verse, wears a veil indicating a screen between mortals, and even gods and goddesses of the earth, and something other we do not understand but feel impelled to worship by verse and song.

Their half-brother Apollo, son of Zeus, is a reminder to Thalia and other muses that play is not enough, that a desire dwells in each of us to compete in contests, to excel. In paintings he is sometimes pictured as playing the lyre, but he will cast it aside in an instant to watch a good footrace or to run in one himself. His competitive instincts are enormous, and he is the sorest loser on record, which makes him far more dangerous than his sisters who are primarily devoted to arts and sciences, learning, sacred song, dance, festival, and fun, which would seem to be enough to satisfy the needs of human normalcy. Yet we forget something bigger than all these together, the desire *to be right*, and, even greater than that, the desire *to win* in sports, politics, business, and even religion and war as in

---

[13] Alpay Kabahali, *Nasreddin Hodja*, trans. Nuket Erasian (Net Turistik Yakinlar A.S., 1999) 15.

"my god is good and yours is bad" and even "my Sunday school is bigger than yours."

It is true that Melpomene holds a sword, but it is a symbol of the tragedy wrought by Apollo when he is unchained from bonds with his sisters. The word "museum" derives from the name given by the ancients to a temple of the muses. We tend to think of the muses as relics of ideas belonging to another age, but the light of learning they represent is, while flickering, still alive, though not as evident as the spirit of Apollo, the sun god of beauty and power.

The goal of Thalia, like that of her sisters, is grace and harmony and delight in being as reflected in family pictures of them with Apollo on Parnassus and Olympia. Though the lords of religion over the ages do not always seem to be aware of it, Thalia may be one of the best friends any faith can have. She is a pagan reminder of the natural joys of dancing, laughing, playing, and singing and that the best place for all is on the holy earth and not in a sacred stadium, the abode of Apollo. As long as Apollo is singing and playing with his half-sisters, essentially muses of the arts and sciences, he—god of beauty, games, colonization, exploration—is fine, a decent member of a family.

When Apollo parts company with them, he picks up a sword or club in a moment's notice. His spirit, for example, ruled over Nazi Germany, symbolized by the attention given to beauty and power but also by the burning of books and intolerance of competing ideas. The movie *Sunshine*, set in Hungary from the days of monarchy until democracy after the Cold War, is centered in part on the story of the flaying of Marsyas (Pan) by Apollo following their celebrated music contest, powerfully illustrating what happens to the Olympics, to justice, and to liberty when Apollo leaves his sisters and travels the world as the only god to worship. *Sunshine* shows that unless sports and religion support or reflect the idea of justice, both are of no account, merely old vehicles without tenor of value to human society or transcendent deity.

In other art, the theme of the music contest, taken from *Metamorphoses* by Ovid, is unforgettably captured in the painting *Marsyas* by Titian and in an antique sculpture by that name, created by the Pergamene school in Asia Minor during the third century B.C. It shows, says Kenneth Clark, "the *Marsyas* hanging with his hands and feet bound to a tree, waiting in terror for the knife. In its origins this myth had expressed the cruel arrogance of the Apollonian idea; but the men of Pergamon…felt enough sympathy with

Marsyas to make his figure into a tragic symbol. The stretched out body is as defenseless as a dead animal in a butcher's shop, and the columnar form allows a concentration, a bare basic simplicity, that was to satisfy the ultimate needs of Michelangelo."[14]

The problem with Apollo is not that he is a sore loser because, being a god, he doesn't know what losing is, a common problem of gods everywhere. The problem is that he is a sore winner. His flaying of an opponent is a perfect example of the *thymos* in contests of all kinds noted by Girard. Even today we speak of athletic contests in which one team "skins another." This is an early illustration of the triumph of the sun god over the god of the earth, a scene reflected repeatedly in art through the ages (in, for example, the *Martydom of Saint Erasmus* by Nicholas Poussin, seventeenth century), with the muscular Apollo holding a club and receiving the praise of those superintending the gutting of the patron saint of those with bowel problems, understandably. We can see the same kind of thing in the daily news, the "skinning" and "gutting" of the have-nots by the haves.

None of this is to claim that gods of nature are perfectly good or that the sky gods are always bad, only that there is a difference in modus operandi in regard to sports and play. While play is generally a thing of the earth, the sun gods love competition inherent in sports with attendant sacrifices of some kind that insure the worship of them. What is required is a vision of a whole picture, which is what the greatest thinkers among us have always tried to provide, such as Otto Rank in the "Self and the Ideal," wherein he identifies the polar opposites between which we are continually swung (or maybe strung)—the Apollonian, which insists that we imitate the models of power and conformity, and the Dionysian, which tells us to rebel and rejoice in our own selves. Since both in extreme are destructive, the one advocating "doing," as in imitation, and the other "being," Rank recommends a third way that he calls the Kantian, "determining thyself from thyself."[15]

This middle or moderate way seems commensurate with the core of major religions and pagan philosophy but not with the extremes of any. It strikes a balance between the impulses of play, *paideia*, and sports with lots of *ludus* or "gratuitous difficulty." With the crisis looming ahead of us in

---

[14] Sir Kenneth Clark, *The Nude: A Study in Ideal Form* (Garden City: Doubleday, 1956) 300–301.

[15] Rank, *The Myth of the Birth of the Hero and Other Writings*, ed. Philip Freund (New York: Vintage Books) 293.

our sports, always a symbol of cultural health or decline, it is time we
started thinking about balance and moderation as the sanest alternative to
over-regulation on the one hand and Dionysian excess on the other.

Sir Kenneth Clark underscores this idea in his discussion of the duality
of Apollo and Marsyas:

> Apollo, who in the early nineteenth century, was lost sight of in
> the smoke of materialism, has become in this century the object of
> positive hostility. From Mexico, from the Congo, even from the
> cemeteries of Tarquinia, those dark gods, of which D. H. Lawrence
> made himself the prophet, have been brought out to extinguish the
> light of reason.... This is the justification of Apollo in his cruel
> triumph over Marsyas. The union of art and reason, in whose names
> so many lifeless works have been executed and so many ludicrous
> sentiments pronounced, is after all a high and necessary aim; but it
> cannot be achieved by negative means, by coolness or
> nonparticipation. It demands a belief as least as violent as the
> impulses it controls; and if today in the sensual wailing of the
> saxophone, Marsyas seems to be avenged, that is because we have
> not the spiritual energy to accept the body and to superintend it.[16]

There is a good argument in the claim that the chief struggle in the
world is always between Apollo and Dionysus as advanced by Nietzsche
and others, but whichever side an individual chooses, the decision will relate
to attitudes toward sports, art, reason, education, and religion, to matters of
control on the one hand and of freedom on the other.

In ancient Greece, at least after a certain period, sports and religion had
so much in common that to speak out against one was to criticize the other.
During the second half of the sixth century B.C., a famous philosopher by
the name of Xenophanes saw what he called "ominous current trends
whether in religion or in athletics."[17] In a similar fashion, Euripides at the
close of the fifth century B.C. saw games and feasts as "useless pleasures" of
no benefit to defense of the city.[18] How many other people shared such
"views in those days," says Robinson, "it is not safe to estimate, but very

---

[16] Clark, *The Nude*, 108.
[17] See Rachel Sargent Robinson, *Sources for the History of Greek Athletics* (Chicago: Ares, 1980) 90.
[18] Ibid., 116–17.

probably, as would be the case today, they were very few."[19] The most memorable denunciation was by Diogenes the Cynic (404–323 B.C.), notorious for his biting scorn and nicknamed the "Mad Socrates" by Plato.

When a winner in the 200-yard race for men in the Isthmian Games joyfully announced his victory, Diogenes informed him he had not become any wiser because he had got ahead of those who were running with him and added that "he would not live any freer from misery." "No, by Zeus," the runner replied, "but I can run faster than any other Greek." "No doubt," said Diogenes, "but not faster than hares or deer—and yet these animals are the most cowardly of all...the same creatures that are the swiftest are likewise the most cowardly of all." After seeing two horses kicking one another and one breaking away, Diogenes went up to the remaining horse and placed a wreath on his head and pronounced him a victor in the games because he had won the kicking contest or pancratium. In this tale he was greeted by cheers by the onlookers who then proceed to poke fun at the athletes.[20]

The form of satire Diogenes uses is theriophily, either showing the superiority of animals over humans or features common to both. He was definitely not Baron de Coubetrin's kind of guy. The stories of the dissidents reveal what Robinson calls a "rhetorical commonplace" among the few critics of the ancient Olympics, but they tell us that even among those on the scene in classic times, there were a few who at least did not consider sports as a religion and more than likely would not do so today, possibly for the same reasons. Generally, and Robinson indicates as much, the criticism was directed at the system of games and not so much at individual athletes, a pattern that seems to prevail over time.

Satire usually attacks on several fronts, and this was the case of the satire of knighthood in the Renaissance. Among the several targets were religious customs, the chivalric code, the cult of manliness, and preoccupation with games and training for battle, as noted earlier in *Gargantua* by Rabelias. The spoofing of knight-errantry is everywhere in the Renaissance as in the mockery of courtly love by Theseus in Chaucer's

---

[19] Ibid., 91.
[20] Ibid., 137–39.

Knight's Tale. Even the size and extravagance of the 200,000-seat stadium where Arcite and Palamon battle seems a tongue-in-cheek commentary on the popular taste of ancient Athens and England of Chaucer's time. It is by far bigger than any we know about in the ancient world and almost twice as large as Michigan Stadium, the largest for college football in the United States. Obviously exaggerating in comparison to the stadia of his day, Chaucer was nevertheless prophetic, knowing how love of sports might grow. While his stadium might be a little big for NASCAR tournaments, it is nearly right for a playoff in Brazil in world soccer.

The title hero of *Don Quixote* by Cervantes and the incomparable Falstaff of Shakespeare play havoc with the stylized heroism of the Renaissance. For Falstaff "discretion turns out to be the better part of valor," and says the dying Quixote to his friends, "Good gentlemen, congratulate me and rejoice with me upon my no longer being Don Quixote de La Mancha but plain Alonso Quixano, surnamed the Good on account of his innocence and simplicity of life. I am now an enemy of that whole tribe of heroes of knight errantry. Now I am aware of my own madness, into which I fell because of reading them and now I abominate and abhor them."[21] The great Don dies but knighthood lives on, spreading around the globe, widening its influence, and keeping its ancient connections with militant religions everywhere of whatever faith. The satire of knighthood survived as well, as seen in Mark Twain, who made of chivalry a major target wherever he found it—in Arthur's England in *A Connecticut Yankee* or in the Confederate South as in *Huckleberry Finn*. He even blamed the Civil War on Sir Walter Scott for filling the Southern mind with the "sham grandeur" of his romances.

The Triangle on the Southern Frontier:
The Preacher, the Trickster, and the Hunter

How has the connection between religion and humor worked in America? Much the same as always, each a check on the other so that religion won't get too serious and humor too playful. Loyal Jones explains the nature of the relation between them, at least in the Appalachia: "We believe in God. We try to believe in goodness, in perfectibility, but

---

[21] Miguel de Cervantes, *Don Quixote*, trans. Tobias Smollett (London, 1975; New York: Farrar, 1986). Adapted translation from Karl F. Thompson, ed., *Classics of the Western World*. vol. 4 (New York: Harcourt, 1988) 516.

underneath is the fear that we are going it alone in the world and getting euchered...pretending that we are worthy and in control. Yet we know that our dignity is a too small hat in the winds of truth. All people know this, but here in this region we keep it uppermost in our minds so that the only reasonable thing to do about it is to laugh —at ourselves and at others who pretend, against odds, that all is well with the human enterprise."[22]

The same perspective on the human condition is echoed throughout Jones's writing: "We may say, for example, of those who aspire to learning, 'preachers and lawyers and buzzard eggs'—there's more hatched than ever come to perfection." One is not surprised that Jones collected the following story told by Will Campbell, a Presbyterian minister and leader in the Civil Rights movement: "A bunch of men were digging a hole in the middle of town. The local character who wasn't too smart came by and asked, 'What you going to put in that hole?' The boss of the job said, 'We're going to round up all the sons of bitches in town and put them in that hole.' The fellow thought for a minute and then said, 'Who's going to cover them up?'"[23]

Southern humor reflects a strong sense of flawed human nature emphasized by Calvinism and summarized by the axiom "In Adam's fall we sinned all." Exaggerated self-denigration becomes the pattern as seen in Mark Twain's quip that his "folks were poor but dishonest" and in the first joke Minnie Pearl pulled on the Grand Ole Opry. When asked by someone if "Brother" had small pox, Minnie replied "no"; "the family had been trying to teach him to eat with a fork."

Jones comments on the mountaineer's love of hunting dogs and of basketball, but we might add that generally speaking, neither hunting nor basketball has become a religion in the mountains excepting perhaps in certain cases, judging from some fans we know and love, who center on Kentucky Wildcat basketball. It needs to be emphasized, though, that just as religion and humor have been inseparable in the South, especially in Appalachia, so have sports and humor. The literature of the Southern frontier, principally the tall tale, is still categorized as "The Humorous and Sporting Writing of the Old Southwest," and much of that humor was anti-

---

[22] Jones, *Laughter in Appalachia: A Festival of Southern Mountain Humor*, ed. Loyal Jones and Billy Ed Wheeler (Little Rock: August House, 1987) 19–20.

[23] Campbell, in *More Laughter in Appalachia: Southern Mountain Humor*, ed. Loyal Jones and Billy Ed Wheeler (Little Rock: August House, 1995) 34.

clerical like that Chaucer's humor. One difference, however, was that on the frontier ministers themselves were involved in the fun.

Practically every yarn in that antebellum body of writing was about humor and play in some form, often the prank, and some aspect of religion was usually part of the plot, as in the classic tale of Sut Lovingood, "A Nat'ral Born Durn'd Fool," letting loose a bunch of lizards up Parson John Bullen's breeches to the delight of the reader since that particular parson deserved it. The parson had some revenge in preaching Sut's funeral using these immortal words: "We air met, my brethering, to bury this ornery cuss. He had hosses, an' he run 'em; he had chickens, an' he fit 'em; he had kiards, an' he played 'em. Let us try to recollect his virtues—ef he had any—and forgit his vices—ef we can. *For of sich air the kingdom of heaven!*"[24]

Sut's tricks are not by any means unique with him, as Cratis Williams, "Mr. Appalachia," has observed. "The pranks that Sut rigged on his enemies have been the stock in trade of his counterparts down to recent times. Such things as turning snakes and lizards loose in churches, throwing nest of hornets in praying congregations howling their sins at the mourner's bench, luring preachers, sheriffs, candidates for office, and school teachers into compromising situations have their local adaptations in the oral traditions of most mountain communities."[25] Moreover, many of these kinds of stories came from Europe as seen in Arne Thompson's *Type and Motif Index*, and some of them are still heard today as in songs by Ray Stevens and stories by Jerry Clower, all reflective of the endless struggle between the limits of order, religious and political, and the delight in mayhem.

The humor here is a form of "schadenfreude," enjoyment obtained from others' troubles. Schadenfruede comes in all kinds of packages, especially in stories of vengeance as in the following, which certainly is not scriptural but not without meaning: "When the Son of God was nailed to the cross and died, he went straight down to hell from the cross and set free all the sinners were in torment. And the devil wept and mourned, for he thought he would get no more sinners for hell. Then God said to him, 'Do not weep, for I shall send you

---

[24] M. Thomas Inge, introduction in George Washington Harris, *Sut Lovingood Yarns* (New Haven: College and University Press Servers, 1966) 24.

[25] Williams, "Sut Lovingood As a Southern Mountaineer" (Appalachian State College Faculty Publication, 1966) 3.

all those who are self-righteous in their condemnation of sinners and hell shall be filled up once more until my return.'"[26]

Parson John Bullen asks that we remember Sut's virtues if he had any. Well, we think he did, along with a lot of faults. He spoke a certain truth, though with a great deal of frivolity and freedom. In creating this "nat'ral born durn'd fool," George Washington Harris was well aware of the verse in Scripture that states, "the fool has said in his heart there is no God" (Ps 14:1; 53:1). Sut may well be aware of the verse, but interestingly and perhaps ironically he is a believer himself as indicated in his rationale for "creating" the book Edmund Wilson called "the most repellent book of any merit in American letters." Says Sut, "Ef eny poor misfortinit devil hu's heart is onder a millstone, hu's raggid children am hungry, an no' bread in the dresser, hu is down in the mud, an' the lucky ones a-tripping him every time he struggles to his all fours, hu hes fed the famishin and is now hungry hissef, hu misfortins foller fas and foller faster, hu is so foot-sore an' weak that he wishes he were at the ferry—ef sich a one kin fine a laugh, jis'one, sich a laugh as is remembered wif his keerless boyhood, a twixt these yere kivers—then, I'll thank God that I *hes* made a book, an' feel that I hev got my pay in full."[27]

As a self-proclaimed fool, Sut makes us aware of our own foolishness, prejudices, and other faults and of the priorities we establish in our lives that reflect neither common sense nor the fruit of the spirit but vanity, ignorance, and greed as in the following: "Whar thar ain't enuf feed, big childer roots little childer outen the troff, an gobbills up that part. Jis' so the yeath over; bishops eats elders, elders eats common peopil, they eats sich cattil es me, I eats possums, possums eats chickens, chickens swallers wums, an wums am content to eat dus, an the dus am the aind of hit all."[28]

That humor of the frontier called anti-clerical is not against the ministry but only against the way some ministers behaved, just as Mark Twain's withering fire was not against religion in general but against religion as practiced in a slave culture, a nation at war with itself, during the scandal-ridden period of reconstruction, followed by what he regarded as our imperial phase. The fire was not against business but against the business practices of the robber barons, not against Congress but against the way

---

[26] Feldman and Kornfield, *Stories of the Spirit, Stories of the Heart*, 228.
[27] Harris, *Sut Lovingood Yarns*, 26.
[28] Ibid., 174.

Congress behaved. In Sut's idea of the chain of being, the challenge of faith is not so much to argue with him but to endeavor to change the conditions of "little childer," the least among us who often get rooted out of the trough merely by coming into the world. In our own time, the "little childer" includes those who on the day of judgment, the final cut for Little League, remain unchosen and left to go home crying with their distressed parents. In the old days of the sand lots and cow pastures this did not happen—or not as much as in our trophy-minded mentality, when in order to look good we have to make others look bad. The sky gods have won again.

The role of religion and even of the ministry cannot be overemphasized in the development of the literature of the old Southwest, which in turn influenced such giants of American letters as Thomas Wolfe, William Faulkner, Robert Penn Warren, Flannery O'Connor, and Eudora Welty, among others. Ministers themselves help write the humor as in the case of H. E. Taliaferro, "a sternly devout Baptist preacher and religious editor" who played a significant role in the formation of the Baptist church in East Tennessee and in Alabama in the years prior to the Civil War. One of the genres engaged in by ministers was the "mock sermon," which poked fun at human nature itself, not just themselves and opposing denominations. The following tale falls into that genre. It was apparently based upon a real sermon by Charles Gentry, a slave preacher living in the 1850s in Surry County, North Carolina, which is the setting for Taliaferro's *Fisher's River Sketches and Characters* (1859). In the excerpt from the tale, note the obvious theme of religion, the subtle satire, and the play of the mind of the tricky slave, a classic type in literature as identified by Frye.

> Beloved bredderin, de white folks ar clean out of it when dey 'firm dat de fust man was a white man. I'm not a-gwine to hab any sich doctering. De fact is, Adam, Cain, Abel, Seth, was all ob 'um black as jet. Now you 'quire how de white man cum. Why, dis a-way. Cain he kill his brudder Abel wid a great big club—he walkin' stick—and God he cum to Cain, and say,
>
> "Cain, where is dy brudder Abel?"
>
> Cain he pout out de lips and say, "I don't know; what ye axin me fur? I ain't my brudder Abel's keeper."
>
> De Lord he gits in airenest, and stomps on de ground and say,
>
> "Cain! You Cain! Whar is dy brudder Abel? I say, Cain! Whar is dy brudder?"

Cain he turn as white as bleach cambric in de face, and de whole race ob Cain dey bin white ebber since. De mark de Lord put on de face of Cain was a white mark. He druv him inter the land ob Nod, and all de white folks hab cum from the land ob Nod, jis' as you've hearn.[29]

On the themes of sports and humor on the frontier, it is probably safe to say that the most influential publication on these subjects during the decades prior to the Civil War was *The Spirit of the Times: A Chronicle of the Turf, Agriculture, Field Sports, Literature, and Stage* (1830–1861). It remains a treasure trove of American popular culture. Its editor, William T. Porter, also edited the most famous collections of humorous and sporting writing of the century, *The Big Bear of Arkansas* (1845) and *A Quarter Race in Old Kentucky* (1846).[30] To be sure, the major theme in these publications was field sport and tall tale, but spiritual themes abound in them as well.

One of the most popular and frequent contributors to *The Spirit of the Times* was Thomas B. Thorpe, primarily remembered as the author of "The Big Bear of Arkansas."[31] He wrote a great deal more and was also a painter of some acclaim. In his several stories on sport, Thorpe revealed great admiration of the hunter but also sympathy for the hunted, which in his view was necessary for the common good of both. While there is overlap between the idea of the hunter and that of the sportsman, there are differences between them. Thorpe's focus is primarily upon the sportsman. Were hunting done solely out of a sense of physical necessity as was the situation with our ancestors for millennia, it would no longer be sport, that is, an aspect of leisure and freedom, but another form of labor. Man hunts, Thorpe suggests, partly because of the need for food but also because of the need for challenge and adventure.

---

[29] H. E. Taliaferro, *The Humor of H.E. Taliaferro,* ed. Raymond C. Craig (Knoxville: University of Tennessee Press, 1987) 146.

[30] For a study of Porter and sources see Norris W. Yates, *William T. Porter and "The Spirit of the Times": A Study of the Big Bear School of Humor* (Baton Rouge: Louisiana State University, 1957).

[31] For a listing of the works of Thorpe, see Milton Rickles, *Humorists of the Old Southwest* (Baton Rouge: Louisiana State University Press, 1962) 255–67. See also Robert J. Higgs, "The Sublime and the Beautiful: The Meaning of Sport in the Collected Sketches of Thomas B. Thorpe," *Southern Studies: An Interdisciplinary Journal of the South* 25/3 (Fall 1986): 235–56.

Because Thorpe places his hunting in the realm of freedom, he exercises the option in telling about the good and bad of the hunter. Above all, the hunter had to have a respect for the prey he sought and even a sense of the "tears of things" to keep from wrongdoing to the game he chased and to the wilderness. Thorpe, while a lover of field sports and admirer of the true sportsman, has recorded in his stories an awful wake of destruction of the game of those who were not true sportsmen. There is no need to share the scenes, but the pictures of the wholesale slaughter of birds, reptiles, and beasts in his stories may be unsurpassed in the work of a single author, bringing up questions of ethics that remain with us to this day.

Supposedly violent athletics offer the possibility of experience of the sublime or the holy with their system of totemic names—Bears, Buffalo and Redskins—and with their emphasis upon inordinate risks and dangers and pain involved, but we stand in stark difference with our ancestors who actually went hunting for the animals and did battle with brave warriors contending for the same territory.

The problem for sports in the nineteenth century as well as in the twentieth and in our current century is identified in the title of Allen Guttmann's book, *From Ritual to Record: The Nature of Modern Sports.* Whereas ancient sports were characterized by ritual, the goal in our ritual-less society is the record. Perhaps record-breaking has always been the goal in both sport and sports in America. We like to say that the winning-is-the-only-thing philosophy is a product of "civilized" society, but the same urge appears to have been there all along as seen in the supposed boast of Davy Crockett, a great and good man in many ways, of the huge number of bears killed beyond human need at the time and even in the urge of Jim Doggett, the hunter of the big bear of Arkansas, to kill the thing the loves.

The spiritual side of sport comes down to ritual, such as that reflected in Faulkner's *The Bear*, the kind of ritual that teaches the old verities with which religion if it is doing its job ought to be concerned. Mainly the purpose of ritual in Faulkner is to teach the right kind of pride with the right kind of humility. In *Bear, Man, and God* one of the contributors is Mircea Eliade in a selection titled "The Pattern of Initiation."[32] From the hunting literature of William Porter and William Faulkner we might gain a better

---

[32] Among many other fine essays in this collection, see Francis Lee Utley, *Bear, Man, and God: Seven Approaches to William Faulkner's The Bear*, ed. Francis Lee Utley, Lynn Z. Bloom, and Arthur F. Kennedy (New York: Random Hoiuse, 1964) 233–60.

idea of how the rituals are supposed to work for tribes and for the world at large.

As in ancient Greece and in the Renaissance, humor, sports, and religion are intertwined, often in elusive and unpredictable ways.

The Eiron and the Alazon

The tricky slave, much like "the nat'ral born durn'd fool" or hell-raising trickster in the tradition of Till Eulenspiegel or Sut Lovingood, is an *eiron*, one who is wiser than he knows or even pretends, a master of self-deprecation and social satire at the same time. Socrates was an *eiron*, from which we get the word "irony," and in certain passages so was Jesus: "Why callest thou me good? None is good, save one, God" (Matt 18:17; Mark 10:18; Luke 18:19). The *eiron*, however, is principally a pagan concept, and the self-deprecation it seems to engender in comic characters such as Sut is not exactly the humility taught in Scripture.

According to *Unger's*, "*humility* for heathen moralists meant meanness of spirit. Christian humility is that grace which makes one think of himself no more highly than he ought to think (Rom 12:3). It requires us to feel that in God's sight we have no merit, and in honor to prefer our brethren to ourselves (Rom 12:10), but does not demand undue self-depreciation or depressing views of oneself, but lowliness of self-estimation, freedom from vanity. It is enjoined of God (Col 3:12; Jas 4:6). The word is about equivalent to *meekness* (Ps 25:9), one of the fruits of the spirit."[33] Just as humility, the one quality the holy absolutely demands, is hard to define, so it is even harder to practice without taking pride in it or competing in the attainment of it as in the following story:

> One day a Rabbi, in a frenzy of religious passion, rushed before the ark, fell to his knees, and started beating his chest, crying, "I'm nobody! I'm nobody!"
>
> The cantor of the synagogue, impressed by this example of spiritual humility, joined the Rabbi on his knees. "I'm nobody! I'm nobody!"

---

[33] Merrill F. Unger, *Unger's Bible Dictionary* (Chicago: The Moody Institute of Chicago, 1970), 507.

The "shamus" (custodian), watching from the corner, couldn't restrain himself. He joined the two on his knees, calling out, "I'm nobody! I'm nobody!"

At which point the Rabbi, nudging the Cantor with his elbow, pointed at the custodian and said, "Look who thinks he is nobody!"[34]

The *eiron* is an archetype much at home on porches of country stores or on benches around courthouse squares, sitting and whittling and listening and biding his time to select the proper words for proper targets. Frye and others identify Will Rogers as an *eiron*, and certainly the term applies to Mark Twain, "the Lincoln of our Literature." Lincoln too was an *eiron*, telling stories about himself in an unflattering manner. A woman once told him that he was the ugliest man she had ever seen. "Well, Madam," he asked, "what am I to do about it?" "You could stay home," she said. Lincoln is also known as the "American Christ" for the many virtues long associated with his character. While not exactly an *eiron*, Jesus used irony often and effectively. Rush Limbaugh, a verbal battler, is more often an *alazon* figure than an *eiron*—on the opposite end of the spectrum of humor from Will Rogers.

In any story, oral or written, the function of the *eiron* is to puncture the illusion of the *alazon*, the self-deceived, the one puffed up with certainty. Says Northrop Frye, "the conception of irony meets us in Aristotle's ethics, where the *eiron* is the man who deprecates himself, as opposed to the *alazon*. Such a man makes himself invulnerable...there is no question that he is the predestined artists just as the *alazon* is one of his predestined victims." The *alazon* figure takes stock in clichés spelled out by doctrinaire people rather than also listening to the promptings of the inner self. The *eiron*, an ally of the holy, knows that all status is fleeting and that to live totally as others expect of us is to ignore the Other. Emily Dickinson is an *eiron* in the highest and best sense of that term. So is Flannery O'Connor. In fact, the collection of O'Connor's works may have the largest population of *eirons* and hence *alazons,* the self-deceived, in modern American literature. Nowhere are there better examples of the use of humor for holy purposes. The writer-critic Robert Drake speaks of the trials O'Connor's characters endure as encounters with "the living Christ."

---

[34] Feldman and Kornfield, *Stories of the Spirit, Stories of the Heart*, 251.

The *eiron* rarely leads a march or a counter march but at the same time is not exactly a rebel without a cause. In addition to being the trickster, he or she is also a symbol of the shadow, the side of the human psyche that seeks to bring attention to the neglected aspects of the self, often spiritual, and thus to integrate all sides of the psyche into a whole and healthy-minded human being. In so doing, the *eiron* draws attention to cultural shadows as well as those of individuals. The *eiron* is not a prophet, except perhaps in the case of Mark Twain, but there are parallels. Like the prophet, the shadow knows, but instead of crying out in the wilderness, the shadow plays pranks in the marketplace and laughs at the results among the foolish who are always its targets, that is, all of us at one time or another as in the anonymous quatrain that serves as one of the epigraphs for *Satire: Spirit and Art* by George A. Test. "The world of fools has such a store, / That he who would not see an ass, / Must abide at home, and bolt the door, / And even break his looking –glass." [35]

In every literary work of verbal aggression or word play between *eiron* and *alazon*, there is a tension not unlike the competition in the world of sports and physical play. Satire can be classified along the same lines Roger Caillois uses in *Man, Play and Games,* as George Test shows. These comparisons between the varieties of satire and games may shed more light on the question of ethics and values raised earlier in chapter 10. Everything looks different when viewed through the prism of humor.

Since we know so little about divine things, we cannot say with certainty that a quality of humor inheres in the holy, but it can be said that Rudolph Otto, who wrote so compellingly about the idea of the holy, certainly had a sense of humor. Among his "endearing qualities," according to translator John W. Harvey, was "an unaffected friendliness...aided by a dry humour." In 1927 in the first of a series of lectures at King's College London on mysticism, "he began with a deprecating remark to the effect that for a foreigner to speak of Mysticism in England was to bring owls to Athens, or, as we should say, coals to Newcastle. Otto spoke with a delightfully impish humour of the theological *naivete* sometimes shown by our professional instructors in religion." [36] From what we know, he seems like an *eiron*.

---

[35] Test, *Satire: Spirit and Art* (Tampa: University of South Florida Press, 1991) 126–49.
[36] *Idea of the Holy*, xii – xiii.

Mark Twain may have been wiser than he knew when he said, "The secret source of humor is not joy but sorrow. There is no humor in heaven."[37] The holy might well be the opposite of humor, yet paradoxically a cause for humor in mortals with beneficent effects upon the soul and maybe the body as well. "He that hath a merry heart hath a continual feast" (Prov 15:15). Joy is probably more akin to grace than to merriment, and while we cannot know the mind of the almighty it would seem that good humor would have some role in fulfilling the counsel to "be of good cheer,"which in the Bible appears so often and with such directness as to seem like a virtual commandment (Matt 9:12; 14:27; Mark 6:60; John 16:33; Acts 23:11; 27:22, 25, 36, for example). Can there be good cheer without good humor? Perhaps and perhaps not.

Much depends on the source of the laughter. In the age of mass media, laugh tracks often dictate why we laugh and when, a process for defining sacred laughter and preserving it. Holy laughter, in scripture, is natural and spontaneous, unrehearsed and unexpected, like that of Abraham and Sarah when they learned they were expecting. We see why it cannot be anything from stupid giggling, even by grown men, to a gargantuan belly laugh triggered by sudden recognition of absurdities in our lives or in the world around us. To us, rightly or wrongly, this does not seem the same as the "holy laughter" now popular in some evangelical circles as an aid to conversion.

As far as we know, "holy laughter" that we see on television was not one of the holy exercises practiced on the American frontier, but it appears closely connected to holy falling, which was a regular feature of the Second Great Revival. There are no absolute guides as to how the holy works or manifests itself, whether the holy descends uninvited or is actuated by the voice of another. Holy laughter and holy falling as theater both seem to depend upon a stimulating agent, and in the case of holy laughter one wonders if an automated laughter machine might be able to produce some of the same results, especially a recording of one who in person previously had congreants rolling in the aisles. As a rule, the holy does not seem to like gimmickry, either in human form or in the form of machines.

Laughter, in fact, faces the same challenge as sports in qualifying for the holy, the absence of vision in comparison to experience and feeling. We might feel differently if we were vibrating hilariously and gasping for breath and holding our sides with hundreds of others at a holy laughter session as

---

[37] *Mark Twain Laughing*, 70.

on TV, but from afar it exhibits a significant degree of mindlessness, even hypnosis. Its adherents are convinced otherwise, enthusiastically providing personal testimony of the healing effects upon their souls.[38]

Humor comes in a wide variety of forms, from jokes about the human body and sexuality on one end to the irony and paradoxes of philosophy and religion on the other. Among the latter examples is that of the holy fool, a paradox that in itself seems inconceivable considering the apparently contradictory uses of the word "fool" and its variants in the Bible and even the apparent incongruities in the definition of the word derived from roots, meaning "bellows" or "bag" and "to blow": "(1) A person lacking in judgment or prudence; (2a) a retainer formerly kept in great households to provide casual entertainment and commonly dressed in motley with caps, bells, and baubles; and (2b) one who is victimized and made to appear foolish."

The last definition offers an understanding if not an explanation of the idea of the "holy fool," and the following verses abound in references to foolishness: "But God hath chosen the foolish things of the world to confound the wise; and God hath chosen the weak things of the world to confound the things which are mighty...and things which are not to bring to naught things that are: That no flesh should glory in his presence" (1:27–29). Champions in sports and in beauty contests, by the way, often try to squirm around this caveat by giving glory to God for their achievements. From one perspective we might admire this expression of humility, yet at the same time we sincerely question whether the creator of an infinite universe really needs or desires such praise and glory.

Another problem emerges. When winners heap too much praise on God, losers begin to wonder what God didn't like about them, adding to the regret of not achieving victory themselves. In this same chapter of Corinthians we learn that, literally taken, there is "a foolishness of God" (v. 25), which may be a figure of speech to reduce in contrast the "wisdom of this world." Or could it mean that there may be an actual foolishness of God, and if so, could it possibly be a spirit of play and infinite leisure as in the creation of Eden?

---

[38] For background and discussion of the features of "holy laughter," see "Rodney Howard Browne and the Toronto Blessing," <http://www.rapidnet.com/~jbeard/bdm/Psychology/holy laugh.htm> (2 March 2004).

It may not seem "wise" to conjoin an idea of foolishness with the idea of the holy, but wherever the holy is involved we enter a unique situation, that governed by the nonrational. Enid Welsford in her acclaimed study *The Fool: His Social and Literary History* illustrates how through the ages the lowly fool has been victimized, sacrificed really, in the service of the great ideas, especially freedom. From a psychological and theological perspective, Elizabeth-Anne Stewart's *Jesus: The Holy Fool* shows how the apparently paradoxical concept is essential to the centering process of healing and rebuilding broken lives. As is often the case, poets, through use of proper metaphors and the spirit of play or imagination, seem to have a way of making the inconceivably complex relatively simple and attainable, as Emily Dickinson does with this idea of the blossoming of the "least" among others even in the twilight of years: "A little madness in the Spring / Is wholesome even for the King, / But God be with the Clown— / Who ponders this tremendous scene— / This whole experiment of Green – / As if it were his own!"

Here too the poet comes to "dwell in possibility," words in the first line of another one of Dickinson's poems. The sacred depends on the sense of *memory*; the holy in contrast reminds us that *possibility* is even more important. "Lest we forget" is a sacred motto; "lest we change" is an admonition from the holy, and perhaps the change we need to make is to lighten up and enjoy the whole experiment of Green, to become, one might dare say, "more foolish."

Sublimation and Transformation Revisited—with a Laugh

In *The Act of Creation: A Study of the Conscious and Unconscious Processes of Humor, Scientific Discovery and Art*, Arthur Koestler, as suggested in the title, places humor on the same level of importance as science and art. All three processes involve "thinking," defined by Robert Frost in "Education by Poetry" as "saying one thing in terms of another." Koestler's view is similar but much more detailed. The routine skill of thinking occurs on "a single plane," but the creative act, according to Koestler, occurs on more than one or where "bisociation" occurs in poetry as seen in the metaphor with its two parts of vehicle and tenor, in science by the equivalency of two things of apparent unlike nature such as energy as a function of mass and the speed of light, and in humor by the intersection of an earthly plane with an abstract or higher plane often associated with religion. The following story Koestler cites is taken from Freud's essay on the comic.

> Chamfort tells a story of a Marquis at the court of Louis XIV who, on entering his wife's boudoir and finding her in the arms of Bishop, walked calmly to the window and went through the motions of blessing the people in the street.
> "What are you doing?" cried the anguished wife.
> "Monseigneur is performing my functions," replied the Marquis, "so I am performing his."[39]

Koestler then proceeds to compare the comedy here with the tragedy of Othello.

> In the tragedy the tension increases until the climax is reached: Othello strangles Desdemona, then it (the tension) ebbs away in a gradual catharsis. As (to quote Aristotle) horror and pity accomplish the purgation of the emotions.... In the Chamfort anecdote, too, the tension mounts as the story progresses, but it never reaches its expected climax. The narrative acts as a channel directing the flow of emotions; when the channel is punctured the emotion gushes out like a liquid through a burst pipe; the tension is suddenly relieved and explodes in laughter.[40]

The anecdote of Chamfort is a story of the possibility of sublimation of violence, which should not surprise us since it is filtered down from Freud. Though he is noted as a Jungian, Anthony Storr, a British psychotherapist, echoes Freud on the question of sublimation: "it is obvious that the encouragement of competition in all possible fields is likely to diminish the kinds of hostility which leads to war rather than to increase it—rivalry between nations can do nothing but good."[41]

Though he was in another field, Konrad Lorenz must have realized that he was in good intellectual company when in 1966 in *On Aggression* he

---

[39] Koestler, *Act of Creation: A Study of the Conscious and Unconscious Processes of Humor, Scientific Discovery, and Art* (New York: MacMillan Company, 1964) 33.

[40] Ibid.

[41] Storr, quoted in Gordon W. Russell, "Psychological Issues in Sports Aggression," *Sports Violence*, ed. Jeffrey H. Goldstein (New York: Springer-Verlag, 1983) 160.

proclaimed, "While some forms of sport, like jousting of medieval knights, may have had an appreciable influence on sexual selection, the main function of sport today lies in the cathartic discharge of aggressive urge; besides that of course it is of the greatest importance in keeping people healthy."[42]

Like other theories of Freud, catharsis trickled down to the man in the street, getting distorted in transit. The popularity of the idea, almost a form of dogma now, can be seen, as Don Atyeo observes, in such statements as the following by the late Dick Schapp in *Sport Magazine* in 1977: "I'd prefer those people got their aggressions out screaming at wrestlers than taking it out on the street. I'm not a psychiatrist and I don't know if it's healthy to do it, but it's healthier for me if they do it in there."[43] The debate goes on, and reversal of views on the issues are not uncommon. Even Lorenz has had second thoughts as mentioned in an April 1976 issue of *Psychology Today*: "Nowadays I have strong doubts whether watching aggressive behavior even in the guise of sport has any cathartic effect at all."[44] Despite a broad spectrum of studies, says Gordon Russell, "there is in the final analysis little evidence to support a catharsis theory; indeed, scientific work appears to point to exactly the opposite: that observing aggression provokes aggression."[45]

Scholars in *From Season to Season* relate modern sports to rituals of primitive man. Lorenz does something more remarkable. He traces our aggressive rituals, that is, our territorial sports, back to the animal kingdom as he does the possible origins of laughter and humor:

> Laughter is not only the overt expression of humor, but it very probably constitutes the phylogenetic base on which it evolved. Laughter resembles militant enthusiasm as well as the triumph ceremony of geese in three essential points: all three are instinctive behavior patterns, all three are derived from aggressive behavior and still retain some of the primal motivation, and all three have a similar social function.... Laughter probably evolved by ritualization of a redirected threatening movement, just as the triumph ceremony did. Like the latter, and like militant enthusiasm, laughter produces a strong fellow feeling among participants and a joint aggressiveness against

---

[42] Lorenz, quoted in Russell, "Psychological Issues," 161.
[43] Schapp, quoted in Atyeo, *The Violence in Sport* (New York: Nostrand Reinhold,1981) 364.
[44] Lorenz, quoted in Atyeo, *The Violence in Sport*, 371.
[45] Russell, "Psychological Issues," 176–77.

outsiders. Heartily laughing together at the same thing forms an immediate bond, much as the enthusiasm for the same ideal does.[46]

"The triumph ceremony of the geese" is visible among victors after highly publicized contests. This might all be tolerable up to some point, a nod to the instinctual need to be right and victorious. It is only when the ceremony of the geese begins to turn into "goose stepping," as practiced by tyranical regimes such as the Nazis, that we have a problem, and one incident is enough for the normal life of a planet, though we have had many.

The humor Lorenz describes above is what we call "sacred," since it sets one group apart from the other. One cannot keep from thinking of Osama Bin Laden in a video laughing with cohorts as he describes the destruction of the Twin Towers, but there are other examples from around the planet. There is, though, another type of humor, far different from that sacred and closely guarded by the "in" group. It is, of course, the humor of the *eiron* or even of the holy fool that seeks to restore a sense of wholeness in oneself by humbling the self in a deprecatory humor. Says Lorenz, "If, in ridiculing insincere ideals, humor is a powerful ally of rational morality, it is even more so in self ridicule.... The power of its persuasion lies in the manner of its appeal: it can make itself heard by ears which, through skepticism and sophistication, are deafened to any direct teaching of morality. In other words, satire is the sort of sermon for today."[47]

Satire, "the stranger in the basement" as it has anonymously been called, was the major weapon in the broad arsenal of Mark Twain. "Good breeding consists in concealing how much we think of ourselves and how little we think of the other person."[48] "Christianity will doubtless survive ten centuries hence—stuffed and in a museum."[49] There are those who say Twain was an atheist. We would disagree. In his genius he had many sides, but whatever else he was, he is one of America's strongest candidates for the rare and distinguished office of the holy fool, a prophet to some and an apostle for both humor and common sense, one who laughed most at himself, which made him so human that he reminds us of the mystery of the divine. What would we have done without him?

---

[46] Lorenz, *On Aggression*, trans. Marjorie Ken Wilson (New York: Harcourt Brace and World, 1966) 284.

[47] Ibid., 286.

[48] Twain, 79.

[49] Ibid, 81

Mark Twain is the polar opposite of Teddy Roosevelt, perhaps the most famous of all American knights, a lover of sport and sports but someone who, we feel, would be appalled by the current sporting scene and who might bring anti-trust legislation against leading organizations were he among us today. Deserving of his sacred place on Mount Rushmore, Teddy had many virtues, but a developed sense of humor does not seem to have been among them. There is little evidence that he laughed at himself and certainly never at Mark Twain, refusing to shake Twain's hand, owing to Twain's satire of him, at ceremonies at Yale when in 1902 both were offered honorary degrees from that august institution.

As in all other modes of human communication, danger lurks in humor of certain kinds, for instance, "schadenfreude" in all its roots and branches, including black comedy, sick jokes, invective, insult, and the curse. A related genre is stupidity humor—blond jokes, ethnic humor, and the like—all designed to elevate the teller of disparaging jokes, almost invariably an *alazon,* above those toward whom they are directed. Certainly such humor is not holy, but it is a matter of opinion if it as reprehensible as some claim who fear that "political correctness" is a larger menace. For the *eiron*, who laughs easily at himself or herself, the issue is not of great moment, knowing that "revenge" from a quiver of many arrows is a certainty, a humbling one for whom the shot is intended. There is a funny thing about becoming humble—it doesn't seem to work unless one does it himself or herself in league with the holy. A battle of wits may be entertaining, but it is always secular or sacred like most wars even when we call them holy.

No claim is made that all humor is healthy, but it is almost innocent compared to forms of seriousness such as what in colloquial German, according to Lorenz, is known as *tierischner Ernst*, which translates as "animal seriousness." It is, he says, "an ever present symptom of megalomania, in fact...one of its causes." Lorenz contends that it at the soul of "militant enthusiasm," which we would add is often visible in territorial sports and in knightly branches of religions. Indeed, it might be viewed as a cousin of "schadenfreude" except that it is not about laughing at the misfortune of others but actually *creating* misfortune for others. Making a religion of sports seems a step in that direction.

One might be inclined to think of humor as nonrational, but Lorenz sees it in an opposite manner. "An amazing parallel between humor and the categorical question is that both balk at logical inconsistencies and incongruities. Acting against reason is not only immoral but, funnily enough, it is very often extremely funny!"[50] Lorenz's trust in the sound sense of humor accounts in part for the title of his final chapter: "Avowal of optimism." He agrees with G. K. Chesterton's prediction "that the religion of the future will be based, to a considerable extent, on a more highly developed and differentiated, subtle form of humor," which, Lorenz adds, "we do not as yet take seriously enough."[51]

Comic Spirit and Holy Spirit: The Same but Otherwise

We have said that the holy spirit and the sporting spirit may move in opposite directions, or with different goals in terms of prizes and gifts, but this may not be the case with the comic spirit in relation to the holy. The bidding of comedy may be to help restore our souls unto harmony with wisdom far superior to our own. Though George Meredith does not mention the humor of Christ, Trueblood feels that Meredith's description of the Comic Spirit "applies perfectly":

> Men's future upon the earth does not attract it (the Comic Spirit); their honesty and shapeliness in the present does; and whenever they wax out of proportion, overblown, affected, pretentious, bombastical, hypocritical, pedantic, fantastically delicate; whenever it sees themselves deceived or hoodwinked, given to run riot in idolatries, drifting into vanities, congregating in absurdities, planning short-sightedly, plotting dementedly; whenever they are at variance with their professions, and violate unwritten and perceptible laws binding them in consideration one to another; whenever they offend sound reason, fair justice, are false in humility and mined with conceit, individually, or in the bulk; the Spirit overhead will humanely malign, and cast an oblique light on them, followed by valleys of silvery laughter. That is the Comic Spirit.[52]

Whereas Mark Twain believed there was no humor in heaven, Trueblood, drawing upon the thinking of Meredith, postulates a connection between God and the Comic Spirit. God's laughter, he says, is "directed at our frailties, but

---

[50] Lorenz, 286–87.
[51] Ibid., 283–84.
[52] Trueblood, *The Humor of Christ*, 54–55.

its purpose is to heal."[53] As for us, we simply don't know what the connections are between God or the holy and humor, much like the mountain woman in a remote cabin who was visited by a census taker. Finding that, as he said, his job was to determine how many people lived in the United States, she responded, "You've come to the wrong place because I don't have any idea." We do know that in the human world the phenomenon of humor exists and that in all climes and times it has an enormous influence upon religion. The most insightful among us such as Meredith and Twain can only speculate what the connections are at the level of the holy. That said, where humor and holy are concerned we suspect that God laughs with us rather than at us. If God didn't, it would seem like schadenfreude which would appear as a bad thing for God to do as it would be for us.

Meredith, as Trueblood observes, coined the term laughter-haters or "misogelastics," which bears a resemblance to haters of ideas or misologists, a term deriving from *Phaedo* where Socrates tells his listeners what a sad fate it is for anyone to hate ideas. The misologists, haters of learning, and misogelastics, says Trueblood, "belong to the same intellectual family."[54] Another name for this group of us is in Kierkegaard's immortal phrase "the stupidly serious"[55] who, to use Lorenz's term, always exhibit "animal seriousness," which in turn breeds "militant enthusiasm." Often, as we all know, comedy, especially on television, in an effort to be funny will instead of being funny become a splendid example of the "stupidly serious" and "militant enthusiasm" evident not only in our violent sports but in just about everything on commercial television.

According to Trueblood, most of the humor of Christ "belongs to what Meredith calls the 'laughter of comedy.' It is not like satire which is a blow in the back or the face but 'is impersonal and of unrivalled politeness, nearer a smile—often no more than a smile.' ...The attack may be strong, when the object is Pharisaic spirit, but it is not an attack upon an individual Pharisee."[56] This important distinction between satire and comedy is echoed by W. H. Auden:

> Satire attempts to show that the behavior of an individual or a group within society violates the laws of ethics or common sense on the

---

[53] Ibid., 55.
[54] Ibid.
[55] Ibid, 22.
[56] Ibid., 51.

assumption that once the majority are aware of the facts, they will become morally indignant and either to compel the violators to mend their ways or render them socially and politically incompetent. Comedy on the other hand is concerned with illusions, and self-deceptions, which all men indulge in, as to what they and the world they live in are really like. And cannot, so long as they remain human, help being. The object of the comic exposure is not a special individual and special social group, but every man or human society as a whole. Satire is angry and optimist—it believes that the evil it attacks can be abolished; comedy is good tempered and pessimistic—it believes that however much we may wish we could, we cannot change human nature and must make the best of a bad job.[57]

The humor of Christ exhibits most if not all of the essential features of comedy, mixed possibly with more elements of satire than Trueblood is willing to acknowledge, and consequently identical in nature to all kinds of humor everywhere, starting with elements of *surprise* and *inevitability,* then, as in poetry or "education by poetry," according to Frost, the "association of two things you don't expect to see associated" or, as Kierkegaard says, "humor is always a concealed pair."[58] This is the essential conclusion of Koestler in his extended study of humor, as we have seen, and of Andrew Newberg and others in *Why God Won't Go Away: Brain Science and the Biology of Belief.* The human brain is so constituted that it cannot refrain from metaphorical thinking, and it doesn't seem to matter whether the thinking pertains to politics, religion, science, humor, or any other human endeavor, especially sports, which, starting with team names, is nothing less than "metaphor city."

Metaphors, though, do not by themselves make a religion, since metaphors can serve seriousness and even super seriousness without speaking a word. In our lives there is another aesthetic function always at work, whether we know it or not, and that is tone, our emotional attitudes toward a subject. In the case of the apologists of sports, the prevailing tone is one of seriousness, as if that is the proper one for all religions, which is hardly if ever the case. One major test for the new Religion of Sports will be to see just how well it can take the heat of humor. Our older religions have endured such scrutiny for a

---

[57] Auden, Introduction, *The Selected Prose and Poetry of Byron* (New York: New American Library, 1966) xi.

[58] Quoted in Trueblood, 50

long time, not in spite of humor, but *because of it*, an irony to be sure. As we shall see in the next chapter, the humorous assault on the new religion has already begun, suggesting to us that sports might be better just as plain old sports rather than as a cultural religion, folk religion, natural religion, and popular religion.

Metaphors and humor both work on the same principle of concealed pairs, as Koestler shows, and what is more unlikely than a pairing of religion and humor, both of which depend upon surprise to be effective? Their relationship is surprising, but it is clear, we hope, that regardless of the religion or time in history, humor has followed in the shadow of religion like a faithful dog, often a watchdog, not so much to keep others at a safe distance as to make sure that the owner stayed on the announced course. Sometimes it is difficult to tell which is more important, the wisdom of the religious message or the mode or media, that is the humor, for it is difficult to imagine one without the other, as Sir Arthur Quiller Couch acknowledged soon after assuming the chair of English literature at the University of Cambridge: "I suppose that if an ordinary man of my age were asked which has better helped him to bear the burs of life—religion or a sense of humor—he would, were he quite honest, be graveled for an answer."[59]

As a sort of epigraph for this chapter on religion and humor and a sense of play, we decided to include the following: "I have always preached.... If the humor came of its own accord and uninvited I have allowed it a place in my sermon, but I was not writing the sermon for the sake of the humor. I should have written the sermon just the same, whether any humor applied for any admission or not. I am saying these vain things in this frank way because I am a dead person speaking from the grave. Even I would be too modest to say them in life. I think we never become really and genuinely our entire and honest selves until we are dead—and not then until we have been dead for years and years. People ought to start dead and then they would be honest so much earlier."[60]

The speaker is Mark Twain.

---

[59] Quoted in Trueblood, 125.
[60] Twain, *The Autobiography of Mark Twain*, ed. Charles Neider (New York: Washington Square Press, 1961) 298.

Chapter 14

The High Seriousness of the Religion of Sports: A Return to Polytheism?

Some people take life serious
In stead of a game to play
If they would not take it so serious
But more like a game to play.
I try to laugh at the hard knocks
Like you get in a base ball game
So wether your with St. Louis or the red Sox
Smile and don't be a shame.[1]

This is a song, grammatical and spelling errors and all, written by Danny Warner, the central character in *Lose with a Smile* (1933) by Ring Lardner. From Booneville, Missouri, Danny is another one of Lardner's Bushers who is not satisfied with an opportunity to play in the major leagues. He also regards himself as a major musical talent waiting to be discovered, a typical Lardner Busher in that regard. Maxwell Geismar writes, "Conceit is the center of Lardner's humanity. The U.S. Champion, master of one field, believed himself master of all, and the U.S. Mediocrity believed himself a champion. In Lardner's view the bombastic American ego always aspired to exceed its own potentialities and all other

---

[1] Ring Lardner, *Lose with a Smile* (New York: Scribner's, 1933) 79.

potentialities too. Beside this contemporary conqueror, Marlowe's mighty Tamburlaine was an Elizabethan Ne'er do well."[2]

Country Boys and that Old-time Humor:
The Busher and the Dumb Athlete

Danny is the familiar *alazon*, the self-deceived, but for purposes of satire, Lardner makes of him an *eiron*, one wiser in some ways than he knows as seen in one of the letters he writes back home from Brooklyn to Mid America.

> Some of the boys has got nick names like wear they come from like 1 of the pitchers Clyde Day but they call him Pea ridge Day because he come from a town name Pea ridge and he was the champion hog caller of Arkansas and when he used to pitch in Brooklyn last year he used to give a hog call after ever ball he throwed but the club made him cut it out because the fans came down on the field every time he gave a call and the club had to hire the champion of Iowa to set up in the stand and call them back.[3]

Here is satire worthy of Jonathan Swift and the extension of a theme of humor from the Southern frontier into the Depression. Satire is ever present in Lardner's fiction, but so is comedy, the side of humor concerned not with illusion and self-deception of one person or group but with the fans in Brooklyn, the folks in Arkansas, Missouri, Iowa, and all of us everywhere. While, as Auden reminds us, satire is angry and optimistic, comedy is pessimistic about the race but still good-tempered as is the legendary Casey Stengel, also a character in Lardner's novel. Even Danny is aware of Stengel's comic genius. In one of his letters, he says Casey is "always sane things like that witch don't make no sense," such as the following:

> Stengel told me he was acquaint it with the mgr of Irving Berlins music company and promise me he would take me there and see whot they thot of that song I wrote Life is just a game of base ball. So we stopped there yesterday noon and Stengel ast to see Mr.

---

[2] Geismar, *Writers in Crisis* (Cambridge MA: Houghton Mifflin, 1943) 7.
[3] Lardner, *Lose with a Smile*, 30.

Schwartz and the girl says they didn't have no Mr. Schwartz and Stengel says what the hell kind of music publishing company is this?

He says Max Carey (manager of the Dodgers) likes you and that if you run out on him now it would just about break his morals. On the other hand you could do a lot worse than play under Harry Splug because he is an expert at training young ball players. So I says I never herd of him and wear did he play ball and Stengel says he didn't play no wear but he used to be in charge of the forrestry dept at the State reform school and took care of the boys that had fell out of the trees.[4]

Just as humor in baseball in the decades of the first half of the last century was often characterized by the myth of the Busher, the comic version of the young man from the country, so was football by the myth of the "dumb athlete"—not "the tramp athlete" whose lineage reaches back to the nineteenth century, but the young man from the mines, the farm, or the ghetto who transformed American college football from the twenties onward. William H. Beezley has collected these kinds of stories in "Counterimages of the Student Athlete in Football Folklore." Here are some samples:

Three professional football players were talking about why they had left college. "I was a senior at Cornell," said the first, "but I wasn't grounded in calculus, so I didn't have the slightest idea what the professor was talking about."

The second said, "Trigonometry did me in. Ran me right out of Kansas State in my Junior year."

The third player, late of Alabama, stared moodily into space. Suddenly he spoke, "Say did you guys ever run into a thing called long division?"[5]

Herman Hickman, who coached at Yale and was noted for his recitation of poetry in the dressing room, also had a great sense of humor. When substitution rules changed after World War II, Hickman said he

---

[4] Ibid., 102, 90–91.

[5] Beezley, *American Sport Culture: The Humanistic Dimension*, ed. Wiley Lee Umphlett (Lewisburg: Bucknell University Press, 1985) 214–15.

would like to see three-platoon football, "one to play on offense, one to play on defense, and one to go to class."[6]

Hickman had been a star player for Bob Neyland at Tennessee, and when some of his Tennessee friends came by his office at Yale and brought a big tackle with them, Hickman said he could see immediately that "he [the tackle] was going to have trouble getting into Yale.... So partly to show off to my friends, I asked, 'How is his Greek?' and they shot back, 'He *is* Greek, it's his English that we're worried about.'"[7]

Says Beezley,

> The recruiting experience gave many prospects their first inkling of a way to escape the drudgery of the mines, farms, and ghettoes. A joke that made the rounds some years ago pokes fun at two immigrant factory hands and their limited vision of football, education, and mobility. In this version the two are talking:
> "Hey Stosh, my oldest boy is going to college. I guess they can't call us stupid Polacks anymore."
> "That's great, Chester. What college is he going to?"
> "Marquette!"
> "Oh, great! What Marquette is that? The A&P Marquette over on Main Street or the National Marquette on Grove Street?"[8]

All of these folk tales involve ethnic and regional stereotyping, but ethnicity and regions are not the target of the humor, and one would have to be dumber than the athletes in the tales to miss the gross exaggeration in all of them. Exaggeration is a major aspect of humor as in that of Christ. In fact, the satire cuts all kinds of ways, poking fun at the colleges, the coaches, and the professors who get caught up in the ruses of helping get players eligible. Consider the economics professor at Ohio State in a classic story of the genre from *University Days* by James Thurber.

The professor, Mr. Bassum, is trying to get Bolenciecwcz, an outstanding player for OSU, to name one means of transportation so he can be eligible for the big game against Illinois. Bolenciecwcz is clueless even as the students in the class make sounds of a bell, whistle, and the escaping

---

[6] Ibid., 215.
[7] Ibid., 216.
[8] Ibid., 217.

steam of a locomotive. Mr. Bassum tries to help by commenting that Bolenciecwcz may choose "any medium, agency, or method of going from one place to another.... You may choose among steam, horse-drawn, or electrically propelled vehicles." He even makes sounds like "Choo-choo-choo" and "*Chuffa* chuffa, *chuffa* chuffa." "Bolenciecwcz, meanwhile, had the look of a man who is being led into a trap."[9] It would not be cricket to reveal the resolution of plot, only to say that the hilarity continues to the end.

In all satire and comedy there is an implied seriousness worthy of our attention, else there would be no cause for the humor at all. Beezley explains what lies behind all this wonderful lore:

> The knowledge that football offered a way to fill the cupboard attracted players to college, while college recruiters used this lure to pull them up from the mines and in from the prairies. Many sons of immigrants have played the game, and many sons of the poor have strapped on shoulder pads. Both possess a drive that comes from having known poverty, and since World War Two there have been very few rich kids who have made it big in sports. Dick Butkus had a simple enough explanation for football: "...football's too rough if you don't really want it. Maybe those rich kids have a different sort of competitive mechanism. They don't need material success." Immigrants, country boys, and ghetto kids recognized that playing football has shorter hours than farms and fewer injuries than steel mills and hardrock mines. In short, football offered a way to a better life.[10]

As we have shown, humor has coexisted with sports, academic art and learning, and religion through the ages, affecting the nature and direction of each and all from time to time. While jokes about the academic qualifications of athletes are still around, the "dumb athlete" has nearly passed from the scene as a comic character in our culture, or if he is still present, he is the one laughing and all the way to the bank. Instead of the buffoon or the comic sidekick to the royal hero as in mythology, the athlete,

---

[9] *The Sporting Spirit: Athletes in Literature and Life*, ed. Robert J. Higgs and Neil D. Isaacs (New York: Harcourt Brace Jovanovich, 1977) 43.

[10] Beezley, *American Sport Culture*, 217.

whether from town or country, has become the prince himself or princess, sophisticate, model, celebrity, talk show guest (and host), author, politician, and, it almost goes without saying, millionaire.

The shift in the image of the athlete started occurring around the middle of the twentieth century, about the time television was arriving on the American scene, and athletes themselves, like colleges and evangelical organizations, started thinking more about money. Something seemed to be happening to the spirit of fun and games in our major sports. In his 1954 biography, *The Tumult and the Shouting*, Grantland Rice, "the champion of all sports writers," offers an insight into the transformation that was taking place in American sports.

> Sports today is, however, much more commercial and much more stereotyped than in my heyday. I doubt if we will ever again have the devil-may-care attitude and spirit of the Golden Twenties, a period of boom, screwballs, and screwball antics. The almighty dollar, or what's left of it, hangs high. The magnificent screwballs have been crowded to the wall. The fleet Washington outfielder who, when asked to race Mickey Mantle against time before a recent Yankee-Senators night game, replied, "I'll do it for five hundred dollars" is testimony to the time.[11]

Note that in Rice's view stereotyping was *just beginning*, with the S in "Stereotyping" as a dollar sign! Suddenly, around mid-century, owing to television, the athlete was groomed as a role model for the young and the perfect persona for advertisers. With the advent of television, the athlete was in the spotlight more than ever, and the burden of images, often conflicting, placed on his or her shoulders was enormous. In the same year as the publication of Rice's book, the Fellowship of Christian Athletes (FCA) was formed with an agenda that involved still more of the athlete's time. No longer was going to church or membership in the Student Christian Association (SCA) enough as far as the spiritual life was concerned—now there was another meeting to attend, usually in the athletic dormitory after study hall.

Of a sudden, the athlete at his or her best was to excel in sports, in academics, and in matters of spirit and character and all within the glare of

---

[11] Rice, *The Tumult and the Shouting* (New York: Dell, 1954) 306.

media. The model in whom all these qualities came together was easy to identify—the Christian knight. On top of everything else, then, he had to be a warrior in training as well, which meant saying goodbye to the shepherd model.

The effects of such pressures were already visible in the highly controversial cribbing scandal at the Military Academy, which in 1951 had one of the strongest teams in the country but still insisted on a regimen that could not, it was said, be handled in a twenty-four-hour day by the likes of Paul Bunyan and Sir Galahad. The same "Bombastic American ego" Maxwell Geismar found in Lardner's ball players was at work in the administration of one of our most revered institutions of learning. Zeus hates those who do too much, yet the same Zeus inspires in mortals the desire to be at the top. This is not the lesson of the one who said, "Take no thought for tomorrow." Andrew Carnegie, himself a notoriously high achiever, says that these "five words spoken by Christ so interpreted, if strictly obeyed, would at one blow strike down all that distinguished man from the beast."[12]

It's tough work staying on the top of the competition, as any champion will confess, and the evidence never goes away. In fact in sports it mounts and mounts, as one could gather from the comments by President George W. Bush in his State of the Union message (2004) on the doping among athletes and the message such habits send to the young. No matter how many times one becomes world champion, the "next" time is always in doubt, the opponent seemingly grinning in the shadows. A few in authority have rebelled against this stylized code that insists on excellence in mind, body, and soul when so much is required in just one of those areas, athletic excellence. In effect, Bush said, "Let's call a halt to all the hype and be honest. Religion and academics will be all right on their own without our endorsement."

The Case of Coach Paul Bear Bryant

In the opening chapter we talked about the significance for any culture of the relation between mind, body, and soul as discussed by Socrates and in America by John Adams and Thomas Jefferson. To find out the state of their union in our schools and our culture, the place to start is sports, which invariably, in classical Greece, the Renaissance, and today, will provide a

---

[12] Carnegie, *The Gospel of Wealth and Other Timely Essays*, ed. Edward C. Kirkland (Cambridge MA: Belknap, 1962) 25.

picture of the health, or lack thereof, of this eternal triangle. For a long time we have listened to philosophers, statesmen, and ministers expatiate on the best balance between the three. Now we must consider another voice, one more popular than ministers or academicians. We speak of the prototype coach, Paul Bear Bryant.

Instead of attempting parity between conventional worship and the religion of sports as the apologists appear to be doing, Bear Bryant deserves our gratitude for at last speaking the truth. If Diogenes is still walking the earth in search of an honest man, he might do well to set his lantern at the feet of a replica of Bryant in the museum on the Tuscaloosa campus. Said Bryant, at least according to legend, "Football is not a religion. It's more important than that."

Football may also be more important than other things as Jay Leno suggests in his commentary on the BCS (Bowl Championship Series). The University of Southern California, though top-rated in the polls, got left out of the assigned competition, which meant, said Leno, that USC meant "Undoubtedly Screwed College." "The formula for ranking teams in the BCS (Bowl Championship Series) is so complicated, even the football players who go to class can't figure it out. Believe me, people are outraged about this. I mean, that Florida thing, that was just about the presidency. This is college football. This is the kind of thing where people go, 'Hey, wait a minute!'"[13]

About the student athlete, Bryant said in the seventies, "I used to go along with the idea that football players on scholarship were 'student-athletes,' which is what the NCAA calls them. Meaning a student first, an athlete second. We were kidding ourselves, trying to make it more palatable to the academicians. We don't have to say that and we shouldn't. At the level we play, the boy is really an athlete first and a student second."[14]

We may not like the way Bryant has demoted religion and academics to a role secondary to sports, even with a note of pride and good riddance in the case of academics. By elevating sports in importance above religion and academics, Bryant went a long way toward making sports sacred, that is, things set apart, which is another way of saying he helped make them more difficult to view in light of the holy. While by definition, the sacred means things set apart, inevitably it means "set above" many other things, like

---

[13] Leno, *Last Night's Late Night Jokes*, Internet – Daily Feature, 9 December 2003.

[14] Bryant, in James A. Michener, *Sports in America* (Greenwood CT: Fawcett, 1976) 254.

academics and learning, the status confirmed by statues, halls of fame, and sports museums, all of which are alien to the idea of the holy. In such instances the idea of the sacred is set above the idea of the holy.

Just as football has been set apart and above so many other features of university life, so too has the so-called "student-athlete," which, as Bryant himself says, should be an "athlete-student." Long ago "student-athletes," praised every Saturday on television by ads from the NCAA, surpassed in popularity and admiration "student-workers," who are far more numerous on campus and whose struggles, though of a different nature, are in the long run every bit as challenging as those of athletes undergoing the agonies of practices and games.[15]

Bryant's influence not only on football but on all sides of the eternal triangle of mind, body, and soul seems fixed, assured in part by a humorous role in the novel *Forest Gump*. In fact, he has entered into apotheosis, and it is questionable whether or not there are any other gods before him, especially in football, a statement we make based to some extent on personal experience. Shortly after the publication of *God in the Stadium: Sports and Religion in America*, by Robert J. Higgs a student who saw it on the shelf at the East Tennessee State University bookstore remarked to his girlfriend, according to sworn testimony, "Oh, look, honey. There's a book about Bear Bryant." About the same time, Andy Rooney didn't help things by proclaiming on *Sixty Minutes* that, whether he even knew about such a publication, he didn't like books with God in the title, but what he does like—and his likes appear to be few—is watching a Big Ten football game from a blimp high over Columbus, Ohio, from what might be called a quasi God-perspective. Andy was even reporting from the blimp. Andy can be funny, but we feel confident in saying that he is no James Thurber, at least in regard to Buckeye football. In regard to using God's name in print on the cover of a book, we do not know whether he would like in titles or anywhere else the names Sam Keen recommends as alternate names for "God."

The figure that Bryant calls the "athlete-student" is a familiar one in American fiction, far more athlete than student, like Forrest Gump, which is not to pass judgment on the character of Forrest. Some of the best people we have ever known could not read or write, but it must be said that they were not in college pretending to be students, however faintly. The athlete-student is a

---

[15] See also John Underwood, "Student-Athletes: The Sham, The Shame," *Sports Illustrated*, 26 May 1980, 36–72.

successor to the dumb athlete of the days of Thurber and Herman Hickman. It's a move up. The athlete-student is no doubt a terrific athlete and maybe a saint of a person, but by definition he is a part-time student and his abode on campus is certainly the athletic dorm, also known on campuses generally as "the Animal House."

In Mark Harris's novel *Bang the Drum Slowly* (1956), the narrator pitcher Henry Wiggen describes his dear friend and catcher Bruce Pearson and Bruce's old college buddy Hut Sut Sutter from SSU (Southern States University) in this manner: "All winter they horsed around in the gymnasium shooting baskets and swinging on the ropes and swimming in the pool, and once a month they took off in a college car and hunted up whore houses, Sutter a regular expert in the matter."[16] Though Henry does not say so, one can easily imagine his adding, "and at night they pitched for pennies in the athletic dorm at the edge of campus." It will be said that Harris exaggerates, which in humor, remember, is a way of getting at the truth.

"The Stranger in the Basement" and the Sacredness of Sports

Another notable product of SSU is T.J. (for Teddy James and also for "Torn Jock") Lambert. Where does T.J. live in the Tennessee college? Obviously in the athletic dorm. The narrator of Dan Jenkins's *Semi-Tough*,[17] Billy Clyde Puckett, another good old boy like Henry Wiggen but Southern, seems to delight in relating T.J.'s gargantuan expertise in passing gas both on the field of play and off. If one were to look for a character reminiscent of the world-beater and ring-tailed roarer out of the wildly imaginative literature of the Old Southwest, there is only one place to turn—the athletic dorm at SSU. Hut Sut Sutter, T.J. Lambert, and the linebacker Frank Howard knew who was so tough he carried a baseball bat with him to the toilet are soulmates filled to overflowing with *thymos*, every one a descendent of the mythical Davy Crockett and one of the three personalities of Mark Twain. T.J. by himself could have provided the gas for a Budweiser commercial at the 2004 Super Bowl.

If there were any thought given to the fragmentation of mind and body in the modern world, especially on the modern campus, we would like to nominate the athletic dorm as a symbol of that condition. Its antecedents are

---

[16] Harris, *Bang the Drum Slowly* (New York: Dell, 1954) 23.

[17] Dan Jenkins, *Semi-Tough* (New York: Signet, 1972).

obvious from the world of religion and war, the monastery and the military barracks. All are things set apart and hence sacred, but not necessarily holy on that account. As for a comprehensive picture of America's popular culture, it is doubtful if Billy Clyde Puckett's report on the description of the Super Bowl as envisioned by Coach Shoat Cooper of the Giants can ever be surpassed.

Shoat, by the way, is himself straight out of the "Big Bear School of Humor" from the Old Southwest. Like Bear Bryant, he is from Arkansas. When he was playing for the NFL, "They say he craved action so much he would beat his head on the locker room wall until they let him loose for the kickoff." He too had *thymos*. He too is an *eiron* as is Billy Clyde. The Super Bowl scene between the Giants and the Jets that Shoat describes and Billy Clyde relates is sacred, but the humor approaches the holy in its irony and ingenuity—satire for the ages—starting with the opening sentences: "Shoat said that both the pre-game show and the halftime show would have a patriotic flavor. 'That can't be anything but good for football,' he said." Now let the ceremonies begin, noting as we go along the inevitable intertwining or the four "occupations" of a leisure-class culture, one, that is, addicted to bragging on itself through symbols of sports, government, warfare, and religion as in *Deus Revelatus*:

> According to Shoat, here is what was going to happen before the game: Several hundred trained birds—all painted red, white, and blue—would be released from cages somewhere and they would fly over the coliseum in the formation of an American flag.
>
> As the red, white, and blue birds flew over, Boke Kellum, the Western television Star, would recite the Declaration of Independence.
>
> Next would be somebody dressed up like Mickey Mouse and somebody else dressed up like Donald Duck joining the actress Camille Virl in singing "God Bless America."
>
> And right in the middle of the singing there would come this Air Force cargo plane to let loose fifty sky divers who would come dropping into the coliseum.
>
> Each sky diver would be dressed up in the regional costume of a state, and he would land in the coliseum in the order in which his state became a United State.
>
> When all this got cleaned up, United States Senator Pete Rozelle, the ex-commissioner of the NFL who invented the Super Bowl, would be driven around the stadium in the car that won last year's

Indianapolis 500. At the wheel would be Lt. Commander Flip
Slammer, the fifteenth astronaut to walk on the moon.

Riding along behind the Indy car, Shoat said, would be two men
on horses. One would be Commissioner Bob Cameron on Luring Funk,
the thoroughbred which won last year's Kentucky Derby. And on the
other horse, Podna (the horse Boke Kellum pretends to ride in the
television series), would be the current president of CBS, a guy named
Woody Snider.

Finally, Shoat said, the teams would be introduced and two
thousand crippled and maimed soldiers on crutches and in wheel chairs
and on stretchers would render the "Star-Spangled Banner."

...Among several other events at halftime, there would be "a
water ballet in the world's largest inflatable swimming pool, a Spanish
fiesta, a Hawaiian luau, a parade stressing the history of the armored
tank, a sing-off between all the glee clubs of all the military academies,
and an actual World War I dogfight in the sky with the Red Baron's
plane getting blown to pieces."

The final event at half time would be the induction into the pro
football hall of fame "of about twenty old stud hosses out of the past"
and the singing of a parody of the "Battle Hymn of the Republic
written by someone out of "the league office" and called "The Game
Goes Marching On" which "might make some people cry." All 92,000
in the LA Coliseum would be presented copies of the lyrics.[18]

Geoffrey Chaucer wrote about people of his time on a pilgrimage to a
holy site. With humor reminiscent of Chaucer's, Dan Jenkins reveals what
happens when pilgrims gather at a modern "holy site" for a national sacrament
supervised and televised by our high priests of media and commerce.

The humor of Jenkins is very much in the mainstream of American
humor as our American humor has been fed by several streams, but they
have merged into one common feature, that of irreverence toward whatever
is highly visible, exalted and clothed in robes of seriousness and certainty as
Constance Rourke explains in her discussion of the contributions of three
key players, the Yankee, the backwoodsman, and the Negro.

The three figures loomed large, not because they represented any
considerable numbers in population, but because something in the nature of

---

[18] (New York: Signet, 1972) 137–38.

each induced an irresistible response. Each had been a wanderer over the land, the Negro a forced and unwilling wanderer. Each in a fashion of his own had broken bands. The Yankee in initial revolt against the parent civilization, the backwoodsman in revolt against all civilization, the Negro in a revolt which was cryptic and submerged but which nonetheless made a perceptive outline. As figures they embodied a deep-lying mood of disseverance, carrying the popular fancy further and further from any fixed or traditional heritage. Their comedy, their irreverent wisdom, their sudden changes and adroit adaptations, provided emblems for a pioneer people who required resilience as a prime trait.[19]

The great humorists are often among the great naysayers whose credo, as Fiedler mentions, is *non servium*, "I will not serve"—not serve that which is presumed to be good or even godly but which, upon closer and more honest, often humorous inspection may be lacking in ways not immediately evident to more optimistic views. Religion, perhaps more than any other human category, has, as reflected, provoked satire through the ages not because of the idea of religion but because of the oppressive practices of religion that followers believe sacred. There is generally some breathing room for a NRM (new religious movement), a honeymoon period when it is allowed to run free in the marketplace of ideas, and the same is true of old alliances in new dress such as Muscular Christianity. With roots going back to knighthood, Muscular Christianity as a hybrid expression of faith came onto the modern scene in the novels of Charles Kingsley and especially in Thomas Hughes's *Tom Brown's School Days* (1857) and his *The Manliness of Christ* (1879).

Satire of the alliance of muscularity—read athleticism—and Christianity was slow in coming, but it arrived with a bang in a novel by our first Nobel Prize winner, Sinclair Lewis. It was called *Elmer Gantry* and about a titular hero who, to use a metaphor of Chaucer, was a "shitten shepherd," which is not to say that all the sheep he tried to lead were "clene" but that all were cleaner than Elmer, whose primary effort was to project an image of purity as a minister. In fact, Elmer eventually becomes the head of the National Association for Purification of the Arts and Press (NAPAP), and among the other many organizations he either heads or becomes prominent in are the Modernistic Education Bureau, the Society for the Rehabilitation of Erring

---

[19] Rourke, *American Humor A Study of National Character* (New York: Doubleday, 1968) 86.

Young Women, and the Dynamos of Democratic Action.[20] In achieving his
success Elmer exhorts his listeners to get on "our team," to make "two yards
for the savior," and he leads them in the "Hallelujah Yell," which he himself
wrote and which is the "first one known in history." "Hallelujah, praise God,
hal, hal, hal! / Hallelujah, praise God, hal, hal, hal! / All together, I feel better, /
Hal, hal, hal, / For salvation of the nation— / Aaaaaaaaaa—*men!*"[21]

Lewis goes to considerable length to contrast Elmer with others in
evangelism or in the ministry, including the man who converted him, Judson
Roberts, "the praying fullback," who has reservations if not regrets over
bringing Elmer onto his team.

> Judson Roberts, ex-football star, state secretary of the Y.M.C.A.
> was on the train to Concordia, Kansas. In the vestibule he had three
> puffs of an illegal cigarette and crushed it out.
>
> No, really, it wasn't bad for him, that Elmer what's his name, to
> get converted. Suppose there *isn't* anything to it. Won't hurt him to cut
> out some of his bad habits for a while, anyway. And how do we know?
> Maybe the Holy Ghost does come down. No more improbable than
> electricity. I do wish I could get over this doubting. I forget it when I've
> got 'em going in an evangelistic meeting, but when I watch a big
> butcher like him, with that damned silly smirk on his jowls—I believe I
> will go into the real estate business. I don't think I am hurting these
> young fellows any, but I do wish I could be honest. Oh, Lordy, Lordy,
> Lordy, I wish I had a good job selling real estate![22]

The difference between Elmer and Frank Shallard, with whom Lewis
clearly sympathizes, is more pronounced, even oppositely. The son of a Baptist
minister and of a woman of a "main line family slightly run to seed," Frank has
in him a good deal of the natural poet and "something of the reasoning and
scientific mind." Instead of Ingersoll, he reads such bootlegged works as
Renan's *Jesus* and Nathaniel Schmidt's *The Prophet of Nazareth*. "Though a
good scholar, he was a thorough failure. He lectured haltingly, he wrote
obscurely, he could not talk to God as though he knew him personally, and he
could not be friendly with numbskulls."[23] In spite of all his doubts and

---

[20] Lewis, *Elmer Gantry* (New York: Harcourt Brace, 1927) 67.
[21] Ibid., 197.
[22] Ibid., 61.
[23] Ibid., 118.

disappointments, "he clung to the church. It was his land, his patriotism. Nebulously and quite impractically and altogether miserably he planned to give his life to a project called 'liberalizing the church from within.'"[24]

The Greater the Glory,
the Greater the Mirth

There are two signs of the arrival of the Religion of Sports on the American scene. One is the general absence of humor in that religion, dominated as it is by a high seriousness in the talk among apologists about athletes being in the zone or getting in the flow. The other is an increase in humor outside it directed at that religion. Among scores of cartoons dealing with the subject is one that shows a man at a hospital desk checking in. The receptionist asks him if he really wants her to put down "NFL" as his religion.

Nothing illustrates the new status of any movement as accurately as the satire cartoonists direct against it. In the world of accounting, for instance, professionals in that field tell us that all the pictorial humor is still directed at white male accountants. That discipline is changing for the better, which means minorities and women will in the not-too-distant future share the spotlight in the spoofing, ironically a sign of progress in equal opportunities. Apologists for the Religion of Sports might be inclined to point to this humor as a sign of the arrival of their religion, but we would urge caution before celebration. The satire of the Religion of Sports "has legs," as is said of stories in journalism, and seems set for a long race, the outcome of which will have bearing on the direction of our national culture.

As the Religion of Sports has developed in the last fifty years, it has imitated the patterns of traditional religion in major ways. Through mass media it has assumed the role of a champion of charity as seen in self-serving ads about contributions to causes, and it has maintained a vigorous campaign as a shaper of character and a promoter of high ideals through ads praising the "student-athlete," not to be confused with the "athlete-student" or "student-worker." In the last decade or so, the religion of sports has even generated discussion about the "feelings of Ultimacy" athletes experience at peak instances of action, leading apologists to speak of holy encounters on the playing field or indoor court.

---

[24] Ibid., 123.

All these things the Church of Sports has been able to accomplish. There is only one thing it has not been able to accomplish. It has not been able to throw off its trail or to leave behind the old watchdog of humor that the familiar religions know like a soulmate and in many instances cherish and use in working together toward a higher good. The old dog of humor, though, has not lost sight of this new religion of sports, and the barking in protest is well under way with no sign of abating.

There are, for example, countless spoofs making fun of the connections of sports and religion such as the following:

Religion is like sports because...: "The larger organizations have colorful, expensive uniforms or 'vestments.' Both religion and sports are centered around large structures to attract crowds. The emphasis and attention are on those under the spotlights, rather than those in the seats. Religion required animal sacrifices for the symbolism of the blood. Most sports require animal sacrifices for the leather, and the risk of blood-letting increases attendance. The 'rich, famous or important' people sit in front seats. If you donate enough money, you can sit in a better seat" and so on through approximately thirty other themes where humorous comparisons are drawn.[25]

One e-mail letter making the rounds takes Dr. Laura to task for indicting homosexuality as mentioned in Leviticus. It also asks her advice on other matters relating to punishment as stipulated in that biblical chapter, both of the following relating to rites in religion and sports, to the "pigskin" and to Super Sunday.

Dear Dr. Laura,
I know from Lev. 11:6–8 that touching the skin of a dead pig makes me unclean, but may I still play football if I wear gloves?
I have a neighbor who insists on working on the Sabbath. Exodus 35:2 clearly states he should be put to death. Am I morally obligated to kill him myself?

---

[25] "Sports: Religion Is Like Sports Because...," <http://www.geocities.com/Athens/Forum/1611/religionislike.html> (2 March 2004).

I know you have studied these things extensively, so I am confident you can help. Thank you again for reminding us that God's word is eternal and unchanging.

Jim

Clearly if death was once demanded on the part of the Lord for those working on the "holy" Sabbath, if Sunday is broadly regarded as our Sabbath, and if the play of professional athletes is a form of work for which they are richly rewarded, then we should give abounding thanks unto the Lord for his growing mercy. No wonder apologists see the Super Bowl as a "religious festival," a time of both play and worship free of the fear of divine decree, free at last, free at last—perhaps.

Even the academic treatment of sports as religion has not been spared as in the following excerpt and paraphrase by Frederick Kiley and J. M. Shuttleworth from Thomas Hornsby Ferrill, "Freud on Football," in *Satire: From Aesop to Buchwald*: "...football is a syndrome of religious rites symbolizing the struggle to preserve the egg of life through the rigors of impending winter." Ferrill notes that "the ceremony begins at the autumnal equinox and culminates on the first day of the New Year with great festivals and bowls of plenty. These festivals are associated with the harvest. Some are dedicated to the flowers such as roses, others to fruits such as oranges, or farm crops such as cotton. There are even festivals dedicated to the animals such as alligators. All of these appear to be special dedications in honor of the sun god."[26]

Fewer things are funnier than daily reports from the world of sports, even when sports are advanced as religion. This is especially true as seen in the stark contrast between wealth in the sports world and the ideal of biblical moderation and poverty, now seen everywhere as a bad mistake on the part of prophets and Jesus, biblical inerrancy apparently a more important theme. One cartoon catches this dilemma brilliantly. It shows Satan with horns and pitchfork appearing in a room before a college prospect with the caption summarizing the situation perfectly: "You have to be kidding. The New Jersey Generals offered me more than that."

This chapter asks two questions: (1) Why at a time when abuses abound in American sports do we insist on viewing them as "religious" or

---

[26] Ferrill, in Don F. Nelson, *Humor in American Literature: A Selected Bibliography* (New York: Garland Publishing Co., 1992) 261.

an ally of religion in the causes of proselytism, as if to imply that religion would be better if it were more sporting? (2) Why the high seriousness in so much exegesis in sports-as-religion texts?

In a thoughtful essay titled "Gods and Games in Modern Culture" in *From Season to Season*, Ronnie D. Kliever observes that "Christian denigration and modern approval of play reinforce each other in separating religion and play in our time. But in traditional cultures, even in those shaped and sustained by Christian sensibilities, religion has been the primary vehicle of human play."[27] Here he is in agreement with David Miller, author of *Gods and Games*, whom he cites and recommends. He is also in agreement with Rene Girard, who in *Violence and the Sacred* writes, "Far from subordinating religion to sport or play (as does Huizinga in *Homo Ludens*), we must subordinate play to religion insofar as it reproduces certain aspects of the sacrificial crisis."[28]

Kliever observes that "religion has lost its control over play," which is as much a loss for religion, he thinks, as for play. "Religion deprived of its play element quickly hardens into sterile rituals and stagnant beliefs."[29] As might be expected, there has been, he points out, a counter movement "among serious Christian theologians." Here is a paradox—"serious" Christian theologians attempting to regain control over "play." Can play be serious? If so, that may be one reason why the church lost "control" over it in the first place. In this regard we might all need to remember Huizinga's argument that play is a higher order than the serious because the playful can be serious but the serious can't be playful. Both may be meaningful if there is some conjunction between them. Humor makes fun only of the "stupidly serious." It cannot satirize the holy since the holy is "inconceivable," but only the sacred parading as the holy.

Kliever notes that "a more visible and powerful recovery of the play element in today's religion can be seen in the charismatic movements that bring entertainment and ecstasy into the very heart of worship." This jubilant expression appears to be play of the spirit and to some extent of the body. It may even be a form of *paideia*, but it is not humor or play of the mind, wit, irony, paradox, or satire, which have been used in support of

---

[27] Kliever, "Gods and Games in Modern Culture," in Joseph Price, *From Season to Season: Sports as American Religion* (Macon GA: Mercer University Press, 2001) 42.

[28] Girard, *Violence and the Sacred*, trans. Patrick Gregory (Baltimore: The Johns Hopkins Press, 1989) 154.

[29] Kliever, "Gods and Games," 43.

gospel aims throughout the long history of the church and even in the Gospels themselves as Elton Trueblood has shown.

We suggest too that even in services where charisma is at work, there may be different motives for the outpouring of song and praise. For instance, "charismatic movements that bring entertainment and ecstasy into the heart of worship" appear to be of a different nature from the African American's experience, in which well-known spirituals exemplify a long history of oppression and collective suffering. We must remember too that there is a silent and still worship that may or may not be a form of inner play. We have reached a point in our society where, just as we confuse activity with leisure, so we are prone to think movement in song or praise, as powerful as it can be, is the most significant form of worship.

If charismatic movements are signs of the holy, as they may well be, then the case for the holy seems improved in similar movements in sports, such as "the wave" or getting in the flow or zone except for one major difference—that of "identification" of the "Other." In mystical experiences of athletes, there seems considerable confusion as to who or what the Other is. In charismatic praise, there seems to be no doubt. The Other is who it has always been: "Lord God of hosts, everlasting from everlasting. If you can't dance, jump about, if you can't sing, make a joyful noise!" Our suggestion is for organized religion to lighten up in the manner of charismatics, that is, without making of play a religion and without doing the same with sports. At other times, the way is to be still and know. In dealing with the holy, no *one* way seems the only way. Sometimes we need to jump for joy, other times to be still and quiet and seek to know, other times to roar with laughter whether profane, secular, sacred or holy. Then, perhaps heretically, we need to doubt in order to live the question at deeper levels.

Obviously our cultural and religious problems are complex, perhaps hopelessly so, but at the heart of them lies the phenomenon of urbanization and commercialization. In rural and small-town America, play, excepting Sunday sports perhaps, was largely under the control of the church. Play and entertainment were both seen in almost in endless variety—box suppers, pie suppers, ice cream socials, cake walks, dinner on the ground, Vacation Bible School with learning another form of play, Easter egg hunts, children's day (which meant acting in pageants—*mimesis*), Christmas plays, "womanless" weddings at the village schoolhouse but under the auspices of church folk, a favorite form of country humor even with the "bride" standing at the altar with "her" baby symbolized by a doll. There were visiting quartets with comedy routines, weekend dances and wiener roasts, and weekend baseball, first on Saturday afternoons, and later on Sundays, violating the Sabbath commandment in the view of some.

On top of everything else was an unwritten requirement for ministers, stemming from the frontier tradition, to be an expert in the telling of tall tales, mainly for front porches of country stores and farm houses but also in the pulpit. The clear implication was that the gospel message could not be passed on without a good dose of humor. At a humor conference at Berea College in the eighties, among the best storytellers were preachers, a fact not surprising to those who know life in rural America.

With the decline of village life in America and the exodus to towns and especially with the advent of television, we turned our souls and hence our freedoms over to experts and professionals in sports, salvation, and humor. It is no accident that the muse of humor, Thalia, is a woman and that she holds in her hand the shepherd's staff. Television slickers have kidnapped her, and it is not difficult to imagine her weeping instead of promoting cheer among her sisters. Amid what passes for humor in the television medium, we often find what would depress a tough-skinned farmer while cleaning the manure trough in his cow barn after a morning milking.

Without self-deprecatory humor, the Religion of Sports will become an even larger target bloated with self-importance and mythological jargon as the commercial athletic establishment increasingly moves toward the practices of the religions of decadent Rome. The shepherd's staff of Thalia could be an effective tool, a magician's wand, of restraining the tyrannical tendencies of her half-brother Apollo, the sun god and the treasured son of the God of Games.

The loss of a sense of humor in mainline religion reflects a larger problem of the church—its growing sacredness, also evident in abounding nationalism and ethnocentrism around the world. While the ties have grown between organized religion and organized sports, religion has increasingly set itself apart from arts and literature and from a rich heritage of mutual concerns as outlined in such books as *Literature and Religion* by Hans Kung and Walter Jens. The same separation or setting apart has occurred between religion and science as reflected in useless arguments on both sides of the debate on evolution. Instead of seeking to be right on such issues and others, even those on foreign policy, the church might do well to follow the divine commission to do good to all people.

In many ways the direction of modern science as reflected in Loren Eisely's poem "Science and the Sense of the Holy," in the thinking of Albert Einstein, and in the wide range of leading scientists over the ages who combined gifted intellect with deep spiritual questing (as outlined in appendix 2 in Arthur Koestler's *Act Of Creation*) could be a model for religion in balancing the demands of the sacred and the holy, in preserving meaningful rites and exploring the dynamics of the soul. Science has had to do battle against the sacred beliefs of the church as well as those within its own domain as seen in the stories of Galileo, Kepler, and many others. Here too is a lesson for sports and religion. Although chaplains now reign in the locker rooms of football teams, one can't keep from wondering about the need for a comedian with equal time, especially if the chaplain lacks talent in that regard.

The sacred is "frozen thought," one definition of instinct and quite different from living thought and creative possibility. Today, science, especially physics, is arguably more spiritual in vision than religion as reflected in such books as *The Spiritual Universe: One Physicist's Vision of Spirit, Soul, Matter, and Self* by Fred Alan Wolf. In every field of human endeavor—art, science, sports, religion—the spirit of the sacred leads to rites of the preservation; the spirit of the holy to a consciousness wider and deeper than ever imagined.

To be sure the best is always some combination of the old and the new, but it may well be the case that organized religion and organized sports, both laden with rites, are our most conservative institutions, which may make them unnecessarily resistant to significant change other than each squeezing the hand of the other a little more tightly every year. The sacred is always defended as in "sacred honor" and "defender of the faith." The holy, in contrast, cannot be defended but only sought, never found but perhaps at times experienced. In regard to the sacred conservatism of both sports and religion, sports apologists do not appear unhappy with the situation as it is.

Universities, no longer under the control of faculty but of corporate folk, are in the throes of Nimrod, winning games of ball, games of enrollment, and games of grantsmanship, and in the throes of Nephilism, emphasizing specialization in trades and technologies at the expense of knowledge of the whole. We worship at the altar of efficiency while refusing to acknowledge the long-term needs of effectiveness. The closeup prevails as the big picture disappears in our universities. Hence there is a wide opening and a need for the church to supplement, if not to lead, the effort toward the highest goals of a civilized world through the study of the best that has been thought and said. To do this, though, the church may have to give up some of its sacredness and maybe even large chunks of dogma to gain a deeper vision of the whole of world society, history, and holiness.

How Many Masters Can One Serve?
Eutrapelia or Polytheism?

What makes sports apologetics so startling is not the novelty of the idea but the development of it by skilled scholars, many of them theologians, into a thesis to be taken seriously in the modern world. We have done no survey, but our speculation is that the reaction to this argument would be ironic. The people who would be most receptive to it are, we suspect, members of the athletic industry in the United States who already see their work in ways deeply meaningful if not moral and spiritual or even overtly religious, considering the almost endless proclamations of clichés along these lines coming from this segment of our culture. The responses of academics across the humanities to this argument, we imagine, would range from curiosity to deep interest and, one would hope, always an appreciation of the spirit of free inquiry, no matter the topic or theme. Where both the thesis and definitions would meet most resistance, we feel reasonably sure, is in the various camps of conservative Christians who generally love and follow sports but who are still not inclined to elevate them to the status of a religion with or without doctrinal portfolio.

To many fundamentalists in the South, at least the many we know, the definitions in *From Season to Season* would be far too liberal for their tastes. They would argue that any religion that did not make the worship of God its sin qua non and emphasize the commandments would be unworthy of the name of religion. We believe they would see the effort here as more evidence of liberalism believed to abound in theological circles, especially "up North" and even more so "up East." Indeed one is reminded of *The Flight of Peter Fromm* by Martin Gardner, the story of a young man with a Pentecostal background from Oklahoma who goes to divinity school in Chicago and eventually loses his faith in evangelism, though he remains a "theist."

This is not to suggest that apologists are engaged in such a mission as the humanist professor who tells the story of Peter Fromm or even whether they are "theists" or not. One of the problems of academics, including theologians, can be summed up by a paraphrase of a poem by Emily Dickinson about a minister: We dwell upon breadth until it argues us narrow. Hence the eternal dilemma of definitions no matter the category, sports or religion. In our passion for clarity of meaning we sometimes define categories so narrowly as to leave out "otherness," or we make our definitions so inclusive as to make them almost as meaningless in understanding distinctions as short views themselves.

The Southern Baptists, for instance, would not be cheered by an argument from any quarter proclaiming sports as an authentic religion of any kind, "folk," "natural," or "popular," even though the Southern Baptist Convention in the year 2000 moved toward the "left"—or would it be to the "right"?—on the issue of how to keep holy the "Lord's Day." In 1963, "the wording of the Convention left no doubt about what was expected. "Sunday should be employed in exercises of spiritual devotion, both public and private, and by refraining from worldly amusements, and resting from secular employments, work of necessity and mercy only being excepted."

The 2000 version opened the door just a crack, which is all that is needed for a sports fan, by referring to "Paul's flexible teaching in Romans 14:5–10: One man esteems one day as better than another, while another man esteems all days alike. Let everyone be fully convinced in his own mind...." The Convention tiptoed around the issue, but the shift in policy was unmistakable. According to Richard N. Ostling, AP Religion Writer, a candid rewrite of the change would run, "Let's admit it. Americans are sports crazy, and this *virtual religion* tempts Southern Baptists as much as others, if not more so."[30]

A fundamental question for followers of the cross, whether fundamentalists or not, is this: Can a person who accepts the commission of the new commandment to love others as oneself compete for a prize in a public place? Apologists avoid this nagging question by considering religion in a broader context than Christianity, Judaism, and other faiths, and, it must be said, in a more narrow context as well, by going to the roots of all religions as found in the myths and rituals of "preliterate man." Such religious breadth existed well before the coming of religious texts or the widespread reading thereof with such "good news" as the Beatitudes, which seem to have little or nothing to do with sports or competition but

---

[30] Ostling, "Southern Baptists Move to the Left on Sunday," <http://www.bpnews.net> (21 September 2002), italics added.

everything to do with the individual in regard to consolation, sharing, and reassurance.

Why is one conventional religion or theology not enough, if one chooses to have a religion at all? To what extent are the established traditions "wrong" in their accessibility to proponents of games of territory and power or for that matter in their opposition to them? What concepts related to religion, the ideas of the "sacred" and the "holy," get warped or stretched as far as common understanding is concerned when traditional religion and sports are placed in the same procrustean bed? What is the *best* relationship in a democracy between traditional religion and sports if sports themselves are also to be viewed as a religion?

The same could be asked of religion and war when war becomes "holy," a question not unrelated to the marriage of sports and religion as seen throughout the ages in the alliance of knighthood in one religion or another. In such a context, knighthood is, among other things, a system of competition, if not conquest, elevating the importance of contests and tournaments that we still use season after season to help celebrate our bounty at the beginning of each new year.

If sports are a religion of one kind or another—cultural, folk, nature, popular—how do they as a religion compete or cooperate with traditional denominations? Can a person serve two masters if the masters are substantially different, if one master says love your neighbor as yourself and another says winning is the only thing? As noted earlier, Price, drawing upon the views of Mircea Eliade, thinks that people may be "simultaneously religious in apparently competing ways." There are other wrinkles still.

Is it possible to maintain multilateral religious affiliations? "Can the proponent of the religion of sports also retain standing within his or her traditional religious affiliation?" Charles Prebish asks. "Ostensibly no!" he responds, reasoning that anyone who identifies sports as his or her religion would be "referring to a *consistent pursuit* that is also *the most important pursuit* and a *religious pursuit.* If this individual were to then state that he or she is also a Jew or a Protestant or a Catholic or whatever," Prebish concluded, "he or she would be referring to *cultural heritage* only, to the complex series of factors that are essentially ethnic and locational rather than religious."[31]

Our argument is that some tension on the matter of fidelity could be eliminated if we simply agreed that sports, in spite of appearances, are not really a religion but an authentic archetype of human action with elements in common not only with religion but with art, work, and war, though not equatable with any. In such a context, sports could be a good thing if handled intelligently but not inherently divine any more than would be the case with work, itself a type of art as in the sense of *homo faber*, man the maker. What needs to come into play in situations between competing allegiances is the classical ideal of *eutrapelia*, "well-turningness" between one endeavor and another as illustrated in the acclaimed book by Hugo Rahner, *Man at Play*.

Drawing upon the writings of Aristotle and Aquinas, Rahner builds a case for both play and seriousness and the happy mean between them for the one who can enjoy both without becoming victimized by either. The *eutrapelos* (well-turning person) avoids the extremes of those who make fun of everything and those who never laugh at anything.[32] The ideal of *eutrapelia* is more complex than it might at first appear, but it has the virtue of allowing a place for humor and play in the world of high seriousness such as that of modern sports.

Perhaps the best way of thinking about *eutrapelia*, Rahner says, lies in an incident he cites from Aquinas, who in the *Summa* recalled an incident in the "Lives of the Fathers" and thus touched on a lovely and profound mystery of the grace of God that "plays" in the world. "It was revealed that a certain joker would be his companion in heaven" And in the same article, Aquinas had the courage—astounding at the time—to open the Christian gates also to actors, to the art of the theatre and to all their patrons, as did later the gentle Francis de Sales....

"Not everything in our civilization is in the hands of the devil and thundering from the pulpit is not always in place." Christians must try to realize, he says, "the Christian ideal of the serious-serene human being at

---

[31] Cited in Price, *From Season to Season*, 229.

[32] Rahner, *Man at Play*, trans. Brian Battershaw and Edward Quinn (New York: Herder and Herder, 1972) 93–94.

play in fine versatility, in *eutrapelia*, in that serene abandonment to the seriousness of God"[33]

While it could be argued that sports is a religion in and of itself, if considered in terms of mythological features common to cultures of antiquity, it is not one that would be publicly applauded in congregations of most conventional denominations, Protestant or Catholic. However, it is one that proselytizers in religion, counterparts in sports of "recruiters" or "birddogs," might quietly find handy in gaining or keeping converts. If a religion or denomination can't have the whole soul of a believer, they can perhaps have half a soul or share a soul and not find themselves left out completely as implied in a cartoon in which one football player is speaking to another: "I'm a converted nose guard. Before that I was a Presbyterian." With football established as an authentic denomination, the player in this cartoon could now say, "I'm a converted nose guard but I am still a Presbyterian." In the eternal struggle and courtship between sports and religion, it might be better for established faiths to gain a tie rather than to lose entirely.

Other indications of the difficulty of serving two masters or having two religions come from the words of two former coaches. Duffey Dougherty of Michigan State, according to Shirl Hoffman, remarked that coaches who held pre-game prayers ought to be made to go to church. The other comes from Tom Landry, who in later years by his own confession prayed on his knees for forgiveness for making a god out of football.

Still we do not rule out the possibility Price proposes. As an example of multiple faiths, one of us knows an impressive family that is deeply committed to matters of the soul and to academic learning. These people attend Baptist, charismatic, and Jewish services every week. If they had time to be avid sports fans, we think Price would say they would be involved in *four* genuine religious traditions. The boys, while also studying Greek, Hebrew, and Chinese, take karate and in their spare time play gleefully with other kids in the backyard, so perhaps they are indeed completing a "Square Deific," to use Whitman's fine phrase.

What is occurring in the example above is an example of *eutrapelia* (well-turningness) and not polytheism, which in our view is what a religion of sports would require. It is not polytheistic for the same person to attend churches of different denominations. It took much of evolutionary history

---

[33] Ibid., 104-5.

for humans to discover gods, and to group them into bunches and monotheism was a longer wait. With the religion of sports, we are headed back toward a religion of glory, toward worship of the sun god, that is, Apollo and all the pantheon of his troop associated with games—Mercury, Hercules, Nike, and her father Zeus, the supreme trickster.

Notice the presence of Zeus in one of the most famous athletic events of the past century, the 1964 heavyweight championship title bout between Sonny Liston and Muhammad Ali, then Cassius Clay. Here is the take of Malcolm X: "'This fight is the truth,' Malcolm told Cassius. 'It's the Cross and the Crescent fighting in the prize ring—for the first time. It's a modern crusade—a Christian and a Muslim fighting each other with television to beam it off Telstar for all the world to see what happens."[34] Zeus was present, clapping his hands not necessarily over the outcome, for he doesn't care who wins. What addicts him is the notion of victory for a prize in a public place. Make no mistake—he is at home in every heart. The fear in honoring Zeus so much, even by other names, is that we will forget the means of dealing with one another aside from sports and war. Already, alternatives seem as preposterous as they did to the reigning King of the Wood three thousand years ago at Nemi. Nothing would suit Zeus more than to make of sports a religion honoring him, as religions of sports always do.

The "Great Hopes" of Civilization: Are Sports and Religion among Them?

Thanks to his keen sense of relevancy and the connection between animal behavior and that of humans, Konrad Lorenz discusses at length the possibilities of sublimation in both sports and humor. He finds no possibility of ventilation in humor disdainful of others, and by his own admission he finds fewer examples of sublimation of violence in sports. Note, too, the absence of sports when Lorenz concludes as follows: "Humor and knowledge are the two great hopes for civilization."[35]

Since religion is also about knowledge, a term or variant thereof that appears in Scripture at least fifteen hundred times, does Lorenz see any hope from religion in the salvation of civilization? The answer would be a definite

---

[34] Budd Schulberg, "The Chinese Boxes of Muhammad Ali," *The Sporting Spirit: Athletes in Literature and Life*, eds. Robert J. Higgs and Neil D. Isaacs (Harcourt Brace jovanovich: New York, 1977), 198.

[35] Lorenz, , 288.

yes if we understand that it does not generate the kind of "militant enthusiasm" that seems to be growing and symbolized in part by the popularity of territorial sports. Instead, "Militant enthusiasm" is common to all religions because, in Lorenz's view, "Militant enthusiasm" also has an evolutionary history apologists draw on to canonize the modern religion of sports. Creationists probably would not put much stock in what Lorenz says since he is a natural scientist and a confirmed Darwinian, as if those facts rule out a reverent sense of mystery on his part, a sense of the holy and a profound sense of ethics. Similarly, Loren Eiseley probably did not find much common ground with creationists even after his several books that reflected the theme of "Science and the Sense of the Holy." In any event, let us note what kind of religion Lorenz has in mind; it is one easily available in every religion on earth and outside of religion too.

> There is a third, more distant hope (in addition to humor and knowledge) based on the possibilities of human evolution…. We know that in the evolution of vertebrates the bond of personal love and friendship was the epoch-making invention created by the great constructors (do not read this as either blind forces or a pantheon of gods) when it became necessary for two or more individuals of an aggressive species to live peacefully together and to work for a common end. We know that human society is built on the foundation of this bond, but we have to recognize the fact that the bond has become too limited to encompass all that it should: it prevents aggression only between those who know each other and are friends, while obviously it is all active hostility between all men of all nations or ideologies that must be stopped.
>
> The obvious conclusion is that love and friendship should embrace all humanity, that we should love all our human brothers indiscriminately. This commandment is not new.[36]

The reference is of course to the new commandment, which would not require a 4,000-pound monument to display or to remember and which would obviate any need for court battles over such actions. How well it squares with territorial sports and the thinking of sports apologists is, like the future of the race, open to question.

---

[36] Ibid., 289-90

As for the chances of religions of compassion to flourish as opposed to religions of violence, and as far as we can tell both apply, there is much that we need to keep in mind, as there is in the case of sports if in the future they too are to play a constructive rather than destructive role in world culture.

Rightly or wrongly, religion throughout history has been given a "license" to deal wholesale, so to speak, with the phenomenon of the holy, to establish rituals in communication with it, to inspire beauty through the recognition of the holy, and to establish or seek to establish ethics based upon promptings from the holy. An argument can be presented that over time the record of the established church is morally abysmal considering the persecutions the church has perpetrated, its narrowness of vision, the self-righteousness and absence of humility the holy demands, the drive for political power, and the unending wars the church has inspired or to which it has lent imprimatur. The claim should not surprise us that, as many assert, the world would be better without organized religion than with it. Perhaps—but before we rush in that direction it would be wise to consider the remark of Benjamin Franklin in his famous letter to Thomas Paine advising him not "to unleash" the tiger in his criticism of organized faith: "If men are so wicked with religion, what would they be if without it?"

It can be argued well that the cruelties committed in the name of religion are not at all what religion, by common understanding, is about. Further, it must be said in fairness that all denominations of the American church have done incalculable good in the world in terms of charity; consolation in grief and loss; spiritual inspiration; establishment of hospitals, missions, and orphanages; provision of opportunities for exercises and play; and a thousand other benefits to society and culture.

Over the long haul of history, sports at first looks as innocently benign as the best face of religion, but the same question needs to be asked of it that Franklin asked of religion: "If men are so wicked with sports, what would they be without them?" The question is unfair in regard to sports, some might say, since sports make up a separate category of human experience from religion. "Ain't it so!" we respond, adding a reminder—since sports have been under control of either church or state or both at once, in Athens, Sparta, Rome, throughout the Renaissance under colonizing powers of England and Spain, in imperial England, Nazi Germany, and Imperial Japan—that whatever is wrong with church or state is ipso facto wrong with sports. Even today when sports are often under the control of business, the credo "winning is the only thing," or more accurately profit is the only thing, holds sway. This first commandment in the world of sports has been adopted by leading corporations with all the arrogance and contempt toward ordinary people that such a policy engenders, not to mention the threat to democracy itself.

Sports at their best are living art, but they are also like art in another interesting way: they are always dependent on sponsors—church, state, corporation, or wealthy individuals—unlike play, which is essentially independent of outside help. This is not to say all sponsors are deserving of Dr. Johnson's definition of a patron, "commonly a wretch who supports with insolence, and is paid with flattery," but at the same time it is good to keep patron in mind this opinion. Sports are useful, which means they serve extrinsic purposes, usually the goal of wealth and often enough the love of it. Play, in contrast, is "useless" but in the old sense of "priceless," its virtues intrinsic in the re-creation of the soul.

"Exercises" are more like sports in that they too tend to be useful in the service of an army, a religion, athletic teams, a philosophy (often Eastern), or even one's health, which is not why we play. Even too much concern for diet or health or for playing well are destructive to the spirit of play, which is Edenic in essence. Let us say that at the least there is not overwhelming evidence that sports, either spiritually or morally, are ready to stand alone as a new religion. They will still need sponsors in addition to fans, and the moral behavior of corporate America does not bode well as far as ethics of the new religion would be concerned.

Sports and religion both might yet prove to be helpful for civilization but only if they abandon the credo that victory in this world is the same as virtue, that winning games of numbers is the only thing or even the most important thing. In the end, sports needs to make sport of itself, as religion at its humble best has always done, and come to remember again that the play *is* the thing. The metaphor that best describes the scramble in sports to get to the top is the pyramid, long associated with the worship of the sun; the metaphor for play is the garden, where in endless variety it may bloom again in all its splendid possibility. The athlete who is part of that sense of play may well compete—but only with himself or herself.

Chapter 15

Apotheosis Versus Atonement

The title of the concluding chapter in *From Season to Season* by Joseph Price is "An American Apotheosis: Sports as a Popular Religion." One must ask whether Price and other apologists are delighted that sports are a religion at last or merely describing the scene for others to ponder. To speak of sports as an "apotheosis" is perhaps accurate in a sense, but it should also be a warning as to the direction American civilization is headed since the word means "deification or the raising of a mortal to the rank of god" as in emperors, kings, and perhaps now athletes and other celebrities of various ilk. In short, such a trend represents just about every concept the American nation has fought against abroad and at home since our beginning, the tendency in the world to make gods of men.

There seems little doubt that we have entered into an apotheosis of sports considering the ubiquity of halls of fame and replays of heroic moments in sports on television networks, while knowledge of literature, including that of Scripture, Christian and otherwise, steadily wanes in the electronic age. Even when the sincere athlete of one sport or another comes to the aid of proselytizing denominations or other sects in the world, his or her presence accentuates the apotheosis of sports even as the case might be made in the proselytism for a religion of atonement. The medium continues to be the message, and the winning athlete, skilled in carrying the torch of victory, is the first choice for religions also vying for first place.

Surprisingly little is said about "atonement" in Scripture. Also, it offers itself to various interpretations depending upon one's faith, but there is little doubt that it depends upon a sense of sacrifice for others by oneself and a desire for the reconciliation between the individual soul and God. "Atonement," says the *Westminster Dictionary of Christian Theology*, "becomes meaningful when there is some sense of brokenness, of disruption, of things being 'out-of-joint,' of falling short, of estrangement from the ideal self, from social well-being, from God." In atonement there is a spirit of surrender or acceptance, in apotheosis of victory. To a large degree but not completely, apotheosis is a quest for ultimacy, atonement for intimacy. As in most other situations, though, things are never completely matters of either/or. All our concepts of the world are intertwined with each other, mutually dependent and often masked as opposites of what they are in essence.

As an example of the need for atonement, Otto cites first the vision of the call of Isaiah and, "less emphatically but quite unmistakably, in the story of the centurion of Capernaum (Luke 7:1-10), and his words, 'I am not worthy that thou shouldest enter under my roof.'" Otto goes on to say:

> Here, then, comes in the felt necessity and longing for "atonement," and all the more strongly when the close presence of the numen, intercourse with it, and enduring possession of it, becomes an object of craving, is even desired as the *summum bonum.*
>
> It amounts to a longing to transcend this sundering unworthiness, given with the self's existence as "creature" and profane natural being. It is an element in the religious consciousness, which, so far from vanishing in the measure in which religion is deepened and heightened, grows on the contrary continually stronger and more marked. Belonging, as it does, wholly to the non-rational side of religion. It may remain latent while, in the course of religious evolution, the rational side at first unfolds and assumes vigorous and definite form; it may retire for a time behind other elements and apparently die away, but only to return more powerfully and insistently than before.[1]

Atonement, in contrast to "apotheosis," is at home with humor and humility, that which is of the earth, as a story from the country illustrates well. A mountaineer is sitting on a log in the woods when a minister comes upon him and implores him to repent, informing him that the end of the world is nigh. "Good," says the mountaineer, "let her Come! I'm out of everything." The mountaineer might be considered the apotheosis of the stoic, and indeed there may be a way that apotheosis and atonement can

---

[1] Otto, *The Idea of the Holy*, 54-55.

work together, made more difficult in an atmosphere of addiction to winning. Much depends on what is being apotheosized and atoned for.

Moby Dick well illustrates how apotheosis and atonement might relate. The one who takes the *Pequod* out to sea is Bulkington, whose appearance so struck Ishmael at the Spouter Inn: "I have seldom seen such brawn in a man. His face was deeply brown and burnt, making his white teeth dazzling by the contrast; while in the deep shadows of his eyes floated some reminiscence that did not seem to give him much joy. His voice at once announced that he was a southerner, and from his fine stature, I thought he must be one of those tall mountaineers from the Alleghenian Ridge in Virginia."[2]

When the *Pequod* sets sail, Melville dwells on the fact, observes F. O. Matthiessen, that Bulkington is at the helm. "Though he has just landed in midwinter from a four years' dangerous voyage, he has unrestingly pushed off again. Melville symbolizes in him the natural seeker for the 'open independence of truth's sea,' and his last words to him are: 'bear thee grimly, demigod! Up from the spray of thy ocean perishing—straight up leaps thy apotheosis!'"[3] Bulkington, one more victim of Ahab's madness, takes the *Pequod* out to sea, but it is another wanderer who lives to tell the tale. Herein lies the meaning of that fish story in terms of the holy, as Loren Eiseley explains in "Science and the Sense of the Holy":

> Ishmael, in contrast to Ahab, is the wandering man, the acceptor of all races and their gods. In contrast to the obsessed Ahab he paints a magnificent picture of the peace that reigned in the giant whale school of the 1840s, the snuffing and grunting about the boats like dogs, loving and being loved, huge mothers gazing in bliss upon their offspring. After hours of staring at those peaceful depths, "Deep down," says Ishmael, "there I still bathe in eternal mildness of joy." The weird, the holy, hangs undisturbed over the whales' huge cradle. Ishmael knows it, others do not.
>
> In the end, when Ahab has done his worst and the *Pequod* with the wounded whale is dragged into the depths amid shrieking seafowl, it is Ishmael, buoyed up on the calked coffin of his cannibal

---

[2] Herman Melville, quoted in F. O. Mattheissen, *The American Renaissance: Art and Expression in the Age of Emerson and Whitman* (New York: Oxford University Press, 1968) 643–44.

[3] Mattheissen, 643–44.

friend Qeequeg, who survives to tell the tale. Like Whitman, like W. H. Hudson, like Thoreau, Ishmael, the wanderer, has noted more of his fellow men than his headstrong pursuer of the white whale, whether "agent" or "principal" within the universe. The tale is not of science, but it symbolizes on a gigantic canvas the struggle between two ways of looking at the universe: the magnification of the poet's mind attempting to see all, while disturbing as little as possible, as opposed to the plunging fury of Ahab with his cry, "Strike, strike through the mask, whatever it may cost in lives and suffering." Within our generation we have seen the one view plead for endangered species and reject the despoliation of the earth. The other has left us lingering in the shadow of atomic disaster.[4]

There is a paradox here. Ishmael the wanderer is the one who is at peace with the whales and the gods from other lands. He redeems Bulkington, who was also a wanderer. Ishmael attains atonement. Through Ahab, Melville illustrates what the alternatives are if we don't change. Melville, according to Stewart, is among the writers in the Christian tradition, showing like his dear friend Hawthorne the consequences of sin and arrogance, especially as revealed in *Moby Dick*.

The holy, as Otto believed and as Melville illustrated, often speaks through art. Ishmael's instruction on the value of atonement comes from nature, from the love of mother whales for their offspring. Here is a word picture of mother and child to go with the sculpture pictured in Eric Neuman's *The Great Mother*, ranging from prehistoric times to the Madonna and Child of Henry Moore.

Ishmael's words offer an archetypal representation of atonement, that is, love, which is also represented by death as in the *pieta* theme that connects to athletic art as discussed in chapter 12. As a friend has observed, if dogs could paint or sculpt, they would create art of mother and pup. Here is perhaps the universal holy scene, one that often involves two beings united in love in Great Time. The sacred aspect of these scenes draws our attention to the participants, whether whales or dogs or humans, to the setting in terms of time or places, which, in the case of the art, shapes the

---

[4] *The Star Thrower*, Intro. W.H. Auden (New York Harcourt Brace Jovanovich, 1978) 199-200.

selection of the medium and the style. For the many variations, though, one thing overarches all—the holy idea of love.

Walt Whitman Speaks

The last thing on the *Pequod* to go beneath the surface is the American flag. It is not necessarily prophetic, but singing "God Bless America" at ball games won't be enough to prevent the disaster suggested by that symbol. We are not ready to lay the possibility of such catastrophe at the feet of Emerson and Whitman for deifying humans, and neither does Randall Stewart, at least not completely, in tracing the stunning evolution of attitudes toward the individual from Emerson's generation celebrating the "I" to the "Me" generation of today. To grasp the seismic transformation in what has occurred regarding our national consciousness, it is necessary to cite at some length Stewart's evidence as presented in *American Literature and Christian Doctrine*.

> The following prayer comes from the *The Book of Common Prayer*, but it could be said, without material change, by all Christians, everywhere.
> Almighty and most merciful Father, we have erred and strayed from thy ways like lost sheep. We have followed too much the devices and desires of our own hearts. We have offended against thy holy laws. We have left undone those things which we ought to have done; and we have done things which we ought not to have done; *and there is no health in us.* But thou, O Lord, have mercy upon us, miserable offenders. Spare thou those O God who confess their faults. Restore thou those who are penitent, according to thy promises declared unto mankind in Christ Jesus our lord. And grant, O most merciful Father, for his sake, that we may hereafter live a godly, righteous, and sober life, to the glory of thy holy name. Amen....
> The importance of the difference between the Christian's prayer and Emerson's cannot be overemphasized. One says, "I am a sinner"; the other, "I am good." One says, "God be merciful, God forgive my sins"; the other, "My godlike qualities are indeed reason for self-congratulation." There can be no doubt, I think, that the Emerson view...became long ago an indistinguishable and almost unconscious part of the "American mind." It slipped in by the back

door. Just as Emerson's "Trust Thyself" became (without his intending that it should) "every man for himself" giving a kind of rough justice to Allen Tate's remark in that Emerson became unwittingly "the prophet of piratical industrialism," and indeed one recalls Emerson saying, "If you build a better mouse trap, the world will beat a path to your door," became the golden text of our competitive economy, so his "I am good, good innately" has suffered a whole succession of noxious sea changes: "I am as good as you"; "I am better than you"; "America is good"; "America is better than any other nation—our prosperity proves it." It is well to remind ourselves occasionally of a text which has not been much quoted in modern times: "Pride goeth before destruction, and a haughty spirit before a fall."[5]

If we ask who or what has played roles in the enshrinement of pride in our "national mind" so that now it is synonymous with virtue, one would have to rank highly sports, media, and religion. Pride is what every team and every coach seek, but not pride in the sense of arrogance, winners always say. Listen, though, to post-game comments of champions; there is little doubt that victory and virtue are regarded as synonymous, that the winning team is loaded with character, and that thanks are due to God for the blessing bestowed, usually, it needs to be remarked, with compliments to the losing coach and team for playing hard and trying.

Twenty-four hours a day, television reminds us that success, often symbolized by the winning athlete, is the key to understanding America's own success in terms of its standing in the world. Televangelism blesses this coalition of sport and state by exploiting the athlete (even better if the athlete is recovering from some addiction) as a material symbol of a spiritual conquest, or vice versa, and wrapping it up in the red, white, and blue of Old Glory. To the mind hungry for numbers of converts or dollars, it seems like a trinity made in heaven—sports, state, and religion. Yet one thing about the union that can't be erased or covered up is its most conspicuous feature—money, also known as power.

Poor Emerson. The man can't win. Stewart blames him for initiating apotheosis in America, the idolization of the human. Also, Charles W. Eliot,

---

[5] Stewart, *American Literature and Christian Doctrine* (Baton Rouge: Louisiana State University Press, 1958) 56–57.

president of Harvard for many years and one of the most distinguished of American educators, attributes to Emerson the creation of athleticism. In 1906, Eliot, struggling all during his presidency with the controversy of sports in the colleges, said, "I find in Emerson the true reason for the athletic cult, given a generation before it existed among us. 'Your boy hates the grammar school and the grades, and loves guns, fishing rods, horses, and boats. Well the boy is right, and you are not fit to direct his bringing up, if your theory leaves out his gymnastic training.... Football, cricket, archery, swimming, skating, climbing, fencing, riding are lessons in the art of power, which it is his main business to learn....' We shall never find a completer justification of athletic sports than that."[6]

If we take literally the language of Eliot, especially the term "athletic cult," then sports were a religion of sorts from the post Civil War Period onward. Emerson no doubt regarded sports and play as secular, maybe even pagan and certainly British, but it was not long, owing to the universal popularity of play, before they entered into an alliance with religion known as Muscular Christianity. Finally, in the late twentieth century, sports decided that it could stand alone as a religion since no deity was necessary and since sports were less violent than religion often is.

If Emerson is John the Baptist of American sports, Teddy Roosevelt is literally the savior, keeping football alive in the first decade of this century amid a controversy centered on deaths and injuries. Just as Eliot had to deal with the heritage of Emerson about sports as education for power, so he had to deal in real time with Teddy on the same issue. He knew Teddy as a boy, he said, and after his election he still knew him as a boy. If there was ever an American seeking apotheosis for his nation, it was Teddy; for his actions, he himself gained apotheosis on Mount Rushmore, though it is doubtful that such glory was what he sought anymore than others enshrined there with him.

The problem, then and now, is not one of kind—keeping sports, religion, education, and the state totally separate—but one of degree. For whatever role they played in the development of American sports in relation to education, it is unlikely that either Emerson or Roosevelt would approve of the current state of things. If they could witness any Super Bowl, our wager is that the reaction of both, maybe in unison, would be, "No! No! No!

---

[6] Charles W. Elliot, *Four American Leaders* (Folcraft PA: Folcraft Library Editions, 1973) 95.

This is not what we envisioned. We both believed in *mens sana in corpore sano* for individuals and for the nation—but not this! We know that *mens sana* is a Christian ideal as well as pagan, but its distinguished pedigree is not why we advocate it. It is just common sense."

It is good to have a towering, controversial figure like Emerson in our past, for we can blame him for just about anything we wish. Because of Emerson, Stewart observes, we have a book like *The Power of Positive Thinking* by Norman Vincent Peale, who proclaimed that if Jesus were alive he would be at the Super Bowl. We can't be sure, but we don't believe that the Jesus of Emerson in his "Divinity School Address" would be present. We are not sure about the Jesus of the televangelists. Whatever Jesus would do depends upon those who have defined him exclusively in sacred time.

In light of the celebrated vision and stature of Whitman, we want to imagine in closing a setting, as mentioned at the beginning, where Whitman, walking alone and singing on a road across his beloved America, comes upon a gathering of modern students around a flagpole holding prayer services and singing "Onward Christian Soldiers," practicing for a half-time program at a football game that Friday night in the American South. We invite ourselves as witnesses to the scene and as interlocutors to find out more about the one occupying center position in the "American Canon." Granting the "Good Grey Poet" the timeless consciousness he claims to possess, here is what we suspect he might say:

"Oh, my children. How wonderful. You are beginning to see the eternal connections of all things, the form, union, plan, happiness, and joy both in the here and now and in the infinite.

"If you read my leaves, you know how I love the stories of the sea and the stories of heroes. That hymn, you know, was sung by British and American crews on ships in the dark, churning waters of the North Atlantic when Churchill met with Roosevelt in the bleakest days our civilization has ever known, the darkness wrought by a scornful cult who thought the body should have dominion over the soul and who had contempt for the old, old cause, that is liberty, the main promise of my dear brother whom you honor by your hymn. 'Many' as I say in my poem in his honor, 'To Him Who Was Crucified,' ...are sounding his name but do not understand him / I do not sound his name but I understand him.' You may find, as Dietrich Bonhoeffer did, that it is necessary in a noisy proclaiming world when faiths collide to practice a secret discipline, but perhaps you will not. It doesn't matter as long as you are driven by love and not by hate.

"Oh, I sense belief in the air all around you and how wonderful belief is in the young, for it is the beginning of the lifelong journey of love which the crucified one asked us to undertake. You pray here in public at a special moment, which my dear brother asked us not to do at special times but at all times, yet at least you gather, hold hands, and acknowledge the yearning power in your souls and longing therein for its proper anchorage. If I seem to contradict myself, it is because I contain multitudes. I will not have a single person left out. Remember what I said to the common prostitute that I would not exclude her 'until the sun excluded' her. Such marvelous language, such gentle thought that I learned in part from my dear brother. Do not speak of him as 'master' for that betrays a residue of royalty still left in the American psyche, which manifests itself too often in American castles and other forms of invidious distinction. Remember that the son of man had no place to lay his head. Instead of 'master,' look upon him as a 'friend' as in another wonderful old hymn quite different from the one you were singing now.

"By the way, I know your event here has just been photographed for the papers and for television. I can see that you love cameras and so do I. I get frustrated when I go to public events where I am featured and one is not available. That is one place where my dear brother and I differ. He would not have loved cameras, almost cherishing solitude it seems, but I do. When I think of America, the land that I love and cherish, I think of the photograph, perhaps one of the eagle or the dalliance of eagles. Oh it is so wonderful to be seen and, especially, heard when one has much to say. I love media of all kinds, especially words and photographs, and theater and opera. So much to love in this abundant land.

"I see you are holding hands around this flagpole as you boys do before kickoff in the ball games. Such a manly thing—and a womanly thing too. I always loved to hold hands, for as I have said I make holy whatever I touch, being divine inside and out as you are too when you come to realize it. I would like to hold hands now except for one minor problem. I will need both to hold my book, *Leaves of Grass*, which I always love to read in the open air to anyone who will listen, so please bring joy to my heart by allowing me to do so here around the great flag I love so much in light of what it has been through and the promise it holds not just for the American soul and body but the human soul and body everywhere for all time.

I could recite without access to print, which would allow me to hold hands with you, but the connections would not be complete without the feel of the book in my hands. I and the book are one. Listen, then, as I read from section 46 of 'Song of Myself,' which is also your song though you may not know it at the present time. We must always strive to see, and the first step toward consciousness is learning to listen. Speech, you see, is the twin of my vision. So, my blessed children, hear these words in this song of freedom:

'I know I have the best of time and space, and was never measured and never will be measured.
I tramp a perpetual journey, (come listen all!)
My signs are a rain-proof coat, good shoes, and a staff cut from the woods,
No friend of mine takes his ease in my chair,
I have no chair, no church, no philosophy,
I lead no man to a dinner table, library, exchange,
But each man and each woman of you I lead upon a knoll,
My left hand hooking you around the waist,
My right hand pointing to landscapes of continents and the public road...
This day before dawn I ascended a hill and look'd at the crowded heaven,
And I said to my spirit *When we become the enfolders of those orbs and the pleasure and the knowledge of everything in them, shall we be fill'd and satisfied then?*
And my spirit said *No, we but level that lift to pass and continue beyond....*
Long have you timidly waded holding a plank by the shore,
Now I will you to be a bold swimmer,
To jump into the sea, rise again, nod to me, shout, and laughingly dash with your hair.'"

As he closes *Leaves*, we imagine him concluding as follows, "Note that the image of the seeker I use is an athletic one, that of the bold swimmer, as I use elsewhere to illustrate the joys of being. I am also a lover of baseball, racing, and everything else about the great outdoors, just everything American and human. Please observe too how the next section of my 'Song' begins:

'I am the teacher of athletes,
He that by me spreads a wider breast than my own proved the width
    of my own,
He most honors my style who learns under it to destroy the
    teacher.'"

Some might say that Whitman, like Jesus, cannot be removed from his
own time, but the spirit of freedom remains relevant in the teachings of both
as well as in those of Saint Paul who, like Whitman, used the symbol of the
child and spiritual athlete to distinguish what is nothing less than the
differences between the sacred and the holy, between material prizes and
gifts, between what we are taught as children to revere in religion, politics,
and culture and what we might as single solitary selves encounter face-to-
face, the mystery of being, one aspect of the holy.

The first question we asked the Great American poet is this: "Which is
the most applicable metaphor in describing the relationship between sports
and religion, peanut butter and jelly or oil and water?" Having the advantage
of cosmic consciousness, he seemed to know all so that nothing coming
from our own time had to be prefaced or introduced.

"Oh, both and neither," he said in this imaginary encounter. "There is
no way to express the separateness of body and soul, for they are one and
inseparable whether the body is still or in motion in vigorous games. Please
know that whether or not sports are a religion is a minor matter, an occasion
for weaker minds to argue concerning God which no one should ever do.
What is of concern is whether or not our games contribute to what I called
the 'divine average,' the good life for all not just a sporting life for a few.

"I must confess I like Deion's better. So original, so bold, so close to
the kitchen sink where I tried to bring the muses. As is often the case, those
who play and work outdoors are more imaginative than the scholars. Peanut
butter and jelly is a more encompassing expression, for it contains oil and
water, but oil and water do not always contain peanut butter and jelly. It
better expresses the inseparable union of body and soul. Even after we die,
as Otto said, we still go on being, which is what I meant, though no one paid
attention, when I said to future generations to look for me in the grass under
their feet. As for the dead, I tell you they are alive and well somewhere, and
I know it."

Whitman continued not so much in a poetic vein as philosophical,
subdued in relation to the exuberance that abounds in his verse. "Since I

have so much to say I do not like to quote others, but my contemporary also from New York, Herman Melville, put into the mouth of his narrator Ishmael these words which apply in regard to religion of sports or any other kind, 'I have no objection to any person's religion, be it what it may, so long as that person does not kill or insult any other person, because that other person don't believe it also.'[7] I also found amusing what Quequeeg seemed in Ishmael's imagination to be saying. 'It's a mutual joint stock world, in all meridians. We cannibals must help these Christians.'

"That was so witty on the part of Herman whom I never met, but I reviewed some of his books for the *Brooklyn Daily Eagle.*

"I would never have said what Ishmael did, 'that Presbyterians and pagans alike…are all somehow dreadfully cracked about the head, and sadly need mending.'[8] It brings a smile to my lips, but I chose to write mending words without focusing so much on the nature of the problems. Herman believed that evil was in the world; I am not so sure and suspect that if there is it only leads toward good."

Seeing a point of entry, we asked him how he felt about the charges made against him by Randal Stewart, about the "apotheosis of man," and read to him certain passages in this regard: "Whitman's world, as I have said before, is man-centered. The apotheosis of man has never been carried farther nor has the apotheosis of the material present. Whitman's 'real objects of today,' which are to supply the inspiration for his 'church' of the future sounds suspiciously like our current technological marvels."

Then we read to him his own words, which, as Stewart had mentioned, Whitman wrote in 1855 in the preface to *Leaves of Grass:* "There will soon be no more priests. Their work is done. They may wait a while, perhaps a generation or two, dropping off by degrees. A superior breed shall take their place, the gangs of kosmos and prophets en masse shall take their place. A new order shall arise and they shall be the priests of man, and every man shall be his own priest. The churches built under their own tutelage shall be the churches of men and women. Through the divinity of themselves shall the kosmos and the new breed of poets be interpreters of men and women and all events and things."[9]

---

[7] Melville, *Moby Dick,* intro. Newton Arvin (New York: Rinehart, 1948) 89.
[8] Ibid., 81.
[9] Stewart, *American Literature and Christian Doctrine,* 64-65.

Whitman was eager to come to his own defense: "I will plead guilty of apotheosis if it means lifting mortals up to new levels of self-respect and opportunity without diluting divinity in the least. My message was unmistakable. I am divine inside and out and every atom that belonged to me as good belongs to you. My goal always was the creation of a 'divine average' where all could sense the power of the god within. I have given voice to the whole race whether they wish to speak or not. If Randall Stewart could have seen the contempt by which the human body was held by the church and the academy in my time and how lowly the ordinary person was regarded, to say nothing of slaves, he might moderate his argument. I was not trying to compete with my dear brother. People like us never compete, especially in virtue. Instead I was trying to get across the idea of divinity in everybody and the inconceivableness in everything, the grass and even the mouse which, as I said, is 'miracle enough to stagger sextillions.' My effort was to make holy not only what I touched but what I saw including the carnage of wholesale fratricide.

"Since I have been accused of so much, I must explain myself even more, so please remain standing. When in the 'Preface' to *Leaves of Grass* I say that priests shall disappear and should, I don't mean that they should be rounded up and carted off or even that they should change their dress. What I mean is that they must become poets and speak wonders with their tongues rather than reciting stale creeds and making motions with their hands or selling the truth like soap. Note what Mr. Huxley said about this in regard to vain repetitions, which you cited earlier. It is not an easy transformation and may never come to pass, which will be sad news for humankind.

"In fact, what I see is the reverse. It is not that poets are better people than priests or of a higher order than humanity. Their function is more one of imagination than repetition. It is not a matter of having visions, but having a vision that will transcend the doctrines and rites that from my perspective should be in a steady state of remission. I know exactly what the remarkable Mr. Einstein meant when he said 'imagination is more important than thinking' and when he spoke of the hope for a 'cosmic religionness' that is not distant, I suspect, from Mr. Bonhoeffer's 'religionless Christianity.' In any event, with doctrine and stultifying ritual, I had absolutely nothing to do. When priests become poets they will still need to practice the old human compassion on a daily basis, as do we all. They cannot sink into sacred routine, though, and must lead rather than following the unenlightened who merely occupy seats of power in politics and sports.

"As for atonement, I fully agree with Mr. Stewart, but atonement I enjoyed every minute of my life not merely in anticipation of death, for there is no such thing. I did not fathom the mystery with which we live but celebrated it. 'I and this mystery here we stand' was what I said. Herman acknowledged the mystery by striking back at it like Ahab who was a big part of himself until he wrote his 'Testament of Acceptance' in *Billy Budd*, a holy story. I didn't focus on differences between me and the Other but became one with the Other in consciousness and in love, 'the kelson of creation.' Somehow, some way, I even affirmed the stacked bodies in Virginia and the dying ones in the hospitals. Even of death I managed to sing. With apotheosis as in separating oneself from God or others, I had nothing to do. For millennia, mortals have spoken of the desire to know God in spirit and when someone finally does, someone like me, they become sacredly suspicious."

We asked, "It seems that your ideas about apotheosis connect to the deification of sports or opened the door for it. Do you see sports as a religion?"

"No. Not any more than all the other 'occupations' I chanted in my songs. When I said there would be no more priests, I didn't mean there would be no more spirit or joy in being but more with gangs of poets to note that spirit and joy. Poets seem absolutely essential to me; priests with their creeds and rites a dying breed, but as I say there is no reason why the latter can't become the former. Much of civilization is a battle between doctrine and imagination, between priests in politics, the old religions, and corporations on the one hand and sincere poets on the other, the true legislators of humankind. To the extent that sports claim status of religion through rituals or vain repetitions, the very petition made in their behalf is hopeless. Compared to war and making a living, sports are trivial matters, and I would not make a religion of any, yet all are the subject of verse, holy verse it is hoped.

"With Virgil, Herman and I sang exquisitely of war, of its heroism and tragedy, and I chanted the poetry of labor, the rhythmic movements of mechanics and farmers, songs of occupations, including the occupation of the presidency, and no one has written as completely and as passionately about sports and play as I. Notice what I said about baseball after the war: 'I see great things in baseball; it's our game—the American game. It will take our people out of doors, fill them with oxygen, give them a larger physical stoicism. Tend to relieve us from being a nervous, dyspeptic set, repair these

losses and be a blessing to us.'[10] Yet of no occupation would I make a so-
called religion, not even of the religions. I do not chant religions—I chant
life."

"Would you go to the Super Bowl if offered the chance?" we asked.

"Only on one condition: That I be allowed to read *Leaves of Grass* at
half-time at midfield without any attendant explosions or competition in
entertainment."

We explained to him that such an invitation would probably never be
forthcoming.

With a smile, he said such narrowness of vision was another reason
why sport would always be set apart from mind and soul, hence sacred but
not holy.

Holy Sermons: When Preachers Become Poets

In an essay called "Selective Attention" published in *Psychology*
(1890), William James says that everyone divides the cosmos between the
"Me" and the "Not-Me," which in light of our discussion are analogous to
the sacred and the holy. It is obvious, we think, that Father Mapple in *Moby
Dick* and Brother Sim Mobberly in James Still's *River of Earth* divide the
cosmos at a huge distance from themselves to partake of the holy as much as
possible but without any pretense to fathom the mind of the "Something"
that is beyond them.

Examples of holy writing abound in Melville as in Father Mapple's
sermon early in the novel and even in the description of Father Mapple
himself. While he was speaking about the sin and repentance of Jonah, "the
howling of the shrieking, slanting storm without seemed to add new power
to the preacher, who, when describing Jonah's sea-storm, seemed tossed by
a storm himself. His deep chest heaved as with a ground-swell; his tossed
arms seemed the warring elements at work; and the thunders that rolled
away off his swarthy brow, and the light leaping from his eye, made all his
simple hearers look on him with a quick fear that was strange to them."
With "manliest humility" he spoke,

---

[10] Whitman, quoted in Lowell Edwin Folsom, "America's 'Hurrah Game': Baseball and
Walt Whitman," *The Iowa Review* 11/23 (1980): 73. See also Toney Frazier, "Whitman,
Eakins and the Athletic Figure in American Art," *Aethlon* 6/2 (Spring 1989): 79–89.

Woe to him whom this world charms from Gospel duty. Woe to him who seeks to pour oil upon the waters when God has brewed them into a gale. Woe to him who seeks to appease rather than to appall! Woe to him whose good name is more than goodness! Woe to him who, in this world, courts not dishonor! Woe to him who would not be true, even though to be false were salvation! Yea, woe to him who as the great Pilot Paul has it, while preaching to others is a castaway![11]

Harry Levin in *The Power of Blackness* has noted that in the whale-chasing scenes, Melville substituted terrestrial imagery for aquatic to catch the sublime action of the mighty sea. In *River of Earth*, James Still has done the reverse in another sermon, which has to rank with one of the most holy in literature in a holy setting, a mountain church in the thirties in Eastern Kentucky as told by the young narrator.

An elder stood in the pulpit. He was lean as a martin pole, thinner even than father. His cheekbones were large, angled from the nub of his chin. He lined a hymn, speaking the words before they were sung, holding the great stick of his arm in the air:
"Come Holy Spirit, heavenly dove
With all thy quickening powers,
Kindle a flame of sacred love
In these cold hearts of ours."
…The singing ended. A fleece of beard rose behind the pulpit, blue-white, blown to one side as though it hung in the wind. A man stood alone, bowed, not yet ready to lift his eyes. He embraced the pulpit block. He pressed his palms gently upon the great Bible, touching the covers as though they were *living flesh*. His eyes shot up green as water under a mossy bank, leaping over the faces turned to him…. [Italics added.]
The preacher raised a finger. He plunged it into the Bible, his eyes roving the benches. When the text was spread before him on the printed page he looked to see what the Lord had chosen. I knew then where his mouth was in the beard growth. "The sea saw it and fled. Jordan was driven back. The mountains skipped like rams and the

---

[11] *Moby Dick*, 46-47

little hills like lambs. Tremble, thou earth...." He snapped the book to. He leaned over the pulpit. "I was borned in a ridge pocket," he said. "I never seed the sun-ball without heisting my chin. My eyes were sot upon the hills from the beginning. Till I come upon the word in this good Book, I used to think a mountain was the standingest object in the sight o' God. Hit says here they go skipping and hopping like sheep, a-rising and a-falling. These hills are jist dirt waves, washing through eternity. My brethren, there ain't a valley so low but what hit'll rise again. They ain't a hill standing so proud but hit'll sink to the low ground o'sorrow. Oh, my children, where air we going on this mighty river of earth, a borning, begetting, and a-dying—the living and the dead riding the waters? Where air it sweeping us?" [12]

Brother Sim Mobberly creates the sense of the holy in the images of mountains quaking and shaking. With the right person in the right setting, that is one way to do it. Another is to evoke awe or epiphany through detailed attention to "smallest things." James Still as a poet is as good as they come in that endeavor as poems such as "Leap, Minnows, Leap" will reveal. Poets, as Eiseley observed, try to make us see large connections without dislocation of the object under view. Like Emerson, Thoreau, and Whitman, whom he admired and often referred to in his works, Eiseley took note of the smallest things in nature, his imagination the "vehicle" that transported him into the domain of the holy as he acknowledges in "Science and the Sense of the Holy."

This same idea is echoed by theologian Belden C. Lane. Among modern poets and writers with this talent, he mentions Annie Dillard, Wendell Berry, and Lewis Thomas who make us see the extraordinary in the ordinary. "The sacred and the profane are ultimately artificial distinctions. Can the foot touch any place where there is no God? Having stalked the holy up narrow paths on windswept slopes, I'm brought full circle by discovering that I have passed it already along every step of the way."[13] One can hear an echo from Henry Thoreau, the man who chased a fox in the snow and played hide-and-seek with a laughing loon.

---

[12] Still, *River of Earth* (New York: Viking Press, 1968) 42–43.

[13] Lane, "The Ordinary as Mask for the Holy," <http://www.religion-online.org/cgi-bin/relsearchd.dll/showarticle?item_id=1422> (2 March 2004).

This tradition of seeing much in little, *multum in parvo*, was illustrated with exceptional power by writers of the American Renaissance, Emerson who sat at the seat of the "commonplace," Thoreau who saw the holy everywhere in nature, Whitman who sang the glories of grass, and Emily Dickinson in poem after poem. In a letter to Thomas Wentworth Higginson, Dickinson in describing the effects on her of poetry was close to the way others have described the holy: "If I feel physically as if the top of my head were taken off, I know that is poetry. These are the only ways I know it. Is there any other way?"

Readers of Dickinson's poems have felt the same effect she describes. Nothing great or small is beyond the vision of the poet, who does not see as others do, finding connection in all that is. Poets dwell in possibility, not in the certainty that doctrine of all kinds seeks to provide. Poets are drawn toward the mystery of the natural frontier of the world, space, mind, and soul. They are transformed by what they observe and experience on their journey. Others, driven by a desire for sacred certainty, fear such mystery and build fortresses of doctrine, law by law. They try to defend their religion by symbols of jewelry, steeples, and stadia. They defend traditions rather than seeking the truth.

Still, the holy beckons, calling each of them by name as it does for all of us, to do the inconceivable, to leave all that we have and, from time to time, return to the wilderness within and without, much like prophets of old. In the spirit of Ishmael, Huck Finn, and Ike McCaslin in *The Bear*, it will be a discovery not of sacred separation from the world but of Otherness in the natural world and in the broader social world as well.

With regard to living well with Otherness, natural, social, or divine, we might keep in mind the words of C.L.R. James: "The last sight of the *Pequod* shows an eagle, symbol of America, the blows of an American Indian. It is impossible to speak more clearly. The social perspectives are not completely hopeless. The survivor is ...saved by a coffin, prepared by the request of another savage.... While Melville sees no solution to the problem of society, he does not say there is none."[14] In other words, he sees no social atonement on the American Horizon. In contrast, Whitman, the

---

[14] "Amercian Writers of the Nineteenth Century," *American Civilization*, quoted in Louis Proyect, "Moby Dick's Finale," htt:///csf.colorado.edu/mail/pen-1/jan98/0803.html. See also chapters 10 and 12 on Melville and Whitman respectively in D. H. Lawrence, *Studies in Classic American Literature* (New York: Doubleday and Co., 1951).

"teacher of Athletes," found atonement in apotheosis, a paradox, a favorite form of expression of the "Good, Grey Poet."

Epilogue

If anything, the religion of sports forces us to reexamine the terms by which sports are validated as a religion, especially by means of the word "holy" and the connection of "holy" to "ultimacy." The word "ultimacy" was used freely in connection with Super Bowl 2004 and with the television show *Survivor* that followed. That was a lot of "ultimacy" for one evening. To us the idea of ultimacy is far removed from the idea of the holy in spite of connections frequently made in that regard by apologists. Considering the widespread use of "holy," "super," and "ultimacy" and the context in which they are used, we would like to conclude our own argument with reminders of what the holy has been and what audacity it takes to alter the basic understanding of that idea as we have known it over the ages, even with the many horrors committed in its name. Here, then, is what we infer the holy has generally meant in terms of relations with others.

The holy reminds us that looks fade and skills deteriorate and warriors die, that neither form nor function nor perfection matter as much as completion and wholeness. St. Paul didn't say "I won the race" but rather "I *finished* the race." The holy encourages us to remember that in the end it is not about how many trophies we capture, souls we win, or jewels we earn for our crown in the hereafter but about these questions: Did we do what we could to help the least of us even when the least of us is ourselves? Did we choose the unchosen to be on our teams and in our lives? Did we give cups of cool water and feed the sheep? We were commissioned to do these things, not to have mystical experiences or to wait for the rapture.

The sacred suggests that God is looking at us. The holy, as Rumi writes, "is nearer to you than the look in your eye," or in the words of Tennyson, as Randall Stewart notes, "closer than breathing, nearer than hands and feet," transcendent yet immediately present at once. The holy invites us, like Ishmael in *Moby Dick*, to seek possibility rather than certainty, to let go of our preconceptions, our vanity, prizes, and public places, because in the end we will all travel light. And what do we know for sure? All we can do is grasp this world lightly and let go of our sacred training wheels with humor, humility, and gratitude.

Appendix I

Religious Dichotomies

Sacred	Holy
The God Idea	God
God Spoke	God Speaks
The Version of the Thing	The Thing Itself
The Vehicle	The Tenor
Sunday School Texts	Holy Bible
Holy Bible	The Holy
Koran	The Holy
Veda/Vedanta	The Holy
The Torah	The Holy
Immanence/Pantheism	Panentheism
Banousia/Idiotes	Arete
Display	Play
Ego	Self
Self	Soul
The Sanhedrin	Prophets
Flags	Values
Values	Ethics
National Boundaries	Infinite Space
The Familiar	The Inconceivable
Passing Time	Great Time
Manners	Mystery
Memory	Possibility
Certainty	Irony/Paradox
Monumentalism	*Multum in Parvo*
Statue of Zeus	*Creation of Adam*
Patriotism	Love of the earth
Law	Justice
Competition	Play

Eros	Agape
Here	There
Talking	Listening
Honor	Honesty
Dulce et decorum est pro patri mori. (It is sweet and fitting to die for one's country)	Thou Shalt Not Kill
Prizes	Gifts
Religion	Life
Tribes	Community
Possessing	Sharing
Praying in Public	Praying in the Closet
Pride	Humility
Seriousness	Humor
Sporting Spirit	Holy Spirit
Stadia	Garden
Garden	Wilderness
Doctrine	Metaphor
Canon	Newness
Apotheosis	Atonement
Instrument	Music
Object	Images
Images	Consciousness
Imitation	Creativity
Following Rules	Wondering
Following Maps	Wandering
Mission	Journey
Halls of Fame	The Redwoods
Celebrity	Anonymity
Settlement /Frontier	Terra Incognita
Money	Knowledge
In the Flow/In the Zone	Being Still
Establishment	The Movement
Super Sunday	Silent Night
Passing a Football	Becoming a Football
Healing at a Distance	Touching
Ultimacy	Intimacy
Nuclear Weapons	Natural Disasters
Me	Not Me
Passion	Compassion
Vengeance	Forgiveness

Glory	Grace
"Onward Christian Soldiers"	"Savior, Like a Shepherd Lead Us"
"Battle Hymn of the Republic"	"Navy Hymn"
Memorializing	Letting Rest in Peace
Pyramid	Garden
The Sun	Sun and Earth
Money	Love

Appendix II

Textual Notes on Comparative Theology

Planks of Orthodoxy
(Protestant and Catholic) in
Christianity

Planks of Orthodoxy in
Church of Sport in
Christendom

1. "Wisdom is the principle thing: therefore get wisdom: and with getting get understanding" (Prov 4:7).

"Winning is not the most important thing; it is the only thing." Variously attributed to "Hurry-up" Yost, Vince Lombardi, and Paul (Bear) Bryant.

2. "For he shall grow up before him as a tender plant, and as a root out of the dry ground: he hath no comeliness; and when we shall see him, there is no beauty that we should desire him" (Isa 53:2).

Jesus was "no sissie and he was no weakling.... He must have been straight, strong, fit, handsome, tender, gracious, courteous...." (Billy Graham). "Graham was sure Christ must have been the most perfect man physically in the history of the world..." (Pollock, *Billy Graham*,168)

3. "Not as the world giveth, give I unto you" (John 14:27).

"God was on our side today."
—Bill Parcells, head coach, New York Giants, following 1991 Superbowl victory.

4. "But when thou prayest, enter into thy closet, and when thou has shut thy door, pray to thy father which is in secret; and thy Father which seeth in secret shall reward thee openly" (Matt 6:6).

A group of New York Giants huddled on sideline praying for their kicker to succeed in playoffs against Forty-Niners and for Bills kicker to fail against them in the Superbowl 1991.

5. "...for your Father knoweth what things ye have need of, before you ask him. After this manner therefore pray ye: 'Our Father which art in heaven...'" (Matt 6:8–9).

"Your son is our quarterback and you are our coach. We sometimes get blitzed by heavy sorrows or red dogged by Satan. Teach us to run the right patterns in our life so we will truly make a touchdown one day through the heavenly gates as the angels and saints cheer us on from the sidelines." —Archbishop Coleman F. Carroll, invocation, Atlanta-Miami football game, 1971.

6. "For bodily exercise profiteth little; but godliness is profitable unto all things" (1 Tim 4:8).

"My work convinces me completely that this ultimate experience occurs regularly in sport" (Charles Prebish, "Teaching Religion and Sport: The Meeting of Sacred and Profane," *Sport in the Classroom*, 145.

7. "Consider the lilies of the field, how they grow; they toil not; neither do they spin" (Matt 5:28). "Therefore take no thought for the morrow" (Matt 5:34).

"Five words spoken by Christ so interpreted, if strictly obeyed, would at one blow strike down all that distinguished man from the beast, 'Take no thought for tomorrow'" (Andrew Carnegie, *The Gospel of Wealth*, 25.)

John Muir encountering a Tennessee mountaineer on his celebrated walk to the Gulf: "…do you not remember that Christ told his disciples to 'consider the lilies how they grow' and compared their beauty with Solomon in all his glory. Now, whose advice am I to take, yours or Christ's? Christ says, 'Consider the lilies.' You say, 'Don't consider them. It isn't worthwhile for any strong-minded man.' This evidently satisfied him and he acknowledged that he had never thought of blossoms in that way before." (Muir, *A Thousand Mile Walk to the Gulf*, 25)

"Few men wanted more intensely to win than Andrew Carnegie. In 1868, at the age of thirty-three, he wrote in an introspective note a sentence of self-analysis: 'Whatever I engage in I push inordinately.' Thirty years later he was trumpeting his triumphs in golf. 'So all goes well. I played eighteen holes today with Taylor. Beat him! Beat Murray Butler Saturday. Beat Franks the day before'" (quoted in Edward G. Kirkland, introduction, *Gospel of Wealth*, vii).

Index